AYODHYA

AYODHYA

CITY OF FAITH,
CITY OF DISCORD

VALAY SINGH

ALEPH

ALEPH

ALEPH BOOK COMPANY
An independent publishing firm
promoted by *Rupa Publications India*

First published in India in 2018
by Aleph Book Company
7/16 Ansari Road, Daryaganj
New Delhi 110 002

ISBN: 978-93-88292-24-5

1 3 5 7 9 10 8 6 4 2

For Didi
for blazing the trail
and
For my parents
who never let their own beliefs get in the way of mine

'The past was erased,
the erasure was forgotten,
the lie became truth.'
—George Orwell, *1984*

CONTENTS

Note to Readers   xi
Introduction   xiii

BOOK I

1 Ayodhya's Early History   3
2 The Ramayana and its Plurality   21
3 The Ramayana in Tribal and Folk Traditions in India and Beyond   36
4 Scripture, Myth And Reality   52
5 Changes to Ayodhya's Religious Landscape   77
6 Ayodhya: 1800–1857   96
7 The Indian Rebellion of 1857   123

BOOK II

8 Independence and its Aftermath   185
9 The Ram Janmabhoomi Movement   200
10 Countdown to 6 December 1992   234
11 Ayodhya Left Behind, India Moves On   253
12 Ayodhya Now   284

Epilogue   365
Acknowledgements   371
Bibliography   373
Index   379

NOTE TO READERS

Most of the interviews for this book were on record while others were under the journalistic rule of 'deep background'. I was allowed to record nearly all of these interviews for the sake of precision. The names of certain interviewees have been withheld at their request out of concern for their safety and security. Writing a 'complete' history is neither desirable nor possible, and thus, this book while being the first agenda-agnostic biography of Ayodhya, only hopes to widen the understanding of the reader.

INTRODUCTION

Why read another book on Ayodhya? This question has to be answered. First, though it is true that Ayodhya has been one of the most written about subjects in the last three decades, the vast range of scholarship, journalistic writing and reportage, and propaganda on it has been limited to a single issue: the dispute over building the Ram temple at the exact spot where Ram is believed to have been born and where a sixteenth-century mosque said to have been built by Mughal emperor Babur stood until 6 December 1992. This book is not only about the dispute. A town that is at least 3,300 years old, Ayodhya's history cannot be confined to or defined by developments of the last one and a half centuries. This is the outer limit; in a more tangible sense, Ayodhya has captured the attention of academia, politics, media and people only in the last three decades (a point echoed by a leading functionary of the Vishwa Hindu Parishad in an interview with me).

Secondly, the existing literature on Ayodhya can be neatly filed into certain broad categories. To start with, there is the 'pro-temple' view that begins with the hypothesis that Babur destroyed a preexisting temple at Ram's birthplace and a mosque was built over its ruins sometime between 1526 and 1528 CE. Some proponents of this theory concede that the temple that existed previously could have been any Hindu temple and not necessarily a Ram temple. As we shall see in the book, this is a crucial concession that needs to be scrutinized more assiduously than it has been so far. The second category is a counter-theory to the pro-temple view, and has been aptly called the 'pro-Babri' position. The advocates of this view argue that a temple did not exist at Ram's birthplace nor was it destroyed by Babur. To prove their point, one of the arguments they use is the fact that there is no mention of the said mosque or the temple either in the *Baburnama* or in the sixteenth-century composition, Tulsidas's *Ramcharitmanas* (*The Psyche of Ram's Life*). However, the proponents of this theory also concede that the mosque did use the spolia of a temple. There is a third view as well, which has begun to assert itself more in the last couple of years. Buddhists in and outside Ayodhya have been arguing that Ayodhya's roots are Buddhist, that the disputed site is of Buddhist origin. And finally, there are those who believe that there is no use fighting over the past; it's best to forget and move on. A section of proponents of this last position also say that a building of a more secular nature, such as a hospital or a library, should be built at the disputed site instead of either a temple or a mosque. This view is a minority view.

Finally, this book needed to be written because it appears that most of the writing on Ayodhya has been driven more by selective agendas than a quest for knowledge. This has done a great disservice to Ayodhya's multilayered and multireligious history. Even when historians have dealt with its history, it is only to prove one of the above-mentioned theories. This book hopes to give readers an unfiltered and continuous stream of historical developments that were either centred in Ayodhya or affected Ayodhya substantively. This is not to say that the book 'sets the record straight'; in fact, it hopes to honestly study available records and present them to the reader in a comprehensible and logical manner. It also hopes that even those who believe in 'setting the record straight' will appreciate that in the case of certain places like Ayodhya—which exist in different realms at the same time—it is neither desirable nor possible to 'set the record straight'. What is possible though is to empathize with the limitations of our methods of historical enquiry and then realize that it is an injustice to define Ayodhya's history to suit contemporary and often self-serving narratives. This book brings together previous scholarship on both sides of the divide. It looks at little known but authentic research as well as books launched by heads of vested parties like the RSS and the BJP. However, to look at Ayodhya only through the history of the disputed site would be doing injustice to the town's fascinating and often silent journey through the ages.

The book follows a chronological and linear narrative and uses as sources a wide spectrum of scholarship, in order to reconstruct as wholly as possible the evolution of Ayodhya over at least three millennia. However, as I am neither a historian nor an archaeologist, I have referred to as many and as diverse secondary sources as possible, in the hope that this will give readers a comprehensive account of Ayodhya's history. This holds true especially for the first 2,000 years of its existence. But the little that we know about this period is enough to conclude that Ayodhya is of great antiquity. It would have been surprising if that were not the case, as the region in which it is situated has been the cradle of civilization for several thousand years.

The book remains true to the early transformation of Ayodhya—or, at least, the idea of it—into an ideal for kingship. It deals with the intimate and enduring association of Ram as an ideal king and later as a near-perfect human being. The intersection of different religious histories either at the physical setting of Ayodhya or in the realm of an illustrative epic is also a significant aspect that is covered in the book.

The last 1,200 years of Ayodhya's history show the transformation of Ayodhya from being an insignificant outpost to a place sought by kings, fakirs, renouncers and reformers.

The book seeks to bring together the various disparate events and developments of the last 150 years that were responsible for launching Ayodhya to centre stage in Indian politics and the political imagination.

In one sense, the history of Ayodhya is a microcosm of the history of the north Indian heartland. In another sense, it is a history of the evolution of Vaishnavism in the Hindu consciousness. In a third sense, it stands for the formation and propagation of an aggressive Hindu cultural and religious consciousness that can be traced all the way back to the advent of the East India Company as a military power in north India in the eighteenth century.

Over the last two decades or so, a singular fixation on corruption and misgovernance has cloaked the rise of communalism and majoritarianism. In India today, secularism and socialism have become contemptible ideas that many liberals have stopped defending. In this sense Ayodhya has come to stand for ground zero in the battle between secularism and religious fundamentalism in India.

One city, many histories.

BOOK I

Chapter 1

AYODHYA'S EARLY HISTORY

The *Nasadiya Sukta*, also known as the 'Creation Hymn', is part of the *Rig Veda* and believed to have been composed in the ninth century BCE. Its simple translation is presented below to show the dilemma that continues to confront historians, archaeologists and all those who are occupied with questions of our past, present and future.

> Who really knows? Who can presume to tell it?
> Whence was it born? Whence issued this creation?
> Even the Gods came after its emergence.
> Then who can tell from whence it came to be?
>
> That out of which creation has arisen,
> whether it held it firm or it did not,
> He who surveys it in the highest heaven,
> He surely knows—or maybe He does not![1]

BEFORE AYODHYA

Ayodhya, once a mound of land bound by the river Sarayu and smaller streams on three sides, has seen its fate change repeatedly. In the minds of millions of devout Hindus there is no doubt that this mound, near Faizabad in Uttar Pradesh, is the same place mentioned as the capital of Lord Ram, the hero of Valmiki's Ramayana. To these devotees it is of little concern that the Ramayana is an epic of mythology and scripture and not a historically verifiable document. It also does not seem to matter to them that the Valmiki Ramayana doesn't seem concerned with giving specific details about Ayodhya or its location or even the lives of its inhabitants during the

---

[1] Raimundo Panikkar, *The Vedic Experience: Mantramanjari: An Anthology of the Vedas for Modern Man and Contemporary Celebration,* New Delhi: Motilal Banarsidass, 2016.

period in which the events of the epic take place—the descriptions that exist are of a nature that can at best be called general.

FERTILE AND CONTESTED

The region lying between the rivers Ganga and Yamuna was considered the granary of ancient India. Similarly, the Gangetic plains, criss-crossed furiously by rivers plummeting down from the Himalayas, remains one of the most significant riverine landscapes of the world and is considered a geobiological microcosm of the Indian subcontinent.[2] Present-day north India, especially areas covering eastern Uttar Pradesh and western Bihar, is overrun by several rivers and consequently densely populated. The region is rich in archaeological findings, indicating that the area has been populated for millennia, a fact now corroborated not by archaeology alone. Modern scientific methods of enquiry into the past are gradually becoming interdisciplinary. One such field is of vegetation history and archaeobotany. The botanical history of a region can give us vital clues about the evolution of particular societies. The history of pollen found from a certain site helps us in understanding the changes that have occurred over time and, crucially, can tell us when people evolved from foraging to farming. Pollen analysis in the Gangetic plains has revealed that farming in the region began around 5000 BCE.

Archaeological studies indicate that millennial climatic cycles or climate patterns coincided with the development of human settlements in this region. By tracing the evolution of Ayodhya's population from pastoralists to small-scale farming to sedentary cultivation, fitting perfectly with the growth of urbanization, these new studies[3] add a new dimension to our existing knowledge and confirm extant theories. Professor Romila Thapar, an authority on the history of ancient India, writes:

> River valleys or the plains created by a river and its tributaries are often optimal areas for the rise of urban centres, particularly at or near nodal points such as the confluence of rivers. The urban civilisation of the Indus system dates to the third millennium BC, that of the Ganges system to the first millennium BC... Land to the east of the Ganges

---

[2]A. Saxena, et al., 'Holocene vegetation and climate change in central Ganga plain: A study based on multiproxy records from Chaudhary-Ka-Tal, Raebareli District, Uttar Pradesh, India', *Quaternary International*, Vol. 371, February 2015.
[3]Ibid.

Delta was also cleared [as found by the aforementioned study], with settlements gradually being established in the first millennium AD.[4]

It is in these cleared lands that the epic Ramayana is believed to have been written and is seemingly situated.

The prehistory of Ayodhya is a matter of speculation, aided by certain facts. These facts have been collected by archaeologists of the Archaeological Survey of India (ASI), the only body in India dedicated to this purpose. Another source of Ayodhya's past is the religious literatures of Buddhism, Hinduism and Jainism.

Five archaeological surveys have been carried out in present-day Ayodhya. The first two were conducted by Britons seeking to establish the historicity of the place. Alexander Cunningham, the founder of the ASI, conducted the first survey in 1862–63. He failed to find any evidence of temples, but did find remnants of Buddhist structures. After him, Alois Anton Fuhrer (who was dismissed from the ASI in 1898 on charges of plagiarism and falsification), surveyed the area in 1889–91 and essentially reiterated the discoveries made by Cunningham. It is only after India's Independence that archaeological surveys threw up substantial evidence revealing the antiquity of Ayodhya. The first excavation after Independence took place in 1969–70 when Professor A. K. Narayan of Banaras Hindu University dug at three places which were not in the immediate vicinity of the Babri Masjid. Narayan's excavations convinced him of 'a strong Buddhist presence in the area under study'.[5] This also pushed habitation in Ayodhya to the fifth century BCE. Since then, excavations have been centred around the Babri Masjid area. The next excavation concluded that the earliest known settlement at Ayodhya went back to the seventh century BCE.[6] These excavations were conducted by Professor B. B. Lal and Professor K. N. Dikshit in 1975–76 under a project called Archaeology of Ramayana Sites. The project was the brainchild of Lal, who had earlier excavated sites that bore the same names as those found in the other great Indian epic, the Mahabharata. Since his early days, Lal had been irked by the then well-accepted notion that

[4]Romila Thapar, *The Penguin History of Early India: From the Origins to AD 1300,* Vol. 1, London: Penguin Books, 2002, p. 41.

[5]Sushil Srivastava, *The Disputed Mosque: A Historical Inquiry,* New Delhi: Vistaar Publications, 1991.

[6]B. K. Thapar, ed., *Indian Archaeology 1976–77: A Review,* New Delhi: Archaeological Survey of India, 1980, pp. 52–53.

'Mahabharata and Ramayana were just figments of Hindu imagination'. So, when he joined the ASI, archaeology became a tool in his hands to prove the historicity of the Hindu epics. The project of excavating Ramayana sites found enthusiastic support from his friend, Professor Nurul Hasan, the minister of education and culture in 1977, who inaugurated the project at a small ceremony in Ayodhya. From the excavation site adjacent to the outer compound wall of the Babri Masjid, Lal and his team found well-fired, highly burnished pieces of Northern Black Polished Ware (NBPW) and associated redware. Similar objects have been found in other parts of India, as well as at most excavated sites across Uttar Pradesh. The objects found by Lal and Dikshit were thin-sectioned and in a variety of shades such as coal black, steel grey, indigo, silver and gold.

Twenty-three years later, the Archaeological Survey of India improved upon the 1978–79 excavation findings by digging across a more extensive area. In 2003, in a report to the High Court of Lucknow, the ASI submitted its findings:

> The Northern Black Polished Ware (NBPW) using people were the first to occupy the disputed site at Ayodhya. During the first millennium B.C. although no structural activities were encountered in the limited area probed, the material culture is represented by terracotta figurines of female deities showing archaic features, beads of terracotta and glass, wheels and fragments of votive tanks etc. The ceramic industry has the collection of NBPW, the main diagnostic trait of the period besides the grey, black slipped and red wares. A round signet with legend in Asokan Brahmi is another important find of this level. On the basis of material equipment and 14 C dates,[7] this period may be assigned to circa 1000 BCE to 300 BCE.[8]

---

[7] 14C or Carbon 14, an isotope of the element carbon, is unstable and weakly radioactive. Plants and animals assimilate Carbon 14 from carbon dioxide throughout their lifetimes. When they die, they stop exchanging carbon with the biosphere and their Carbon 14 content then starts to decrease at a rate determined by the law of radioactive decay. Radiocarbon dating is essentially a method designed to measure residual radioactivity. By knowing how much Carbon 14 is left in a sample, the age of the organism when it died can be known. It must be noted though that radiocarbon dating results indicate when the organism was alive but not when a material from that organism was used.

[8] Hindu Vivek Kendra, 'Summary of archaeological findings at Ayodhya' in Ranjana Agnihotra, ed., *Sri Ram Janmbhoomi Ayodhya Unpunished Conspiracy: Brutal Killing, Mischief and Interpolation*, Chennai: Notion Press, 2017.

The 'disputed site' referred to in the ASI report is where the Babri Masjid once stood and inside which the Ram Lalla (infant Ram) idol had been placed by Hindu activists in 1949. The Babri Masjid was demolished on 6 December 1992 by a large mob of Hindu rioters organized by the Vishva Hindu Parishad (VHP) to clear the way to build a temple for Ram. A large section of Hindus believe that the mosque had been constructed over the exact location where Ram was born. Presently, a makeshift temple containing the idols of Ram and his consort Sita stands on the site under the watch of hundreds of armed guards.

In 2003, excavations were conducted over much of the area that was previously covered by the Babri Masjid and Hindu shrines like the Ram Chabutra (a raised platform or dais) and Sita Rasoi (kitchen). The area lying under the makeshift temple was not excavated as per the orders of the court.

These excavations discovered four more periods of human habitation between the seventh century BCE and seventh century CE. These were the Sung (also called Sunga) period (second to first century BCE), marked by typical terracotta figurines of the mother goddess, humans and animals, beads, hairpins and engravers. It was during this time that the first signs of structural activity were found in Ayodhya. The founder of the Sung dynasty was a king-slayer Brahmin general in the Mauryan empire called Pushpamitra Sung. In Ayodhya, local tradition says that he declared a price of one gold coin for the head of one Buddhist.[9] He is believed to have initiated a Brahmin campaign to wipe out Buddhist rule from north India.[10]

After the Sungs, who did not hold sway over Ayodhya for very long, came the invading Kushans (first to third century CE). They built more than their predecessors and the ASI excavators found evidence of massive structures of unknown nature.[11] They also found antimony rods, terracotta figurines—indicative of a more advanced society—hairpins and bangles.

The Guptas (320–550 CE), who succeeded the Kushans, were better empire builders as is affirmed by the evidence of city-like societies found all over India, especially in Uttar Pradesh, from their reign. There is not much archaeological proof of their presence in Ayodhya; but in Lucknow and Fatehpur, the ASI has found Gupta-period structures like roads and enclosures,

---

[9] Another version of this story has Pushpamitra declaring a price of one gold coin for the head of a Buddhist in present-day Sialkot in Pakistan.

[10] Upinder Singh, *Political Violence in Ancient India*, Cambridge (Mass.): Harvard University Press, 2017, pp. 172–74.

[11] *ASI Report 2002-03: Ayodhya Excavation*, pp. 39 and 270.

and redware pottery such as short-necked water vessels, surahis, lipped bowls, lids with various knobs, long-necked spouted vases and carinated bowls.

EVOLUTION OF AYODHYA AS A POLITICAL CENTRE

Before empires, there were smaller units of political organizations in the area, as the case in much of north India. The smallest unit was the gram or the village. And before that there were hunter-gatherers and pastoralists. Although we can merely speculate about the lives of people in earlier times and civilizations, archaeological findings occasionally give us some clues. For instance, we know that the Northern Black Polished Ware civilization that flourished in north India was 'better off' than its predecessors, who presumably were forest dwellers (Vanvasis or Adivasis), surviving on roots, fruits and meat. But the change from hunter-gatherer was not uniform across the groups. While Vanvasis continued to live in the jungle, other groups of people, generally identified as 'Vedic people', progressed through agriculture and trade.

Gradually, instead of crafting items of daily use from bones and wood, societies evolved to using bronze in the second millennium BCE, and then iron in the period from approximately 1500–200 BCE. The corresponding pottery cultures known to us as ochre coloured ware, painted greyware and NBPW reveal a similar development of human societies in India. And Ayodhya, being identified largely with NBPW and associated grey and redware, has not been exempt from this coexistence of varying human societies. Expounding on the contribution of preceding cultures, Professor B. B. Lal notes:

> Their contribution to material life is no less significant. The Painted Grey Ware people, with their iron technology, are the first to have brought about a revolution in the settlement pattern in the Ganges-Jamuna basin—the Madhyadesa of old. Their predecessors in this region, namely, the copper-hoard people, seem to have been merely sporadic occupants, leaving hardly any mark on the civilization to be. Further, it is the Painted Grey Ware period that brought northern India to the threshold of what is known as the second urbanization. The glory lost through the fall of the Indus Civilization was regained after a lapse of nearly 1,000 years by the immediate descendants of the Painted Grey Ware people, namely the Northern Black Polished Ware people. On the solid foundation laid by the Painted Grey Ware people

arose the superstructure in which during the sixth and fifth centuries BC there flourished not only the legendary Mahajanapadas ruled by kings like Udayana, Prasenjit and Bimbisara, but also the great religious teachers, Mahavira and Buddha.[12]

These great personalities, the empire-builder, Bimbisara, who laid the foundation of the Mauryan empire, the renouncer, Buddha, and the initiator of a religion based on compassion for all life, Mahavira—all fought, preached or proselytized in the lush plains of present-day Uttar Pradesh.

An account of Ayodhya's prehistory must also include the community of Nishads,[13] who survive to this day and live along the banks of the Sarayu, Ganga, Gomti, Yamuna, Son and other rivers in Uttar Pradesh. The Ramayana mentions the Nishad 'local lord', Guha, who helps Ram cross the Ganga to continue towards present-day Allahabad on his way to exile in the forests of central India. The Nishad king is described by Valmiki thus:

> …the king of this region was a man named Guha, he was a Nisada and famed for his strength and courage. He was a good friend of Rama's. As soon as he heard that Rama had arrived in his kingdom, accompanied by the elders, his ministers and his family, he hurried to meet him.[14]

Guha beseeches Ram to treat 'this place' (not a city or a town) as 'his own city', but Ram politely refuses and continues with Lakshman and Sita on his journey. The Nishad king spends the night armed with his bow talking to Lakshman while Sita and Ram sleep. The next day the trio continue their journey into the forest while Guha and Sumantara (Ram's father Dasharatha's adviser) return to their respective places.

In the Ramayana, mentions of the people of Ayodhya—other than the ruling dynasts—are hard to come across. For example, there is no mention of the clan or caste or family name of any charioteer, but there are scores

---

[12]B. B. Lal, 'The painted grey ware culture of the iron age' in A. H. Dani and V. M. Masson, eds., *History of Civilizations of Central Asia*, Vol. 1, Paris: UNESCO Publishing, 1992, p. 440.

[13]Romila Thapar in her essay, 'Of histories and identities', describes a Brahmanical myth about the origin of Nishads: 'It tells of Vena the ruler who having stopped performing brahmanical rituals was killed by the brahmans. But a ruler was necessary. So they churned the left thigh of Vena and a short, ugly, dark man with bloodshot eyes emerged and they called him Nishad. He was banished to the forest and was associated with the Pulinda, Shabara, Bhilla and other forest dwellers, and also the rakshasas, the demons.' Romila Thapar, *The Past as Present: Forging Contemporary Identities through History*, New Delhi: Aleph Book Company, 2014, p. 55.

[14]Valmiki, *The Ramayana*, Arshia Sattar, trans., New Delhi: Penguin Books India, 2000, p. 161.

of references to charioteers in the Ayodhya Kand (section on Ayodhya) of
the Ramayana. Are we to assume then, that these drivers of royal chariots
belonged to the ruling clan, or that they were so insignificant as to not
merit being mentioned by name? What existed before the family of Ikshvaku,
Ram's ancestor, started ruling over Ayodhya? Were there other kings or clan
leaders in the region that they vanquished? Or did they defeat those who
lived in the forest and were from a different culture altogether? Answers to
these questions are still being sought. However, one aspect of the region
in pre-historical times that we do have some clarity on is that it produced
agricultural surplus, which was a pre-requisite for early state systems and
urbanization. Thapar believes:

> The population of the *doab* [the region lying between the Ganga
> and the Yamuna, roughly corresponding to present-day western Uttar
> Pradesh and Punjab], though small, slowly expanded. From staying
> close to the banks of rivers, some settlements moved into the interior
> where they cleared land for cultivation. This may have been an escape
> from floods or a more venturesome encroachment into forests. The
> small settlements linked to Ochre Colour Pottery were more frequent
> in the upper *doab*. The Painted Grey Ware settlements had a wider
> distribution in the *doab* and larger sites often occur on the edge of
> *jheels*, or lakes from natural depressions or as ox-bow lakes.[15]

Such settlements are still found all over India as well as in other parts of the
world. Writing about the development of communities further east in the
Gangetic plains, Thapar observes:

> ...wet-rice cultivation provided a high yield, even if it was more
> labour intensive. Although sedentary cultivation came to dominate the
> landscape, it did not eliminate hunter-gatherers, pastoralists and shifting
> cultivators. Closely placed small settlements of the PGW gave way to
> the appreciably larger settlements and at longer distances these were
> associated with sites and levels of the NBPW which herald incipient
> urbanism.[16]

As we have seen earlier, surplus produce and irrigation are considered to
be the main factors needed for the creation of early state systems and

---

[15]Thapar, *The Penguin History of Early India: From the Origins to AD 1300*, p. 140.
[16]Ibid.

urbanization. But they are not enough, as the production of foodgrains, control over its distribution, as well as irrigation systems, all require the management of a labour force and its handlers. The structure of settlements is also a pointer to urbanization. The village was the smallest unit, then came exchange centres or marketplaces known as nigams. River fords such as Sringaverapura (nearly 150 kilometres from Ayodhya), and river ports such as Patligrama enabled trade and exchange. Then came the nagaras, or towns, and the mahanagara—a large, well-established city like Kaushambi (200 kilometres away from Ayodhya).

According to the Valmiki Ramayana, Ayodhya was Ram's capital city and it is described as having palaces, wide streets and mansions. It also had an army and was rich in material goods. But what was the process of evolution from small settlements to planned towns? What was the corresponding change in social and political organization?

We are yet to come across archaeological evidence to support the belief that present-day Ayodhya was indeed a large town or the capital of a kingdom. Kingdoms themselves existed at a nascent stage at this time and were in contestation with Ganasanghas, or clan-based chiefdoms. While kingdoms such as the Sung and Kushan were concentrated in the Gangetic plains, the chiefdoms were dominant in the periphery of these kingdoms, bordering the Himalayan foothills, and in the south of the plains towards northwest India, Punjab and in central and western parts of India.

Coming back to the development of kingdoms in the Gangetic plains, clan loyalty, which was essential for chiefdoms, had weakened and, in turn, made way for caste loyalties and consequently, loyalty to the king. Professor Thapar writes, 'The competition between elites in the kingdom and the earlier rivalry between brahmans and kshatriyas was gradually having to contend with what was to become a new phenomenon in the towns—the rise of wealthy traders.'[17]

With trade becoming increasingly important, the kings had to share power with the traders and that brought about a change in statecraft. New alliances were formed through marriages; for example, Bimbisara (558–493 BCE) realized the potential of state-controlled revenue and married the daughter of a high-status family of Vaishali as well as Princess Kosala Devi of the ruling family of Kosala. Here it is important to mention that scholars like Vishnubandhu Pathak, on the basis of the Puranas and epics like

---

[17]Ibid., p. 151.

Valmiki's Ramayana, propound that the Buddha, Ram and Ram's ancestors, Ikshvaku, Mandhata, Sagara and Harishchandra, lived in the pre-Mauryan (322–185 BCE) kingdom of Kosala. As a result, Kosala is also one of the names used for Ayodhya.

In the Ramayana too, there are examples of marriage alliances with neighbouring kingdoms. Ram's wife Sita was from the neighbouring state of Videha while his half-brother Bharat's mother was from a kingdom called Kekaya (identified with present-day Punjab), although it is important to reiterate that the Ramayana is an epic and not a historical document.

AN ARCHAEOLOGIST'S READING OF VALMIKI'S AYODHYA

Since Valmiki's Ramayana is frequently cited in the context of Ayodhya, it is of interest to know what archeologists think of it. H. D. Sankalia, a giant among Indian achaeologists and a pioneer in excavation techniques, in his 1982 book, *The Ramayana in Historical Perspective*, wrote a brilliant analysis of Ram's city as described in the Ramayana:

> Whatever be the nature of the first or the earliest Ayodhya, a village or a city, its description, as it appears in the *Critical Édition of the Ramayan*, is of a well laid out city, with arterial roads—a *rajamarga* or a *patha*, fortification all round, and in addition a ditch or *parikha*. Within the city, there were various kinds of buildings: *harmya*, *prasada*, *vesma*, and *rimana*. Some of these were seven or eight stories (*attalaka*) high.
>
> There were checkposts (*gulma*), parks and gardens, besides drinking houses (*pana-grhas*), houses for recreation (*krida-grhas*). There were shops or bazars, where all sorts of things could be had, and the godown stocked with paddy. The merchandise was brought from far and near, by ox-drawn carts, as well as on camelback.
>
> No detailed description of a single house is available, nor any inkling given as to how these were built—with mud, mudbricks, pakka bricks, and lime or stone. Nor are we told how they were roofed: with tiles or simply thatched.[18]

Sankalia therefore infers that some of the houses briefly described in the Valmiki Ramayana were not only very large and had several rooms, but also that some of them could be entered while being seated in a chariot.

---

[18]H. D. Sankalia, *The Ramayana in Historical Perspective*, New Delhi: Macmillan India, 1982, pp. 49–50.

And that 'all the three queens of Dasaratha, as well as his son Rāma, lived in separate houses'.[19]

Turning his attention to the grandiose temples described by Valmiki, Sankalia wrote:

> ...as far as the structural history of temples is concerned, there were no temples with tall *sikharas* before the 6th century A.D. Fa-hien, who visited Ayodhyā in the fifth century, did see a Buddhist *stupa*, whereas two centuries later, Hiuen-tsang [Yuan Chwang] noticed more than a hundred monasteries with thousands of Mahāyāna and Hinayāna Buddhists, and only ten Deva temples.[20]

According to Sankalia:

> ...if the excavations so far conducted in India, outside the Indus Valley and the Panjab are any guide, the earliest houses at Ayodhya—whatever be that period, perhaps not earlier than the eighth century B.C., if the account in the *Aitareya Brahmana* is indeed correct (viz., that it was a village, even in the time of Hariscandra, one of the kings mentioned in the *Puranas*)—could not be better than mud huts, exactly as we see in the villages near Ayodhyā today.[21]

His deduction is also substantiated by an episode in the Valmiki Ramayana, which describes Ram's mother, Kaushalya, fainting when she hears about Ram's banishment, as a result, of which her body is covered with dust. Sankalia concludes from this that, 'Though nowhere are we told how the houses were built, such covering with dust is not possible, nor expected, on a well-made floor, of a house built with baked bricks or stone. Hence, this unconscious reference possibly tells us that the houses were nothing but mud huts in the earliest Ayodhyā.'[22]

ABSENCE OF EVIDENCE ON THE GROUND

Sankalia's conclusions deserve to be taken seriously for if houses were anything but mud huts in the earliest Ayodhya, archaeologists would have come across their remains. But the story of Ram doesn't need archaeological

---

[19]Ibid., p. 50.

[20]Ibid., pp. 50–51.

[21]Ibid., pp. 51–52.

[22]Ibid., p. 52.

structures to propagate itself and Sankalia's critique of generalities in the description of Ayodhya in the Ramayana is worthless for the believer. A booklet titled *Shri Ram Janambhoomi ka Raktranjit Itihas* (*The Blood-soaked History of Shri Ram's Birthplace*) by Ranjana Sarvesh, which is widely available in Ayodhya, is the perfect go-to guide for the credulous pilgrim. This simplified, effulgent glorification of Ram's Ayodhya takes the reader to the golden age of Lord Ram. For instance, the booklet declares, 'Nine lakh years before present time, in the fourth stage of Treta Yuga, God of Gods, the ideal Shri Ram took birth at this very spot. Needless to say, his place of birth was a massive palace laden with precious gems.'[23] Quoting Valmiki, the booklet adds:

> Mountain-like palaces adorned the site, which also had leisure-homes for women, the beauty of which was so enthralling that it seemed this city is the city of god. The royal palace was of golden colour and heaps of gems could be found lying everywhere. Wherever you looked you saw sky-high seven-storey houses. They were of such a kind that it seemed they were the flying homes of the sages returning from heaven itself, and those who lived in these homes were the best of men. Such was the radiance of Ayodhya in the past, but after Ram left it for Saket it became desolate…[24]

Though there is little in the booklet that would stand up to scholarly scrutiny, the fact is that it is the single most popular text on the history of Ayodhya sold in contemporary Ayodhya.

AYODHYA, SAKET AND BUDDHA

The Saket that Ram sets out for is a city of gods, a divine abode or heaven from where he has come to watch 'the tamasha of the world'. However, Saket is also known as another name for the earthly Ayodhya. How Ayodhya acquired the name of Saket or, equally plausibly, how Saket became Ayodhya (we cannot ascertain which happened first), is a fascinating journey through pre-Christian era north India. This journey is illuminated in patches, but for the most part, remains shrouded in darkness.

In his essay, 'The Rise of Ayodhya as a Place of Pigrimage', cultural historian and Indologist Hans Bakker writes that 'Säketa, the name generally

---

[23] Ranjana Sarvesh Mishra, *Shri Ram Janmabhoomi ka Raktranjit Itihas*, Ayodhya: Ram Milan Tiwari, p. 6.
[24] Ibid.

given to the Ayodhyä of Brahmanic literature in Buddhist sources, was already an important centre of civilised India as early as the sixth century B.C.[25]

Around the fifth century BCE, in the kingdom of Kosala, lay a busy town at the intersection of two major routes, one going from Sravasti in the north to Pratishthana (Maharashtra) in the south, and the other going to Taxila in the west from Rajagriha (Uttar Pradesh) in the east. This town was Saket and its king was Prasenjit, who ruled from his capital, Sravasti, about 80 kilometres from Saket. Prasenjit is also known as the king of Kosala which is, as mentioned earlier, now acknowledged to be yet another name for Ayodhya. As trade flourished in the region, Saket came to be coveted by the neighbouring kingdoms of Kashi (Banaras) and Magadha. The Magadha king Ajatashatru annexed Saket and it remained a part of the Magadha empire until its fall in 200 BCE. Although Saket remained a business centre for 300 years (485–200 BCE) it never grew as a political centre, but it continued to attract to its bounteous gardens preachers like Buddha and Mahavira, who proselytized there.

Was Saket located in present-day Ayodhya? We don't know that but we do know Saket had become a large and important city in the time of the Buddha, as is evidenced by accounts of his several visits there.[26] It is generally agreed upon by scholars that Buddha lived in the sixth century BCE. Historians Thakur Prasad Varma and Swaraj Prakash Gupta in their book, *Ayodhya ka Itihas evam Purattatva* (*Ayodhya's History and Archaeology*) published by the Indian History and Culture Society in 2001, claim that 'the places at which Buddha resided in Saket include Ajjanayan and Tikandivan and Kalakarma, a hostel for Buddha's students, which was situated in Saket and where he stayed'. They add, 'Kalak was married to a woman named Chulsabhaddh and when Buddha gave him *diksha* or took him as a student, Kalak gifted Kalakarma to him',[27] in accordance with the custom of followers giving away lands and gardens to Buddha once they joined his order.

---

[25]Hans Bakker, 'The rise of Ayodhy as a place of pilgrimage', *Indo-Iranian Journal*, Vol. 24, No. 2, 1982, p. 103, JSTOR, <www.jstor.org/stable/24653635>.

[26]Ibid. Hans Bakker quotes from the Buddhist *Dhammapada* (*Collection of Buddha's Sayings*), an account of a festival held in 'Ayodhya-Saketa during the reign of Pasenadi [another name for King Prasenjit]. This was an annual event of a profane nature called the *Vivatanakkhatta* or "Public Day". The young unmarried daughters of the most distinguished families would make their way on foot and unclothed to the river Sarayu, in view of a row of ksatriya boys and others who each threw a garland of flowers'.

[27]T. P. Verma, S. P. Gupta, *Ayodhya ka Itihas evam Purattatva*, p. 35.

Historian Sushil Srivastava also underscores the confusion around
Ayodhya and Saket being the same place in his book, *The Disputed Mosque:
A Historical Inquiry*. He writes:

> Rhys David who [also] depended on Buddhist sources, does not
> agree that 'Saketa' and 'Ayyojha' are the same. However [Alexander]
> Cunningham, [Pandurang Vaman] Kane and B. C. Law agree that the
> two cities are virtually identical. In some of the sources in which
> Ayojjha figures, the place is said to be situated on the bank of the
> river Ganga... It is amazing when we realise that places where the
> Buddha lived are frequently mentioned, such as Anjana, Tikandaki
> and Kalakarma, but never Ayojjha. Again, we do not have any epic
> literature which refers exclusively to that quarter of the town i.e.
> Ayojjha, and never to the town of Saketa.[28]

Going beyond Buddhist traditions, Srivastava uses Jain sources to argue that
Saket and Ayodhya were, in fact, not the same place. He writes:

> A similar situation is demonstrated by the older parts of the Jaina
> canon. In most of the *angas* [Jain religious texts] and *upangas* [sub-
> sections of Jain religious texts], Saeya (Sageya) figures prominently,
> having been visited by Mahavira, whereas Ayojjha is mentioned only
> once, when it is said to be the capital of the north-west district of
> Gandhilvatti, of the largely mythological country of Mahavidesha.[29]

Even though many historians—and several texts—attest to Saket and
Ayodhya being one and the same place, there is no consensus on it. With
the passing of time and the coming of new rulers the legend of Saket and
Ayodhya being one gained more strength. The Gupta ruler Skandagupta
(Skanda means spilling or spurting, a likely allusion to bloodshed) was a
prolific conqueror who succeeded Kumaragupta I and presided over the
Gupta empire for twelve years (455–467 CE). It is also believed that during
the time of the Guptas there was a Brahmanical revival and the town of Saket
reacquired prominence. Scholars hold the belief that Gupta kings consciously
worked to increase the importance of Ayodhya because they wanted to use
the idea of the avatar of Ram to support their deification of kings.

An inscription found near Karamdanda, a village situated 24 kilometres

---

[28]Sushil Srivastava, *The Disputed Mosque*, p. 55.
[29]Ibid.

southwest of Ayodhya, says that in 436 CE, Prithvisena, a former governor and minister, who was the then commander-in-chief of Emperor Kumaragupta I (415–455 CE), made an offering to certain Brahmins of Ayodhya. The occasion was a religious procession and the inscription also clarifies that Prithvisena was not a devotee of Vishnu but of Shiva.[30]

Skandagupta as emperor is credited with many military victories, including one over the Hunas,[31] who were a formidable threat at the time. And it is thought that he rewarded himself by assuming the title of 'Vikramaditya' (stronger than the sun).[32] Skandagupta is also believed to have moved the capital of the Guptas from Pataliputra (Patna) to Saketa. Bestowing greatness upon themselves seems to have been a universally common practice among kings—the Western world especially is full of laudatory titles such as Frederick II, the Wonder of the World, Beast of the Apocalypse; Suleiman[33] the Magnificent; and Constantine the Great. Skandagupta, too, was not immune to this syndrome. Hans Bakker believes that:

> ...the vanquisher of the Hunas, Skandagupta, liked to compare himself with Ram and the choice of Saketa as the new capital might have offered good opportunity to invigorate the ideology of his power. The restoration of the capital of yore, the renascence of the glory of Iksvaku, was a theme that was prominent in circles attached to the Gupta court of this time.[34]

---

[30]Srivastava, *The Disputed Mosque.*

[31]See Raghavendra Vajpeyi, 'A critique of the Huna invasion theory', *Proceedings of the Indian History Congress*, Vol. 39, 1978, pp. 62–66. JSTOR <www.jstor.org/stable/44139333> and R. P. Tripathi, 'Bhitari pillar inscription of Skandagupta—a note on Ganga-Dhvanih', *Proceedings of the Indian History Congress*, Vol. 39, 1978, pp. 1010–14, JSTOR <www.jstor.org/stable/44139451>.

[32]A local legend in Ayodhya narrated to me by Mahant Satyendra Das, the mahant of the Ram Janmabhoomi temple, speaks of a king, Vikramaditya who, having lost his way, was resting under a tree on a mound by the Sarayu. The king saw a black man on a black horse enter the river and emerge glowing like the sun. Curious, Vikramaditya asked the man on the horse about him and the place, to which the man replied, 'I am Prayagraj, the king of tirthas (holy places), and this [is] Ram's lost city, Ayodhya.' Then, Prayagraj told the king to go to a cow, bow to her and follow the cow. Prayagraj told him that the spot where milk would begin to flow from the cow's udders was the exact place where Ram took birth. Subsequently, Vikramaditya built 360 temples in Ayodhya. (Historians dismiss this as a myth.)

[33]Suleiman's lost tomb was discovered in 2016 in a small Hungarian town nearly 500 years after his death.

[34]Hans Bakkar, *Ayodhyā: Part I*, Groningen: Institute of Indian Studies, University of Groningen, 1984, p. 30.

And one of the more effective ways of furthering an ideology has always been through literature. Therefore, writes Bakker:

> Kalidasa who lived in the middle of the 5th century AD, may have projected the actual events in the realm of saga by relating in the *Raghuvamsa* [Raghu is another name for Ram], the story of Rama's son Kusa returning to the capital of his forebears in order to restore her ancient magnificence. By the explicit identification of Ayodhya with Saketa, the poet might have endeavoured to endorse the aspirations of his patron, the Gupta emperor.[35]

Kalidasa, it seems, was successful in rebranding Saket as Ayodhya.[36] But his 'Raghuvamsa', too, is devoid of any details (except the mention of the river Sarayu), which could have helped us in establishing the precise historicity of Ayodhya, or Saket for that matter. Archaeologist B. B. Lal, too, failed to discover any meaningful traces of Gupta rule at present-day Ayodhya. He observed:

> It is rather remarkable that the Gupta period is not significantly indicated at this site [Ramkot area of Ayodhya]—a fact also noticed in the first season's dig in 1975.
>
> After the early historic deposits there is a break in occupation, with considerable debris and pit formations before the site was again occupied around the eleventh century.[37]

The Gupta empire went into decline at the same time as Skandagupta's death, within three decades of which the Hunas overran much of their empire in the northwest. By the early seventh century CE the last Gupta king had been decimated. With that, Ayodhya (Saket) began its steady descent into political oblivion. Srivastava aptly sums up this period:

> However, the loss of its position of eminence did not imply a decline in its importance as a town. Huien-tsang visited the capital of the kingdom of O-yu-to during the reign of King Harsha of

---

[35]Ibid.

[36]The first postgraduate college in the Ayodhya–Faizabad region was established in 1951 by Acharya Narendra Dev, a socialist, Baba Raghav Das, a sanatani Hindu, and Pandit Parmeshwar Nath Sapru. The college is called K. S. Saket Post Graduation College. There are hundreds of commercial establishments in Ayodhya–Faizabad that use the name Saket to brand themselves.

[37]B. K. Thapar, ed., *Indian Archaeology 1976–77: A Review*, pp. 53.

Kanauj (AD 636–640). At that time Ayodhya had become a part of Kanauj and it is probable that it might have been the seat of a feudatory vassal or merely an administrative officer. Huien-tsang wrote about the prosperity of Ayodhya and maintained that until that time it was a famous centre of Buddhist activity.[38]

AYODHYA 'LOST' AGAIN

The four centuries after the death of King Harsha of Kannauj, Ayodhya was rife with continuous warring between kingdoms across north India. However, Kannauj remained a political centre and was ruled by Gurjara–Pratiharas as well as the Gahadvalas. Based in Kannauj, Gahadvalas did pay obeisance to Ayodhya as a local holy pilgrimage. This is known through inscriptions from the time of their reign. One of the inscriptions left by a Gahadvala king, Chandradeva, records the donation of a large gift to a group of 500 Brahmins from Ayodhya in 1093 CE. According to the inscription, the donation was completed only after veneration of the sun, Shiva and ritual worship of Vasudeva (father of Krishna).[39] Hans Bakker reckons that because there is no mention of Ram in the list of deities mentioned in this inscription, Ayodhya was not a site of Ram's worship in the eleventh century CE.

It needs to be mentioned here that there is not much evidence to link these dynasties with direct rule over Ayodhya except for a stone inscription found by karsevaks in the debris of the Babri Masjid after its destruction in 1992.[40] According to that inscription, comprising twenty lines, the Gahadvala king Govinda Chandra repelled Western intruders and built a magnificent temple dedicated to Vishnu-Hari[41] at the same spot in Ayodhya where the Babri Masjid was built. This inscription has become a raison d'être for those who insist that a temple existed before the Babri Masjid was built over it, and hence, justify the demolition of the mosque.

The deepest study, as also the most casual reading of Ayodhya's known early history, leaves one similarly mystified. Unlike other holy cities such as Kashi or Jerusalem there are no definite markers, records or substantial archaeological remains that help us in unravelling, deconstructing or even

---

[38]Srivastava, *The Disputed Mosque*, p. 62.
[39]Ibid.
[40]The authenticity of this stone inscription remains inconclusive.
[41]Ram is an avatar or incarnation of Vishnu.

accurately reimagining ancient Ayodhya. In the fog of its prehistory, fragments of pottery, solitary figurines, myths, passing references, occasional inscriptions and holy literature provide fugacious glimmers of human existence. The many-sided 'truth' lies scattered, perhaps irredeemably, among these remains, the only witness to all of it being the river Sarayu. According to historians like Srivastava, the period between 650–1050 CE is one of darkness in Ayodhya's history, and 'it is in the case of such darkness that myths are generally thrown up to fill the blanks'.[42]

However, in the minds of Ram's followers the epic continues to be 'lived' as vibrantly as it was first imagined by Valmiki. There is arguably no other epic in the world that has so many retellings and so many versions. The hydra-headed nature of the story is what lends itself to so many narratives that shift with time, the context of its retelling and the agenda of its narrator. But more importantly, it is its survivability that is the most significant sign of the Ramayana's antiquity as well as its almost universal appeal. Perhaps, the utopian allure of Ram's Ayodhya is much more vivid than any verifiable facts of its history.

---

[42]Srivastava, *The Disputed Mosque*, p. 62.

Chapter 2

THE RAMAYANA AND ITS PLURALITY

VARIATIONS ON AN EPIC THEME

A story can be retold in countless ways. This is true of the Ramayana which has several versions and interpretations. Buddhists and Jains have rewritten the Ramayana to suit their own ideology. A comparative reading of these different Ramayanas along with the Valmiki and Tulsidas versions throws up some obvious patterns. The central themes for the Jains are Deeksha and Nirvan (renunciation and liberation), for Valmiki and Tulsidas they are Dharma (duty) and Brahminism, while the Dashrath Jatakas of Buddhism are smaller in scale and more practical in outlook. Besides these variations there are several differences in the religious structure of these tellings.

It is highly likely that the Ramayana left India's present shores even before it reached the four corners of the country. So far, the generally accepted chronology of the diffusion of the Ramayana is as follows: Valmiki's was composed in the period 500 BCE–300 CE, Kamban's Tamil Ramayana in the twelfth century, Hemchandra's *Trishashthi Shalaka Purusha Carita* (*Lives of Sixty-three Great Men*) or the Jain Ramayana in the twelfth century, Krittivas's Bengali Ramayana in the fourteenth century and Tulsidas's Ramayana in the sixteenth century in Awadhi Hindi. This is not an exhaustive compilation, only an indicative one. In the Jain tradition alone there are at least fifteen Ramayanas that are preserved with reverence and care. Leaving aside the first Jain Ramayana—*Pauma Cariya* by Vimalasuri, which is undated—the rest are from the seventh to the seventeenth centuries. I have studied the popular versions of the different Ramayanas in the belief that by doing so I could understand the attitudes of the people who believe in them. The Ramayana's intrinsic plurality is also reflected in how many times and by how many different agents it has been co-opted, rewritten, revised and retold. The distinctive feature of the Bengali Ramayana by Krittivas is a

Ram who doesn't curb expression of his emotions and feelings. He may have been called 'weak-kneed' for this but he is true to his emotional side. In the Ramayana of Tulsidas, the softer attributes of Ram are covered with masculine qualities of 'keeping your feelings always in check'. While Valmiki's Ram was a hero-prince, in Tulsidas's version he is the all-knowing god who has descended to earth to witness the 'theatre of the world'. Most Hindus who profess to know the Ramayana know it through its recitation either by a religious elder at home or through its public staging. Few have read Tulsidas's *Ramcharitmanas*, and fewer still have read Valmiki's poem. In many cases even the reciters of Tulsidas's Ramayana are unaware that it is a retelling of the Ramayana of Valmiki. And almost nobody is aware of the influence of the Adhyatma Ramayana on Tulsidas's version. Later, we will see a rich and representative range of the hundreds of Ramayanas that exist or have existed in the past. From its influence on the folklore of central India to its various versions that still prevail among the tribes of Odisha, Chhattisgarh, Madhya Pradesh and Jharkhand, an attempt has been made to show the distinctiveness of the Ram-katha, or Ram's story, as it spread across the subcontinent and beyond. The Assamese folk versions of the Ramayana, as well as those in Mizoram and other states in the Northeast, will also be touched upon. The presence of Ramayana episodes in Telugu and Kannada folk literature also feature in this chapter. The effort is to show the Ramayana's ability to be woven into local narratives while still maintaining its overarching design.

The plurality of the Ramayana exists and grows even today. Much like Western epics that have been repackaged as slick 3D movies, the Ramayana's characters are in the process of being reimagined as modern superheroes of the digital age. And it should not be forgotten that since its inception (which could have origins in folk traditions), the Ramayana has been used for both entertainment and religious purposes.

To understand the plurality of the Ramayana, one needs to appreciate its inherent ability to be localized. It can be called the first truly glocalized story. Wherever it went, it was adapted to local mores and customs. The basic shell remained largely unchanged. In fact, the differences in the Ramayana date back to the second century CE when it broke up into two recensions, the southern Indian and the northern Indian. Later, the northern recension was further divided into northwestern and northeastern recensions. The southern recension, which is best exemplified by Kamban's *Ramavataram*, known as the Tamil Ramayana, has an equally old history. There is evidence of the Ramayana in the second century in the Tamil epic *Shilappadikaram* and in another pre-Kamban work of Vaishnavite importance, the *Nalayira Divya Prabandham* (sixth to ninth century CE). It's almost as if as soon as it was born the Ramayana story started travelling. Buddhism and Jainism too couldn't ignore its existence—they made it their own. This makes it difficult to establish Valmiki as the original author of the epic.

In any case, in the Ramayana attributed to him, Valmiki is shown as having heard the story from Narada, a divine personage. Was it Buddhist or did it belong to the successor of the Vedic religion? There is no scientific way to establish this. However, there is evidence of the Ramayana being looked upon as a fable to emulate, a utopia to fight for and a template to consolidate kingly power, especially when it is incipient. From Java in Indonesia to Mongolia at the roof of the world, from Tamil Nadu in south India to Kashmir in the north, the Ramayana has touched and absorbed local traditions like no other epic. Unsurprisingly, Ram's saga continues to be staged, recited, carved into stone, sung and performed.

DASHRATH JATAKA—BUDDHIST RAMAYANA

Some scholars believe that the Dashrath Jataka, which is set in Banaras and not Ayodhya, is the oldest version of the Ramayana while others argue that it was written after Valmiki's. There is inadequate evidence for both assertions and this matter remains inconclusive. Others argue that it was probably an oral folk tradition, which was compiled into an epic-poem by Valmiki. Be that as it may, unlike the voluminous Ramayana by Valmiki, the Dashrath Jataka is a less than 2,000-word tale. It talks about how to deal with your inner demons, with grief and joy, with pain and relief. In it, the Buddha starts narrating the story of one of his previous lives (as Rama Pandita) to relieve the pain of a grieving householder who has just lost his father. In this rendering, a scheming stepmother causes Ram's exile to make her son Bharat the king. Sita is a sister of Ram, presumably born of one of Dasharatha's 16,000 wives. She becomes his queen-consort once they return to Banaras and Ram becomes the king.[43] This is a highly condensed version of the already short tale. But, the Theravada Buddhist Ramayana tradition is not a monolith and the Dashrath Jataka is just one tradition in Buddhism; the other is a fusion of classical Hindu Ramayanas, the Jain

---

[43] *The Jataka, Vol. IV,* W. H. D. Rouse, trans., *Sacredtexts.com* <http://www.sacred-texts.com/bud/j4/j4025.htm>.

Ramayana and the Buddhist Jataka. This tradition, which draws heavily
from Hindu gods like Indra, seems to have developed in an area identified
as 'greater Laos, from Yunan in the north through Laos and northeastern
Thailand to the borders of Cambodia in the south'.[44] Out of this tradition
has emerged the voluminous Laotian version of the Ramayana called *Phra
Lak Phra Lam*.

VALMIKI'S RAMAYANA

Let us begin by looking at what is widely believed, particularly by Hindus,
to be the first telling of the Ramayana. Valmiki's Ramayana is a story about
a prince of the kingdom of Kosal (capital: Ayodhya) who is denied his
rightful claim to the throne by his envious stepmother and is made to live
in a forest for fourteen years. His wife and brother accompany him to this
exile. While in the forest Ram and his brother Lakshman spurn and injure
a lusty Surpanakha, sister of Lanka's king, Ravan. Moved by Surpanakha's
sisterly exhortations (and his own lust, according to Tulsidas), Ravan abducts
Sita and takes her to Lanka. Ram and Lakshman gradually raise an army
made up of other kings and tribes and defeat Ravan in battle. Sita is rescued
and goes through an ordeal by fire to prove her purity. The trio then return
to Ayodhya. During their fourteen years of exile Ram, Lakshman and Sita
meet an array of characters. Some of those common to most versions of the
Ramayana found in India are Nishad Raj Guha, the tribal king who helps
the trio cross the river; Sumantra, Dasharatha's confidant; the sages Vashishta
and Vishwamitra; Sabari, the old tribal woman they meet in the forest;
Sugriv, Bali and Angad of Kishkindha; Jabali, the sage who lectures Ram on
pragmatism and rationality; and Ravan's siblings, Vibhishan and Surpanakha,
among others. This is the indivisible basic plot of Valmiki's Ramayana which
has been changed and adapted in different versions. Valmiki's Ramayana
consists of seven different sections or 'books' called kands. These are Bala
(childhood), Ayodhya, the Aranya (forest), Kishkindha (Sugriv's kingdom),
Sundara (beautiful), the Yuddha (battle) and the Uttara (the sequel). The first
book, the 'Bala Kand', pertains to the birth of Ram and the last, the 'Uttara
Kand', deals with events, like Sita's banishment, that happen after Ram, Sita
and Lakshman return to Ayodhya. The 'Uttara Kand' is also where Ram's

---

[44]Frank E. Reynolds, 'Three Ramayana, Rama Jataka and Ramakien: A comparative study
of Hindu and Buddhist traditions', in Paula Richman, ed., *Many Ramayanas: The Diversity
of a Narrative Tradition in South Asia*, New Delhi: Oxford University Press, 1994, p. 53.

divinity as an avatar of Vishnu is established. These two books are believed to have been added later.

RAMAVATARAM OR KAMBA RAMAYANA

Preceding Tulsidas's *Ramcharitmanas* by four centuries, the Tamil poet Kamban's twelfth-century retelling of Valmiki's Ramayana, *Ramavataram,* is a work of poetic excellence suffused with the spirit of devotion, or bhakti. It clearly portrays Ram as a god and not only a hero.

The book contains only six sections and ends with the return of Ram, Sita and Lakshman to Ayodhya; there is no Uttara Kand, and thus no mention of the Luv–Kush story and Sita's banishment. The retelling follows the Valmiki Ramayana in plot, but gives the characters a poetic spin; it also sanitizes episodes like Sita's abduction by Ravan. Instead of showing Sita being grabbed by her hair, Kamban makes Ravan transplant the whole plot of land on which Ram, Sita and Lakshman's hut stood, thereby eliminating the need for Ravan to make physical contact with Sita. C. Rajagopalachari's translation of Kamban's Ramayana, *Bharat Milap*, illustrates its aesthetic and poetic qualities and brings out the following salient points:

- Ayodhyavasis—the entire city of Ayodhya—go to the forest to meet Ram, Sita and Lakshman. He calls it the revenge of the city on the forest.
- After Bharat and the rest of his kutumb (family) and city people leave Chitrakoot, Ram is unable to live there in peace as the memories of his family and Bharat haunt him greatly.
- Rajagopalachari says that for Kamban, Guha is perhaps even greater than Lakshman in his bhakti for Ram. He says, 'the devotees of Kamban may well look upon Kamban as an incarnation of Guha'.[45]

ADHYATMA RAMAYANA

The Adhyatma Ramayana is a part of the Brahmanda Purana, a canonical text of the Vaishnavas written in Sanskrit. 'Adhyatma' means spiritual in Sanskrit and the book is written in the form of a dialogue between Shiva and his consort, Parvati. It seeks to answer some of the questions pertaining to the divinity of Ram and explains why Ram, an avatar of Vishnu, had to

---

[45]C. Rajagopalachari, *Bharat Milap: From the Tamil Ramayana of Kamban*, New Delhi: Publications Division, Ministry of Information and Broadcasting, Government of India, 1967, p. 24.

undergo the suffering and tribulations depicted in the Valmiki Ramayana. This book is also divided into seven sections, or books, and comprises nearly 4,200 verses. According to Lala Baij Nath, who translated it into English in the early 1900s, 'nothing is known of its author or as to who he was or where he flourished. The internal evidence furnished by it, however, points out to a modern origin, after the system of worship inculcated by the Tantras had come into vogue.' Baij Nath places the Adhyatma Ramayana to be later than the fourteenth century. But, reflectively, he adds that 'the Indian Pandit or sadhu does not trouble himself with these questions of chronology, nor cares to examine the language or the style of the book he venerates'. And, further critiquing the lack of scientific enquiry among pandits, Baij Nath says, 'if it (Adhyatma Ramayana or any other Holy Book) serves his purpose, either of devotion or as the giver of livelihood, as it does, it is quite sufficient'.[46]

The Adhyatma Ramayana follows Valmiki in script and the differences that exist are because the Adhyatma establishes Ram's divinity at the beginning itself. Thus, the many human failings in the story are explained by the Vedantic concept of Anadi Ayigya, which means 'primal ignorance' or 'beginningless error'. Significantly, the Adhyatma differs from Valmiki's rendition by describing Ram as the best of men, and 'tries to show how, in spite of the few failings of humanity, one can rise to godhead by setting before him the noble ideal of truth and duty as Ram did'.[47] The Adhyatma Ramayana was composed in Sanskrit and this limited its reach mainly to Brahmins. Other Ramayanas that were written in Sanskrit include the Adbhuta Ramayana, the Ananda Ramayana and the Bhusundi Ramayana.

JAIN RAMAYANAS

The main motif of Jain Ramayanas is to challenge the fantastical tales present in the Valmiki Ramayana. The earliest known Jain Ramayana is the *Pauma Cariya* of Vimalasuri, composed sometime in the first century CE. Since then there have been a number of Jain Ramayanas. The one that is discussed here is the *Trishashthi Shalaka Purusha Caritra* of Acharya Hemchandra, dating to the twelfth century. It eulogizes the twenty-four tirthankars or religious teachers of Jainism. Hemchandra's Ramayana also

---

[46]*The Adhyatma Ramayana*, Rai Bahadur Lala Baij Nath, trans., Allahabad: Oriental Books Reprint Corporation, 1913, p. i.
[47]Ibid.

follows Vimalasuri's self-defined purpose in writing the Ramayana: '...to give the true facts of what happened instead of the lies and silly stories, contrary to reason and belief, with which the existing narrative is replete'.[48] Hemchandra's version, too, is full of practical wisdom and clearly forbade the killing of women as well as of cows. It starts by introducing Ram, Lakshman and Ravan in the same sentence because to the Jains, all three were followers of the Jain faith.

Below are listed some of the main Ramayana recensions in the Jain tradition:

1. *Pauma Cariya*—Vimalasuri
2. *Vasudevabindi*—Sanghadasa (seventh century CE)
4. *Padmapurana*—Ravisena (seventh century CE)
5. *PadmaCharit*—Svayambhu (mid-eighth century CE)
6. *Chaupanna Mahapurusecharita*—Silacharya (mid-ninth century CE)
7. *Uttarapurana*—Gunabhadra (ninth century CE)
8. *Brihatkathakosa*—Harisena (tenth century CE)
9. *Mahapurana*—Pashupadanta (late tenth century CE)
10. *Mahavali*—Bhadrasvera (eleventh century CE)
11. *Yoga-shastra-Svopanjinni-vritti*—Hemchandra (twelfth century CE)
12. *Trishashthi Shalaka Purusha Caritra*—Hemchandra (twelfth century CE)
13. *Satrunjaya Mahatmya*—Dhaneswar (fourteenth century CE)
14. *Puryachadradayapurana*—Krishnadasa (1528 CE)
15. *Ramacharita*—Devavijaynagir (1596 CE)
16. *Laghu Trisastisalakapurusha Charitra*—Meghavijay (1700 CE)[49]

Unlike in the other Ramayanas, in the Jain Ramayana, Ram married several times after returning to Ayodhya. Lakshman had 16,000 wives, who gave him 250 sons. Ram had four wives: Sita, Prabhawati, Ratinibha and Shridhama.

THE BENGALI RAMAYANA BY KRITTIVAS OJHA

Written in the fifteenth century by Krittivas Ojha, this retelling of Valmiki's Ramayana brings out the social milieu and mores of the time when it was written. Profuse in bhakti or devotional aspects, the Bengali or Krittivasi

---

[48]Romila Thapar, *The Past Before Us*, New Delhi: OrientBlackswan, 2013, p. 249.
[49]Sisir Kumar Das, *A History of Indian Literature, 500–1399: From Courtly to the Popular*, New Delhi: Sahitya Akademi, 2005, p. 121.

Ramayana portrays Ram in a 'softer' light, with more humane attributes. Reflecting the influence of the female-worship tradition in Bengal, the retelling also seeks to signify the power of the 'chastity' of women like Sita.

Another Bengali epic, *Meghnad Badh Kavya* (*The Saga of Meghnad's Killing*) focuses on the killing of Meghnad, Ravan's brother, who fought bravely till the very end of his life against Ram, Lakshman and their army. The poem, written by Michael Madhusudan Dutta,[50] was first published in 1861.

TULSIDAS'S *RAMCHARITMANAS*

Goswami Tulsidas, who is revered as a saint-poet in Hindi-speaking parts of India, is believed to have finished writing his *Ramcharitmanas* (*The Psyche of Ram's Life*), some time before the end of the sixteenth century. He is said to have lived in the time of Mughal emperor Akbar's reign, and composed the text in Awadhi, a dialect spoken in parts of eastern and central Uttar Pradesh and in Nepal's Terai region. While he was alive, Tulsidas, who spent most of his life in Banaras, was ostracized by local Brahmins for writing the Ramayana in the language of the masses. Today, it is considered to be the Bible of the Hindus—Brahmins and non-Brahmins alike. However, many Hindus are not aware that *Ramcharitmanas* is not simply a translation of the Valmiki version, but a different retelling altogether. The Tulsidas Ramayana, like the Adhyatma Ramayana, uses the 'Anadi Avidya' or 'beginningless error' technique to explain all the mortal follies of the Ramayana. According to Baij Nath, Tulsidas 'adopts the theory of *avidya* and resorts to it whenever it suits his purpose. For instance, like the Adhyatma, before her abduction by Ravan, he makes the real Sita enter the fire and [an] illusory Sita, play all the subsequent parts in the drama'.[51]

TULSIDAS AND THE BABRI MASJID CONTROVERSY

The Babri mosque in Ayodhya is said to have been constructed by Mir Baqi, a commander of the first Mughal emperor, Zahiruddin Babur, in 1528. This information was recorded on an inscription on the walls of the mosque. Tulsidas neither mentions the destruction of a temple that marked the exact birthplace of Ram nor the construction of the Babri mosque over its ruins.

---

[50]Amid a spate of incidents of vandalism of statues of Dr B. R. Ambedkar by right-wing upper-caste Hindu groups, Datta's statue too was vandalized on 9 March 2018 in Raniganj in West Bengal. See Koushik Dutta, 'Vandalism virus spreads, now poet's statue defaced in Bengal', *Hindustan Times*, 10 March 2018.
[51]The Adhyatma Ramayana, Baij Nath, p. ii.

For the proponents of the theory that no temple was destroyed to build the Babri mosque, the absence of any mention by Tulsidas is hard evidence. But to the pro-Ram temple destruction theorists, Tulsidas's omission is irrelevant. Koenraad Elst, a Belgian author and avowed sympathizer of Hindu nationalists, writes in his book, *Ayodhya: The Case Against the Temple*:

> Thus, poet Tulsidas, author of the main devotional work on Rama in Hindi, the *Ramcharitmanas*, is often cited as remaining silent regarding the alleged temple demolition. But this proves little, when you keep in mind that in his day (ca. 1600 AD) the construction of the Babri Masjid at the site (1528 AD according to the inscription on the mosque itself) was a long-accomplished fact, and that the same Tulsidas doesn't mention any of the numerous temple demolitions even in his own Varanasi. As a rewriter of ancient traditions, Tulsidas was just not a reporter on recent events at all; he does not even mention his own most famous contemporary, the enlightened Emperor Akbar.[52]

Based on their interpretation of some of his verses, others claim that Tulsidas did mention the demolition in *Ramcharitmanas*.[53]

A COMPARATIVE ANALYSIS OF DIFFERENT RAMAYANAS

To appreciate the richness of the Ramayana's plurality—the Valmiki Ramayana, Kamban's Ramayana, Tulsidas's *Ramcharitmanas*, the Thai Ramayana Ramakien, and Hemchandra's Jain Ramayana—let us examine characteristics and distinctiveness across different versions.

DIFFERENCE BETWEEN TULSIDAS'S AND VALMIKI'S RAMAYANA

For millions of Ram worshippers, his humanity, humaneness and humility comes across in a brief encounter Ram, Sita and Laksman have with a kevat (boatman) when they reach the Ganga. This encounter is mentioned only by Tulsidas. In the Valmiki Ramayana, there is no dialogue between Ram and the kevat, as there is only an empty boat tied to the shore and no boatman in it.

In the Valmiki Ramayana, after Ram crosses the river it is said that he

---

[52]Koenraad Elst, *Ayodhya: The Case Against the Temple*, New Delhi: Voice of India, 2002, p. 11.

[53]Nityānanda Miśra, 'Tulsi Dasji described demolition of original Ram Mandir in 1528', *Google Groups*, September 2012 <https://groups.google.com/forum/#!topic/bvparishat/X9xQiS5HhUs>.

performs the 'evening worship'. Worship of whom and in what manner is not stated. Whereas in Tulsidas's version, after trying and failing to convince the kevat to accept a jewelled ring as a token of appreciation for helping them cross the river, Ram takes a bath and prays to Shiva. Shiva worship seems to be an integral part of the life of Tulsidas's Ram. This perhaps reflects the context or the setting of Tulsidas's time. Shaivas and Vaishnavas had been quarrelling for a long time when Tulsidas wrote his Ramayana.

In a way, Tulsidas builds on the presence of Shiva in the Valmiki Ramayana but takes it much further by uniting Shiva worship and Ram worship in his version. The Tulsidas Ramayana opens with Shiva narrating the story of Ram to Parvati, and throughout the story, Shiva worship remains a constant feature.

MANTHARA'S BEATING

In the scene in Valmiki's Ramayana when Shatrughan (Lakshman's twin brother) is about to strike a deadly blow against Manthara, a hunchbacked maid, Bharat scolds him for raising his hand on a woman. Bharat says, 'Control yourself! Women should be protected from assault from all creatures! I would have killed vile Kaikeyi had I not known that the righteous Ram would condemn me for killing my mother. If Ram hears that we have killed this hunchback, he will never speak to us again.'[54] Admonished by Bharat, Shatrughan lets the maid go.

In Tulsidas's Ramayana, the same scene is described with the gory details of Manthara's injuries as a raging Shatrughan drags her across the floor. The Tulsidas version also skips the admonition Bharat gives Shatrughan over assaulting a woman. Tulsidas's version of the same scene is as follows:

> Angered at seeing the bejewelled hunchback Manthara, Shatrugan lands a powerful kick on her hunch. Screaming, she falls on the floor... her hunch is busted, her head splits open, her teeth broken and blood oozes out of her mouth. She asks, 'What did I do to get this beating? I did you good but this is how you treat me?' This further fuels Shatrugan's rage and he grabs her by her hair and starts dragging her across the floor. At this moment the reservoir of kindness [Bharat] saves her and both brothers leave to meet Kausalya.[55]

---

[54]Valmiki, The Ramayana, Arshia Sattar, trans., p. 191.
[55]Translated by the author from *Shri Ramcharitmanas*, Gorakhpur: Gita Press, 2015, p. 479.

Tulsidas also emphasizes the kindness of Ram who accepts all kinds of lowlife sinners or outcastes after they bow to him. They can all receive his love and blessing if they are truly and fully devoted to him. This is perhaps the most remarkable feature of his version of the Ramayana: that Ram worship is not conditional, it doesn't have strict rules of admission. Ram, as an avatar of Vishnu, is even made to embrace the lowly Nishad; the message is—anybody can win Ram's love. To this extent, Tulsidas's Ramayana can be compared with Kamban's Ramayana in Tamil.

BHARAT FAILS TO CONVINCE RAM TO RETURN TO AYODHYA

The closing scene of 'Bharat Milap', a chapter of the Ramayana, depicts Bharat travelling with his family, army and the people of Ayodhya to Chitrakoot at the borders of the Dandaka forest, where Ram, Sita and Lakshman are staying, to persuade Ram to return to Ayodhya and rule as king.

In the Valmiki Ramayana, as this chapter is about to end, Bharat, torn apart by his love and devotion for Ram, has begun to realize that his older brother is not going to return to Ayodhya. Feeling more and more helpless and growing desperate, Bharat does what little brothers do—he holds his breath and threatens self-harm. Bharat addresses Sumantra, the late Dasharatha's charioteer and confidant:

> Bring sacred grass O Charioteer,
> And strew it on the level here,
> For I will sit and watch his [Ram's] face,
> Until I win my brother's grace.
> Like a robbed Brahmin will I lie[56]
> Nor taste of food, nor turn my eye,
> In front of Ram's leafy cot,
> And till he yield will leave him not.[57]

Bharat, seeing Sumantra wavering in front of Ram, himself spreads the sacred grass in haste. Ram then chides Bharat for besieging him like a commoner, as it is unbecoming of a king. Bharat, feeling alone in his attempt to sway Ram's mind, turns to the people of Ayodhya who have been

---

[56]A practice, which had frequently been described under the name of dharna by European travellers to India,
[57]Ralph T. H Griffith, trans., *The Rámáyan of Válmíki,* London: Trübner & Co., 1870–74, p. 221.

standing around witnessing this tense and dramatic scene unfold. Bharat says, 'O people, join your prayers with mine, And so his stubborn heart incline.'

It is a testing moment for the people of Ayodhya who travelled so far to bring their beloved Ram back to rule Ayodhya. It is a test because by now they too have realized the absolute devotion Ram has to his dead father and his promise to him (what is often described as Dharma in the epic). They have seen his commitment and resolve to stay in the forest for the fourteen years of exile. The ordinary people of Valmiki's Ayodhya perhaps realized, more than the sages and more than the brothers Bharat and Shatrughan, that Ram was sure of his decision, and perhaps they also respected him now for his steadfastness to his conviction. In an almost volte-face, the people reply to Bharat:

> 'Full well is Ram known to us.
> Right is the word he speaks,
> And he is faithful to his sire's decree,
> Nor can we rushly venture now,
> To turn him from his proposed vow.'
> Then Ram spoke:
> 'O Bharat, heed
> Thy virtuous friends and mark their rede
> Mark well what I and they advise,
> And duty view with cleaner eyes.
> Thy hand on mine, O hero, place,
> Touch water, and thy sin efface!'
> Then Bharat rose: his hand he dipped,
> And purifying water sipped
> 'Each citizen,' he cried, 'give ear;
> Attend each counsellor and peer.
> My mother planned, by me untaught,
> To win the sway I never sought;
> 'Ne'er Raghu's son could I despise,
> In duty's lore supremely wise.'[58]

Here Bharat tries another trick to force Ram to change his decision, he continues:

---

[58]Ibid.

'Now if obedience to our sire
This dwelling in the wood require,
I, till the destined years be spent,
Will dwell alone on banishment.'[59]

Ram dismisses this entreaty completely but assures Bharat that upon his return after fourteen years he will reign as king.

In the Tulsidas Ramayana, on the other hand, it is Bharat himself who realizes the folly of his campaign to change Ram's mind. Bharat is shown by Tulsidas as first trying all kinds of appeals and supplications. Muni Vashisht, King Janak, Janak's wife, Ram's mother, all of them are shown as trying to get Ram to change his mind. Finally when it dawns on them, particularly on Bharat, that Ram's purpose and intent (to save Indra's capital Amravati from Ravan) is higher than their selfish love, it is Bharat who gives in to Ram's conviction and then almost as if he had always known the outcome, asks Ram's permission to visit the various holy sites in Chitrakoot before he consecrates Ram as king and rules in his stead or in his sandals.

The difference between Tulsidas and Valmiki's Ramayana is not in the story, characters and narrative style alone. It is not restricted to Ram being a god and god-like. It is also to do with how the authors have depicted the people of Ayodhya. For instance, in Valmiki's Ramayana, the author acknowledges the agency of the people of Ayodhya and their appreciation of Ram's resolve to keep his and his father's word. He does so by showing that when Bharat seeks the people's support in a final effort to change Ram's mind through 'little brother blackmail', they deny it to him and instead back Ram's vow to complete his exile. By the time Tulsidas came to write his Ramayana, kingship was so deeply entrenched that he makes no effort to acknowledge the people of Ayodhya except as extras or props on a stage. They have no agency whatsoever except, of course, when some are shown gossiping about Sita's morality.

JAVALI'S SPEECH OMITTED IN TULSIDAS'S RAMAYANA
In the Valmiki Ramayana, Ram is told by one of his father's priests, Javali, to not accept his father's wish to go into exile. He says:

'Hail, Raghu's princely son, dismiss
A thought so weak and vain as this...

---

[59]Ibid.

… Enjoy, my lord, the present bliss,
And things unseen from thought dismiss.
Let this advice thy bosom move,
The counsel sage which all approve;
To Bharat's earnest prayer incline,
And take the rule so justly thine.'[60]

SHABARI EPISODE

The encounter between Ram and Shabari, an elderly tribal woman he meets in the forest, is used by Tulsidas only to highlight various kinds of devotion to Ram. He has Ram telling Shabari how to win his favour:

- By listening to sermons by saints.
- By love for Ram's story.
- By serving gurus without pride and ego.
- By praising Ram's various qualities without malice.
- By chanting Ram-mantra and having strong faith in Ram.
- By controlling your urges, by being polite, by not being involved in many things and by serving saints and sages practising their dharma.
- By viewing the whole world as devoted to Ram and considering saints even greater than Ram.
- By being content with what you have and not even dreaming of seeing the faults of others.
- By being 'simple', being without malice and having heartfelt faith in Ram
- By neither feeling happiness nor sadness.

AUBREY MENEN'S RAMAYANA

The story of Ram continues to be rewritten and retold. Today, several translations of the Ramayana exist in English and other foreign languages, and many more are in the process of being written. The Ramayana story is being propagated through radio shows and TV programmes. In India, one of the first orginal takes on the Ramayana in English was by Aubrey Menen. His *Rama Retold* was first published in 1956. It is an iconoclastic portrayal of the epic and spares only Ravan in its scathing and humorous depiction of the story. Menen attacks the flaws of Brahminical ideology as well as the

---

[60]Ibid., p. 217.

inherent patriarchy embedded in the Ramayana. Jawaharlal Nehru banned
the book in India and it remains banned till today.

SULEIMAN CHARITRA BY KALYAN MALLA

A recent translation of a fifteenth- to sixteenth-century Sanskrit text, *Suleiman
Charitra,* deserves a mention here because it is set in Ayodhya when it was
under the Lodi dynasty which preceded the Mughals. It was translated into
English only in 2015. The author says that it was written at the orders of
'Prince Lad Khan, the son of King Ahmad, the Lodhi ruler of Ayodhya'. Its
author, Kalyan Malla, lauds the Lodi 'chieftains with profuse panegyrics' and
Malla describes himself as a leading poet in Ahmad Khan's court. However,
the similarity with the Ramayana is limited to its setting in Ayodhya. The rest
of the story comprises Judaic and Biblical themes, and tales drawn from the
Arabian Nights.[61]

RAMAYANA'S PLURALITY AND AYODHYA

It would be simpler to imagine Ayodhya in Uttar Pradesh as the lively
source of the propagation of the Ramayana, where temples and monasteries
have churned out priests, stocked libraries and trained reciters so that they
spread the Ramayana to the ends of the world. Ayodhya, either abandoned
or ignored for most of known history, has not been as fortunate as the
Ramayana story, which was propagated by bards, traders and kings. While
towns like Shravasti, Banaras and Pataliputra boast a rich and long history of
kingdoms, Ayodhya's glory emanates from being the city of Ram on paper.
It was a paper-capital, a paper-city, an abstraction to most who heard the
story.

In Ayodhya, no doubt people, mainly sadhus, lived in the forests
surrounded by monkeys and carried on with their sadhna (worship), but
it was not an episcopal headquarters which produced customized Ramayanas.

---

[61]Kalyan Malla, *Suleiman Charitra,* A. N. D. Haksar, trans., New Delhi: Penguin Books, 2015.

Chapter 3

THE RAMAYANA IN TRIBAL AND FOLK
TRADITIONS IN INDIA AND BEYOND

The spread of the Ramayana story among the different tribes of India is a fascinating process of diffusion through interaction with the 'greater Hindu tradition' in the form of travelling mendicants called Gossains. Though increased 'Sanksritization', a process through which traditionally non-Hindu tribes are absorbed into Hinduism, has made many of the tribal Ramayanas extinct, researchers have documented hundreds of different Ramayanas in the various tribal and folk traditions across the subcontinent. K. S. Singh, co-editor of an anthology called *Rama-katha in Tribal and Folk Traditions of India*, recalls in his introduction that as a young researcher in the 1960s, he found songs and stories which showed the extent to which the Ramayana had been internalized. This chapter deals with some of the tribal and folk traditions that underscore the plurality of the Ramayana and the different ways in which it was re-adapted by communities.

TRIBAL RAMAYANAS

Though tribal groups vary from each other, their common existential basis in relation to the more prosperous and powerful Hindu tradition makes them interpret the Ramayana in similar ways.[62] Thus, in its bare bones form, the tribal Ramayana story consists of a mighty ruler named Ravan who ruled over the entire universe in which all living creatures were 'at the mercy of his desire'.[63] Ravan was both cruel and despotic; he exploited the weak tribals who finally prayed to the Almighty to save them by killing Ravan. Pleased

---

[62]N. N. Vyas, 'The tribal view of the Ramayana: an exercise in the anthropology of knowledge' in K. S. Singh and Birendranath Datta, eds., *Rama-katha in Tribal and Folk Traditions of India, Proceedings of a Seminar*, Kolkata: Anthropological Society of India and Seagull Books, 1993.

[63]Ibid., p. 12.

with their prayers, God descended on the world as Rama, their saviour.

A tribal magician-priest ensured the birth of a son to Dasharatha, who was cursed with childlessness. Once the four sons were born, the priest demanded two sons in his service. Dasharatha, as promised, gave him the two younger sons. 'But since rulers, according to the tribal Ramayan, always tell lies and practice deceit, the priest realised the fraud and took the first two sons—Rama and Lakshmana—away to the forest.'[64]

Similarly, in tribal retellings, Sita is not the daughter of a king who resided in a palace with all imaginable comforts but lived in a thatched hut with her father, Janak. One day, while busy spreading cow dung on the mud floor of the small courtyard outside their hut, she discovers the favourite bow of the tribe. Being in a hurry, she effortlessly manages to move the famous bow out of her way. When Janak finds out that his daughter was able to lift the bow which many men couldn't, he resolves to get her married only to somebody who can 'break the mighty bow into two pieces. Ram performed this act and was married to her'.[65]

Another common feature in many tribal Ramayanas is the presence of Vaishnava ideas of morality and piety. Alcohol and sex outside marriage were often looked down upon and were woven into the story in a way that made them appear to be the cause of the tribals' woes.

RAVANAVAMSI GONDS

In the origin myth of the Gond tribe of Garhmandla in central India, the first human being, a Gond, was born from the union of Shiva and Parvati. A Gond couple, who lived near Ravan's kingdom, had been cursed by Shiva in their previous birth that they would remain childless till they drank Ram's charandoka (water used to wash Ram's feet). The couple waited for Ram and when he finally arrived to battle Ravan, they washed his feet and drank the water. Ram said to them, 'You will be known as Ravanavamsi Gonds, you will have three sons, Alko, Talko, and Karcho.' Subsequently, when returning after vanquishing Ravan, Ram brought some Gond people along with him to Ayodhya. They came to be known as Suryavamsi Gonds (Gonds of the Solar clan) and were said to have kinship with the Ravanavamsi Gonds.[66]

---

[64]Ibid., p. 13.

[65]Ibid.

[66]M. K. Mishra, 'Influence of the Ramayana tradition on the folklore of central India' in Singh and Datta, eds., *Rama-katha in Tribal and Folk Traditions of India*, pp. 17–18.

A MYTH OF THE BONDA TRIBE

Now numbering less than 12,000 (according to the 2011 census of India), the Bonda people are found in the remote hilly areas of Malkangiri district in Odisha. A myth prevalent among them in the first half of the twentieth century weaves in a rather contrived explanation for their custom of not covering their bodies. The story goes that while Ram was in the forest with Lakshman and Sita, they encountered a group of Bonda women who laughed at them because they found it amusing that one female was moving about with two males, and also because Sita's clothes were too thin to cover her private parts. An enraged Sita, whose clothes were provided by Brahma, cursed the amused women, 'You Bonda women will never use cloth and even if you do, your body will never tolerate the heat of the cloth.'[67]

In such myths, scholars contend that 'the tribes have tried to project their ancestors as contemporaries of Rama and that this shows the wide reach of Rama-story amongst the autochthonous tribals of the different regions of India'.[68] It can be argued, equally plausibly, that such origin myths were themselves a result of the 'Sanskritization' of tribes during their interaction with the Hindu tradition.

THE BANSGEET OF ODISHA AND CHHATTISGARH

Bansgeet literally means bamboo song. The bans is a three-feet-long bamboo pipe with five holes in it, similar to a long flute. The Gaur or the milkman caste found in Odisha's Kalahandi district are believed to have been the first to perform their own version of the Ram story in the form of an epic song that was played on the bans. The Ram story is localized with a village farmer, Kotrabaina, and his wife Ramela playing the roles of Ram and Sita. The king of that region was a lustful tyrant given to abducting beautiful women. Once, finding Ramela alone, the king's soldiers forcibly take her to their king. The same night, Kotrabaina sees what had happened in a dream. Like the rescue of Sita by Ram, Kotrabaina galvanizes his army of twelve lakh bulls and twelve lakh sheep, along with a magical bull named Kurmul Sandh and sheep named Ultia Gadra, and attacks the king in order to free Ramela. Once freed, the Gaur society, like the people of Ayodhya in the Ramayana, refuse to accept Ramela until she passes a chastity test. A localized version of this bansgeet is found in Chhattisgarh too.

---

[67]Ibid., p. 18.
[68]Ibid.

BAIGA LAKSHMAN'S ORDEAL BY FIRE

Most Ramayanas and Ram-stories mention the ordeals by fire that Sita had to undergo to prove her purity. But a totally different kind of ordeal-by-fire story was found to be prevalent among the Baigas, a primitive tribal group in central India.

The gist of the story relates to Ram's suspicion that Sita and Lakshman were having an affair. When confronted by Ram, Lakshman protests and offers to go through a fire test to prove his innocence. Ram agrees and makes his brother go through circles of fire through which he emerges unharmed.

According to sociologists, the purpose of making Lakshman go through the fire test was to 'solve a social problem' among the Baigas.[69] The 'social problem' was the custom of licentious relations between the brother's wife and his younger brother. Thus the story of a chaste Lakshman serves to present an ideal of 'moral' behaviour from which Baiga society can draw inspiration.[70]

BHILODI RAMAYANA OR THE BHIL RAMAYANA

The Bhils are one of the largest tribal groups found in states like Andhra Pradesh, Madhya Pradesh, Rajasthan, Maharashtra and Gujarat. In the Panch Mahal area of Gujarat and Rajasthan, the Bhils performed their own version of the Ramayana. It comprised seventeen different songs, 'a penultimate bhajan and an ultimate arti'.[71] The Bhils believe that Valmiki was a Bhil called Valio Bhil; the opening song of the Bhil Ramayana describes Valmiki's story first and then comes to Ram. The remaining sixteen songs cover the entire Ramayana up to the point when Ram, Lakshman and Sita return to Ayodhya. It is in the bhajan, or song of worship, that the moral overtones of purity and piety appear. In it 'there are references to Bhil habits of drinking, and in the last arti, they [the singers] fall at the feet of Rama'.[72]

MONKEY-EATING BIRHORS' RAM STORY

Found mainly in the states of Jharkhand, West Bengal, Odisha and Chhattisgarh, the Birhors are an almost extinct primitive tribal group

---

[69]Ibid., p. 26.
[70]Ibid.
[71]T. B. Naik, 'Rama-katha among the Tribes of India' in Singh and Datta, eds., *Rama-katha in Tribal and Folk Traditions of India*, pp. 31–32.
[72]Ibid., p. 33.

who have traditionally survived by gathering fruits and hunting animals, including baboons and monkeys. Over time, with the influence of Hindu traditions and customs, they have managed to weave into their version of the Ram-story a plot that legitimizes the consumption of monkey meat. 'The story goes that when Ravan took Sita away to Lanka, Ram, Lakshman and Hanuman went there to rescue her.'[73] Birhors were living in those parts, too. When Ravan failed to capture Hanuman, he took help from the Birhors, but they too failed. Hanuman, taking pity on them, told them the trick to catching him and when they did, he asked them to set him on fire. Hanuman then proceeded to set Ravan's Lanka on fire and went to Ram and asked him, 'who will dispose my body when I die?' 'The Birhors who trapped you, they and their progeny will eat you and your kind,' replied Ram.[74]

RAMAYANA IN FOLK SONGS

In folk songs in Awadhi and Bhojpuri, two dialects from eastern Uttar Pradesh and Bihar, Ram is portrayed as an ordinary man. At other times, he is a village boy who plays along the banks of the Sarayu. Sita, on the other hand, is said to be the daughter of Ravan, who abandons her to prevent her from becoming the cause of his death, as prophesied by the sage Narad. She is discovered by King Janak when he himself takes up the plough during a severe drought. In Bhojpuri songs, it is Janak's wife who ploughs the fields, stark naked, in the middle of the night (this practice continues to this day, where women plough the field naked either to appease or to shame the gods).[75]

RAMAYANA STORIES IN TELUGU FOLK SONGS: THE PLIGHT OF URMILA

'Urmiladevi Nidra' (Urmiladevi's Coma-like Sleep)[76] is a popular ballad sung by women in Andhra Pradesh and Telangana. This song seeks to redress the complete marginalization of Urmila, Lakshman's wife and a younger sister to Sita. The Telugu folk tradition seems to have preserved her memory. Urmila's wish to accompany Lakshman into exile along with Sita and Ram

---

[73]Ibid., p. 47.

[74]Ibid., pp. 47–48.

[75]K. D. Upadhyaya, 'The story of Rama in the folk tradition of the Hindi region' in Singh and Datta, eds., *Rama-katha in Tribal and Folk Traditions of India*, pp. 68–69.

[76]D. Rama Raju, 'Versions of Ramayana stories in Telugu folk literature' in Singh and Datta, eds., *Rama-katha in Tribal and Folk Traditions of India*, p. 85.

was rejected by Lakshman, who quoted sacred injunctions:

> The younger sister-in-law shall not tread
> The same ground traversed by the eldest brother-in-law.
> She shall not be within earshot of him.
> How can I take you, to follow them?

Urmila stays behind in Ayodhya and out of loneliness and the pain of separation from her husband, slips into a coma.

When Ram, Sita and Lakshman return, instead of heading straight to meet Urmila, Lakshman continues to remain in the service of his elder brother until the coronation. It is only when Sita tells him to check on his wife that Lakshman finally goes to her. What follows is a poignant scene in which Urmila, who had been asleep for fourteen years, remonstrates at the 'sudden presence of an intruder in her private chamber'.[77] She says:

> O Sir, who are you? Why this outrage?
> Wandering in lanes and bylanes,
> Why did you commit this mistake?
> Why did you intrude into this solitary chamber?
> If my sire King Janaka learns about this
> He will order your punishment.
> If my sister and her husband know about this,
> Danger to your life is imminent.
> If her brother-in-law was here now,
> He would not allow you to survive.[78]

RAMAYANA IN FOLK TRADITIONS IN ASSAM AND NORTHEAST INDIA

The most well-known Assamese Ramayana is the one composed by Madhav Kandali in the fourteenth century. It is considered to be largely a translation of the Valmiki Ramayana and is 'hailed for its faithfulness'.[79] But Kandali too could not resist including what is considered an interpolation of existing folklore, which goes as follows. One day during the exile, as Ram was sleeping with his head resting on Sita's lap, a raven was drawn to her extraordinarily beautiful breasts. The raven started pecking at them but Sita,

---

[77]Ibid., p. 87.
[78]Ibid.
[79]Birendranath Datta, 'Rama-katha in Assam and its neighbourhood: popular and folk traditions', in Singh and Datta, eds., *Rama-katha in Tribal and Folk Traditions of India*, p. 120.

anxious not to wake Ram from his sleep, neither moved nor cried out. When Ram woke up and found out what had happened he shot an arrow at the raven and blinded it in one eye. 'Since then it is believed that the raven sees with only one eye.'[80]

Another story that appears in the oral tradition in Assam but is not present in any other Ram-katha pertains to Sita's chastity after Ram's victory. Here, instead of putting Sita through a fire test, 'Ram asks her to produce witnesses in her support'.[81] Sita calls the sun and the moon as her witnesses; the sun promptly vouches for her conduct during the day but 'pleads ignorance about the happenings of the night when he is absent'.[82] The moon too testifies in Sita's favour on all nights except the night of the new moon when he is not present. Thus, on account of that one night, Sita's innocence remains unproven and Ram banishes her to the forest.

Some other Ramayanas that need to be mentioned here even though they might not be extant any more are the Karbi Ramayana of the Karbi tribe, the Mizo (Lushai) Ramayana in Mizoram, the Khamti Ramayana and the Ramayana of the Lalungs (Tiwas).[83]

THE RAMAYANA STORY IN PERSIAN AND URDU

Persian translations of the Ramayana can be traced back to Mughal times. Historian Abd al-Qadir Badauni translated the Valmiki Ramayana into Persian at the orders of Akbar between 1584 and 1589. During Emperor Jahangir's reign (1605–1627), the Ramayana was translated into Persian by Girdharidas. Later, *Ramayana Faizi* was composed during Emperor Shah Jahan's reign (1628–1658). The *Tarjuma-e-Ramayan* by Gopal was also written in the seventeenth century. Chandrabhan Bedil composed a concise translation of the Valmiki Ramayana in 1685, followed by a more complete translation in 1693. Another translation, *Ramayan Amar Prakash*, by Lala Amar Singh, appeared at the beginning of the eighteenth century in 1705. Lala Amanat Rai translated the Valmiki Ramayana in 1754. Mullah Masih composed the last known Ramayana in Persian in 1898. It is possible that

---

[80]Ibid.

[81]Ibid., p 124.

[82]Ibid.

[83]Swami Parampanthi, Bangovinda, et al., 'The Ramayana: Its influence on the tribal life of north-east India' in Singh and Datta, eds., *Rama-katha in Tribal and Folk Traditions of India*, p. 164.

Masih was a Christian as his version of the Ramayana contains biblical characters like Jesus and Mary.[84]

The earliest known Ramayana story in Urdu dates back to 1864. It was written by Munshi Jagannath Lal Khushtar and published by Nawal Kishore Press, Allahabad. It came to be known as Khushtar Ramayana and begins with the words 'Bismillah ir Rehman ir Rahim'. Inspired by the epic's eternality, another translator, Jogeshwar Nath 'Betab' Bareilvi called his translation the *Amar Kahani*. Scores of other translations of parts of the Ramayana were done in the nineteenth century and were named after their authors. These include *Ulfat ki Ramayana*, *Rahmat ki Ramayana*, and the more famous *Chakbast ki Ramayana*. Brij Narayan Chakbast was born in Faizabad in 1882. His renderings of certain episodes in the Ramayana remain etched in the memory of the people of Awadh. The episode describing the departure of Ram from Ayodhya is specially remembered for its evocative depiction:

Rukhsat huwa woh baap se lekar khuda ka naam
Raah-e wafa ki manzil-e awwal hui tamaam

(He took leave of his father taking the name of God
And thus the first stage of the path of loyalty was crossed)[85]

Similarly, 'Kaushalya's lament at her son going away to exile, too, is expressed in a language that could only have emerged from the beating heart of Hindustan'.

Kis tarah ban mein ankhon ke taare ko bhej duun
Jogi bana ke raj-dulare ko bhej duun

(How can I send the light of my eyes to the forest?
How can I turn my prince into a mendicant and send him away?)[86]

These are just some of the compositions and versions of the stories from the Ramayana that were translated and rendered into Urdu. 'According to a comprehensive study of Ram-katha in Urdu by the late Ali Jawad Zaidi, there were over 300 such versions, many from the Awadh region alone, and several

---

[84]Camille Bulcke, *Ramkatha: Utpatti aur Vikas*, Prayag: Hindi Parishad Prakashan, 1950.
[85]Rakshanda Jalil, 'The Ballad of Ram-e-Hind: revisiting the Urdu versions of Ramayana that once lit up the stage', *Indian Express*, 24 September 2017.
[86]Ibid.

written in the style of marsiya-goi popularized by Anees and Dabeer.'[87]

RAMAKIEN OR THE THAI RAMAYANA

The Thai Ramayana or the Ramakien is a dance-drama influenced by the aesthetics of and for eighteenth-century Thailand. For centuries, Thai kings have appended Sanskritic Rama titles to their names. Since the first millennium of the Common Era, Thai kingdoms and their capitals have been named after places and characters in the Ramayana.

Prince Subhadradis Diskul (1923–2003) was the great-grandson of Rama IV (Mongkut), who remodelled the Thai education system and is also known as the father of Thai history. Subhadradis Diskul, too, turned to history early in his life and produced many works of importance. About the Thai Ramayana tradition he writes, 'the story of the Ramayana has been very popular in Thailand... *Ramakien* which probably derives from the word Ramakirti in Sanskrit. The word Rama existed already during the Sukhothai period (about AD 1250–1450).'[88]

References to the story of the Ramayana go back to the Ayutthaya period (1350–1767 CE). However, the dance dramas are of recent origin— they cannot be placed before 1767 CE, as all surviving manuscripts are of later origin.

According to Diskul:

> King Rama I of the Bangkok period (1782–1809) composed the whole story of the Ramayana for a dance drama but it was King Rama II, his son (1809–1824), who composed the most popular story for dancing. King Mongkut (Subhadradis Diskul's great-grandfather) or Rama IV (1851–1868) wrote certain episodes of the Ramayan and it was King Vajiravudh or Rama VI (1910–1925) who was very much interested in Sanskrit literature and composed certain episodes of the Ramayan for dancing.[89]

The Ramayana that Mongkut wrote is a beautiful assimilation of the Valmiki Ramayana as well as the other, often later, Ramayanas that reached Thailand after a process of acculturation through medieval Southeast Asia.

---

[87]Ibid.
[88]Subhadradis Diskul, 'The difference between Valmiki Ramayana and the Thai version of Ramayana (Ramakirti) of King Rama I of Thailand (1782–1809)', p. 113.
[89]Ibid.

Pusa Sri, an activist who works on children's issues in Thailand, has an interesting take on the dominant values in Thai culture. She believes that despite the westernization, modernization and rapid transformation of general life in Thailand, children are expected to be obedient. Obedience to parents, mainly to the father, is the defining feature of ordinary Thai life and children are reared according to this ideal. She was speaking on the sidelines of a conference on children's rights in Thailand and saw violence against children sometimes emanate from such moral ideals. 'Children live under too much pressure and surrounded by modern media commodities. They might dress up like Justin Bieber but at home they are expected to be the ideal obedient son and daughter.'[90]

Unquestioned obedience is one of the obvious moral lessons of the Ramayana tale, whether it is of Ram to Dasharatha, of Lakshman to Ram, of Sita, of Ram to societal pressure and of Dasharatha to his own words. This is true for Thailand too; perhaps obedience has been a precondition to primogeniture everywhere. The Thai dynasty has passed on from eldest son to eldest son for more than 300 years.

RAM–SITA ENCOUNTER

Given the localized nature of Ramayana retellings it is not surprising that the Thai Ramayana has an interesting twist in the tale of Ram winning Sita's hand for marriage. Before reaching the venue of the public contest among princes to win the right to marry Sita, Ram and Lakshman are called to her father's palace. On their way Ram and Sita happen to see each other, and it is the proverbial love at first sight. Lakshman is summoned first to try lifting the divine bow, but knowing fully well that Ram has already fallen in love with Sita he deliberately fails at lifting it. Ram then easily lifts the bow, and thus, Sita and Ram are united.

ORIGIN OF AYODHYA IN THE THAI RAMAYANA

According to the Ramakien, Ishwar/Shiva decided to make the child found by Narayen in a lotus flower at the bottom of the sea the first king of the world. This boy eventually becomes the founder of the Narayen clan/dynasty. It was also decided that the boy's rule should begin from Jambudeep. Following Ishwar's orders to build a beautiful capital, Indra came to Jambudeep and met with four rishis—Achangari, Yugagra, Dah and Yag.

---

[90]Interview with Pusa Sri, Thailand, September–October 2016.

The rishis suggested that the capital should be established in Dvaravati forest. Indra then made this the capital and named it using the initials of the four rishis: thus the name Ayodhya.

AYODHYA IN THAILAND

In October 2016, eleven white elephants brought from Ayutthuya in trucks, trot-danced to the gates of the royal palace in Bangkok and knelt to pay respect to the deceased king Bhumibol Adulyadej. It is believed that Ayutthuya was based on the Ayodhya of the Ramayana and shows the once widespread influence of pantheistic Hinduism in Thailand (then Siam) since at least the latter half of the first millennium of the Common Era. Bound by a large river on three sides, old maps of Ayutthuya bear a striking geographical resemblance to Ayodhya as described in the epic, and also to present-day Ayodhya. This might have led some writers like Lala Sitaram to believe that the Ayutthuya of Siam was founded by Kshatriya families who 'left Ayodhya because of persecution of Muslims around the 1300s'.[91] By the fourteenth century rulers who followed Islam had conquered much of the Gangetic and Yamuna deltas, and what is now Ayodhya under the Emperor Qaiqabad of Delhi, as the Hindu kingdoms had long lost control over the region.

CHAKRI KINGS AND THEIR 'RAMA' TITLE

At the time of his death on 13 October 2016 at the age of eighty-nine, King Bhumibol Adulyadej or Rama IX of Thailand was the longest ruling head of state in history. First-time visitors to Thailand would note the ubiquitous presence of King Bhumibol's portrait, from taxis to parks to shops and even people's homes. Observant visitors who are Hindu would perhaps be surprised by the countless road signs bearing the title 'Rama IX'.

This has been the official title of Thai kings since 1782.[92] Bhumibol was worshipped as the 'father of the land' and as a king-god. Royal families in countries like India look up to how successfully Bhumibol and his ancestors have made democracy monarchy-friendly.

But unlike India, Thailand has never been colonized. The Chakri dynasty

---

[91]Lala Sitaram, *Ayodhya ka Itihas*, New Delhi: Arya Book Depot, 1932, 2001, 2015, p.112.
[92]The practice of designating them and their successors as Rama I, Rama II and so on was not established until the time of Rama VI, who thought that Thai names were too difficult for foreigners to remember.

that Bhumibol belonged to is comparatively young. It was founded only in the late eighteenth century by Thongduang, a powerful general of King Thaksin of Thonburi (derived from the Pali for Dhana, or wealth, and puri, or fortress, which is now one of the fifty districts that make up Bangkok).

King Thaksin made Thonburi the capital of his kingdom in 1768 after wresting it back from the Burmese in the aftermath of Ayutthuya's destruction by the Burmese. The kingdom of Ayutthuya had lasted for 400 years.

In 1350 CE, the Ayutthuya kingdom had been shifted about 150 kilometres north of present-day Bangkok by a man who had also used the legitimizing power of Ram by calling himself King Ramathabodi (from the order of Rama). Ekkathat, the thirty-third and last monarch of Ayutthuya, was defeated by the Burmese in April 1767.

THE ROLE OF KINGS

The Thai Rama dynasty is not Hindu by any measure. It follows Theravada Buddhism which has incorporated many Hindu elements including the Shaivite 'Holy jewel' or lingam. What is helpful in understanding the hydra-headed epic and its various uses, is the role of kings, since it is a story of a prince denied his throne. So in a way, it is only right that kings have been using the Ramayana to their own ends. The only religion of kings is to rule. And in the case of King Rama I, he rewrote the Ramayana, commissioned a set of murals depicting episodes from his Ramakien and popularized its performances along with the traditional forms of Buddhist worship in Thailand. Like many other kings, he too legitimized his own rule by incorporating the 'Glory of Rama' into the Thai idea of royal power. Thus, by reorienting the same kernel of a prince suffering in exile only to return to claim his legitimate throne, Rama I established a dynasty that continues to dominate Thai life to this day.

RAMAYANA AND KINGSHIP

Like Thai kings, Rajput kings in medieval Rajasthan too envisioned themselves as Ram, the epitome of duty and propriety. The earliest example of a ruler projecting himself as Ram comes in the late seventeenth century from the kingdom of Mewar. Comprising 120 miniature paintings in the Rajput style, this Ramayana survives in the British Library in London. The Ramayana was painted at the orders of the Mewar ruler, Rana Jagat Singh (r.1628–1652). The Mewar ruler commissioned the Ramayana at a time when Mughals had established themselves as the supreme power in north India. The rana's great fort of Chittor in Rajasthan had been ransacked and the library burnt to the ground.[93] According to historian William Dalrymple:

> Years later, when the Ranas re-established their capital at Udaipur, the Mewar Ramayana was commissioned by Rana Jagat Singh as part of the effort to rebuild his family's library, and it may have been under his influence that the manuscript came to link the Mewar dynasty with Rama (from whom it claimed descent), while connecting the demon Ravana with the Mughals.[94]

That perhaps explains why colourful paintings show Ravan taking a ceremonial bath in what resembles a royal Mughal tent. He is also painted standing at the window of his palace like the Mughal emperors Jahangir and Shah Jahan did when their subjects wished to have their darshan (audience).

The second example is of a later origin but is also against the backdrop of Mughal rule. In 1708, when Jai Singh, the Kachvaha ruler of Amer, set forth for battle against the Mughal troops, he depicted himself as Ram setting out to battle against Ravan. In 'Ramavilaskavyam' (Poem of the Sports of Ram), a poem composed around the events of the battle of Sambar, Jai Singh is 'portrayed as the quintessential dharmic king...for Jaisingh is identified with Rama, Vishnu this time not embodied to kill Ravan but the Mughal troops, called the Yavanas or Mlecchas, foreigners and barbarians. Whereas the emperor himself, the lord of those intruders, is mentioned in a rather subdued way and as an honourable opponent,' it is also said that 'Rama had incarnated himself as Jaisingh to destroy the family of the Yavanas.'[95]

AYUTTHUYA FADES AWAY, 'RAMA' THRIVES

In the wake of Ayutthuya's destruction, a new Ramayana and a new dynasty arose under Thongduang whose descendants continue to 'rule' Thailand today. The father of Thongduang, who founded the Chakri (derived from the Sanskrit 'Chakravartin') dynasty, worked in the royal court of Ayutthuya. Thongduang later assisted King Thaksin in establishing his smaller kingdom of Thonburi, and in a sense, reunifying Thailand (then Siam) after the fall

---

[93]William Dalrymple,. 'All Indian life is here', *The Guardian*, 23 August 2008.
[94]Ibid.
[95]Monika Horstmann, 'Visions of kingship in the twilight of Mughal rule', *2005 Gonda Lecture*, Amsterdam: Royal Netherlands Academy of Arts and Sciences, 2006.

of Ayutthuya. This was also enabled by the Burmese facing defeats at home by the Chinese. When King Thaksin died, Thongduang founded his own dynasty at Rattanakosin (now Bangkok). Later on, building on the long tradition of Siamese kingdoms like Sukhothai and Ayutthuya, he named himself Ramathibodi, just like the first king of Ayutthuya.

HOW 'HINDU' IS THE THAI RAMAYANA?

A reading of the Thai Ramayana reveals a strong Hindu influence. Hindu gods dominate the scene: Shiva is the supreme god, creator and upholder of the world, he is present throughout the Thai Ramayana while Vishnu is in the forefront of the story as he manifests as Ram at Shiva's request.

But the Thai Ramayana is not a Hinduized story. Scholar Frank Reynolds, in a comparison of the Ramakien with Hindu and Buddhist Ramayanas, has written:

> When in the late 18th century, a stable new dynasty was established with its capital at Bangkok, one of the prime concerns of the King Rama I was to reconstruct the religious and cultural life of the country. One of the major components in that reconstructive effort was his own specifically ordered and personally supervised composition of a new crystallisation of the Rama story called *Ramakien.*[96]

The Thai king Rama I who produced the Ramakien was not only a Buddhist king but was also a great patron of the religion. At the time he got this version written Thai Buddhists were adopting many Hindu elements and revising authoritative Buddhist texts by including Shiva and Vishnu in the Buddhist religious cosmos.

When Hindu chauvinists take pride in the imperial glory of Hinduism, they forget to mention the transformation of Shaivite and Vaishnavite traditions by Theravada Buddhism. And what makes the Thai version unambiguously non-Hindu is the absence of hierarchical, Brahmanical and dualistic elements. On the contrary, it contains Buddhist sensibilities, karmic explanations and Buddhist attitudes towards life, and gives much greater importance to Indra, who has come to be reviled in the Hindu Ramayana tradition.[97]

---

[96]Reynolds, 'Ramayana, Rama Jataka, Ramakien: A comparative study of Hindu and Buddhist traditions', pp. 55–56.
[97]Ibid.

The hierarchy and the 'irrationalism' of the medieval Hindu Ramayana seem to have been on the mind of King Rama I when he warned his people against viewing the Ramayana literally. In an epilogue attached to the Ramakien, he wrote, 'The writing of the Ramakien was done in accordance with a traditional tale, it is not of abiding importance; rather, it has been written to be used on celebrative occasions. Those who hear it and see it performed should not be deluded. Rather they should be mindful of impermanence.'[98] The word that Rama I uses for delusion is 'lailong', which is a direct translation of the Pali 'moha', a term that refers to one of the three main Buddhist vices (delusion, anger and greed). For impermanence he uses the word 'anitchang', a transliteration of the Pali term 'anicca', or impermanence. The use of Pali underscores the predominant Buddhist influence on the Ramakien because Pali was the language of the earliest literature of Buddhism and the sacred texts of Theravada Buddhism.

The Thai Ramayana, owing to Buddhist influence, is unapologetic, unpretentious and, given the localized nature of Ramayana tellings, it is unsurprising that it is full of twists that don't exist in the Valmiki or Tulsidas versions. For example, in the Thai Ramayana, Kumbhakarna (Ravan's ferocious brother, depicted as humongous and lazy in the Tulsidas's *Ramcharitmanas*-inspired TV series that was aired in the late 1980s) is shown to be a knowledgeable man who is an upholder of justice, and who in the end fights for his brotherly affection towards Ravan. When he first faces his enemies, Ram, Lakshman, Angad, Vibhishan, etc., he tells them to win an intellectual duel with him. He asks Ram four questions:

1. Who is a foolish sadhu?
2. Which elephant has straight tusks/teeth?
3. Who is a clever woman?
4. Who is a wicked/cruel human being?

Kumbhakarna challenges Ram to answer these questions and prove that he is an incarnation of Narayan (Vishnu). Ram fails to answer but in a face-saving attempt Angad speaks up and says, 'Of course Ram knows the answers but he wants to check if you have the right answers, so tell us the answer.'[99] Kumbhakarna gives them the answers.

1. Ram is the foolish sadhu who left Sita alone in the jungle.

---

[98]Ibid.
[99]Swami Satyanand Puri, *Ramkirti*, Gangaprasad Upadhyay, trans., pp. 80–81.

2. Daskanth (Ravan) is the elephant with straight tusks for he covets another's woman.
3. Sanmanakha (Surpanakha) is the clever woman for planning revenge in this manner.
4. Vibhek (Vibhishana) is the wicked man for betraying his country and master.

At least in this regard, the Thai Ramayana is more like the Jain Ramayana, which also paints Kumbhakarna in a positive light. Thus it would seem that the Thai version is influenced more by Jain thought, which in turn contains Buddhist influences. And yet, it cannot be called a Buddhist tale because the story is not presented as an incident in one of the previous births of Buddha.

To further buttress this point: in the Tulsidas version there is no scope for such berating of Ram as done by Kumbhakarna. Ram is a god and is flawless. Whatever errors he makes are attributed to anadi avidya, a device that Tulsidas uses freely in his Ramayana. This allows him to deal with episodes in the Valmiki Ramayana that cannot be completely removed but also cannot be justified as the doings of Ram, the ideal man, to the audience of sixteenth-century north India. Thus, he adds elaborate twists. For instance, using the omniscience of Ram, Tulsidas has him secretly tell Sita, when Lakshman is away in the jungle, to create a living, breathing replica of herself (duplicate Sita) and that she (the real Sita) should go into the protective care of the fire goddess (Agni), because the Ram of Tulsidas knows that she will soon be abducted by Ravan.

Chapter 4

SCRIPTURE, MYTH AND REALITY

Ascending anachronism means pushing an event or occurrence to a time in the past. This is often accompanied by the idealization of that time as a period when things were perfect. The more the event is pushed back into the past the more legitimizing power it acquires. Muslims hark back to the time of the Prophet, Christians to the time of Jesus, Buddhists remember Buddha, Jains the time of Mahavir, and Hindus today are told that in the time of king-god Ram, Ayodhya was the best capital in the world where all lived happily and peacefully. The example of Ram Rajya, or Ram's rule, was often cited by Mahatma Gandhi. It is interesting that Gandhi could use Ram Rajya to galvanize all communities and not just Hindus, which once again reflects the plurality of the Ramayana tradition. Ram was called Imam-e-Hind by Iqbal, the famous Urdu poet who later wrote the national anthem of Pakistan.[100] It is impossible to establish when Ram Rajya prevailed, if it indeed did. Those who believe in the historicity of Ram Rajya place its birth around 5114 BCE[101] on the basis of astro-archaeology, although using planetary positions to establish historicity is yet to be recognized as a reliable method.

The material evidence of Ram Rajya in the Ayodhya of today is negligible, as we have seen in the first chapter. Perhaps the Ayodhya of Ram was a different place that now lies submerged under the Sarayu, as suggested to me by K. N. Govindacharya, a former ideologue of the Rashtriya Swayamsevak Sangh (RSS). The paucity of evidence of the kingly Ram has been replaced by faith in the godly Ram, and thus, the Ayodhya of today encapsulates both Ram-Rajya and Ram worship.

---

[100]Rakshanda Jalil, 'The Ballad of Ram-e-Hind: revisiting the Urdu versions of Ramayana that once lit up the stage', *Indian Express*, 24 September 2017.
[101]Pushkar Bhatnagar, *Dating the Era of Lord Ram,* New Delhi: Rupa Publications, 2004, p. 18.

We cannot scientifically establish the historicity of Ram Rajya, but we shall attempt the same for Ram worship in Ayodhya.

In today's Ayodhya, the legends around Ram stretch time to limits that are impossible to wrap one's head around. Visitors, educated and unlettered, rich and poor, are told by local guides, 'It has been nine lakh fifty-six thousand years since Ram left Ayodhya. Therefore, obviously, nothing remains from that time. The temples that you see today were built by King Vikramaditya of Ujjain. He brought a Kamdhenu (wish-fulfilling) cow from Banaras, made the cow circumambulate Ayodhya and wherever the cow dropped dung, he excavated those places and at these places he built the temples.' A slightly different version of this story is what Mahant Satyendra Das, the head priest of the Ram Janmabhoomi temple, tells me. According to him, it was not dung but milk from the cow's udders that marked the 'holy' spots. Wherever the cow spilled milk, Vikramaditya built a temple. Nar Singh Pandey, a local guide, continues, 'Hanumangarhi, Ram Janmabhoomi, Kanak Bhavan, Sita Rasoi and Dashrath Mahal were built by Vikramaditya. Later on, many temples were built by people. In Ayodhya, every year a couple of new temples come up.'

Ram is said to have left Ayodhya for heaven nine lakh fifty-six thousand years ago, taking his subjects who loved him dearly along with him. Thus, Ayodhya became desolate and remained so until Vikramaditya—whose own historicity remains unestablished—found it and resettled it. Pro-temple historian Thakur Prasad Verma writes about this legend in his book, *Ayodhya ka Itihas evam Purattatva,* and also in the ASI's magazine, *Purattatva.* 'Who was this Vikramaditya? Nothing can be said with certitude about him. According to tradition, Vikramaditya was a king of Ujjain in the Gardhabhilla dynasty and who instituted the Hindu calendar known as Vikram Samvat in 57 BCE. There is no evidence of him ever visiting Ayodhya.'[102]

Verma also explores the possibility of Chandragupta II being the Vikramaditya of Nar Singh Pandey's tour but concludes that the legend 'can neither be rejected nor verified'.[103] Be that as it may, the guides of Ayodhya believe it and so do the priests.

At the Vishva Hindu Parishad (VHP)-run stone-cutting workshop which also houses a mini gallery exhibiting the VHP-approved version of Ayodhya's

---

[102]T. P. Verma and S. P. Gupta, *Ayodhya ka Itihas evam Purattatva*, New Delhi: Indian Council of Historical Research, 2001, p. 74.
[103]Ibid.

history, Nar Singh Pandey continues, 'Babur destroyed the temple in 1526 with the help of cannons because the temple was so strong that his army couldn't destroy it without them. The mosque that he then built over the ruins used the blood of 176,000 Hindus to prepare the mud mortar. One lakh seventy-six thousand,' he emphasizes the number of Hindus who presumably died protecting the Ram temple. Information about the exact number of martyrs is doled out with astonishing confidence and regularity by many local guides. Pandey's claims made at the VHP workshop seem even more astounding given that historians and archaeologists have been looking for decades for signs of the grand temple and have come up with nothing but controversial finds. On the other hand, there are examples of destroyed temples at other sites in India, including Bijai Mandal and Ashapuri near Bhopal, where the broken and scattered remains of temples are overwhelmingly visible. They are undeniable, eliciting the attention of even the most uninterested and unsympathetic observer. No such remains are to be found in Ayodhya.

'Where is all that rubble?' John Stratton Hawley, a professor of religion at Barnard College, New York, had asked when he visited Ayodhya in January 1993, just a month after the demolition of the Babri Masjid. He was told that the 'vast Hindu crowd took it away...as souvenirs and objects of veneration'.[104] This is partially correct, but it doesn't explain the virtual absence of huge building blocks of stone or any other remnants of the great mosque of Babur, said to have been constructed from the ruins of an equally great—if not greater—Hindu temple. As Hawley noted, the answer is quite simple: 'The mosque was not actually constructed of such stones. It predated the fine mosques of Mathura and Banaras and used a more modest medium: large bricks of the Jaunpuri style.'[105] Ayodhya may not have any grand ruins of the Babri Masjid or any other majestic structure, but it does have other interesting layers of religious history.

The Buddha is believed to have preached from Mani Parbat, a mound of earth on the periphery of Ayodhya. Today, Mani Parbat has become part of the local Ramayana lore. It is said to be a fallen portion of the hill that contained the Sanjeevani herb that Hanuman was transporting from the Himalayas to the battlefront in the war with Ravan.

---

[104]John Stratton Hawley and Vasudha Narayanan, *The Life of Hinduism*, New Delhi: Aleph Book Company, 2018, p. 259.
[105]Ibid., pp. 262–63.

Deshraj Upadhyay, a local expert on the region's history who works in the Dr Ram Manohar Lohia Awadh University in Faizabad and has published a book on the 'statue art history' of this region, explains the origins of the Mani Parbat tale:

> When Buddha used to visit Saket (Ayodhya) he used to stay in Pubbaram Vihar which is the Pali distortion of Purvaram Vihar (earlier it was Ram's Vihar). Thus it is clear that the place was associated with Ram in the time of Buddha.[106] Later on, in the time of Nandaram of Krishna dynasty a small stupa was built there which was enlarged in the time of Ashoka. With the decline of Buddhism the hump became abandoned by Hindus till the Vaishnava tradition turned it into a Ramayanic spot in the Mughal era.[107]

This kind of appropriation by the Vaishnava[108] tradition is seen also in the case of the oldest known temple in Ayodhya—the Nageshwarnath Temple on the banks of the Sarayu. This temple is dedicated to Shiva, and the shivling there is said to have been installed by Kush, Ram's son, as a sign of gratitude to a Naga-kanya who helped him find his bangle which had fallen in the Sarayu.

And so it goes on in Ayodhya. The guides, often from the community of 'Pandas', are young boys who work part-time to promote this hybrid but indisputably Vaishnava history of Ayodhya. Nar Singh Pandey too is in his first year of college and is preparing to appear for an exam that will get him a government job. These guides are aware of Ayodhya's Buddhist history but reluctant to acknowledge it. And some of them admit that, being untrained in history, they are unqualified to comment on any non-Hindu aspect of the region. Many of them were in fact born after the Babri Masjid was demolished in 1992. Thus, to them, Ayodhya is what the

---

[106]Such name-distortion-based history is not very reliable. Such name linkages are used to show that the Ramesses dynasty of ancient Egypt is also linked to Ram and are called Vaishnavas (See 'Shri Rama and the Vedic history of the world' <http://lordrama.co.in/sri-rama-and-vedic-history-of-the-world.html>). More work needs to be done in this area.

[107]Behind Mani Parbat lies the mazaar (mausoleum) of Hazrat Sheesh Paigambar, said to be the son of Adam and Eve. The mazaar is worshipped by both Hindus and Muslims.

[108]Followers of Ramanuj among the Vaishnavas started a sect called Sri Vaishnavism which was strict about rules of commensality and maintaining caste distinctions when it came to becoming a guru. I am using Vaishnavism as an overarching ideology instead of specifying which sect of Vaishnavism each time in order to maintain ease of understanding.

VHP has made it to be. However, there are many people who acknowledge that Ram worship in Ayodhya is a phenomenon that gained prominence in the Mughal period (1526–1857).

Pawan Singh, a vociferous proponent of the theory that Jains are the real ancestors of Hindus, is one such person who doesn't shy away from talking about the non-Hindu, non-Ram history of Ayodhya. He has been managing a prominent dharamshala (pilgrim hostel) for many decades and is well respected for his good nature and efficiency in running the sprawling place. 'When the first tirthankar of Jains, Rishabh Dev, is clearly mentioned as an ancestor of Ram-ji why can't Hindus accept Jains as their ancestors instead of fighting with them?' Pawan Singh is referring to a well-known fact about Ayodhya's links with Jainism. Out of their twenty-three spiritual teachers or tirthankars, five (seven, according to scholars like Hans Bakker) are believed by Jains to have been born in Ayodhya, and three of them in not too distant Banaras. Jains believe that Ayodhya means a place 'without war' and Awadh means a place where there is 'no killing'. The Jain temple of Ajitnath is the grandest and most beautiful of all the temples in the town and the statue of Rishabh Dev sits in a park named after the Buddha on the river-facing side of Ayodhya. It is one of the most scenic spots in the town, from where the stunning Awadh ki Shaam (sunset in Awadh) can be best enjoyed. Like elsewhere, Jain temples in Ayodhya are not only the grandest but also the best maintained. However, it is possible to spend several days in Ayodhya without ever hearing of its Jain history, as I would myself discover. And therefore this unsolicited declaration by Pawan Singh, a Ram-bhakt, was all the more unusual.

For Hindu pilgrims, this much can be said without a doubt—no matter which god the people of this region come to worship in Ayodhya, their visit isn't complete without a dip in the river Sarayu, the only uncontested constant in the history of Ayodhya. The river's importance to worship subsumes religious and sectarian differences. As we have seen earlier, the Sarayu is mentioned in an eleventh-century inscription by Chandradeva, a Gahadvala king of Kannauj, in which he proclaimed a massive land grant to 500 Brahmins after bathing in the river at Swargdwar, the place where Ram ascended to heaven along with the entire population of Ayodhya. This is the 'first evidence' pointing to Ayodhya as a holy place.[109] However, Ram worship was still at least 500 years away.

---

[109]Hans Bakker, 'The rise of Ayodhya as a place of pilgrimage', p. 109.

THE CULT OF RAM

The Ramayana's conversion into a divine or holy text began in the second millennium CE. Ram was not always worshipped as a god even though the worship of Ram certainly preceded the emergence of present-day Ayodhya as a centre of Ram worship. Moreover, it was after Tulsidas's version of the Ramayana appeared in the sixteenth to seventeenth century that Ayodhya became an important centre of pilgrimage in north India and Ram worship grew rapidly. In the following centuries, it would become the most dominant cult, if not the most prevalent one among Hindus.

Ram embodies many values that are attributed to India itself, such as tolerance, secularism, social harmony, equality, moral propriety and courage. As the Bharatiya Janata Party's (BJP) Atal Bihari Vajpayee said, Ram is also to many 'the symbol of India's cultural heritage and its national ethos'.[110] 'Ram-bharose', or 'thanks to Ram', is a common phrase heard in high-rises as well as weekly haats. Ram has come to be synonymous with God, at least since the time of the poet-saint Kabir (who was a disciple of Tulsidas).

It was not always so. Ram worship erupted slowly and quite late in Indian religious history (as evidenced by most Ram temples and Ramayani art dating from the medieval period) and the Ayodhya of today offers us reason to believe that it developed even later as a place of Ram worship. The power of the Ram story as a legitimizing force was used in the fifth century by Vikramaditya (Skandagupta) when he moved his capital from Pataliputra to Saket (Ayodhya). Saket, till then a town with Buddhist and Jain histories, now became the Ayodhya of the Gupta king. After the fall of the Guptas, Ayodhya too faded away till the Gahadvalas rose to power in the aftermath of Ghaznavid raids.[111] Bear in mind that this was a time of intense conflict between raiding Muslim armies from the northwest and regional struggles between Hindu kings. It is against the backdrop of a strife-torn political-social landscape that Vaishnavism began to emerge as a religious cult that would subsume many other sects in Hindu life. Some scholars believe that the Gahadvalas built five Vishnu temples in Ayodhya

---

[110] Atal Bihari Vajpayee, 'My musings from Kumarakom–I: time to resolve problems of the past', *The Hindu*, 2 January 2001.
[111] Vasudha Paramasivan, 'Yah Ayodhya vah Ayodhya: earthly and cosmic journeys in the Anand-Lahari' in Heidi Pauwels, ed., *Patronage and Popularisation, Pilgrimage and Procession: Channels of Transcultural Translation and Transmission in Early Modern South Asia; Papers in Honour of Monika Hortsmann*, Wiesbaden: Harrassowitz Verlag, 2009, pp. 101–16.

that survived till the time of Aurangzeb.[112] However, it is baffling that even after extensive excavations, so little has been discovered of their remains.

Till at least the 1700s, Ayodhya was a regional military centre of the Mughal empire, from where the nawabs of Awadh ruled. It had been in the wilderness for centuries, the continuous armed struggle between the Delhi Sultanate and its feudatories kept the region in turmoil and despite or probably because of that, Ayodhya attracted only the religiously and spiritually inclined of all faiths. In fact, this aspect of Ayodhya needs to be appreciated much more than it has been. Like most pilgrim spots, some parts of today's Ayodhya offer the spiritual minded, the seeker of peace and the renunciate solace and solitude.

As we have seen earlier, Nageshwarnath, the oldest temple in Ayodhya, is dedicated to Shiva, and as in most of the country, Shiva worship preceded the cult of Ram in Ayodhya as well.[113] Shiva is a peer of Vishnu and hence there cannot be a direct comparison between him and Ram, who is the seventh incarnation of Vishnu.[114] The six incarnations that precede him are Matsya or the fish avatar, Kurma or tortoise, Varaha or boar, Narasimha or half-man, half-lion, Vaman or the dwarf, and Parshuram or the priest with an axe. Then comes Ram, followed by Krishna of the Mahabharata, and after him, in the Vaishnava tradition, the Buddha as the ninth avatar of Vishnu. The tenth and final avatar is Kalki, a man on a white winged horse; he is to appear at the end of the present cosmic age.

AYODHYA IN THE VAISHNAVA TRADITION

The followers of Shiva are known as Shaivas whereas those of Vishnu are known as Vaishnavas. Since any history of Ayodhya requires us to understand the development of Hinduism as a religion, we will take a detour here to see what the Vaishnava tradition says about its development, in north India in particular. In Vaishnava literature, there are numerous accounts of

---

[112]Ibid.

[113]An inscription on a shivling dated 435–36 CE records a gift for the worship of Mahadeva (another name for Shiva). This shivling was found in the village Karamdande in Faizabad district (Meenakshi Jain, *Rama and Ayodhya*, New Delhi: Aryan Books International, 2013, p. 95).

[114]However, from the Valmiki Ramayana, where Shiva is supposed to have asked Vishnu to manifest as Ram to kill Ravan to the *Ramcharitmanas* of Tulsidas, where Shiva is shown to be worshipping Ram and narrating the Ramayana to his consort Parvati, *Ramcharitmanas* marks the ultimate adoption of Shiva by Vaishnavism.

Ayodhya being wrested miraculously from the control of Shaivite monks with the help of Vaishnava saints. According to the biography of one such saint, Shri Devmurari, written by another saint of the same order, Pandit Ramtahal Das, Vaishnavism had to overcome the violent and deadly obstacle of Shaivaism in north India. In a subsection titled 'Uttar Bharat mein Shri Vaishnavta ka Prachar Kaise Hua?' (How did Shri Vaishnavism spread in north India?), the author starts by outlining the regions where Vaishnavism prevailed in the time of Devmurari. Ramtahal Das lists Bengal, western Punjab and Marwar as centres of Vaishnavism but states that eastern states and the region of Mithila were still out of its reach. It is from western India that Vaishnava saints came and brought eastern regions under Vaishnavite influence. The writer categorically states that no holy Vaishnavite centre pre-dates *Bhaktamal*[115] in 'poorv Pradesh' and that if there were a centre it would have certainly been mentioned in *Bhaktamal*. Elaborating the context in which Vaishnavism was beset against a violent and entrenched Shaivism, Ramtahal Das writes, 'right at the beginning, to fight the growing influence of Buddhism, Bhagwan Shri Shankaracharya-ji raised a *Dashnam* army comprising of different divisions. Their names were Aranya, Giri, Van, Bharti Sagar, etc... This army defeated Buddhism and created the resurgence of Sanatan Dharma which was later on fully accomplished by Shri Ramanuj Swamy.'[116]

Devmurari, said to be a contemporary of Emperor Akbar (r.1556–1605), wrote in his biography that after the threat of Buddhism was dealt with and Vaishnavism was emerging as a major force, the same Dashnam army raised by Shankaracharya turned against Vaishnava saints.

At this point, the section explaining the spread of Vaishnavism traces the conquest of south India by Vaishnava saints through sorcery and magic. It says, 'with the help of the *"Suparnastra yantra"* Shri Varvar Muni eradicated the Dashnam army from the south of India forever. Since then, the Shaivaites made the country north of the Vindhyas their stronghold while in the south they still don't have any presence.'[117]

---

[115] *Bhaktamal* is a compilation of the biographies of Vaishnav saints believed to have been composed in the first half of the seventeenth century by Nabhadas, a Ramanandi ascetic.

[116] Ramanujcharya is credited with starting the cult of Ram bhakti, which was later established by his disciple Ramanand, which is thence known as the Ramanand sect or sampraday. See Pandit Ramtahal Dasji, *Shri DevMurariji ki Jeevani Tatha Shri Guru Parampara Prakash*, 1938, p. 74.

[117] Ibid.

But north India was still a dangerous region for followers of Vishnu. According to a legend, corroborated by interviews with several Vaishnava saints in Ayodhya, 'if 500 Vaishnavs used to go to the north only 50 would return'. Ramtahal Das also confirms this in Devmurari's biography: 'the Dashnamis, with the help of north Indian kings started attacking Vaishnav saints who used to venture northwards for pilgrimages. It was the time of Muslim rulers and they had decreed that the sects be allowed to settle their scores without interference.'[118]

The author then describes the enmity against Vaishnavas which prevailed to the extent that the 'daily ritual of Shaivas was to kill four Vaishnavas before doing datoon [brushing teeth]' and on days when they couldn't find a Vaishnava to kill the Shaivas would make voodoo-like doll-Vaishnavas out of dough and slit their throats. 'Things were so bad that lakhs of brave men were killed, many in sectarian pitched battles, during that time it was not possible for a tilak wearing Vaishnava to be alive without hiding themselves. When priests from the south used to come to the north for pilgrimages they used to wash [off] their tilak before leaving their dwelling places and when asked by a Shaiva about their identity they pretended they were Shaivas too in order to save their lives,' writes Pandit Ramtahal Das.[119]

Pandit Ramtahal Das, himself a Vaishnava, displays remarkable neutrality when writing about the historicity of the Vaishnava tradition. He asserts that if there was indeed a Ram or Vaishnava centre in Awadh at the time of Nabhadas (circa 1600) it would certainly have been mentioned in his *Bhaktamal*.

Ramtahal Das's biography of Devmurari written in the hagiographic style, credits him with first pushing Shaivaites out of the area of Prayag (the Hindu name of Allahabad) and then deeper into Awadh and eastern Uttar Pradesh. Though he doesn't give the precise dates of Devmurari's lifetime, Das describes an encounter between Emperor Akbar and Devmurari. It pertains to the 'divine' help that Akbar got from Devmurari in building the largest fort of his career. This fort, situated near the confluence of the Yamuna and the Ganga was named Allabas or God's blessing.[120] And it was Devmurari, according to the biography, who established the first site of Vaishnavas near Prayag.

---

[118]Ibid., pp. 74–75.
[119]Ibid., p. 75.
[120]Present-day Allahabad derives its name from this fort.

Das also lists at least 269 places around India, a large number of them in the southern states, as the holy sites that Devmurari used to 'mentally visit' every day. Among the ninety-one places defined as the main seats of Vaishnava saints, Dakshin Ayodhya or the southern Ayodhya in Palakkad, Kerala, finds a mention. In the extended list of holy places, several other places linked with the Ramayana are to be found. Among these remaining 178 places 'Shri Ayodhya Sarayu' is mentioned and Nageshwarnath, along with Swargdwar, are also featured. At the end of the list, Ramtahal Das concludes, as if to allay any doubts, 'today's Ayodhya did not exist'.[121] From this, one is encouraged to infer that if the birthplace of Ram was known to Devmurari or his predecessors, it would have been included in this list of pilgrimages. More significantly, Devmurari's biography and its version of the Shaiva-Vaishnava conflict points to a deep Shaiva-Vaishnava fault line in late medieval north India. As we shall see later in the book, the advent of the British East India Company as a military power coincides with the growth of the Vaishnava Ramanandi movement in Ayodhya, as in much of north India.

RAM WORSHIP IN AYODHYA

Ram worship was not and is not restricted to Ram's supposed birthplace alone. Ram has been identified with Ayodhya as a whole, not merely a particular spot in Ayodhya. A fact affirmed by the Gahadvala inscription mentioned earlier. It was issued by the Gahadvala king Chandradeva who was a Shiva devotee. Besides the sacredness of Ayodhya in its entirety, the inscription underscores the greater importance of the Swargdwar area where he worshipped, and the river Sarayu. It read:

> After making a resolve at Ayodhya in the Uttara-Kosala country on the Amavasayu day of the Asvina month of the Vikram era 1150, i.e. on 23rd of October 1093 AD Chandradeva took bath on the day of the solar eclipse on the confluence of the sin-effacing Sarayu-Ghaghru at the Svarga-dvary ghata and made oblations with rituals to gods, sages, human beings, spirits and ancestors.
>
> Then he worshipped the Sun god who dispels darkness and provides unlimited heat, and after paying obeisance to the earth, water, fire, air and sky he performed ritualistic exercise in honour of Lord

---

[121] Ramtahal Dasji, *Shri DevMurariji ki Jeevani Tatha Shri Guru Parampara Prakash*, p. 36.

Siva who appears like the snow-shine and has the red body and is the master of all medicines (herbs) and wears the crescent on his forehead. Then he worshipped Lord Vasudeva[122], the protector of all the three worlds. Thereafter, he made a pinda-offering to his ancestors.[123]

None of the inscriptions from the Gahadvala era (eleventh century) mention Ram as a god nor do they contain any evidence of Ram worship in present-day Ayodhya during their reign.

AYODHYA MAHATMYA OR 'AYODHYA'S GLORY'

Mahatmyas are texts that glorify deities and holy places. Besides acting as holy maps of a place they also expound the benefits that can be got by performing pilgrimages and certain rituals. Simply put, they can be understood as manuals (mainly for priests) on how to derive holy benefits through ritual worship. They are usually a part of the several Puranas that are variously dated from the first half of the first millennium to fourteenth century CE.

As with the Ramayana, the Puranas and the Mahatmyas are not texts set in stone. They have been revised and innovated upon at various stages so as to make necessary changes keeping in view the concerns of the religious elite of the time. Scholars Cornelia Dimmitt and J. A. B. Buitenen have described this nature of the Puranas in a simple analogy in their book, *Classical Hindu Mythology: A Reader in the Sanskrit Puranas*. They write that, 'It is as if they (Puranas) were libraries to which new volumes have been continuously added, not necessarily at the end of the shelf, but randomly.'[124]

The Ayodhya Mahatmya is often cited by scholars to be a part of the Skanda Purana, one of the eighteen mahapuranas that, as mentioned earlier, have been dated differently. The Skanda Purana is considered the longest with nearly 81,000 verses. It is named after Skanda (also known as Kartikeya or Murugan), the son of Shiva and Parvati. The earliest or the oldest version of this text dates to the seventh century, roughly coinciding with the eclipse of Buddhism by Shaivite resurgence. However, most of the 81,000 verses seem to have been added much later. The historicity of Purana literature has always been taken with copious amounts of salt; this,

---

[122]Vasudeva is another name for Krishna, an incarnation of Vishnu.

[123]Kunal Kishore, *Ayodhya Revisited*, New Delhi: Ocean Books, 2016, p. 52.

[124]Cornelia Dimmitt and J. A. B. Buitenen, *Classical Hindu Mythology: A Reader in the Sanskrit Puranas*, New Delhi: Sri Satguru Publications, 1998, p. 5.

however, has not deterred many scholars who believe in the antiquity of the Ram cult and Ram's birthplace in present-day Ayodhya from citing the Ayodhya Mahatmya of the Skanda Purana as proof of Ram worship in Ayodhya being of ancient origin. Surprisingly, scholars of this inclination insist on the seventh-century origin of the Skanda Purana as proof of continuous Ayodhya-Ram worship, completely forgetting the dynamic nature of the Puranas, and also ignoring the obvious fact that the Skanda Purana has been undergoing changes since it was first composed.

However, a careful analysis of both the Puranas and the development of Hinduism reveals that the revisions or additions in the Puranas cannot be called random even though that's how they would appear to somebody trying to understand their evolution in isolation.

In the Skanda Purana, the Ayodhya Mahatmya is found in the section on Vaishnavism, and deals with the moksha-giving qualities of worshipping Ram at Ayodhya. Much quibbling had taken place over the dating of the Skanda Purana in the years leading up to the demolition of the Babri Masjid in 1992.

Two and a half decades later, the bickering over legendary figures and undated Puranas composed by unknown writers continues. First, let us look at the pro-temple scholarship represented here by the work of Kunal Kishore, who after painstaking research produced a voluminous book in 2016. He reiterates Dutch Indologist Hans Bakker's view by saying that the Ayodhya Mahatmya dates to the close of the thirteenth century or the beginning of the fourteenth century. Hans Bakker believes it was then that the Ayodhya Mahatmya was inserted into the Vaishnava section of the Skanda Purana along with Venkatachala Mahatmya (Tirupati), the Badrikasrama Mahatmya (Badrinath) and the Purusottamaksetra Mahatmya (Jagannath Puri).

If we accept this date, then Ayodhya as a place of Ram worship goes back to the fourteenth century. However, as pointed out earlier, no evidence besides this is to be found in the sectarian literature of the Vaishnavas. Therefore, it appears that Ram worship can be traced to a later date in Ayodhya. Establishing the genesis of Ram worship in Ayodhya is not an easy task but it is made a little easier by focusing on Vaishnava literature. The worship of Ram in Ayodhya is intrinsically linked with the sub-sectarian Ramanandi movement in the larger Vaishnava or Sri Vaishnava tradition at the cusp of the seventeenth and eighteenth centuries. And as we shall see in a later chapter, Ayodhya's growth as a major centre of Ramanandis heralds the identification of a particular spot in Ayodhya as Ram's exact birthplace.

AYODHYA: 1100 CE ONWARDS

The last known Hindu king to have been mentioned with regard to Ayodhya was Govindchandra Gahadvala in the eleventh century, after which it came under the rule of the various Muslim kingdoms and remained so until the British brutally overthrew the liberal Awadh nawabs in 1856. In the interregnum of roughly 800 years, several Muslim governors were appointed to Awadh.

In Ayodhya, the first notable incident during the early decades of the Sultanate period pertains to the destruction of the Jain temple of Adinath by Makhdum Shah Juran Ghori, the younger brother of Muhammad Ghori, sultan of the Ghurid empire. However, one of the last surviving chiefs of the Gahadvala dynasty, Bartuh, led a resistance which was successful in defeating Shah Juran's large army. Shah Juran today lies buried in an unmarked grave on the premises of the Adinath Jain temple. This event is believed to have taken place some time after 1192 CE.[125] Three decades later in 1226 CE, Bartuh was killed and the region of Awadh came under Malik Nasiruddin, the son of Sultan Iltutmish of Delhi. Unfortunately, the history of the early medieval period is illuminated by records of conquests, deaths of important persons and the occasional crowning of rulers. Therefore, the next landmark in Ayodhya's early medieval past is the death of Sultan Iltutmish in 1236 CE. The power vacuum left behind by his death lasted a decade during which four rulers were slain as soon as they were crowned.

In 1246 CE, Nasiruddin Mahmud, Iltutmish's grandson, ascended to the throne, and soon an improbable event in Indian royal history occurred. His mother, Malk-i-Jahan, chose to remarry a court noble who was then put in charge of overseeing the revenues of Awadh. Her decision continues to intrigue historians, for she relinquished the power she would have acquired in Delhi and moved to a provincial outpost. It could be that she grew weary of the bloodlust and deadly power games that plagued the Mamluk (Slave) dynasty and sought to spend the rest of her life in the bounteous serenity of Ayodhya, which was soon to acquire fame for its gardens, salubrious qualities and spiritual solace among the new rulers of India. Her new husband, Qutlugh Khan, a headstrong noble, started ruling Ayodhya as his own kingdom and ignored the farmans of Delhi. Soon a force was sent by Sultan Nasiruddin Mahmud's powerful prime minister, Ulugh Khan (who later became famous as Balban), to subdue this disobedient governor. A new

---

[125]Kishore, *Ayodhya Revisited.*

governor, Tabar Khan, was appointed while Qutlugh managed to escape.

The breathless pace of empire building continued and as Balban's power rose in the Delhi court so did his mercilessness. When Amin Khan, the new governor of Ayodhya, was defeated in a battle by a recalcitrant Tugrail Beg, the governor of Bengal, Balban ordered that Amin Khan be punished by being hanged from the gate of Ayodhya. This was in 1279 CE.

AMIR KHUSRAU, 'THE PARROT OF HINDUSTAN', COMES TO AYODHYA

Born in Patiali near Etah in Uttar Pradesh, Amir Khusrau (1253–1325 CE) moved to Delhi with his mother in 1260 CE. In 1287 CE, he took service with a noble in Balban's court with whom he moved to Ayodhya. Khusrau was both a swordsman and a prolific poet. He presaged the great poets of India and his genius is still celebrated in literary festivals around the world, especially in the subcontinent. His timeless poetry survives and grows with every new generation. Effortlessly combining his mixed roots (Turkish and Indian), he invented a style of poetry called Rekhta (Persian and Hindi) to reach out to the masses as well as the elite:

> Kaafire ishq ishqam muslamani mara darkaar neest
> Har range man tare gashta haazate junnar neest[126]
>
> (I am the worshipper of love, I don't need to be a Muslim
> My rags are the thread, I don't need the sacred thread)

After reaching Ayodhya with his master, who was given the governorship of Awadh, Khusrau wrote to his unnamed friend with longing but also with stunningly real descriptions of his new home's natural beauty:

> What a town! Nay it is not a town; it is all a great garden.
> It does not possess much but is so rich with inner peace.
> It is a town which adorns, the good earth.
> Its suburbs call out to you, go free!
> The blissful stream running under its feet quench
> One; wayfarers thirst through the eyes.
> Happiness here knows no bounds; every leaf and
> every flower, pours out nectar-eternal.
> Look at its orchards—all laden with

---

[126]Malik Muhammad, 'Amir Khusrau ka rashtra prem' in Malik Muhammad, ed., *Amir Khusrau Bhavamatmak Ekta Ke Agradoot*, 1975, p. 82.

Uninhibited fruits so laden with that branches bow down.
The choicest of fruits here, appear to have been nursed,
And nurtured by the Hands of the creator...
Fruits like grapes, pomegranates, oranges—they are all,
all gold, when you hold them...
And like them there are hundreds whose very names,
in Hindavi make the lips sweet and mouth full of taste...[127]

Thirteen years before Khusrau reached Ayodhya in 1274 CE, a family of Pashmina traders living there was blessed with a son whose tomb is now the centre of a burgeoning settlement in the heart of south Delhi. Syed Nasiruddin Mahmud Al Hassani, who later became a Sufi saint known as Chirag-e-Dehlavi, is now remembered by a small tomb that marks the spot of his birth. It lies under a bunch of neem trees behind the Adinath temple that is said to have been destroyed by Shah Juran Ghori. Chirag Dehlavi moved to Delhi in his middle age where he eventually became the successor of Nizamuddin Auliya. Chirag Dehlavi's tomb was ordered to be built by Firoz Shah Tughlaq, a patron of Sufism. The tomb lies in ruins in the neighbourhood of Chirag Dilli.

PATRICIDE AVERTED IN AYODHYA

Once again, Amir Khusrau's presence in Ayodhya affords us a glimpse of an emotional and unexpected encounter between a governor father and his emperor son who were on the verge of battle at the orders of prime minister Balban (who, as we have seen earlier, had Amin Khan hanged at Ayodhya's gate) of the Delhi Sultanate. In 1288 CE, just a year after Khusrau had moved to Ayodhya, in Delhi, Sultan Muizzuddin Kaikabad, who was barely out of his teens, was persuaded by Balban to subdue his father, Nasiruddin Bughra Khan, who had declared himself the independent ruler of Bengal. Their armies stood on opposite sides of the Sarayu River, ready to face each other in battle. Whether it was a twist of fate or the magic of the place, this patricidal war was averted and son and father united in a teary embrace. Amir Khusrau, a witness to this happy reunion, recorded it in his moving masterpiece, 'Qiranus Sadain'.

For about five decades after this episode not much of note occurs in Ayodhya till a new governor takes over under the Tughlaq dynasty

---

[127] Ameer Hasan Abidi, 'Awadh at the times of Amir Khusrau' (as reflected in 'Firaqnaama') *Commemoration Vol.*, ed. Zoe Ansari, National Amir Khusrau Society, 1999, pp. 42–43.

(1320–1414 CE). Ainu-I-Mulk, in line with Muhammad bin Tughlaq's general policy of communal harmony, developed Ayodhya into a prosperous province that made significant contributions of provisions and money during famine to another part of the Tughlaq empire in 1337 CE. He also oversaw the construction of a separate quarters for Muslims between present-day Swargdwar and Shah Madar.[128] Incidentally, and we will discuss this later in the book, at present there is a mosque in the Mughalpura neighbourhood of Ayodhya (not very far from the disputed site) which is known as the mosque of Shah Madar (dated by a marble plate on it that reads 1438 CE). While there are a number of mosques in the Ayodhya–Faizabad region that have the same architecture as the Babri Masjid, this particular mosque seems to bear the closest resemblance to it.

Muhammad bin Tughlaq's reign was important to Ayodhya, as under him, the first Hindu governor was appointed in the 1340s. The unhindered presence of Shaiva ascetics, called jogis, has also been recorded during his time. Muslims were also present in significant numbers. Not much else is known about Kishan, the Hindu governor, except that his ascension to the post was scoffed at by Muslim elites. Kunal Kishore refers to this in his book by quoting a Sultanate period Muslim thinker, Ziauddin Barani's *Fatwa-i-Jahandiri:*

> Low born people are not to be taught reading and writing, for plenty of disorders arise owing the skill of the low born in knowledge. The disorders into which the affairs of the state are thrown are due to the acts and wards of the low born who have become skilled.[129]

Kishan's appointment seems to have been shortlived as there is evidence that Malik Amul-ul-Malik Multani was the governor of Ayodhya from 1325 to 1351 CE. During his reign, many 'noble families settled in Avadh and it is certain that there was a great deal of construction'.[130] It is also believed that Malik built his palace near the banks of the Sarayu, the ruins of which existed till at least 1990.[131]

In 1359, Firoz Shah Tughlaq shifted the capital of Awadh from Ayodhya to Jaunpur which was founded in memory of his predecessor and cousin,

---

[128]Kishore, *Ayodhya Revisited,* p. 481.
[129]Ibid., p. 482.
[130]Srivastava, *The Disputed Mosque,* p. 91.
[131]Ibid.

Sultan Muhammad bin Tughlaq, who was also called Muhammad Juna.[132] Firoz Shah Tughlaq himself lies buried in an octagonal tomb in Delhi's Hauz Khas Village. There lies another age-old link between Delhi and arguably its most important province of Awadh.

JAUNPUR: AWADH'S NEW CAPITAL

Jaunpur's Sharqi kingdom was founded by a eunuch named Malik Sarvar who took matters into his own hands between the death of Firoz Shah Tughlaq in 1388 CE and the imminent invasion by Tamerlane in 1398. The Sharqi dynasty officially came into being after the death of the last Tughlaq king, Muhammad Shah IV, in 1394 CE. Sharqi means winds from the southeast in Arabic and the dynasty was so named because it was the title given to Malik Sarvar, an efficient administrator and patron of music, literature and the arts. As Jaunpur's stature as an independent kingdom grew by leaps and bounds, Ayodhya yet again slipped into a quiet and ascetic corner.

The stellar contribution of the kingdom of Jaunpur in a short life of eighty-five years resonates even today in the form of the many ragas in the Khayal genre of Hindustani classical music. However, the Sharqi architecture of Jaunpur exceeds all other aspects of this kingdom's achievements. Many experts believe that the Babri Masjid dated from the time of the Sharqi dynasty, which preceded Babur by nearly a hundred years.

AYODHYA DURING THE LODI PERIOD (1451–1526)

In less than a hundred years, the Sharqis were overthrown by another Afghan dynasty that took control of Delhi, the Lodis.

Bahlul Lodi ascended the throne of Delhi in 1451 and captured Jaunpur in 1479. He appointed his eldest son, Barbak Shah, as the governor of Jaunpur and made his nephew, Muhammad Farmuli, the subedar (provincial governor) of Awadh in 1489 CE.[133]

The Farmulis would be the de facto rulers of Ayodhya from 1489 CE until the defeat of their Lodi masters by Babur in the Battle of Panipat in 1528 CE. After that battle Bayazid Farmuli, a descendant of Muhammad Farmuli, was reappointed as the chief of Awadh by Babur.

---

[132]Sanjukta Dasgupta and Raj Shekhar Basu, eds., *Narratives from the Margins: Aspects of Adivasi History in India*, New Delhi: Primus Books, 2012.
[133]Kishore, *Ayodhya Revisited*.

Here, the narrative starts getting blurred. Did Babur come to Ayodhya at all? Did he order the destruction of a temple and have a mosque built in its place? Kunal Kishore believes and argues that there was a temple before the mosque, but he denies that Babur even ventured close to Ayodhya.

After studying Babur's memoirs, Kishore concludes: 'That on 28th March 1528 AD when Babur dismounted 2 or 3 kos [1 kos=3.2 kilometres] from Aud above the confluence of the Ghaghra and Sarda rivers he was 115 km away from Ayodhya.' He adds, 'there Babur and his expedition team stayed for a few days to settle the affairs of Aud.'[134] What was this settling of the affairs of Aud? Here many historians have made flights of imagination. They have written that Babur went to Ayodhya on the advice of Musa Ashiqan, where he directed Mir Baqi to demolish the Janma-sthana (birthplace) temple and build a mosque there. Finally answering what 'settling the affairs of Aud' meant, Kishore writes, 'But this is totally improbable because the governor or king of Ayodhya was not a Hindu. He was Shaikh Bayazid who was an Afghan and on the run. Therefore, Babur had to make arrangement for the successful chase of...Bayazid and by deploying armed forces and officers to capture them he settled the affairs of Aud.'[135]

A source which could have settled the debate over Babur's visit to Ayodhya is the emperor's own journal. But, frustratingly, Babur's diary is of no use, as the period (28 March–June 1528) during which Babur visited Ayodhya and the mosque was supposedly built at his bidding is absent from his daily journal. Babur died in December 1530. However, even if Babur did not go to Ayodhya, he could have ordered the mosque's construction through one of his commanders. The inscription on the inner wall of the Babri Masjid said that it was built by Mir Baqi at the orders of Babur Shah. However, we are yet to find any evidence that a temple was destroyed to build the mosque.

Historian Sushil Srivastava believes that the 'style of architecture of the Babri Masjid raises doubts regarding the contention that Babur had the mosque constructed in 1528'.[136] Many scholars and other experts share his view, which is based on the similarities between other Sharqi era buildings in and around Awadh. In Jaunpur, which is nearly 150 kilometres away, the Attala Masjid bears a resemblance to the now demolished Babri Masjid

---

[134]Ibid., p. 215.
[135]Ibid., pp. 215–16.
[136]Srivastava, *The Disputed Mosque*, p. 90.

when it was viewed from the western side. The proponents of this point of view explain the presence of inscriptions that clearly said a masjid was built at the orders of Babur by theorizing that it is possible that it was the ruins of a Sharqi-era masjid which were repaired and the new masjid rechristened Babri Masjid by Mir Baqi, Babur's commander.

The period after Babur's death in 1530 once again turns into a dimly lit patch of history. After Humayun reconquered Delhi, Awadh and Jaunpur remained in the hands of Afghan nobles and Ayodhya came again under the Mughals only in 1559 during the time of Akbar, Babur's grandson.

Akbar's reign (1556–1605) stimulated religious life in his empire which spanned most of north India. Besides Islam and the various sects under it, among Hindus, Krishna worship and Ram worship too grew under Akbar's direct and indirect patronage and many new temples were constructed by his Hindu chiefs and officials. A case in point being the Govinda Deva Temple at Vrindavan which was built by Raja Man Singh of Amber in 1590 during Akbar's reign.

In 1605, Jahangir was crowned the emperor after Akbar's death. Jahangir largely followed the liberal policies of his father, but when required to subdue a Hindu enemy chief, he did not refrain from destroying his place of worship.[137]

William Finch, an English traveller who visited Ayodhya within a decade of Jahangir's ascension to the Mughal throne, noted several myths with regard to Ram during his visit. He met Brahmins who showed him certain ancient ruins of the castle of Ramchand. He mentions the existence of a cave on the farther side of the Sarayu at a distance of two miles, and that people went there to collect sacred 'graines of rice as blacke as gun-powder'. Local guides also told him that people believed the ashes of Ramchand were supposed to be buried there and that the cave was '...so spacious and full of turnings within that a man may well lose himself there'. However, the construction of the Babri mosque over Ram's birthplace temple was one story that doesn't find mention in Finch's travel diary.[138] According to Kunal Kishore, it was during Aurangzeb's time (1658–1707 CE) that the temple believed to mark Ram's birthplace was destroyed and the mosque

---

[137]Richard M. Eaton, 'Temple desecration and Indo-Muslim States', *Frontline*, 5 January 2001.
[138]William Finch, 'Early travels in India 1583–1619' in William Foster, ed., *Early Travels in India*, London: Oxford University Press, 1921, p. 176.

constructed over it. However, his theory is not borne out by historical records of that time. Nevertheless, Kishore wishes to be made a party in the legal case pertaining to the Ram Janmabhoomi–Babri Masjid on the basis of this theory.

The debate over Babri Masjid's construction is far from settled, but, from Finch's account, as from other sources, it appears that by the time Aurangzeb was crowned the Mughal emperor in 1658, Ayodhya had become well known as a place of Ram worship.[139] After Aurangzeb's death in 1707, political anarchy prevailed over much of north India, which as we shall soon see, proved to be an enabling environment for the Vaishnava takeover of Ayodhya.

EVOLUTION OF AYODHYA AS A RAMANANDI CENTRE

On 17 November 2015, Ashok Singhal, the VHP's international working president and its most prominent face, died in a hospital in Gurgaon. According to Hindu custom, his ashes were immersed at various holy places like Sangam in Prayag (Allahabad), Haridwar, Banaras, Ujjain and Meerut. Singhal's death was mourned by those who, like him, were part of the Ram temple movement of the 1980s and 1990s. Among the many places where his ashes were immersed in Rajasthan, one place stands out for its importance to both Ayodhya and the Vaishnava tradition—Galta, near Jaipur.

The VHP was launched by the Rashtriya Swayamsevak Sangh (RSS) under the leadership of M. S. Golwalkar in 1964, in an effort to unite, politically, the diverse sects and groups that make up Hindu society. The VHP, as far as the Ram Janmabhoomi Movement was concerned, successfully achieved that. By imbuing Ram and his place of birth with political meaning, both were turned into symbols for the Hindu nationalist cause. The story of Galta is important to understanding how the two most widespread Hindu sects existed with relation to each other in the past, and more importantly, to understand the emergence of the Ramanandi subsect in the Vaishnava tradition.

Galta, in the wake of Aurangzeb's death in 1707, emerged as the strongest centre of Vaishnavas under the patronage of King Jai Singh II of Jaipur. In 1713 CE, at a conference hosted at Galta's Hanuman temple, its chief mahant, Swami Balanand, took two breakthrough decisions which would have far-reaching implications for Ayodhya. The first decision was the arming of the four Vaishnava sects to counter the increasing attacks

---

by Shaiva monks,[140] and the second was to disallow persons from non-Brahmin and non-Kshatriya castes from becoming gurus. William R. Pinch, the author of *Peasants and Monks in British India*, an important work that traces the history of armed ascetics in Indian history, writes, '…the arming of bairagis [followers of Vishnu] was the product of a conscious decision made in 1713 by leaders of the four main Vaishnava sampraday—often referred to collectively as the *chatuh-sampraday*, namely the orders organized around the teachings of Vishnuswami, Madhvacharya, Nimbarkacharya and Ramanujacharya (in which Ramanandis were included).

Significantly, the Galta meeting in 1713 also marked the emergence of Ramanandis (those who look to Swami Ramanand for inspiration) as the dominant force not only among the followers of Ramanujacharya's teachings, but among Vaishnavas in north India generally.'[141]

RAMANANDA: VAISHNAVISM'S RADICAL REFORMER

The Ramanandi sect started as a reform movement within the Ramanuj-centred Sri Sampradaya sect in Vaishnavism. Ramanand's own origins are a matter of debate, although not so for the Ramanandis themselves.[142] To them, the accepted history is that he was born in Prayag in 1300 CE. He learnt under the guidance of one Raghavananda, a Ramanuji guru. However, because Ramanand is said to have accepted disciples from all castes including Shudras, he was thrown out of the Sri Sampradaya of caste-conscious Ramanujis. Ramanandis dispute this and hold that Swami Ramanand broke away from the Sri Sampradaya of Ramanujis and started his own sect which admitted ascetics from all castes and also allowed them to become gurus in the sect. Their tradition records that twelve of his disciples became important gurus. These twelve included those born in the cobbler, weaver and barber castes, as well as others. A thirteenth devotee—a

---

[140]According to Indologist and anthropologist Richard Burghart, 'In the early 18th century the Sannyasis encircled and captured Ayodhya on the very birthday of Lord Ram thereby routing the Ramanandi ascetics from the birthplace of their tutelary deity. According to the sectarian bards the loss of Ayodhya provoked the leaders of the Vaisnavite sects to call the conference at Galata.' Burghart, 'The founding of the Ramanandi sect', *Ethnohistory*, Vol. 25, No. 2, 1978, pp. 121–39. JSTOR <www.jstor.org/stable/481036>.

[141]William R. Pinch, *Peasants and Monks in British India*, Berkeley: University of California Press, 1996, p. 17.

[142]Richard Burghart has collated four different spiritual genealogies of Ramanand in his work, 'The founding of the Ramanandi sect'.

woman named Padmavati—was also said to have been initiated as a disciple by Ramananda. The strict adherence to caste rules by Ramanujis deprived a large section of devotees from becoming priests or even simply enjoying commensal equality within the Sri Sampradaya. In a way, it was this 'assimilative' nature of Ramanand that caused the Ram cult to grow exponentially in later centuries, as all castes—high, low and untouchables—became free to practise and preach Ram's life and its lessons. Tulsidas's *Ramcharitmanas* became the guiding text for the Ramanandis. Though the *Ramcharitmanas* is criticized[143] for being anti-Dalit, anti-tribal and anti-women, the fact remains that, as a text of the Bhakti period, it upheld the same values that placed God as the subject of complete surrender and loving devotion. Within fifty years of the Galta conference Ramanandis were emerging as an independent force who could take on the might of the Shaiva ascetics.

AYODHYA'S EXTINCT SHAIVA–VAISHNAVA FAULT LINE

To most Indians, sadhus or ascetics are itinerant men of God who are expected to be devoid of materialist attachments. Generally speaking, very few people associate them with violence, except during the large bathing festival of the Kumbh melas when the media tell us about 'turf wars' and 'pitched battles' between 'naga sadhus'. This heavy-handed, broad-stroke portrayal makes these periodic conflicts look like petty disputes over privilege and favour by the government. Occasionally, there is an insightful report that details the conflict's history with records of 'bloody battles' in which hundreds of sadhus perished. What remains concealed is a deeper fault line with a long history between Shaiva Sanyasis and Vaishnava Bairagis. While sanyasis primarily worship Shiva and Shakti along with Hanuman as a 'super-yogi', Vaishnavas revere Vishnu and his avatars, like Ram and Krishna. The Shaiva tradition is older, and till the eighteenth century, Shaivas held predominance over religious places in north India. Vaishnavas and Shaivas have been competitors for three resources that are necessary for their sustenance and growth as religious sects—devotees and disciples, pilgrimage routes and pilgrimage centres, and political patronage[144]—all three were to be found in abundance in the Awadh and Gangetic regions.

It was Shaiva ascetics who first came to acquire political patronage

---

[143]Bharat Dogra, 'Rereading the Ramayana', *The Statesman*, 18 October 2015.
[144]Ibid.

under various empires. They were feared in wars because, unlike common soldiers, they had no fear of death and this made them preferred allies. When they won battles, they also won the right to administer north India's holy places like Haridwar, Prayag and even Ayodhya. But in medieval India, Ramanandis were struggling to dislodge the Shaiva dominance in north India. Indologist and anthropologist R. Burghart found that, 'The competition for control over pilgrimage routes and pilgrimage centers led to outright battles between the Ramanandi sect and the Dasnami sect of Sannyasis in which the Ramanandi sect did not fare so well.'[145] However, by the end of the eighteenth century, Shaivas had been ousted from Ayodhya, though they still maintained a stronger position up north, at the foot of the Himalayas.

An eyewitness account (the first in English) by Captain Thomas Hardwicke, a British officer, provides a vivid glimpse of the martial Shaiva ascetics at the Haridwar Kumbh Mela in 1796. At that time, Haridwar was under the control of the Marathas. Capturing the prevailing power dynamics between Shaivas and Vaishnavas, Hardwicke recorded:

> The Gosain (Shaiva monks)...are the first here in point of numbers and power...in the early part of the fair, this sect of *faqirs* erected the standard of superiority and proclaimed themselves regulators of the police.... They published an edict, prohibited all other tribes from entering the place with their swords or arms of any other description... The Vairagis, who were the next powerful sect, gave up the point, and next followed their example. Thus the Gosains paraded with their swords and shields, while every other tribe carried only bamboos through the fair.
>
> The ruling power was consequently held by the priests of the Gosains, distinguished by the appellation of *Mahants*, and during the continuance of the fair, the police was under their authority, and all duties levied and collected by them...no part is remitted to the Maratha State.[146]

Burghart ascertains the same trajectory of the inter-sect conflict. He notes:

> In 1760 the Dasnami ascetics captured Hardwar and it was not until

---

[145]Burghart, 'The founding of the Ramanandi sect'.
[146]Thomas Hardwicke, 'Narrative of a journey of Sirinagar', *Asiatic Researches*, Vol. VI, qtd. in Jadunath Sarkar, *A History Of Dasnami Naga Sanyasis*, New Delhi: Sri Panchayati Akhara Mahanirvani, p. 101.

the British administered the district that the Ramanandi ascetics were able to return to this pilgrimage center. In 1789 a battle erupted over the bathing rights at the Kasi Sangam on the Godavri River in which reportedly 12,000 ascetics lost their lives.[147]

In the nineteenth century, the Shaivas would have been decisively overshadowed by Vaishnava Ramanandis. The Marathas' interests in north India, and those of the British East India Company would together mean the end of the supremacy of the Shaiva ascetics. This would also coincide with the gradual disintegration of the Mughal empire till 1858.

The death of Aurangzeb in 1707 plunged the Mughal kingdom into a crisis from which it never recovered. Mughal feudatory kingdoms like Bengal, Awadh and Hyderabad became all but independent of the central authority in Delhi and each served its own interests first. The striking growth of the Marathas under Baji Rao I—who in two decades of his rule (1720–1740) expanded the kingdom tenfold in terms of territory—would act as the second pincer, the British forces expanding from east being the first.[148] Indeed, the most crucial development was the advent of the British East India Company as a military power in the Indian subcontinent. Over the eighteenth century these factors together, perhaps inadvertently but decisively, shaped the history of Ayodhya, as of India itself.

Here it has to be borne in mind that Ayodhya had by the 1700s become an important religious place for Muslims too. Several Sufis had roots in the province and Ayodhya itself had become associated with the legends of prophets Shish, Nuh and Ibrahim. Scores of other Sufi saints like Shah Madar, Badi Bua and Nasiruddin Chirag Dehlavi had found in Ayodhya both a temporal and a spiritual home. According to legend, Tulsidas too had lived here briefly and started writing his *Ramcharitmanas* on the banks of the Sarayu. He later moved to Banaras and settled there. Why Tulsidas did not mention the Ram Janmabhoomi temple in his epic is a question that, as we have seen, is often asked, as it was during his lifetime that the Babri Masjid is said to have been built after the Ram temple was razed. His omission must be all the more shocking to those who believe in the history provided by the VHP and its offshoot, the RSS. According to the VHP version of history, 375,000 Hindus were killed by

---

[147]Burghart, 'The founding of the Ramanandi sect'. .
[148]Bernard Law Montogomery, *The Concise History of Warfare*, New York: William Morrow & Co, 1983, p. 132.

Babur's army while trying to protect the Ram Janmabhoomi temple. It is certainly incomprehensible why a writer of Tulsidas's genius would fail to mention such an epic catastrophe. Or perhaps the massacre theory is a later, more recent creation to serve the VHP's agenda of a Hindu Nation.[149] Even without the component of Muslim brutality, the *Ramcharitmanas* contributed to the spread of Ram worship in north India like no other text before it had done. Composed in Awadhi, the language of the masses, it soon captured the hearts and minds of the people after it was written, sometime in the second half of the sixteenth century.

---

[149]Tanika Sarkar, 'Who rules India? A few notes on the Hindu Right', *Revista Canaria de Estudios Ingleses*, 76; April 2018, pp. 223–39 <https://riull.ull.es/xmlui/bitstream/handle/915/7568/16%20Tanika%20Sarkar.pdf?sequence=3&isAllowed=y> and Audrey Truschke, 'It is high time we discarded the pernicious myth of India's medieval Muslim "villains"', *The Wire*, 11 January 2017.

Chapter 5

CHANGES TO AYODHYA'S
RELIGIOUS LANDSCAPE

AYODHYA IN THE EIGHTEENTH CENTURY: A NEW DYNASTY

Zooming out once again to get an overview of the political situation that prevailed in north India in the eighteenth century, we find a weakened Delhi-based Mughal empire besieged by Afghan, Rajput, Jat, Rohilla and Maratha kings. As no one kingdom was strong enough to defeat all the others, alliances fell apart as quickly as they were brokered. The province of Awadh too was in constant turmoil and the small settlement of Ayodhya was about to enter a defining period of its history. Mughal emperor Farukh Siyar appointed two little-known Hindus as governors of Awadh in quick sucession. The first Hindu governor was Chabile Ram. After his death in 1719 CE, his nephew Girdhar Bahadur was appointed governor and it is believed that under him and through the urging of Jai Singh II of Jaipur, a Vaishnava revival commenced in Ayodhya.[150] In the 1713 Galta[151] conference Ramanandis had proclaimed themselves as a sect independent of the Ramanujis. Within a decade they began making their presence felt in Shaiva strongholds like Prayag, Kashi and Ayodhya. It is not known how much aid they received from the two Hindu governors of Ayodhya between 1713 and 1722 CE, but for Ayodhya's evolution as a Ramanandi centre, a decisive change was to happen in 1722 CE, when Mughal emperor Muhammad Shah appointed his minister Mir Muhammad Khan the governor of Awadh. Mir Muhammad Khan adopted the title of Saadat Khan and built the Qila Mubarak in Ayodhya. Qila Mubarak

---

[150]Kishore, *Ayodhya Revisited.*

[151]Galta's mahants are Ramanuji householders as opposed to the Ramanandi celibates of Ayodhya.

was a small fortress that afforded a clear view of the river Sarayu and beyond. According to tradition, it was in Saadat Khan's time that the first land grants to Ramanandi Akharas were made. Adopting a generous and accommodating attitude towards the Ramanandi ascetics (henceforth called Ramanandi Bairagis), Saadat Khan permitted his diwan Dayashankar, to support the construction of both Shaiva and Vaishnava temples. His army still relied on Shaiva warriors in battles. though in the course of history the ruins of his mud fort were occupied by Ramanandis, which is now known as Lakshman Qila.

Saadat Khan's successor, Abu-i-Mansoor Khan Safdarjung (1739–1754), moved the capital a few kilometres west to what was first known as 'Bangla', a name derived from the wooden mansions built there for the new seat of the province. Later, it came to be known as Faizabad; it is now a divisional headquarters. During Safdarjung's time, his deputy governor Diwan Nawal Rai commissioned the building of a temple of Lakshmi and also of the ancient Nageshwarnath on the banks of the Sarayu. The Nageshwarnath temple remains one of the most popular temples in Ayodhya today. Going by the available records of Awadh, in the eighteenth century, Hindus (Shaivas and Vaishnavas) and Muslims were mutually respectful of each other's religion and strove to harmonize their differences. It is not an exaggeration to say that most of the medieval rulers prioritized power over prayer. After the temporary disruption caused by Aurangzeb's fanatical zeal, with Safdarjung as governor of Awadh and prime minister of the Mughal empire, this tendency had revived. To succeed at the Mughal court in Delhi, Safdarjung expeditiously allied with the Jats of Bharatpur as well as the Marathas. He is still remembered for being bipartisan towards both communities and counted Hindus among his most trusted advisers. Nawal Rai, who died fighting the Rohillas, was the 'first assistant and head of the military and civil administration of the whole of his dominion... His Diwan in the *subas* (provinces) and his *vakil* at the imperial court in Delhi were Raja Ram Narayan and Raja Laxmi Narayan respectively.'[152] Till at least the middle of 1752, Safdarjung was away from his province most of the time. As the wazir, or prime minister, of the Mughal emperor Ahmad Shah, he was needed in Delhi to thwart the Rohillas and their Afghan kinsman, Ahmad Shah Abdali. When Safdarjung's forces were besieged in the Allahabad Fort

---

[152] A. L. Srivastava, *The First Two Nawabs of Awadh*, Agra: Shiva Lal Agarwala and Co. Ltd., 1954, p. 244.

early on in 1751,[153] his subordinate kings, Raja Prathipati of Pratapgarh and Raja Balwant Singh of Banaras, had helped the Pathans. To avenge these acts of betrayal, Safdarjung adopted an equally perfidious revenge. He sent the Raja of Pratapgarh a friendly letter asking him to meet him and seek pardon. The raja complied and appeared in Safdarjung's camp in Sultanpur, nearly 70 kilometres south of Ayodhya. The cunning wazir kept the raja distracted with small talk and at an opportune moment gave the signal to his trusted bodyguard, who swiftly sank a dagger into the raja's abdomen. Safdarjung later turned towards Banaras to mete out justice to the other opportunist, Raja Balwant Singh, who, having been forewarned about the fate of Prathipati, refused to come in person and seek pardon from the Awadh governor.

Before restoring order by making an example out of the raja of Pratapgarh, Safdarjung had already had to ward off the invasive Marathas under Malhar Rao who was an expert at 'running with the hare and hunting with the hound'.[154] Even though the second Pathan war in 1751 had been victorious for the Awadh governor, it was won with the help of the Marathas, who under the guise of asking for the right to worship at holy places, demanded the rich cities of Kashi (Banaras), Prayag (Allahabad) and Awadh (Ayodhya). Safdarjung rejected their demand on the grounds of it being untenable to the security of his province.[155]

In any case, Maratha chief Malhar Rao's wish to rebuild the Vishveshwar temple which had been demolished by Aurangzeb was opposed by the Brahmins of Kashi who feared that this would endanger their lives. Interestingly, Malhar Rao made no mention of reconstructing temples in either Allahabad or Ayodhya.[156]

THE BRITISH EAST INDIA COMPANY AND AYODHYA

In the middle of the eighteenth century, the Hindu religious landscape of Ayodhya was to change because of events that were outside its domain and control. Nine hundred kilometres east from Ayodhya, on the banks of the river Bhagirathi, lies the small town of Palashi, in Bengal. Here in 1757,

---

[153]At the Allahabad siege, Shuja's commander Ismail Beg was helped by the daring Nagas under Rajendragiri Gosain, the guru of Umragiri and Anupgiri.

[154]Kalika-Ranjan Qanungo, *History of the Jats: Contribution to the History of Northern India, to the Death of Mirza Najaf Khan, 1782*, New Delhi: Low Price Publications, 2003, p. 136.

[155]Ibid.

[156]Ibid.

the British East India Company defeated Siraj-ud-daulah, the nawab of Bengal, after his army chief, Mir Jafar, was bribed and enticed to become the next nawab by Colonel Robert Clive. Many Indians remember this victory with bitterness as it marked the beginning of India's colonization. But it also marked the birth of a modern consciousness of India being one country. After the Battle of Plassey, the British also won the Battle of Buxar in 1764 and were poised to steadily chip away at the sovereignty of the Mughal empire. First, they set their sights on Awadh, one of the richest provinces of Mughal India. Fed by glacial rivers, the region and its people had developed a distinct self-reliance. From pre-Mauryan times, this fertile land had been coveted by every conqueror, and the British were the latest power drawn to it. As it turned out, they got Awadh without a battle. The victory in the Battle of Buxar had given the British a strategic foothold in north India. Ranged against the British army were Mughal emperor Shah Alam II, Awadh's governor, and Mughal prime minister Shuja-ud-daulah (Safdarjung's successor), and the new nawab of Bengal, Mir Qasim, who had turned against the British even though he owed his position to them. After the defeat, Shuja-ud-daulah, considered the best informed man in India at the time because of the large spy network at his command, was pursued by British forces and survived only because of the intervention of Anupgiri Gosain, the leader of the Shaiva army that was in his service. Shuja, determined to avenge his defeat, planned another attack on the British forces with the help of the Maratha chief, Malhar, but was defeated again on 3 May 1765 in Kara, Allahabad.

SHAIVA FIGHTERS AND NAWABS OF AWADH

The common factor in the reigns of the first three Shia governors of Awadh was the presence of Shaiva Gosain armies. A decade earlier, in 1755, when Shuja-ud-daulah was consolidating his rule, Gosain chief Umraogiri, who was also known as Himmat Bahadur, supported him against persistent attacks by Afghan pathans led by Ismail Khan Kabuli. The pathans of Awadh still nursed hopes of establishing themselves as kings, and what stood in their path was the army of Shaiva Gosains (also called Nagas) who had built a reputation for winning many a lost war.[157]

Ismail Khan, keen to establish his supremacy in the province, decided to

---

[157]Jadunath Sarkar, *History of Dasnami Sampraday*, Daraganj: Sri Panchayati Akhara Mahanirvani, p. 148.

get rid of the Shaiva Gosains. The vagrant Shuja gave him the opportunity between 1754 and 1764 CE. Here it is worth noting that this episode has been narrated differently by historians. Jadunath Sarkar treats it as an example of the Naga loyalty for Shuja against the backdrop of a power tussle whereas Lala Sitaram portrays this as an example of 'people power' against a Muslim ruler.

Jadunath Sarkar writes:

Second to none in influence in Oudh after the death of Safdarjung, this Ismail Khan looked about for means to establish his virtual supremacy in the state. He found that the Nagas, being the loyal adherents of Shuja, were the chief obstacle in his path and determined to root them out. The ruler of Oudh was a dissolute youth; struck by the beauty of a Khatri girl of Faizabad, he sought to get possession of her and when other means failed, Shuja employed the Nagas under the service of the Gossain chiefs, Anupgiri and Umraogiri. At once the whole city was stirred by agitation against the young ruler and his accomplices, the Nagas. Ismail Khan entered into a league with the leaders of the Mughalia troops; at his instigation Muhammad Quli Khan, governor of Allahabad, marched towards Lucknow. The only body of men who stood by Shuja at this hour were the Gosain brothers with their followers. Ismail Khan now asked Shuja to absolve himself of the heinous guilt by dismissing the Nagas from their services. The latter understood the motive behind this seemingly just proposal and refused to disband them. A civil war seemed inevitable but Shuja's mother brought her influence to bear upon the Diwan Ramnarain and weaned him from the rebel group. Ismail Khan and the Mughal sardars too thereupon submitted, partly out of consideration for the sentiment of Begam Sadrunissa and partly out of the fear of a clash with the Naga arms in which victory was not certain.[158]

The same episode was portrayed by Lala Sitaram in his *Ayodhya ka Itihas*:

An incident from the time of Shuja-ud-daulah is being given here to show that even though a Muslim ruler's authority was supreme, the people were capable of revolting against his atrocities.

---

[158]Ibid., p. 149.

Once while on a walk, Shuja-ud-daulah saw a Khatri beauty and immediately wanted to have her. He called the Gosain chief Himmat Bahadur and expressed his desire. After three days, the Nagas forcibly brought her to Shuja who then fulfilled his heart's desire. On her return home she narrated her ordeal which caused the Khatris to approach Diwan Ram Narain and threaten him with mass desertion. The news reached Ismail Khan Kabuli who sympathising with them decided to get the Nagas punished for this crime. But the mother of Shuja intervened and told the Diwan to not make a fuss about a matter so small. Thereafter, the Khatris were somehow persuaded to stay and the chapter was closed.[159]

Nowhere does Lala Sitaram mention the power tussle involving two Muslim chieftains and their respective Hindu supporters that is brought out so well by Jadunath Sarkar. It is in such nuances that the history of Ayodhya can truly be traced.

THE GROWTH OF RAM'S CULT IN AYODHYA

Shuja-ud-daulah died at the age of forty-three in January 1775. His three-decade-long reign was dotted with constant warfare, the emergence of two bigger powers—the Marathas/Peshwas and the British—and the unjust and financially crippling treaties with the British who were guaranteed by the bankers of Banaras.

Five years before Shuja-ud-daulah died, Joseph Tiefenthaler, an Austrian Jesuit priest escaping prosecution from the Portuguese in Goa, travelled to Agra from north India. Tiefenthaler came to Ayodhya while on a tour of Awadh between 1766 and 1771. He collected anecdotes and observations in a book, *Description Historique et Géographique de l'Inde*. The Babri mosque featured in this book and it is clear from his account that he was accompanied by local guides and perhaps the caretaker of the mosque. Following in the footsteps of William Finch, his English counterpart 150 years earlier, Tiefenthaler noted a new set of legends and customs, including one about Ram's birthplace. According to Tiefenthaler, locals in Ayodhya believed that:

> Emperor Aurangzeb got the fortress called Ram Kot demolished and got constructed at the same place, a Muslim temple (masjid) with three domes. Some believe that it was constructed by 'Babbar'. Fourteen

---

black stone pillars can be seen there, which existed at the site of the fortress. Twelve of these pillars now support the interior arcades of the mosque while two of the 12 (pillars) are placed at the entrance of the cloister, two others are part of the tomb of some 'Moor'. It was narrated that these pillars, or rather the debris of the pillars skilfully made were brought from the island of Lanca or Selendip (called Ceylon by the Europeans) by Hanuman, the king of monkeys.[160]

Tiefenthaler described Ram's Cradle as follows:

On the left is seen a square chest, raised five inches from the ground covered with lime, about 5 ells in length but not more than 4 in breadth.

The Hindus call it Bedi, the cradle. The reason for this is that once upon a time, there was a house in this place where Befohan was born in the form of Rama besides his three brothers. Subsequently, Aurangzeb or according to another belief, Babbar, got this place destroyed in order to deny them the opportunity of practising their superstitions. However, there still exists some superstitious cult in some place. For example, in the place where native house of Rama existed, they go around three times and prostrate on the floor.[161]

AYODHYA'S IMMINENT VAISHNAVA CONQUEST

Tiefenthaler's visit marks the time in Ayodhya's history when Shaiva Gosain influence was waning and Vaishnava Bairagis had started asserting themselves. Tiefenthaler's arrival in Ayodhya is likely to have occurred around the same time when the Gosain chief Anupgiri was reassessing his own options in the light of Shuja's humiliation by the British. Tiefenthaler was in Ayodhya some time after Shuja's second defeat in 1765 in alliance with the Marathas. At this time the Gosain army was in the service of Bharatpur's Jat ruler, Jawahir Singh, and was not present in Awadh.

Shaiva–Vaishnava enmity had never had clear rules of engagement; like mortal enemies they struck at each other whenever and however possible. The presence of the Gosain brothers in their vicinity afforded one Vaishnava an opportunity to plot their assassination. When Jawahir Singh and the

---

[160]Joseph Tiefenthaler, *Description Historique et* Géographique de *l'Inde*, Berlin: Spener, 1786, p. .

[161]Kishore, *Ayodhya Revisited*, p. 147.

Gosains were in Malwa, a plot to assassinate Anupgiri and his brother Umraogiri was hatched at the behest of Ramakrishna, a disciple of Galta's chief mahant, Balanand.

> Suspecting the gosains of intriguing with the Marathas...Jawahir Singh ordered an assassination attempt on Anupgiri and Umraogiri under the cover of darkness. Also in the Jat service at this time, and probably responsible for poisoning Jawahir's mind against the gosains was Ramakrishna mahant, a powerful Vaishnava bairagi commander of Jaipur and a chela of the well known Balanand Swami.[162]

The brothers survived the attempt and Anupgiri Gosain avenged it by 'dismantling a pavilion honouring the Jat king on the outskirts of the Vaishnava pilgrimage center of Mathura and used the materials for the construction of a ghat at Vrindaban to commemorate his own name'.[163] By making a ghat in his name in Vaishnava Vrindaban, Anupgiri served the ultimate insult to his Vaishnava Ramanandi foes. Back in Awadh though, the Gosains were soon to drift away, first from Shuja, and then from his son, Asaf-ud-daulah. What started as a slowly widening rift with Shuja's second defeat at Kara became a quick separation with the capitulation of Asaf to the British. The British East India Company had by now cast its net on Asaf-ud-daulah, the young nawab-wazir, who was often overshadowed by his influential mother, Umat-uz-Zohra or Bahu Begum.

AWADH UNDER ASAF-UD-DAULAH: MOTHER VERSUS SON

Muhammad Faiz Bakhsh, a contemporary of Asaf employed with the Bahu Begum in Faizabad, in his memoirs titled *Tarikh Farah Bakhsh*[164] (*The Enchanting History*), describes Asaf as being of dissolute character and surrounded by naked rustics and fakirs whose brothers and fathers had themselves worked the plough.[165] He elaborates at length on the unending machinations of Asaf and his acolytes to get as much money out of his

---

[162]William R. Pinch, *Warrior Ascetics and Indian Empires*, Cambridge: Cambridge University Press, 2006, p. 112.

[163]Ibid.

[164]It was translated by William Hoey who found it in the possession of a drug vendor who was using it to wrap drugs.

[165]This pejorative reference to men whose fathers and brothers 'had worked the plough' points to the gradual rise of the landowning intermediate castes like the Kurmis and Pandeys. The naked fakirs most likely refers to armed Hindu ascetics called Bairagis.

mother as possible. The memoirs are the only existing record of life in Faizabad in the wake of Shuja-ud-daulah's death. Surprisingly or perhaps not so, Ayodhya doesn't find mention in them. In fact, the memoirs give the impression that Ayodhya remained obscure and unimportant to the rulers, perhaps because it had been considered a wilderness and a mainly 'Hindu' place since the time of Safdarjung, who had moved the capital to Bangla or Faizabad in 1722.

The two times that Ayodhya does feature in *Tarikh Farah Baksh* is with regard to a dispute over the ownership of an estate of which it was a part. Ayodhya was part of Mahal Haveli Avadh,[166] an estate passed on to Asaf-ud-daulah after Shuja's death, and after Asaf's death, it became a part of a struggle between two jealous nobles. Finally, Bahu Begum prevailed and granted it to her own trusted man.

Faiz Bakhsh's memoirs capture successfully the genesis of the decay that set in soon after Shuja's death. Asaf, unlike his father who was both an able warrior and administrator, took little interest in the affairs of the kingdom, and by the age of thirty-three, he had grown accustomed to a sybaritic life of pleasure. Within days of his father's death he started asking his mother for money to maintain his retinue of wastrels, fakirs and upstarts.

1775: AWADH'S CAPITAL MOVES TO LUCKNOW

It was to counter his mother's overbearing, if somewhat justifiable, presence in Faizabad, that Asaf thought of moving the capital to Lucknow. First though, he set up his court at Mahdi Ghat on the road to Lucknow from where he blackmailed her into giving him six lakh rupees. A month later, he wanted more and this almost caused bloodshed between the troops of the new nawab-wazir and those of his mother, the Bahu Begum. Faiz Bakhsh's account of this episode is more sympathetic to the mother, as he was in her service, but Asaf's greed and tales of his degeneration are attested to by other accounts. Despite being his critic, Faiz Bakhsh also recognizes generosity to be Asaf's only redeeming grace.

But it appears that Asaf wanted to practise generosity by relying on his mother's inheritance rather than on his own endeavours. Bahu Begum, after giving Asaf six lakh rupees within days of her husband's death, realized that no amount of money would be sufficient to bankroll her son's dissolute ways.

The rift between mother and son was perhaps widened by the presence

---

[166]Mahal is the Urdu equivalent of estate.

of Bahu Begum's trusted eunuchs like Jawahar Ali Khan, who realized that their prosperity depended on Bahu Begum's wealth. On Asaf's side the eunuchs had their equivalents in cronies like Murtaza Khan, who constantly poisoned Asaf's ears about the Bahu Begum and her eunuchs.

In 1775, by Asaf's order the court had moved to Lucknow which was being developed into a capital that sought to rival the by now fading eminence of Shahjahanabad (Delhi). But Asaf's departure from Faizabad was neither graceful nor peaceful.

It took Asaf only a month to exhaust the money given by his mother so he dispatched Murtaza Khan to ask for more. Bahu Begum very reluctantly parted with another four lakhs and became permanently embittered with her son. Writing about the time when Asaf returned to Faizabad briefly, Faiz Bakhsh portrays the sudden change that had taken place since the death of Shuja:

> What a change I saw, when Asafuddaulah returned on this occasion to Faizabad. In the time of Shujauddaulah no one dared to go about armed even with a penknife, and all who came to see him passed on foot within the armorial gate…and I had never seen an exception even among the courtiers, the highest military officers and the eunuchs, who came specially on business with Shujauddaulah. But now naked rustics, whose fathers and brothers with their own hands guiding the plough, were enrolled in the regiments as regulars and rode about as Asafuddaulah's orderlies and were allowed to go in and out of the Baradari [a building, usually with twelve doors], and the Nawab's own court, riding on horseback.
>
> And around nawab-wazir's palanquin there rode in disorderly fashion, on state horses with grand caparisons, Bhawani Singh, Moti Singh, Hulas Singh, Nawaz Singh, and Maiku Singh. Such was the change within two months![167]

Among these, it can be safely speculated that Nawaz Singh hailed from a family of Hindus who had converted to Islam or at least he had had another good reason to use a Muslim first name. The other, more probable possibility is that Nawaz Singh belonged to a new group at Asaf's court,

---

[167]*Memoirs of Faizabad, Being a Translation of the 'Tarikh-i-*Farahbakhsh' *of Muhammad Faiz Bakhsh: 1722-1781*, William Hoey, trans., Lucknow: New Royal Book Company, 2005, p. 21.

which was made up of 'peasant soldiers', who were derisively called Tilangi Rajas or Trooper Rajas (to underscore the irony of soldiers becoming kings). However, the Tilangis considered themselves Rajputs, and they had successfully thwarted Asaf's plan to anoint some Ayodhya Kurmis as rajas.[168]

Ayodhya Kurmis[169] is the name that came to be used for those land-owning Kurmis who claimed Kshatriya status on the basis of an Ayodhya-centred consciousness of their origins. But this claim was not uncontested, as some Ayodhya Kurmis from Parraona in Gorakhpur found out when the Rajputs in Asaf's court objected to them being made kings and thereby attaining Kshatriya status. These 'Awadhia Kurmi' communities were spread over parts of Bihar and eastern UP, over the area known as Bhojpur. If the Muslims were fighting for position and power in the court, the Hindus were too involved in contests related to their own claims over status in the Hindu order.

Interestingly, after Asaf's ascension to the throne of Awadh in 1775, the Kurmis, 'naked faqirs' and in many cases the Tilangis themselves became beneficiaries of Ayodhya's almost total identification as a geocultural hub of Vaishnava belief. The Ramanandi Bairagis who had begun displacing the Shaiva sanyasis in the first half of the eighteenth century, too, had established their stronghold in Ayodhya by the time of Asaf-ud-daulah's death in 1797 CE.

The Ramanandis' philosophy of inclusion coupled with Asaf's 'permissive program of social mobility'[170] would impart a big push to jati or caste reform based on an Ayodhya-centred image of themselves. This aspect will be dealt with later when we trace the rapid development of the Vaishnava pilgrimage complex during the British period; for now, let us return to the time when Asaf ordered an armed assault on his mother's palace to recover her hidden treasure.

THE BRITISH AVERT A MOTHER-SON CLASH IN FAIZABAD

After moving to Lucknow in 1775, Asaf, in a drunken haze, agreed to a plan to extricate the Begum's treasure before it was usurped by her eunuchs. A force was dispatched under Asaf's trusted man, Mukhtaruddaula,

---

[168]Pinch, *Peasants and Monks in British India*, p. 53.

[169]Kurmi is a caste group found in north Indian states like Bihar, UP and MP, among others.

[170]Pinch, *Peasants and Monks in British India*, p. 53.

accompanied by John Bristow, the British Resident at Lucknow.

The Begum refused to part with any more of her money. Mukhtaruddaula threatened to use force and the Begum too prepared her own army of three regiments and irregulars. A bloody battle between mother and son's troops was averted by the intervention of Bristow, who convinced the Begum to pay enough and get an assurance from her son that there would be no more financial demands. Faiz Bakhsh, who was present at the time of this extortion of Bahu Begum, writes:

> After this consultation and lapse of a week the Begum gave in, and the sum of sixty laks of rupees was agreed upon. Sixteen laks already given and eight laks now given were disbursed from her treasury. The writer himself produced 30,000 rupees from his office-chest and included it in the eight laks. In all twenty-four laks were paid in cash.[171]

The rest of the money was paid by Bahu Begum in movable and immovable assets like elephants and jewellery. In return, the begum made the British Resident and the representatives of Asaf sign a deed in the name of God that barred him from making any more demands of money or estates.

By brokering this truce, the British, with one stroke, had become the arbiters of a compromise between mother and son. John Bristow was one of the first Britons to exploit the differences between them. Warren Hastings, the Governor General of the Company, extracted twenty-six lakh rupees from Asaf in return for some estates. Later, the estates were confiscated (Hastings was eventually found guilty of fraud by a British court).

Once Asaf-ud-daulah was in the virtual control of the British, they prevailed upon him to get rid of the Shaiva warriors or Gosains from his army. William Pinch notes that:

> Company officials reviled the gosains and doggedly strove to distance them from the service of Asaf-ud-daulah. Part of their distaste was due to the ongoing skirmishes with similarly accoutred sanyasis and fakirs in Bengal during the latter part of the eighteenth century. But much of it had to do with British apprehensions about the 'undue' influence (and mischievous intentions) of the gosains in north Indian affairs.[172]

As a result, soon after he took over as nawab, Asaf-ud-daulah, who was in

---

[171]Faiz Bakhsh, *Tarikh Farah Bakhsh*, p. 27.
[172]Pinch, *Warrior Ascetics and Indian Empires*, p. 113.

any case unable to afford the expensive Shaiva army, allowed the Gosain chief Anupgiri alias Himmat Bahadur to leave his service and join Mirza Najaf Khan, the regent of Delhi. By the end of 1775, the Gosains had completely quit the service of Awadh's fourth nawab, Asaf-ud-daulah.

AYODHYA'S REVIVAL DURING THE REIGN OF AWADH NAWABS

Nawab Asaf-ud-daulah's kingdom was dependent on the British for its security and survival. Realizing this, Asaf chose to direct his resources towards maintaining stability and developing trade within the kingdom. During his time Ayodhya witnessed a revival of sorts under Asaf's trusted official, Diwan Tikait Rai, who oversaw the construction of several ghats and temples. Lala Sitaram, the first British-era chronicler of Ayodhya's history, writes approvingly of Asaf and Tikait Rai's contribution to Ayodhya in *Ayodhya ka Itihas*. 'He was famous for giving large donations. Thousands of rupees were given to Brahmans from the royal treasury. Ayodhya's Hanumangarhi was built during his time and stands as a testament to his religious good.'[173] Evidently, Asaf's munificence was indiscriminate. Among his cohorts were many Hindus of 'low' castes as well as fakirs.

The resurgent Marathas in the south of Awadh were also an indirect but ultimately favourable factor in the growth of Ayodhya as a major pilgrim centre controlled by Ramanandis. In 1787, Maratha general Mahadji Scindia had successfully intervened to reduce the pilgrim tax at the Hindu centres in Awadh, including Ayodhya. To counter more Maratha demands Asaf's policy seems to have been to increase his patronage of Hindu establishments in his kingdom.

This was not very different from what Shuja-ud-daulah had also done to deal with the Marathas, who were demanding control of Ayodhya, Banaras and Prayag, as these were Hindu holy places. During Shuja's reign (1754–1775), a number of Ramanandi temples had come up in Ayodhya. Besides, his move to shift the capital from Ayodhya to Faizabad had created a lot of goodwill among Hindus. On his watch, several Muslim nobles donated lands to various Hindu priests to build temples and ashrams. Notable among these were the Khaki Akhada, Mahanirvani Akhada, Niralambi sect and the expansion of the temple complex atop Hanumangarhi.

It is believed that Asaf, who was the first Awadh-born nawab, commenced the construction of Lucknow's famous Bara Imambara as a relief measure

---

[173]Sitaram, *Ayodhya ka Itihas*, p. 121.

against drought, and since then it has acquired the somewhat disturbing monicker of 'a monument to hunger'.

A couplet from that time even equates him with God.

Jis ko na de Maula
Usko de Asafudaula

(To whom God does not give
Asaf-ud-daulah will give)[174]

Nawab Asaf-ud-daulah died in 1797. In the next sixty years or so, Awadh came to be ruled by seven nawabs. Barring a few exceptions, all of them continued to patronize religious bodies and individuals. The court at Lucknow acquired fame for its patronage of poetry, dance and music, and war became a distant memory. A syncretic Hindustani culture thrived and its extent was epitomized by the last king of Awadh, Wajid Ali Shah, who in 1855 while responding to a complaint pertaining to a religious dispute between Hindus and Muslims over a place of worship, is believed to have said:

Hum ishq ke bande hain mazhab se nahin waqif
Gar Kaaba hua tuh kya, butkhana hua, tuh kya?

(I am a man of love, not familiar with religion
What of it, be it the Kaaba or the temple?)[175]

While the nawabs and their nobles may have largely espoused religious plurality and tolerance, the undercurrents in both Hindu and Muslim tensions were showing the emergence of radical positions. In 1855, during the time of Wajid Ali Shah, matters came to a head when the Bairagis of Hanumangarhi and Muslims led by a fanatic maulvi of Amethi met in a bloody face-off over the existence of a demolished mosque on the top of Hanumangarhi. This dispute—which arose against the backdrop of British plans for Awadh's annexation and their constant meddling to scuttle Hindu–Muslim harmony—was also the first time that the Babri Masjid finds a mention in official correspondence during the British period.

---

[174]Darogah Haji Abbas Ali, *An Illustrated Historical Album of the Rajas and Taluqdars of Oudh*, Allahabad: North-western Provinces and Oudh Government Press, 1880, p. xi.
[175]Kunal Kishore, *Ayodhya Revisited*, p. 616.

THE BRITISH ROLE IN AYODHYA, RAMANANDI ASSERTION AND THE NAWAB OF AWADH

In the last two decades of the 1700s, Ayodhya had emerged as an important Vaishnava pilgrimage site. There is barely any evidence to relate the precise nature of developments in Ayodhya but we do know that some important akharas of the Vaishnavas had been established, and that in the larger arena of religion in India, Vaishnavas were emerging as a superior force. In Ayodhya and surrounding areas, this Vaishnava thrust was led by the Ramanandis who had opened the doors to God and godhead to practically everybody, Shudras included. Their policy of unrestricted access allowed men and women of hitherto prohibited castes to become priests and followers. This had understandably caused a social revolution and Ayodhya, being the seat of Ramanandis, began to acquire the prominence that had eluded it since, mythically speaking, Ram's departure in Treta Yug.

Whether and to what extent the plurality policy of the Awadh nawabs influenced the outlook of the Ayodhya Ramanandis is a matter for another study; however, one visible and lasting impact of nawabi patronage has been the fish emblem that adorns all older Ramanandi temples and monastries. In fact, besides the many commonalities that are only expected to be found in a people who share the same geography and culture, the fish emblem has transcended all barriers of caste and religion. The facades of temples and mosques that came up during the nawabi period proudly bear this emblem.

The fish emblem's story dates back to the time of Saadat Khan, the first governor of Awadh between 1722–1739 CE. While crossing a swollen Ganga at Farrukhabad in a boat, a fish jumped out of the water and landed on his lap. Considering this a good omen, Saadat Khan preserved the fish. Till the time of Wajid Ali Shah, the last nawab of Awadh, the same fish-skeleton is said to have been stored in the royal treasury. This is how the fish came to be the royal emblem of the Awadh dynasty.[176] The present state emblem of UP bears testament to the inclusive times of the not-so-distant past. When India became independent, the fish emblem was retained with the addition of a bow (symbol of Ram) as the state symbol of the then United Provinces (now Uttar Pradesh).

The process of social change in the Ramanandi sect, as well as Hinduism in general, was aided by the British and 'their idea of God' which was based on a devotional, worshipful outlook towards religion and all things

---

[176]Yatindra Mishra, ed., *Shehernama Faizabad*, New Delhi: Vani Prakashan, 2016.

holy.[177] Armed ascetics like the soldiering Shaiva Gosains did not conform
to their idea of religious monks. As William Pinch notes:

> The British application, unconscious or otherwise, of a normative
> conception of religion served to structure their own actions and
> decisions with respect to armed ascetics. The British were not in
> the main overly concerned with the task of convincing them of the
> correctness of their Enlightenment[178] conception of religion. They did
> not have to be...[179]

The British found the Vaishnava values of complete devotion to a personal
God to be more in line with their own ideas of religion. As opposed to
the militant, extremely ambitious and war-like Shaiva ascetics, the British
found common ground with Vaishnavas. William Pinch also corroborates
the commonality between Vaishnavism and the British; he writes: '...a major
strand of Indian religious reform was tending in the same general direction
as late medieval, early modern Christianity, and had been for some time. And
the purveyors of that Indian religious reform also took a dim view of men
who encroached upon the terrain of God.'[180] Here the purveyors referred
to are the Vaishnava saints and priests who scorned at the practices of the
Shaiva ascetics. In fact, the revulsion to certain Shaiva sects (like the Nath
Yogis of Gorakhpur) because of their tantric practices such as drinking one's
own urine, eating human flesh, etc., is still as strong as it was back then.[181]

But for the British East India Company, the biggest problem with Shaiva
ascetics was not their peculiar, sometimes unpleasant, practices and privations.
They had, during their decades-long pacification of Bengal, experienced the
intensity of the fighting sanyasis and fakirs first-hand. Below is an instance
of the killing power of the armed ascetics as recorded by a Major James
Rennell on 20 August 1766.[182] Rennell and his troops had ambushed a
party of these ascetics and Rennell himself was grievously wounded in the
encounter. Having recovered six months later, he wrote:

---

[177]John Bossy, *Christianity in the West, 1400–1700*, New York: Oxford University Press,
1987.

[178]An eighteenth-century period of social, cultural and religious renaissance in Europe.

[179]Pinch, *Warrior Ascetics and Indian Empires*, p. 12.

[180]Ibid.

[181]Interview with Mahant Gyan Das, Hanumangarhi, Ayodhya.

[182]He later became the first Surveyor-General of India. He is also credited with making
the first accurate map of India.

...the Sanyashy Faqirs (part of the same tribe which plundered Dacca in Cossim Ally's time) were in arms to the number of 7 or 800 at the time I was surveying Baar (a small province near Boutan) and had taken and plundered the capital of that name within a few coss of my route... I came up with Morrison immediately after he had defeated the Sanashys in a pitched Battle.... Our Escorte, which were a few Horse, rode off, and the Enemy drawn with Sabres immediately surrounded us. Morrison escaped unhurt, Richards, my Brother officer, received only a slight Wound, and fought his Way off; my Armenian Assistant was killed, and the Sepoy Adjutant much wounded... I was put in a Palankeen, and Morrison made an attack on the Enemy and cut most of them to Pieces. I was now in a most shocking Condition indeed, being deprived of the Use of both my Arms...a cut of a Sable (*sic*) had cut thro' my right Shoulder Bone, and laid me open for nearly a Foot down the Back, cutting thro' and wounding some of my Ribs. I had besides a Cut on the left Elbow which took off the Muscular part of the breadth of a Hand, a Stab in the Arm and a large Cut on my head.[183]

Rennell's account is valuable for his own terrified account as well as the trajectory of armed asceticism after the arrival of the British in India.

In neighbouring Awadh too, the British had seen the death-defying and game-changing frenzied bravery of the soldiering ascetics in the battles of Buxar, Allahabad, Panipat and against the Rohillas. Therefore, once both Bengal and Awadh came into their protection, the British thought it prudent to get rid of them.

By the 1780s, the British were comfortably ensconced in Fort William[184] at Calcutta and at Lucknow, the new capital of Awadh. To improve their administration, they began a serious study of the people and the land that they had come to control in a matter of a few decades. Thus began the documentation of local traditions and fables, especially relevant as we will see in the case of religious sites like Ayodhya.

So too everything from flora to fauna, butterflies, ancient ruins, agriculture, natural produce, fishes, customs of the 'natives', their beliefs and gods, all were examined and documented so that the British East India Company could make sense of their new dominion.

---

[183]La Touch E., ed., *The Journals of Major James Rennell First Surveyor-General of India, 1764–1767*, Calcutta: Asiatic Society, 1910.

[184]Built by the 'unstable sociopath', Lord Robert Clive in 1781.

'BRITISH SURVEYS' FOR THE SAKE OF ADMINISTRATION

It is through such a survey done by a surgeon and botanist in 1813–14 CE, that we are able to partially trace the evolution of Ayodhya as a Ramanandi centre in eastern Uttar Pradesh. Francis Buchanan, a Scotsman who travelled through Patna, Shahbad and Gorakhpur, besides other districts of Gangetic Bihar and eastern Uttar Pradesh, enumerated religious sects with the thoroughness of a botanist. Although some of his Bengal surveys have been criticized for statistical shortcomings, his work on the religious sects and their followers has been found valuable by scholars.[185]

Ayodhya at this time was seeing a heightened concentration of Ramanandis. This is also borne out by Buchanan's survey which found the number of Ramanandi gurus ascending as he moved westwards from Patna to Ayodhya. In his accounts of the Ramanandis, Buchanan found that the priests stressed upon their followers a strict moral code and adherence to a daily regimen of prayer and physical exercise; they also forbade meat and alcohol. Observance of such Vaishnava traditions gave them, untouchables included, 'a substantial aura of self-respect', he concluded.[186]

Thus, while Shaiva ascetics often became free of all social and moral obligations and focused on immortality through discipline and transformation into gods themselves, the Ramanandis emphasized the devotional and abstinential aspect of worship.

At the same time, the socio-religious changes taking place in the entire region of eastern Uttar Pradesh were being felt in Ayodhya. This was only natural given that the Shaiva Gosain army led by the Giri brothers had moved out of Awadh, and the new nawab Asaf-ud-daulah had also turned his benevolence on the Ramanandis. Buchanan also noted that Buxar, less than 300 kilometres from Ayodhya, had become a big centre of Ramanandis. In Buxar, he found that while some gurus are Brahmins, 'most are shudras'.[187]

This was in character with the liberal rules of access of the Ramanandi Sampraday. This point about the birth-origins of Ramanandis and whether it mattered was something I brought up with various mahants of Ayodhya—and all of them rejected any notion of casteism in their respective akharas.

While the Ramanandis were gaining a large number of followers, they

---

[185]Pinch, *Peasants and Monks in British India.*
[186]Ibid., p. 22.
[187]Ibid.

were also being scorned for their apparent lack of respect for the orthodox rules of priesthood. Buchanan noted in his survey, 'men of impure of vile tribes, who wish to be thought better than their neighbours, and who abstain from meat, fish, and spirituous liquors, are called Bhakat (devotees), and at the recommendation of the Vairagis, who are their gurus have given up an indulgence of their appetites'.[188] Thus, recourse to a pure lifestyle was promoted as a way to enhance one's social standing and status.

Unsurprisingly, the British had found in the Ramanandis a relatable order of monks given their Enlightenment-influenced dispositions. Earlier in 1773, Governor General Warren Hastings had banned all 'Biraugies and Sunnasses' from Company-ruled Bengal with the exception of those ascetics who resided in one place and quietly observed their religious functions. In fact, by the first decade of the 1800s, most of the Gosain armies had been disbanded by the British, and their soldiers had melted back into their non-soldierly vocations. Faced with shrinking prospects of survival as Shaiva ascetics, some were also quietly acquiring Vaishnava moorings. Meanwhile in Ayodhya, the Ramanandis were biding their time to reclaim in totality their very own Jerusalem or Mecca.

---

[188]Ibid.

Chapter 6

AYODHYA: 1800-1857

A glimpse of life during this period in Ayodhya is hard to come by, but rare interstices in the form of British gazettes give us fleeting insights. Published in 1828, Walter Hamilton's gazette is devoid of any specific details. But it does capture the general attributes of Awadh—the province and Ayodhya. Written twenty-six years before the great rebellion of 1857 and almost an equal number after the Treaty of 1801, it describes the Hindus of the province as:

> ...a very superior race, both in their bodily strength and mental faculties, to those of Bengal and the districts south of Calcutta... Rajpoots or military class here generally exceed Europeans in stature, have robust frames, and are possessed of many valuable qualities in a military point of view. From the long predominance of the Mahomedans a considerable proportion of the inhabitants profess that religion, and from both persuasions a great number of the Company's best sepoys are procured.[189]

This is also perhaps how the moniker of Awadh being 'a nursery of sepoys' came into being. About Ayodhya, the town of Ram, Hamilton writes:

> This town is esteemed as one of the most sacred places of antiquity.
>
> Pilgrims resort to this vicinity, where the remains of the ancient city of Oude, the capital of the great Rama, are still to be seen; but whatever may have been its former magnificence it now exhibits nothing but a shapeless mass of ruins. The modern town extends a considerable way along the banks of the Goggra, adjoining Fyzabad, and is tolerably well peopled; but inland it is a mass of rubbish and

---

[189]Walter Hamilton, *The East India Gazetteer*, Vol. II, London: Parbury, Allen and Co., 1828, p. 349.

jungle, among which are the reputed sites of temples dedicated to Rama, Seeta, his wife, Lakshman, his general, and Hunimaun (a large monkey), his prime minister. The religious mendicants who perform the pilgrimage to Oude are chiefly of the Ramata [Ramawat] sect, who walk round the temples and idols, bathe in the holy pools, and perform the customary ceremonies.[190]

It is noteworthy that Hamilton finds not one temple worthy enough to be described in detail. He merely sums up the religious affiliation—belonging to the Ramanandi Ramawat sect—of the monks, and his account also makes no mention of Ram's birthplace temple or the Hanumangarhi or even the ancient Nageshwarnath temple. Hamilton recorded what he saw, and perhaps this was all there was to be found: a town in the wilderness, within which lay ruins that had come to be woven with cobwebs and legends of Ram. The majority of Ayodhya's population stayed close to the river, and some isolated temples had come up across the inland keorah (a tree used for perfumes and spices) forests. In short, it was (unlike it is now) a place shorn of the humdrum of a big pilgrim centre or the buzz of the religious bazaar of other Hindu centres like Haridwar and Banaras.

FIRST BATTLE OVER A PLACE OF WORSHIP IN AYODHYA

The year 1855 was momentous in the history of Ayodhya. It is often cited as the year in which the recorded history of the Ram Janmabhoomi–Babri Masjid dispute commences. It should also be seen as a marker of the half-truths that have come to systematically shroud the vexed issue. This is because in 1855, the bloody conflict that took place was not over the supposed birthplace of Ram.[191] It was over the Hanumangarhi temple and the claims by certain Sunnis that the Bairagis of Hanumangarhi had destroyed a mosque that existed atop it. The Muslims charged on the Hanumangarhi but were repelled and routed. They hid inside the mosque of Babur that lay at a distance of less than a kilometre from Hanumangarhi. In this way, the site of the Babri Masjid became embroiled in the dispute over Hanumangarhi. At the time of the 1855 riot, the Bairagis had not claimed the Babri mosque as the birthplace of Ram. It was only much later that the conflict of 1855 came to be associated primarily with the Babri Masjid instead of the Hanumangarhi temple. Today, it is widely believed that the

---

[190]Ibid., p. 353.
[191]Kishore, *Ayodhya Revisited*.

first recorded Hindu struggle for Ram's birthplace dates back to the events of 1855.

It is ironic that despite voluminous British and other contemporary records of the incident, it is this falsified version that is accepted as the 'truth'. There are however, some incontrovertible facts about it:

Firstly, that the Muslims claimed that there was a mosque on Hanumangarhi and that it was destroyed by the Bairagis.

Secondly, that there took place a bloody battle in which Muslims were routed and that they took shelter in the Babri mosque.

And finally, at least till the 1855 dispute, the Babri Masjid had not been claimed as Ram's birthplace.

HANUMANGARHI: AYODHYA'S PRE-EMINENT TEMPLE

What are the events of 1855 that are fairly well documented?

Hanumangarhi, a temple of Hanuman, Ram's most devout devotee, is built atop a small hillock that also happens to be the highest point in Ayodhya. Today, it is a well-fortified temple, with fourteen cannons adorning its ramparts. At its foot live hundreds of Bairagis, the more important ones live in modern buildings equipped with all conveniences. It is the most favoured temple for the lakhs of devotees who visit Ayodhya every year. For them a trip to Ayodhya has always meant a dip in the Sarayu, followed by a visit to Nageshwarnath and Hanumangarhi. Hanuman is special even to Ram; therefore it is no surprise that for Hindu pilgrims too, he is sometimes revered more than Ram himself.

Even though Hanuman is identified with Ram by most lay devotees, he is claimed by both Vaishnavas and Shaivas (in fact to lay devotees, Ram, Shankar, Vishnu, Hanuman and Ganesh are all forms of the same god).

Devdutt Pattanaik, in some ways a modern version of Valmiki himself, explains Hanuman's all-round appeal thus:

> According to Shaivites, Shiva himself descended as Hanuman to destroy Ravana, an errant Shiva-bhakta. They said that Ravana had offered his ten heads to Shiva and obtained boons that made him very powerful. But as Rudra, Shiva has eleven forms. Ravana's offering of ten heads satisfied ten forms of Rudra. The eleventh unhappy Rudra took birth as Hanuman to kill Ravana. Hence Hanuman is also Raudreya.
>
> To establish their superiority, Vishnu-worshippers argued that

Hanuman, hence Shiva, obeyed instructions given by Vishnu. To counter this, Shiva-worshippers said that without Hanuman's help, Ram would never have found Sita. In many stories, it is Hanuman who enables the killing of Ravana. For example, in one Telugu retelling, despite knowing that Ravana's life resided in his navel, Ram shot only at the head of Ravana as he was too proud a warrior to shoot below the neck. So Hanuman sucked in air into his lungs and caused the wind to shift direction causing Ram's arrow to turn and strike Ravana's navel. Association with Shiva, and with celibacy, was reinforced by Hanuman's association with the various ascetic schools of Hinduism, from the Nath-jogis who followed the path of Matsyendranath from around 1,000 years ago, to the Vedantic mathas who followed Madhva-acharya from around 700 years ago, to Sant Ramdas who inspired many Maratha warriors 400 years ago. The latter sages, especially during the bhakti period, introduced the idea of connecting celibacy with service; you give up your worldly pleasures and work for the worldly aspirations of society. Just as the hermit Shiva becomes the householder Shankara for the benefit of Humanity, they spoke of how the ascetic Hanuman became Ram's servant for the benefit of society.[192]

So, irrespective of whether it was the Bairagis or the Shaiva Sanyasis or Nath-Yogis who were the orginal founders of Hanumangarhi, at the time of the 1855 conflict, Ayodhya and Hanumangarhi both had become centres of the Ramanandis.

Land was first allotted to one Abhayaram Das of Hanumangarhi in the time of Saadat Khan, who, as we have seen earlier, was the first governor of Awadh, between 1722–1739 CE. Subsequently, his successors, Safdarjung as well as Shuja-ud-daulah, supported the temple's construction with more revenue land grants. Finally, in the time of Asaf-ud-daulah, the Hanumangarhi temple was completed. It is important to note here that according to tradition, the first land grant made to Hanumangarhi was after the Galta conference of 1718 CE, and the completion of Hanumangarhi happened only in 1799 CE under Diwan Tikait Rai during Asaf-ud-daulah's governorship of Awadh. Asaf-ud-daulah, as we have seen, moved the capital even further away from Ayodhya—from Faizabad to Lucknow. Earlier, Safdarjung had

---

[192]Pattanaik, Devdutt, *My Hanuman Chalisa*, New Delhi: Rupa Publications, 2018, p.16.

moved the capital from Ayodhya to Faizabad. Some writers find the shifting
of the capital as evidence of the Muslim nawabs recognizing the Hindu
pre-eminence of Ayodhya. There is no evidence to suggest that this was
the reason, but from a strategic point of view, Faizabad would have made
more sense as it was more suited for the founding of a capital with its
vast plains and the river Sarayu's wide channel protecting it in the west.

1855 CONFLICT: THE WEAKENING POWER OF LUCKNOW AND INCREASING BRITISH INTERFERENCE

By 1855, the British had become the de facto rulers of Awadh. British
troops were present in places like Faizabad, Lucknow and Gorakhpur to
ensure the stability of areas under their direct control. With the help of
a large spy network, the British officers ensured that they were in step
with the developments in the province. In February 1855, the Resident
of Lucknow, Major General G. B. Outram of the Awadh Frontier Police,
had written to Wajid Ali Shah, warning him of a 'dreadful breach of peace'
by Muslims led by one Shah Ghulam Hussein.[193] Muslim fundamentalists
in north India had gained much currency owing to the weakening of the
absolute supremacy of rulers. In Awadh, the situation was a little more
suitable for people like Hussein, given that the rulers of the province were
Shia and a large number of the Muslim population were Sunni. In addition
to this, there existed a historical rivalry between the mostly Sunni Afghan-
origin Pathans and the more recent arrivals, non-Afghani Shias. But more
than anything it was the defiance of rulers by religious leaders that incited
the conflict. Muslim religious preachers had started to blame the godlessness
of the rulers for the enslavement by the British, and openly preached jihad.

The letter Major General Outram to the King of Awadh, Wajid Ali
Shah, dated 8 February 1855, stated with the certitude of foreknowledge
and forewarning:

> ...it appears that Shah Ghulam Hussein has assembled a large force
> of Musulmans at Kotuaha in the neighbourhood of Fyzabad and is
> intent upon committing some dreadful breach of the peace and is
> determined to destroy and ruin the Hunnooman Ghurrie which is

---

[193]Three maulvis or Muslim priests feature in reference to Faizabad and the 1857 mutiny.
Ghulam Hussein; Ameer Ali of Amethi who was killed by the Awadh forces while on a
march to attack Hanumangarhi; Maulvi Ahmadulah Shah who appeared in Faizabad in
1856 and was imprisoned by the British for his anti-British speeches.

inhabited by Hindoos... His Lieutt. [astt.] called the Maulvee Sahib is even more diabolically inclined and ready for strife—hence the mendicants and devotees, who are there at Hunnooman Ghuree in defence of their lives have been obliged to arm themselves... therefore the Resident feeling exceedingly anxious on this subject entreats His Majesty to despatch a very swift camel messenger with all possible speed, to convey to the King's servants, most peremptory orders to cause the immediate apprehension of Ghulam Hussein and his coadjutors...[194]

Maulvi Ghulam Hussein claimed to his followers that the Bairagis of Hanumangarhi had destroyed a mosque atop that hillock which needed to be redressed by rebuilding it. A large number of Muslims gathered on his side in support of this cause, and having the confidence of belonging to the religion of the ruler, charged at the 70-feet-high Hanumangarhi on 28 July 1855. With help from Hindus from surrounding areas, the Bairagis and the more militant Naga sadhus (Vaishnavas), repulsed this attack and routed the maulvi and his followers. The Muslims retreated to the Babri Masjid, which was then attacked by the Bairagis. More than sixty-five Muslims were killed and the Bairagis allegedly held possession of the mosque for three days.[195] The bodies of Ghulam Hussein's men (he managed to escape) were buried around the mosque and the area later came to be known as Ganj Shaheeda, or Martyr's Place or Quarters.

Captain A. P. Orr, who as the British officer in charge of the troops stationed in Faizabad, acting on intelligence about the impending attack, had secured a temporary peace between the Bairagis and Shah's followers a day earlier. The peace he had secured was by dint of placing his troops between the Hanumangarhi and the Babri Masjid. Orr expected reinforcements the following day; however, as he realized later, the few buildings that existed then were all filled with the supporters of the Bairagis. Having prevented violence for a day by invoking the power of the king and the British Resident, Orr returned to his house at night.

Ghulam Hussein and his band of 'fanatic' followers used the Babri Masjid as the launching place for the attack that finally took place on 28 July 1855 at around 1 p.m. A. P. Orr's first-person account gives us an

---

[194]Surinder Kaur and Sher Singh, *Hanuman Gurhie Ayodhya: Incident, 28th July, 1855* (*Root Cause of Babari Masjid Dispute*), New Delhi: Institute of Objective Studies, 2011, p. 27.
[195]Interview with Khaliq Khan, Faizabad Hilal Committee.

insight into how the British viewed the entire episode. After the battle,
Orr in a letter to his superior, G. K. Weston, superintendent of the Awadh
Frontier Police, wrote:

> ...with regard to Shah's people all our remonstrances were of no avail;
> persuasion, entreaty, threats, all were lost on these fanatics. On the
> other hand the Byragees were perfectly willing to listen to us and to
> obey the government orders...the answer that we last obtained from
> the Shah's people was that at the time of Johur Nemaz [Muslim prayer
> after mid-day] they would attack the Byragees and not listen to further
> proposals as they could no longer restrain the Ghazees [volunteers
> ready to die in a religious cause].[196]

By the morning of 28 July 1855, Orr's small force had been augmented
by more troops led by Captain Hearsey, another officer, and in all they had
150 men and a few guns. Deciding not to intervene, they moved to a better
vantage point from where the imminent battle between the two parties
could be observed. Orr continues:

> ...the Mahomedans may at the outset have numbered 4 or 500 men,
> the Byragees with their allies more than 8000. The leaders of the
> Shah's party were soon laid prostrate while endeavouring to cheer
> on their men towards the Hunooman Gurrie, the greater portion of
> the Shah's allies i.e Mahomedan inhabitants of Oude and of Fyzabad
> fled on every side and his own immediate followers together with few
> friends who still remained staunch to him, retreated.[197]

The maulvi and his Ghazees were badly routed and they ran back to the
masjid 'pursued by the Hindoos'.

In the letter, Orr records for the first time the use of the Babri Masjid
as a hiding place by the retreating followers of Ghulam Hussein.

That day a general massacre of those hiding in the masjid took place.
Orr described it as a 'deadly contest', in which 'the Byragees yelling and
furious though obstinately resisted closing on the Musjid hemmed it in
on every side and after a few desperate efforts stormed it and gave no
quarter'. Orr records that seventy of the Shah's people were killed, 'and as

---

[196]Kaur and Singh, *Hanuman Gurhie Ayodhya*, pp. 30–31.
[197]Ibid., pp. 31–32.

many perhaps or more of the Byragees and their allies'.[198]

Watching the massacre from a distance as a passive observer needed to be explained to his superiors, and Orr did so by suggesting that their numbers were too few and thus if they had intervened, and failed, a general insurrection would have been likely. 'Thus we remained passive though during the whole of this fray we endeavoured by every means in our power to restore peace,'[199] Orr wrote. Hostilities were briefly interrupted because of a monsoon storm and during this short break, Orr tried to get the Muslims in the masjid to take shelter in his position which was defended by small cannons and guns, but they refused to do so. Soon enough the rain stopped and fighting resumed, which ended only when all the Muslims were either dead or had escaped.

The concluding part of Orr's letter—in which he demarcates the different equations at play in this affair—is more important. He writes that the nawab's local nazim or agent of the district, Aghai Ally Khan, was a Shia and Ghulam Hussein and his followers Sunni; therefore a compromise would not have been reached. About the Hindu leadership, Orr wrote, 'as to Raja Maun Singh, his followers openly espoused the cause of the Byragees, his claims to impartiality must therefore be much questioned'. Raja Man Singh was in charge of Sultanpore under which Oude (or Ayodhya) also fell.

Another reason for Orr to not intervene in the battle was that he doubted the loyalties of his Hindu and Muslim soldiers if he ordered them into a three-way fight. Thus, the first bloody battle in Ayodhya came to an end, with a cynical British force overseeing it from a vantage point. And once all seventy odd Muslims and many more Hindus were killed, Orr seemed to justify his inaction; in characteristically colonial style, he blamed the Hindus and Muslims for their own deaths. Orr reasoned, 'in conclusion though none can more than ourselves regret that so many blind misguided creatures have been so summarily disposed of, yet, it may truly be said that their blood is on their own head'.[200] This—as British history in India vindicates—was a pattern: the British were somehow always 'too few in number' to prevent a massacre of Indians by Indians.

---

[198]Ibid., p. 32.
[199]Ibid.
[200]Ibid., p.35 .

TRIPARTITE COMMISSION OF ENQUIRY

A series of letters, secret communiqués and meetings followed the massacre at Faizabad. In August 1855, the British and the nawab were so completely occupied with this matter that not a day passed without the Resident, G. B. Outram, weighing in on this issue, either in letters to Governor General Lord Dalhousie in Calcutta, or in meetings with Wajid Ali Shah, even as he continued to exchange reports and instructions with his subordinates like Orr.

It seems the nawab had been warned about the possibility of such violence before it occurred and it was brought up by Resident Outram when he met Wajid Ali Shah on 1 August 1855 at a conference held at a palace called Zard Kothi. The nawab was surprised to learn this and denied any prior knowledge at which point Outram produced a copy of an earlier letter of warning.

The nawab, cautious not to appear to be siding with the Hindus, did not, at first, agree with the Resident's suggestion of setting up a tripartite commission of enquiry made up of 'Hindus, Muslims and a Christian judge'. The nawab's own view was to first allow for a cooling of tempers on both sides before such a step was taken. Given the rising anger in his Muslim subjects against the massacre of Muslims in Ayodhya, the nawab was worried about a backlash.

Outram, taking up the cudgels on behalf of Hindus, reminded the nawab that over two-thirds of Awadh's population was Hindu and that it wouldn't be wise to give them any cause for enmity. The Hindu chiefs were powerful and would not remain quiet and unmoved if 'the contest were renewed and any further outrages were committed on shrines which *from time immemorial* had been held by them as peculiarly sacred'.[201]

The nawab having been persuaded by Outram, issued instructions for the constitution of a commission comprising Captain Alexander Orr (who had watched the bloody battle), Raja Man Singh and Chukledar Aghai Ally Khan to 'commence an immediate investigation into all the particulars connected with the melancholy loss of life—assuring all parties that they should have a patient hearing and most complete redress'.[202] This tripartite commission of enquiry became the first such body to be appointed in the case of Ayodhya.

---

[201]Ibid., p. 39.
[202]Ibid., p. 41.

Almost 150 years later, another commission of enquiry would be set up by the Government of India, under its archaeology wing, but as we shall see, it would have nothing to do with Hanumangarhi or the alleged destruction of a mosque on it. In a remarkable diversion from the original, primeval source of dispute the masjid from which Captain Orr said the Muslims launched their attack on Hanumangarhi would become the site of the same claims and counterclaims. After the 1857 rebellion and the victory of the British to 1980s–1990s India, Hindus would go on to expand their claims to argue that the mosque referred to by Orr was built exactly atop Ram's birthplace, while Muslims would deny this by saying it was a concocted story.

Back in 1855, Outram, the cautious Resident, after getting the commission of enquiry constituted, set about ensuring that the military presence of the British remained strong in Lucknow. He also detailed the entire sequence of events in a letter to Governor General Dalhousie and brought him abreast of the happenings. On 4 August, three days after his meeting with Wajid Ali Shah, Outram stated that the removal of any troops from Lucknow would be hazardous to peace and stability given the high state of vengeful excitement that he claimed the Muslims were in. He also seems to have acted against the advice of his officer, Captain A. P. Orr, by getting the king to set up the commission under Man Singh and Aghai Ally Khan. Orr believed that the two neither got along nor could they be trusted to act above their religious affiliations. Patting both himself and the Hindus on the back, Outram omitted this fact from his letter to Dalhousie. He wrote:

> I hope the mixed commission consisting of Captain Orr, Aghai Ally Khan and Rajah Maun Singh possessing as it does an equal Mahomeddan and Hindoo element with a Christian Umpire may inspire confidence so as to induce the belligerents to submit to their mediation; for the victorious Hindoos have heretofore displayed the most praiseworthy forbearance and the humbled Mahomedan factions are more likely now to listen to reason.[203]

Reverting to his fears about the possible fallout of the withdrawal of troops, he concluded his letter by saying:

---

[203]Ibid., p. 45.

...but certainly any weakening of the British troops at Lucknow at this juncture when such exaggerated reports of the success of the Sunthal rebels prevail and the already reduced strength of the Cawnporre Brigade is known would be highly dangerous as calculated to encourage the excited Hindoos who form 4/5th of the Oude population to aim at higher objects.[204]

It appears that Outram knew quite well that he was playing with fire. While he was endeavouring to implement a British plan to annex Awadh, he wanted to be careful not to allow the situation to go out of control. The violence over Hanumangarhi had given the British another pretext to decry the Awadh king, but if not handled with care, Hindu fury and Muslim anger could turn into a general insurrection against the British as well.

In Ayodhya, things were moving at a fast pace in the usually quiet temple town. Since the massacre by the Bairagis and their supporters—mostly men from neighbouring villages, the Muslims of Ayodhya had moved out to other safer places. At the same time, the news of this defeat was bringing in Muslims from neighbouring districts to Faizabad every day. The usually more hardline Pathans among them had united under the banner of two maulvis, Ameer Ali and Ramzan Ali of Amethi, who were now said to be marching towards Ayodhya. Through hurriedly written letters, Outram and Wajid Ali Shah had informed each other of the developments at almost the same time. Outram pleaded with the king to direct his servants to ensure that the events of July were not repeated, he implored the king to order the stopping of 'Pathans and others who are bent in proceeding to Fyzabad and especially to cause the arrest of the two Maulavees'. Wajid Ali Shah, the nawab-king of Awadh, equally concerned by the threat of more violence along religious lines, wrote to Resident Outram:

> ...it appears from newswriters' reports that numerous Hindoos and Musulmans are flocking into that place from all sides and that many more are determined to join them. The King is most anxious to put an end to this rupture and therefore entreats the Resident to be good enough to address the various Magistrates of adjacent districts to prevent bodies of armed devotees whether Hindoo or Mahomedan from entering Oude and to take steps to forbid their coming.[205]

---

[204] Ibid., 45–46.
[205] Ibid., p. 49.

Wajid Ali Shah's tone makes it clear who the real ruler of Awadh was. The districts from which the mobs were flocking were all in the traditional zone of Ayodhya's religious influence. There were also Muslim strongholds in the list sent by Wajid Ali Shah. Gorakhpur, Jaunpur, Allahabad, Fatehpur, Kanpur, Farrukhabad, Shahjahanpur and Azamgarh were the chief regions of Sunni populations and these were governed by British magistrates; thus the nawab hoped that his request to Outram, if fulfilled, would deprive the maulvis of Amethi from gaining more followers.

Meanwhile, the Bairagis of Hanumangarhi had signed a bond alluding to their complete willingness to abide by the findings of the tripartite commission of enquiry, whatever they may be. Under Mahant Bilramdass, three other priests put their signature to this bond in which they also spoke of past friendships and a willingness to compromise. Interestingly, the Hanumangarhi priests who were Ramanandis belonging to the Nirvani Akhada did not object to the presence of Aghai Ally Khan. They perhaps knew that as a Shia Muslim, he was not going to be overtly excited by the prospect of Sunni claims. Hindus favoured a Shia over a Sunni member in the enquiry commission and, as Captain Orr had believed, Muslims themselves being largely Sunni, did not trust Aghai Ally Khan because of his Shia persuasion.

Irrespective of all this, the bond signed by Hanumangarhi priests on 10 August 1855 must have brought peace to the mind of the avowedly irreligious and secular Wajid Ali Shah.

The bond promised that:

> ...having in view our former friendship and acquaintance we declare we have no enmity towards them [Gholam Hussein and others], and agreeing to Aghai Alee Khan, Rajah Maun Singh, Captain Orr as our arbitrators we solemnly swear by Mahabir [another name for Hanuman] and hereby write that we will not on any account create any disturbance or tumult on condition that no one molests us or abuses us. All the Byragees who are of our tribe will not do anything contrary to what we have written...if we act contrary to what we have written we confess that we are deserving of whatever punishment may decree[206].

In Lucknow, the nawab, anxious to avoid a confrontation with the maulvis,

---

[206]Ibid., p. 51.

sought the help of the influential chiefs of neighbouring Hadergarh and Gosainganj. The nawab wanted them to persuade the Muslims at Amethi to desist from marching to Ayodhya. In his communiqué to Outram on 11 August 1855, Wajid Ali Shah also apprised him of his plan of seeking religious opinion on how to tackle the belligerent maulvis. On the whole, the nawab appeared to be confident that his plan of peaceful resolution would work, obviating the need for arrests and violence. The king's seeking of religious sanction was made necessary because of the nature of the maulvis' campaign. In order to enlist more followers they had declared a planned revenge-attack on Hanumangarhi a jihad, or religious crusade, against infidels. The king was aware that a jihad could be declared only by the king in a Muslim-ruled country; his plan was to counter the maulvis theologically and take the wind out of their proposed jihad. Ever careful, Wajid Ali Shah concluded his note to Outram with the words 'but the future is in the disposal of God'.

This, however, was not enough for Outram to repose faith in Wajid Ali Shah's abilities. Outram was also acting on his own secret intelligence which said that the nawab was only buying time and that once the Sawan mela[207] in Ayodhya was over, he had promised the maulvis that the mosque would be rebuilt in Hanumangarhi.

In Faizabad, Captain Orr had his ear to the ground. Consistent with the first report he sent to his superior police officer, G. K. Weston, the superintendent of the Awadh Frontier Force, Orr again advised against any immediate enquiries by the tripartite commission. In this he was echoing Nawab Wajid Ali Shah's own instinct. However, Orr also warned about the effect of the presence of certain Muslims in Faizabad.

On 11 August 1855, the same day that the king informed the Resident of his aversion to arresting the maulvis, Orr wrote to G. K. Weston again regarding certain decisions taken by the committee comprising Aghai Ally Khan, Raja Maun Singh, Captain A. P. Orr and Captain J. Hearsey. He opened his letter by stating forthrightly that 'it would not be safe in the present state of affairs to institute enquiries regarding the existence in the midst of Hanooman Gurrie of a Musjid'.

Ameer Ali, the radical preacher who had vowed to avenge the deaths of Muslims in Ayodhya, was gathering numbers for his jihad near Amethi.

---

[207]The sawan mela is one of the three melas held in Ayodhya every year, it is held in the month of July and marks the start of the rains.

Meanwhile, certain Muslim notables said to be deputed by the court in Lucknow, were in Faizabad and Ayodhya. They were conducting their own enquiry and were collecting signatures and testimonies vouching for the existence of the mosque in Hanumangarhi. As we will see later in the book, such campaigns continue to take place in contemporary Ayodhya.

Captain Orr also worried about the adverse effect these persons were having in an already tense atmosphere. In the same letter Orr categorically mentions the danger posed by the presence of these 'notables' and requests his superior to ensure that they are removed from there.

'INDEPENDENT' ENQUIRY FINDS MOSQUE AT HANUMANGARHI

Captain Orr's fears about the independent enquiries by the notables from the Lucknow court proved to be justified as the next day, on 12 August 1855, Outram, the Resident, received another communiqué from the king of Oude. Along with the dispatch, the king had also sent for his perusal the documents collected through the above-mentioned notables' efforts.

The king's letter summed up the findings thus:

> The purports of these papers is that *A MOSQUE WAS BUILT BY ONE OF THE FORMER SOVEREIGNS OF DELHIE*, that this fact is notorious, that *in the days of Borhanool Muk* [Saadat Ali Khan I] *Sobahdar of Oude, there was a quarrel of the same kind* but the Hindoos subsequently declared that they had no intention of meddling with the mosque. One witness who declares he is 104 years old asserts that he has repeatedly seen the mosque. *One Chuprasee Dhunnee Singh, a Hindoo, declares that he saw the mosque in the time of Hakeem Mehudee who was a minister in the days of Nusseeruddeen Hyder (1827–1837), one Chedee, a Hindoo, declares he has often seen the Musjid.* The tenor of all these papers casts all the blame on the Hindoos and details their atrocities—two leaves of the Koran which were found on one of the slain is sent for His Majesty's inspection; they have been trampled upon, burnt and torn.[208]

The note then proceeds to record the various crimes committed by Hindus, including destroying the tomb of Khwaja Huttee Shah and slaying a pig in the mosque while it was in their possession. It ends by describing the genesis of the Hindus' aggression and says that, 'the Hindoos first began to interfere

---

[208]Ibid., pp. 57–58.

and became powerful when the district of Sultanpore fell into the hands of Durshan Singh Chukledar[209] and their encroachments commenced and have progressed'.[210]

The next day, Resident Outram responded with disdain to these documents and summarily declared them to be 'untrue' in a letter to the king. While doing so he employed the age-old argument of 'obtained under duress and coercion' that is used against suspicious affidavits and testimonies.

The Resident wrote, 'His Majesty must be well aware that it is very easy for interested parties to obtain seals and signatures to any representations they may choose to make in the heat of religious excitement and doubtless the opposite party would easily obtain similar testimony in support of their assertions.'[211] The Resident then declared the documents and the claims made by the nawab-king to be baseless. He also goes on to dismiss the claims about the slaying of a pig, desecration of the Quran, and destruction of Khwaja Huttee's tomb in Hanumangarhi. He explained his dismissal saying:

> The enclosed representations are obviously *untrue* in one particular in as much as they attribute the whole of the blame to Hindoos, whereas it is notorious and moreover officially reported by Capt Orr that they were ready to submit their grievances to the King's decision, even when victorious they abstained from all violence and from the commission of any excesses and enormities. His Majesty can not fail to be convinced of the truth of this when His Majesty peruses the bond signed by the leaders of the Byragees in which they profess their readiness to submit to terms and which reached the King yesterday. It is well known that the Mahomedans would not listen to reason and that they began the conflict.[212]

The Resident then concludes that 'the alleged atrocities of the Byragees such as trampling on the Kuran and the sacrifice of swine (in the musjid) may prove equally unfounded and baseless'.

Though Outram doesn't specify the mosque he is referring to, it could only either be the one atop Hanumangarhi, which was destroyed by the Bairagis, or the Babri Masjid from where the Muslims had launched

---

[209]Darshan Singh, a peasant-soldier who was the ancestor of Raja Man Singh.

[210]Kaur and Singh, *Hanuman Gurhie Ayodhya*, pp. 58–59.

[211]Ibid., p. 63.

[212]Ibid., p. 64.

the attack. In 1855, curiously enough, no extant British record of the Hanumangarhi conflict identifies the said mosque as Ram Janmabhoomi.

The next day, on 15 August 1855, Captain Orr reported to Superintendent Weston a series of steps he had taken for the officially appointed tripartite commission to carry on its work. Owing to the sawan mela a large number of Hindus had gathered in Ayodhya. As the presence of thousands of Hindus had increased the risk of violence erupting again, the commission had been unable to make probes regarding the existence of a masjid on Hanumangarhi. Therefore, Orr finally decided that Raja Man Singh should conduct 'private and strict enquiries as to the existence of the supposed Musjid and to report the result of his personal researches, which would eventually be verified' by other members of the committee. The reason Orr gave for reposing such faith in Man Singh was curious and contradictory to his own earlier view regarding Man Singh's impartiality. Orr said, 'the Rajah being of the Hindoo persuasion could more easily effect the object the Committee had in view than any other of its members'.[213] In July, Orr had cited the same 'Hindu persuasion' to report to Weston the untrustworthiness of Man Singh. But now, Man Singh had become fit to be trusted again and he lived up to the expectations of the British by quickly completing his 'private and strict' probe. As Orr put it in his letter:

> Raja Maun Singh had succeeded, not only in obtaining the desired information stating that to the best of his belief no Musjid existed in the Gurrie, but also obtained from the Mahunt Byragees of Hannooman Gurrie two papers signed and sealed by them, by which they bind themselves to allow the Committee to make any investigations necessary to satisfy the demands of the government.[214]

Having obtained this bond, and armed with Man Singh's findings, the committee called a public meeting of prominent Muslims of Faizabad–Ayodhya and surrounding areas in Gulab Bari, the magnificently built tomb of Shuja-ud-daulah. The purpose of this meeting was to give Muslims an opportunity to put forward their claims, grievances and evidence regarding the mosque in contention. A large number of Muslims had fled Ayodhya after the massacre in July, and now a number of them spoke up to say that even if such a masjid existed, it was in the domain of the king of Oude to

---

[213]Ibid., p. 66.
[214]Ibid.

recover it. All that these Muslims 'now wished was to obtain some security of life and property in order to return to their homes at Awudh, which they have abandoned since the late disturbance', wrote Orr. [215]

Interestingly, it was also decided that the individuals who had claimed to have seen the masjid, including the Hindus Chedee Singh and Dhunee Singh, should be taken to Hanumangarhi, asked to show the spot where the masjid stood, and prove the veracity of their assertions. Orr reported to his superior Weston that this was now possible as the Hanumangarhi priests had agreed to 'allow us to dig open any one spot pointed out by the Mahomedans as containing their Musjid'.[216] If there was a quid pro quo deal affected by Raja Man Singh with the priests, Orr's letter doesn't reveal it. Seemingly satisfied with the committee's work so far, Orr concluded that 'surely such an investigation will satisfy the most bigoted'.[217]

Outram was pleased to hear that Orr had been successful in defusing the situation with the help of Man Singh and Aghai Ally Khan. Outram transmitted the contents of Orr's letter to Governor General Dalhousie in Calcutta. As Lucknow was under his direct supervision, he also added the latest update on the situation there:

> *In this city especially the excitement was very great. War with the Hindoos was openly preached in the mosques* in spite of the exertions of the authority to prevent it and fanatic moolahs erected the standard of Islam at *Qurcita* 7 miles distant where all true Moslams were urged to assemble. Some hundreds did so and thousands in this city who were prepared to join, were with difficulty deterred by the most stringent measures of the Government.[218]

Outram's self-serving portrayal of the situation at Lucknow and Ayodhya was only partially true. Indeed, the Muslim clergy, including some Shia priests, were by now roused by the British-backed handling of the Hanumangarhi situation. Just a week after Outram had shared his satisfaction at the abatement of the conflict, a mujtahid, a high priest or Shia imam, raised the hackles of the British once again.

Spies brought news that after the Eid celebrations at Asaf-ud-daulah's

---

[215]Ibid., p. 67.
[216]Ibid.
[217]Ibid.
[218]Ibid., p. 69.

Imambara, the high priest had openly showered curses on Aghai Ally Khan, a member of the Hanumangarhi committee, and alleged that he, a Shia, had accepted bribes to favour the Hindus. Many notables from Wajid Ali Shah's court were present on this occasion but remained silent.

Four days later, on 28 August, the Hanooman Ghuree Commission's petition was received by Wajid Ali Shah. The commission had concluded its work and was ready to present itself and the various witnesses and deponents it had examined to the king in Lucknow. Orr, the unofficial head of the commission, also wrote to Weston, forwarding with the letter the various depositions collected by the king's committee under Maulvi Hafizullah, the eleven depositions given to the tripartite committee (including Orr, Man Singh and others), the statement of a Muslim bricklayer, Joomun Khan, bonds furnished by the priests of Hanumangarhi, sunuds (royal grants) furnished by the priests of Hanumangarhi, and the committee's urz-dasht (written petition).

The findings of the other so-called independent committee led by maulvis Hafizullah and Nihaluddeen were rejected as false and fake by Orr. He considered them as having been 'preconsented' and full of discrepancies.[219]

The sunuds shown by the Hanumangarhi priests on the other hand were taken to be legitimate and because 'no reference whatsoever is made to the existence of a Musjid, neither within nor near the precincts of the Gurhee'.[220] Orr thought it was proof that no masjid could have existed there.

Orr further stated that the deposition of Joomun Khan corroborated his conclusions. Moreover, according to Orr, more proof lay in the

> ...depositions furnished by two of the Mahunts of the Guree, they contain total denial of the Musjid having ever existed, with a shrewd and in my opinion just remark, that had a Musjid stood in their Gurree at all events within the last 25 or 30 years would it not have been remarked by the Kotwal of the City Mirza Mooneem Beg, whom they cite, as having on more than one occasion visited their building.[221]

Finally, Orr clinches the anti-mosque argument by stating that even those Muslims who had claimed to have seen and even prayed in the mosque

---

[219]Ibid., p. 76.
[220]Ibid.
[221]Ibid., p. 77.

at Hanumangarhi were unable to point to the spot where it could have existed. Some even blundered by pointing out a directionally implausible spot as Muslims offer prayer while facing the west. Thus Orr concluded with certitude:

> no traces however slight of such a building now exist... In fact it seems of itself improbable that two buildings consecrated to such opposite creeds, could ever have stood in so close proximity—and is it not moreover extraordinary that during so many years, that is at the very lowest calculation from the time of Munsoor Ali Khan Soobadar of Oudh, to the present period, no one, either ruler or subject should with the exception of Shah Ghulam Hussein and his followers, have taken cognizance of such matter had they been worthy of consideration.[222]

Thus, the claims of Muslims being deemed bogus, fake and time-barred, were rejected and the commission sought to close the matter.

Upon learning the outcome of the commission's enquiry, Maulvi Ameer Ali, who had reached Lucknow and was under house arrest, set out on his jihad once again. With more than 200 devoted followers the maulvi seemed to have been discreetly supported by the Shia clergy in addition to the Sunni clergy. In order to halt his march, Wajid Ali Shah dispatched some envoys who were able to convince the maulvi to postpone it for the time being and allow the peaceful resolution of the dispute. Ameer Ali was also warned that if he disobeyed the nawab's order, he would be forcibly restrained. What Wajid Ali Shah had in mind was a plan that would 'satisfy all parties'. The proposal was radical; it suggested 'that the King should build a mosque resting on one wall, but outside of the ghuree...and the dividing wall be so raised as to prevent either Moslem or Hindoos interfering with each other, or either party even seeing into the others' place of worship'.[223] Wajid Ali Shah also stated that Hanumangarhi priests would be suitably awarded any reasonable demands of land if they agreed to this proposal. Resident Outram reported these details to Dalhousie with scepticism about the success of the proposal.

In Calcutta, upon learning of the developments in Awadh, Governor General Dalhousie stressed that this was 'further proof, if further proof

---

[222]Ibid., p. 78.
[223]Ibid., p. 86.

were necessary, of the unfitness of the King of Oude and of his Durbar
to hold the powers of Government in that country and fortify the opinion
which I lately submitted to the Hon'ble Court that the administration
should be entirely taken out of their hands'.[224] The British were preparing
the ground to annex Awadh and the Hanumangarhi incident was being
woven into that plan.

Back in Ayodhya, Orr, who was tasked with getting the Hanumangarhi
priests to agree to the king's compromise formula, failed to convince them.
Orr conveyed his failure to Outram, who transmitted it to Dalhousie on 16
September. The Bairagis, reported Outram, declared 'that if it is attempted
to build a Mosque adjoining the Hunooman Ghuree, they will vacate the
place and at the same time desert every one of the temples of Awudh,
which in other words really means that they are prepared to resist any
such attempt to the death, for never in life would they abandon these holy
shrines'.[225] Rhetoric was building up again on both sides—on three sides
if one includes the British, who were desperately hoping to convert this
conflict into a dramatic cause so that they could annex Awadh.

When Outram met with Wajid Ali Shah a few days later on 29
September, he tried his utmost to impress upon him the need to take
immediate action to restrain Maulvi Ameer Ali. No doubt this would have
made Wajid Ali Shah extremely unpopular among his co-religionists in the
court and outside. He was aware that any action by him that was perceived to
be anti-Islam would make his position even more untenable. Unsympathetic
to Wajid Ali Shah's predicament, Outram also alleged that the nawab-king
had made a secret pledge to Ameer Ali about the construction of the
mosque at an appropriate time even though Wajid Ali Shah had dismissed
such allegations as 'preposterous'. The nawab-king was convinced that the
matter could be resolved to the satisfaction of all. In order to buy more
time, he now proposed the formation of a second commission comprising
an equal number of Hindus and Muslims. It seems from Outram's account
that Wajid Ali Shah was not convinced of the Bairagis' version of the dispute.
According to the minutes of a meeting between Outram and him, the king
believed, 'much misconception prevailed…as to the sanctity of the ground
generally known as Hanooman Guree—in fact—but a very small portion
of it was sacred, the rest having been quietly added by the Hindoos to the

---

[224]Ibid., p. 91.
[225]Ibid., p. 93.

ground granted by His Majesty's ancestors more than a century ago'.[226]

And therefore, Wajid Ali Shah expected the Hindus to agree to the proposal of sharing the space atop Hanumangarhi with a mosque. Outram agreed but added a caveat. The minutes of that meeting record him issuing a warning to the king of Oude.

> The Resident declared that he would be delighted to learn that the Hindoos could be persuaded to yield compliance but he did not hesitate to warn His Majesty against any such attempt to take even one yard of ground without the fullest and most unqualified consent of the Hindoos—on no other ground could His Majesty attempt to build the Musjid without lighting up the flames of civil discord in his territories.[227]

What Wajid Ali Shah really thought of the British Resident's very sensible but obvious word of caution is not known but he assured him that nothing would be done by force.

Meanwhile, Ameer Ali who was still camped on the road to Ayodhya, thought of keeping his ghazis (crusaders) motivated by letting them loose on Hindus and Shias. While stationed near Saheliya, a village that now falls in Barabanki district, his followers, 'annoyed at the blowing of Sunks [conch shells] in the temples belonging to Roopnarain and Salikram Brahmins of Saheli',[228] attacked the place and destroyed all the idols and threw them into the adjacent pond. The Brahmins, together with their families, fled to Calcutta, according to a dispatch dated 4 October from the Resident's office. Besides mentioning the attack on Hindus the same set of dispatches also informed the Governor General in Calcutta that 'the report is confirmed that a fight had taken place between the Syeeds of Zaidpore (20 kilometres from Saheli) and Ameer Ali's followers, in consequence of the Maulavi having endeavoured to prevent the Syeeds carrying their Tazeahs in procession until the Musjid should be built in the Hanooman Ghuree, 8 men were killed and 6 wounded on both sides'.[229]

The dispatch by Outram on 4 October was significant as it not only reported the maulvi's communal excesses but also because it reported that

---

[226]Ibid., p. 103.
[227]Ibid.
[228]Ibid., p. 115.
[229]Ibid.

Wajid Ali Shah, responding to the spate of conflicts involving the maulvi's militia and Hindus—and in one case Shias—had deputed mainly Hindu troops to march to Hanumangarhi and protect it. It also conveyed a rising degree of alarm among the general population which was evidenced by the fact that the richer families of Faizabad and Ayodhya were relocating their women and children in anticipation of violence.

MAULVI AMEER ALI'S END DRAWS NEAR

Between 5 October and 8 November a number of events took place that brought an end to Maulvi Ameer Ali's campaign. His patience exhausted, Ameer Ali gave up on Wajid Ali Shah keeping his reported promise to build the mosque atop Hanumangarhi. The king too had all but abandoned hopes of a peaceful resolution, and now he gave clear orders to intercept the maulvi en route to Ayodhya. On 5 October, Outram reported to Lucknow that it was generally believed 'that the assault on the Hanooman Ghuree will take place on the 40th day of Mohurram (23 October)'.[230]

In Hanumangarhi, the Bairagis were fortifying their defences and making small holes in the walls of the temple-fortress through which arms could be fired. The word on the street in Ayodhya, Faizabad and Lucknow was that Hanumagarhi was also receiving aid from the kingdoms of Gwalior, Jodhpur and the local talukdars or chiefs of Awadh. Amidst this buildup, Raja Man Singh brought a delegation of Hanumangarhi priests to Lucknow.

The maulvi, still camped on the road to Ayodhya, was also being joined by hordes of Muslim men. In a last-ditch effort to strike a compromise, the king's deputies met him and once again beseeched him to defer his march. Writing disapprovingly about it, Outram informed Calcutta on 7 October that after much persuasion and 'begging', Ameer Ali was 'induced to grant a further respite of 5 days—if, however, on the Friday next, some steps shall not have been taken by the Durbar, he intends then to proceed to Bansa...eastward of Saheli, and there raise the standard of Islam'.[231]

The maulvi had relented, but only a little. Unbeknownst to him at the time, his predicament was to worsen soon. Outram was totally against the constitution of another commission of enquiry and had rejected the nawab's request to join such a commission if it were formed. His reason

---

[230]Ibid., p. 120.
[231]Outram letter to Calcutta dated 11 October 1855, Kaur and Singh, *Hanuman Gurhie Ayodhya*, pp.123–24.

being: 'he [Wajid Ali Shah] supposed the British Government would be
bound to support the subsequent measures of the Durbar for enforcing
the decree of the Committee whatever that might be. As I had reason
[not specified] to believe that bribery would be employed to induce the
Hindoo members to betray their trust, it behoved me I conceived for that
reason particularly but also under any circumstances, to reject the overture
in explicit terms.'[232]

The British had practically come to rule Awadh in the eighty years
since the Battle of Buxar in 1775. Gradually, they had also come to acquire
a network of spies that was spread deep and wide across the province
as well as in other parts of India. A letter dated 15 October reflects the
astuteness with which the East India Company ran its intelligence network.
On the basis of information provided by a clerk in a government office in
Faizabad, Outram listed the number of local Hindu chiefs who were ready
to support the Bairagis of Hanumangarhi; some of them had also offered
money. Outram wrote, 'among others from whom letters and pecuniary
contributions have been received, he [the clerk-spy] enumerates the Rajahs
of Bansee, Pyrespore, Ramnuggur, Dumeree, Souhan—Ranee of Dairwa—
and Maharajahs of Gwalior and Joudhpore'.[233]

On the same day, Governor General Dalhousie in Fort William, Calcutta,
drew up a note that both summarized the developments in Awadh and
laid down British policy for future events. He authorized Outram to use
'decided language' to convey the displeasure of the British government should
Wajid Ali Shah 'either direct or not prevent an attack on the Hindoos'.
He declared that such a neglect of duty would make the king regret his
inaction. Dalhousie approved the actions of the Resident at Lucknow along
with his own and patted himself on the back for his commitment to always
acting in the interests of the British government. Wajid Ali Shah's decision
to dispatch Hindu troops for the protection of Hanumangarhi was lauded
by Dalhousie. That rare praise was overshadowed by his severe criticism of
the 'feebleness and falseness' of the king of Oude.[234]

And with the characteristic duplicity that defined the era of the British
East India Company, Dalhousie noted, 'the King of Oude having permitted

---

[232]Ibid., p.125.

[233]Bansee and Dairwa (Dewa) are on the Faizabad–Lucknow road whereas Ramnuggar
(Ramnagar) and Pyraspore (Paraspur) are trans-Ghaggra towns, all lying within a
100-kilometre radius of Ayodhya.

[234]Kaur and Singh, *Hanuman Gurhie Ayodhya*, pp. 129–30.

the rise of the present disorders at Awudh near to Fyzabad and having permitted flagrant wrong to be done to the Hindoos, not only contrary to the advice of the resident, but in defiance of his warnings and his resistance, the British troops ought upon no account to be moved to the assistance of the royal troops if hostilities should again break out at Awudh'.[235] If Orr and Hearsey had refrained from interfering in the July clash because of being 'few in number', now they were explicitly ordered to stay out of it. Dalhousie seemed to have been hoping that Awadh would soon be engulfed in communal bloodshed, and to make sure it was not impeded by the interference of British troops, he directed his officers to stand by, just as they had done in July when Shah Ghulam Hussein had attacked Hanumangarhi. At that time, it was Muslims who had been massacred. But for Dalhousie, it was not Hindu versus Muslim or right versus wrong. The sole concern was how to justify the annexation of Awadh by the British government.

Therefore, the main purport of his note was the Treaty of 1801, which gave control of more than half of Awadh's richest cultivable lands in return for an annual stipend to the nawab of Awadh. It also bound the British to defend Awadh against external and internal aggressions. This, technically, stood in the way of the annexation of Awadh, even though many British acts of omission and commission had left the treaty all but abrogated. Now, in the event of the explosion of further violence between Hindus and Muslims, the British would have found a dramatic justification to annex the province.[236] Towards that end, it was also imperative that communal anarchy defeat the writ of the king of Awadh as well as its largely harmonious social culture.

AMEER ALI SUFFERS A SETBACK

Therefore, upon receiving Outram's letter dated 17 October, Dalhousie must have felt a tinge of disappointment. Outram, who was cast in the same colonial die as his Governor General, reported two instances of Muslim landords refusing to join the maulvi's crusade. One of them, Shujat Ali of Masauli in Barabanki district, was said to have declared to the maulvi that 'he said his prayers five times a day, and kept all fasts like a true Moslem, but as to disobeying the order of the King who is a true believer like himself,

---

[235]Ibid., p. 131.
[236]Ibid., p. 130.

or going to certain death at Ajoodhea, he chose to decline'.[237] Razabaksh, another Muslim landholder in Barabanki, rejected the maulvi's inducements on similar grounds. It was not just a sense of communal harmony that drove the general public and landlords to snub Ameer Ali. The king of Oude had issued a proclamation warning all who supported the fanatic crusade of dire consequences. The proclamation and its translation were made available to Outram who forwarded it to Calcutta on 18 October. The proclamation stated:

> ...that whoever may have ventured to quit his Amaldaree, Talookdaree, or Zamindarees to join the rebels shall have his houses and property seized by our soldiers, and whoever may be on the point of going to the rebels is to be restrained, and wherever either of the above-mentioned parties presumes to refuse obedience to our orders or to abandon his vile intentions, shall be punished by the imprisonment of his family and relatives who are to be forwarded to the capital, and by the demolition of their houses and property; whoever chooses to return home in peace shall not be molested in any way...[238]

On 19 October, Outram had reported to Calcutta that the maulvi had decided to proceed with his march towards Ayodhya and was ready to battle the king's troops if they tried to stop him. Unaware of either the proclamation or the maulvi's march, the secretary to the Government of India at Fort William in Calcutta had dispatched a set of instructions to Outram in Lucknow on 20 October. They wanted him to clearly state to the nawab of Awadh that the government would never agree to a second commission, and even if formed, 'the Government will never approve of a mosque being built in the Hanooman Ghuree or near to it'.[239]

The king's proclamation was successful in restraining Muslims from joining Ameer Ali's jihad. A letter from Outram, dated 6 November, notes 'that the effect of the proclamation has been most satisfactory, scarcely an individual from the British districts [land ceded under the Treaty of 1801] having joined the large assemblages of Mahomedans or Hindoos which have been threatening the peace of Oude for some time past'. Outram was now 'hopeful' of a speedy and peaceful resolution of the dispute, and he

---

[237]Ibod., p. 133.
[238]Ibid., p. 136.
[239]Ibid., p. 139.

was 'happy' to report it.[240] But it would have been a cause of some alarm for the Governor General who was banking on an imminent breakdown of peace and order.

THE BATTLE OF DHAURAHRA

The next day (7 November) began unexpectedly for the British troops and officers who were tasked with monitoring Maulvi Ameer Ali and his zealous followers. For the maulvi it was the day of reckoning which began in a planned way. At Dariabad, he gave the slip to the British troops led by Colonel Barlow and got a lead of an hour before his absence was discovered. The maulvi's plan seems to have been to attack Hanumangarhi on Diwali, which was going to fall on 9 November. The maulvi's selection of the day could have not been loaded with more symbolism. Diwali marks the day Ram, the exiled prince of Ayodhya, returned home after defeating Ravan at the culmination of fourteen years of banishment, along with his wife Sita and brother Lakshman. In Ayodhya, the day before Diwali is celebrated as Hanuman Jayanti, or the birthday of Hanuman. Unlike in the rest of the country where Hanuman Jayanti falls in the summer, in Ayodhya it is pegged to Diwali which falls in the winter.

According to an account written by a junior officer named Lieutenant Catania, British troops caught up with the maulvi's militia at Dhaurahra, a small village situated near Rudauli. Ameer Ali's force of ghazis was resting under the shade of some trees when Colonel Barlow sent some Indian troopers to tell him to return to Dariabad, and 'that if he persisted to advance',[241] they would fire on him. The maulvi defied the warning and resumed the march after midday prayers. Catania writes:

> ...the 2-9 Pounders attached to our Corps were the only guns that had come up, the rest with the Najeebs and other Telangah Regiments not having arrived. They were immediately placed into position, and laid by Col. Barlow, the Infantry supporting them, the order to fire was given as soon as the enemy was within range, they as instantaneously returned the compliment, and thus the action became general...[242]

---

[240]Ibid., p. 141. Like now, it wasn't uncommon then for official communication to be 'tracked' or even leaked by couriers for a good reward. Therefore, non-secret official letters seldom contained anything that might indict the government in any way.

[241]Kishore, *Ayodhya Revisited*, also Kaur and Singh, *Hanuman Gurhie Ayodhya*, p. 143.

[242]Ibid.

Maulvi Ameer Ali got his head cut off by an Indian sepoy, all other recruits of his cause fought to the death, asking for no quarter nor giving one.[243] In this way Barlow, Catania and their force of 300 soldiers, Indian and British, had successfully eliminated the threat of the maulvi's band of 'fanatics' in a bloody battle near Rudauli which lies nearly 40 kilometres from Faizabad. Lasting for two hours, it ended with the death of Ameer Ali and more than 400 of his followers. About eighty men belonging to the other side were also killed. Ameer Ali's dead were buried in four large pits in nearby Rudauli. The British-led troops, too, were exhausted by the long and bloody day. Most had had nothing to eat. After the battle they marched on to camp at Mahmudpur where they took care of their dead and wounded. It is here that Catania recorded the details of the battle and its aftermath on 8 November, the eve of Diwali. In the letter detailing this narrow and lucky victory, he indicted the nawab's troops for not showing up. This battle would be an enduring end of the conflict over Hanumangarhi but that night, on the eve of Diwali, Catania feared a reprisal and an unprecedented outbreak of communal violence. He wrote, 'it is rumoured that affairs are not yet settled and the Mahomedans are again assembling, if this prove correct, I fancy we have yet a great deal to do'.[244] Soon after receiving Catania's letter, Lucknow Resident Outram travelled to the British headquarters at Fort William in Calcutta.

---

[243]Ibid.
[244]Ibid., p. 145.

Chapter 7

THE INDIAN REBELLION OF 1857

The British were masters of self-righteous deception. They were covetous of Indian wealth but at the same time they pretended to be guided only by the interests of people. Their unfair treaties with the nawabs of Awadh had, over the course of seven decades, reduced the province to a virtual state of anarchy. The people, especially the zamindars and nobles, knew that the nawab's authority existed only in name and that real control rested with the Company sarkar and his agent, the Resident. Thus existed two authorities: the nawab and his government and the British officers deployed throughout the province along with garrisons of troops maintained by the British but paid for by the nawab. This dichotomous and fundamentally flawed arrangement had somehow existed for several decades.

The British East India Company had begun its systematic campaign to undermine the authority of the nawab of Awadh soon after the death of Asaf-ud-daulah in 1797. In 1801, just four years after Asaf-ud-daulah's demise, the British signed a treaty with his successor, Saadat Ali Khan II. This treaty gave the British control of half of all the fertile lands in Awadh.

Less than a decade before the Treaty of 1801 was signed, Thomas Twining, a British East India Company official (today better known as the founder of the Twinings Tea company) who toured the country between Calcutta and Delhi in 1793 CE, had noted the extraordinary sums of money that were being spent by the nawab on his personal indulgences. While residing at the Awadh court, Twining wondered why the then British Resident seemed to condone it.

> It seemed surprising that the British Resident at the Court of Lucnow did not interfere, as a friend, to prevent his later interference as an enemy; that he did not state to the Nabob that such improvident expenditure might embarrass his finances, and thus, causing delay in the payment of the instalments to the Company's troops at Cawnpore

and Futtighur, afford a pretext for taking possession of his kingdom, or of a part of it. But a proceeding so ambitious and violent was as yet, probably, as little in the premeditation of the present Government of Calcutta as of the Nabob, though realised soon after under another administration.[245]

No doubt the nawabs, and post-1817, the kings of Awadh, were big spenders. Like the Mughals of Delhi, they too lavished upon themseves the most extravagant luxuries. It's not that the British themselves were unaware of the long-term effect of this scheme of slow decay of the Awadh court and its rule. They in fact seemed to welcome the degradation of the court and its power. Within a couple of decades of the Treaty of 1801, the nawabs had been reduced to mere functionaries who had a limited role of approving the 'guidance and counsel' of the British East India Company. The descendants of the great Safdarjung, the first nawab of Awadh, had virtually become prisoners of their British-funded decadence.

ANNEXATION OF AWADH

By 1855, the British East India Company was impatient to annex Awadh, ostensibly in the interests of Awadh's people given the incompetence and lacklustre rule of the nawab. After the Battle of Dhaurahra in which Ameer Ali was killed and the threat of a second attack on Hanumangarhi eliminated, Outram, the Resident at Lucknow, had travelled to the headquarters of the British East India Company in Fort William in Calcutta. After a prolonged stay there, he returned on 31 January 1856 with a scheme to annex Awadh. The plan was to take over the entire financial and administrative management of the province with guarantees of financial and physical security to King Wajid Ali Shah and his family. Outram had been authorized by the governing council in Calcutta to offer up to Rs 18 lakh annually to Wajid Ali Shah in exchange for an amicable acceptance of giving up his throne.

In fact, the British, under Governor General Lord Dalhousie, an imperious and arrogant man, had come up with two plans of annexation. The first was to induce the king of Awadh to vest the whole civil and military administration of his territories forever in the government of the East India Company, on the following conditions:

---

[245]Thomas Twining, *Travels in India a Hundred Years Ago, With a Visit to the United States*, London: J. R. Osgood, McIlvaine & Co., 1893, p. 312.

a. that such territories shall not be incorporated with the Indian territories of the British Crown, but shall remain (nominally) under the sovereignty of the King;

b. that the King shall retain his royal title and position; that provision shall be made for the maintenance of his honour and dignity; and for the support of the Royal family, by adequate annual stipends; and

c. that the revenues of Oude shall be applied first to the civil and military charges of the government of the Province, secondly to the payment of the stipends aforesaid, thirdly to the improvement of the Province and if any residue remain, fourthly to the general improvement of the Indian empire.

With British colonial thoroughness, the plan also specified the consequences in the event the nawab of Awadh, Wajid Ali Shah, failed to give up his throne. The plan stated:

> Should all efforts to induce the King to agree to this proposal fail, his Lordship recommends that the treaty of 1801, having been violated by the king and his predecessors, be declared to be wholly dissolved, and that all amicable engagements between the East India Company and the Court of Lucknow be declared an end; whereupon the Resident at Lucknow shall quit the territory of Oude and shall withdraw the whole subsidiary force within the British frontier.[246]

Even before Outram had presented the plan for annexation to Wajid Ali Shah, on 23 January 1856, Dalhousie had written a condescending and self-absolving letter to the nawab of Awadh. In the letter, Dalhousie first praised the British, bemoaned the inefficiency of the nawab and his ancestors, and finally warned him of the consequences of resisting the annexation. Dalhousie wrote:

> It has now become my most painful duty to inform Your Majesty that the British government, influenced by a regard for its reputation among the nations, and still more by the obligations which, many years ago, it took upon itself in relation to the people of Oude, can no longer lend its countenance and support to a Government whose

---

[246] *Oude: Papers Relating to Oude*, London: Harrison and Sons, 1856, p. 204.

existence is the fruitful source of misrule, oppression, and misery, to all who live under its control.[247]

As events would show later, the people of Awadh would eventually suffer a much more monstrous and worse taxation system under the British Raj. And the cruel and bizarre taxes levied on poor farmers would eventually cause a peasant uprising, with its rallying point at Ayodhya. The peasant uprising was led by a Ramayan-reciter—Fiji-returned Baba Ramchandra, as we will see in a later section.

In his letter, Dalhousie continued to lament the failure of the nawabs:

These hopes and expectations, however, have been grievously disappointed. From the earliest period of the connection above referred to, the government of Oude has been notorious for its abuse of power, for gross misrule, and for the oppression of its subjects; and successive Governors-Government have felt it to be their duty to bring to the notice of the Rulers of Oude the disorders and evils which prevailed under the ruinous system of their administration, the impoverishment and desolation with which the kingdom was threatened and the deplorable condition of misery and insecurity to which the people of Oude were reduced.[248]

When Outram reached Lucknow on 31 January 1856, he first called on Ali Naqi Khan, Wajid Ali Shah's prime minister. He apprised him of the imminent annexation and to the general litany of reasons of economic rot was added the charge of 'lawlessness'. The assault on Hanumangarhi by Muslims (both Sunnis and Shias) in July 1855 had only strengthened the British ruse of anarchy and breakdown of law and order.

On 7 February, the British annexed Awadh. Wajid Ali Shah offered neither resistance nor acceptance and announced his plan to go to London on 12 March to make his case to the king of England. However, he could not go beyond Calcutta where he was to stay until his death in 1887 in Matia Burz, a small fortress, under British guard. The people of Lucknow were devastated as they were the first to witness the changed behaviour of the British who had so far respected the sovereignty of the king. The departure of their king meant the end of their world, of essentially everything they had come to take for granted. The court of Wajid Ali Shah and his

---

[247]Ibid, p. 244.
[248]Ibid.

predecessors supported lakhs of people and the status quo that had held for generations was suddenly under threat. These fears moved people to compose poems, songs and couplets of desperation; musicians who earlier composed eulogies and sang paeans to the glory of the king now sang of the pain of their king's loss. Two of the more common refrains were:

Raja Praja mil mil Roven, hil mil Rove Sara Sansar
Hai Gayo Pardes ko Raja, chhor apna ghar Sansar

(Noble and peasant all wept together and all the world wept and wailed
Alas, the king bid adieu to his home and has gone to a foreign land)

Hazrat jate hain London, hum-pe krupa karo Raghunandon

(His Highness is going to London, O' God be kind to us)[249]

The annexation of Awadh, and the tension and skirmishes leading up to it, sealed the fate of composite culture and amity that had existed between the Hindus and Muslims of the region. In the years to come the divisions between the communities would deepen. A general unrest was also beginning to spread which would come to a head just a couple of years later. As we know, Wajid Ali Shah never returned to Lucknow. He died in Calcutta in 1887 while still living off his annual pension of 12 lakh rupees. After the annexation, the British Residency in Lucknow began an immediate eviction of royal families from their palaces like Chhattar Manzil. The British also razed a number of buildings with magnificent architecture including the Bhim ka Akhara and the house of poet Mir Taqi Mir in order to lay a railway line. By the winter of 1856, anger was rising among ordinary people and nobles alike. Many landholders and chiefs who had been deprived of their hereditary lands by the British plotted against them. Raja Man Singh had established contact with Nana Saheb of Kanpur[250] and together they had come to an understanding with the court of Delhi that once the British were overthrown, Hindus would be permitted the use of the Sanskrit Devnagri script, which had been prohibited until then.[251] Man

---

[249]Roshan Taqui, *Lucknow 1857: The Two Wars of Lucknow, Dusk of an Era*, Lucknow: New Royal Book Company, 2001, p. 30. Later, the poetic outburst would be replaced by an armed insurrection.
[250]Adopted son of the last Maratha Peshwa, Baji Rao II.
[251]Taqui, *Lucknow 1857*.

Singh and Nana Saheb were to fall out soon after this and the former in fact would decisively take the side of the British when the revolt was fully under way a year later. While Nana Saheb of Kanpur was demonized for his role in the massacre of British non-combatants, including women and children, Man Singh was invested in by the British as a rough-weather friend and given the title of maharaja and a knighthood. No descendants of Nana Saheb survive while the house of Man Singh has flourished and lives on till today.

In the wake of Wajid Ali Shah's dethronement, as his former courtiers and officers deliberated upon a course of action, a year had passed.

FAIZABAD: BEGINNING OF THE REVOLT IN AWADH

In 1855, it was the fanatical zeal of Maulvi Shah Ghulam Hussein that started the communal flare-up over a mosque in Hanumangarhi. After the annexation and the relative quietude that prevailed from February 1856 to February 1857, it was another maulvi who descended on the old capital of Awadh and immediately gave cause for the British to be alarmed.

Almost to the day when two years earlier Captain Orr had informed his superiors about the threat Shah Ghulam Hussein posed to law and order in Faizabad–Ayodhya, another British officer wrote to his superiors about the presence of Maulvi Ahmad Ulla Shah who was inciting people against the annexation. After failing to induce the maulvi to surrender his weapons, a fight broke out which left the British-led troops and the maulvi injured. With the maulvi lodged in the military hospital, Deputy Commissioner Forbes wrote, 'with respect to him, little reliable information has yet been gathered. On the Bazaar he is styled Sikandar Shah. He speaks and understands English, though imperfectly. And though he states that he came from the Madras side of India...'[252] The maulvi was a belligerent man: when a British lieutenant had assured him that if he left the town his weapons would be returned to him, the maulvi had replied that he would leave when he had some phursat (leisure).

While in hospital, the maulvi was being helped by a Muslim doctor named Najaf Ali who used to smuggle home-made food to him, and 'fed him with his own hands'.[253] Three months later in May 1857, this daring doctor assisted Ahmad Ulla Shah in escaping from the Faizabad jail

---

[252]Ibid., p. 42.
[253]Ibid.

by obtaining for him the full uniform of a British colonel posted there. Ahmad Ulla Shah subsequently became the leader of a large faction of rebels and is remembered as one of the leaders of India's First War of Independence. After the fall of Lucknow in 1858, Shah's collaborator, Najaf Ali, was captured and summarily executed by the British in November that year.

HANUMANGARHI BAIRAGIS RETURN THE FAVOUR
By the last week of April 1857, the rebellion had spread to all major towns of Awadh and the British were busy strengthening their entrenchments in the Residency building at Lucknow in anticipation of the mutinous soldiers who were congregating and heading to Lucknow. Many small chieftains and landlords were raising militias to fight the British. Incensed by the summary settlements that deprived them of the hereditary rights over their lands, a large number of landlords and soldiers were also attracted by the prospect of partaking in the plunder of the quarter million rupees worth of treasure that was present in the Residency.[254] Some talukdars were still hedging their bets and trying to ascertain which side looked more likely to emerge the winner. In the midst of this general insurrection that looked like doomsday to the English officers besieged in Lucknow, there appeared some solace around the middle of June 1857. Lieutenant General McLeod Iness, who was present at the time, wrote in his book, *Lucknow and Oude in the Mutiny,* about the unexpected support that the besieged Britishers received. The British feared that there would be a shortage of food owing to being surrounded by hostile villages around Lucknow, but as Iness wrote, not all of Awadh was against them:

> The districts were meanwhile remaining quiet; food was pouring in from the country; the Talookdars were either playing a friendly part or giving no trouble. Supplies were being received from the most unexpected quarters, such as the Mohunts of the Hunnooman Gurhee, and the family of the Bhow Begum.[255]

This outpouring of support was perhaps due to the gratitude that the British government had earned through their acts with regard to the 1855 violence

---

[254]McLeod Iness, *Lucknow and Oude in the Mutiny: A Narrative and a Study*, London: A. D. Innes and Co., 1895.

[255]Ibid., p. 94.

and lingering memories of the handling of Bahu Begum's personal estate in 1775. As we have seen earlier, they had helped the widow of Shuja-ud-daulah in negotiating a handsome pension for herself and her dependants. And, more recently, they had openly sided with the Hanumangarhi mahants during the months-long dispute in 1855. According to Patrick Carnegy, an officer who compiled a *Historical Sketch of Tehsil Fyzabad and Zilla Fyzabad* in 1870, the priests of Hanumangarhi were also provided a grant of Rs 1,000 by the commissioner, Colonel Goldley, for the protection of British officers and their families after the outbreak of rebellion in Faizabad.

THE RISE OF MAN SINGH

Man Singh was one of the talukdars who switched to the British side early on. Iness notes that Man Singh came over to their side around April of 1857.

> ...a Talookdar and ex-Amil [high-ranking official under the Nawab], who had hitherto tried to play a double game, and to stand well with both the British and the rebels, now openly tendered his allegiance to the Government and held his fort of Shahgunge [Shahganj] in their interests. The enemy soon appeared before his fort and besieged it, and there he remained till relieved in June.[256]

It was also Man Singh, who given his proximity, seems to have arranged for the food supplies that were sent by the priests of Hanumangarhi.

Originally named Hanuman Singh, Man Singh would by the end of the mutiny be made a maharaja and given the prized lands of Ayodhya. His successor, Pratap Narayan Singh Bahadur, would be awarded the title of Ayodhya Naresh, or the Lord of Ayodhya. Man Singh was not from the Solar clan nor a descendant of Ram; his family background was neither rich nor illustrious. Born to an impoverished Sakaldip Brahmin family of Bhojpur, his journey to the throne of Ramchandra's mythical kingdom can best be described as the audacity of hope. It was a childless uncle, Bakhtawar (meaning fortunate in Urdu) Singh, who made Man Singh successor to his estate of Mahdona. Bakhtawar Singh had acquired the title of raja and the estate during Saadat Ali Khan's reign (1798-1814). Bakhtawar was a trooper in the Bengal Regular Cavalry and was 'serving in this capacity at Lucknow', where:

---

[256]Ibid., p. 296.

his fine figure and manly bearing attracted the notice of Nawab Sadut Ali Khan, who having obtained his discharge, appointed him a Jemadar [junior officer] of cavalry, and shortly afterwards made him a Risaldar [commander of a mounted troop]. After the death of Sadut Ali, Bakhtwur Singh secured the favour of Ghazi-us-din Hyder, the first king of Oudh, which led to his further advancement, and to the acquisition of the title of Raja. This title was subsequently granted in perpetuity by Mahomed Ali Shah, when he also turned the Mehdona property into a Raj or estate.[257]

Beginning from the small estate of Mehdona, the family came to acquire many more territories through violent struggles, deceit and court intrigues. By 1827, Darshan Singh, Man Singh's father and brother of Bakhtawar Singh, had gained control of Salon, Baiswara and the Nizamat (a kind of court during the rule of the British East India Company) of Sultanpore which included Faizabad and Ayodhya.

It was a stunning ascent of the feudal hierarchy of nineteenth-century Awadh. It was against this family background that Man Singh stepped forward for the protection of Hanumangarhi in 1855. This decision had made both him and the British popular among the Hindus of the region. And, as a man trusted by the British, Man Singh had also come to represent the Rajputs' concerns. Thus, when he openly declared support for the British in 1857, some Rajput landlords, too, followed suit, or at the very least, remained neutral. But, Man Singh's influence on Rajputs was limited—a large number of rebels and their leaders were Rajput chiefs with unchallenged claims to royalty. Unlike Man Singh, whose history went back to only a few decades, men like Rana Beni Madho, the legendary Rajput chief who eluded the British till the very end of the revolt in 1858, hailed from thoroughly established families with much older histories of rule.

The British had calculated accurately the outcome of supporting the Hindus over the Muslims in the 1855 conflict over Hanumangarhi. It was now easy for them and their beneficiaries like Man Singh to demand support against the rebel chiefs. Iness summed up the fruits of the British handling of the Hanumangarhi conflict in characteristic style:

---

[257]P. Carnegy, *Historical Sketch of Tehsil Fyzabad, Zillah Fyzabad*, Lucknow: Oudh Government Press, 1870, p. 4.

This episode destroyed any latent reluctance that there might otherwise have been to remove the Nuwab from the rulership of the province; but it had also two other notable results. One was that the Hindoos of Oude, including the Rajpoot chiefs, knowing the part played in the crisis by the English Resident, became especially well disposed towards the British. The other was that Rajah Maun Singh, hitherto one of the most detested of the Amils, having come forward with his followers to the defence of the Hunnooman Gurhee, and posed as the champion of Hindooism, lost much of his unpopularity, and acquired the respect of the Rajpoots to such a degree as to enable him to act during the Mutiny as the representative and leader of the community.[258]

Man Singh's star was to rise further. His influence would peak after the last matchlocks were fired at the end of 1858.

MAN SINGH GETS AYODHYA FOR SUPPORTING THE BRITISH

Earlier in 1857, Man Singh was trying to interpret what was going on and hoping that he was right. The 'deluge', as the British had described the revolt that spread through a swathe of north and east India, had swamped chiefs like Man Singh too. They were surrounded by soldiers who had revolted and now expected their hereditary chiefs to join them in throwing off the yoke of Company Sarkar. The soldiers were men who had nothing left to lose, having committed the cardinal sin of betraying their British masters. Men like Man Singh, on the other hand, owed their prosperity and power to the Company and its officers. Though still serving the nawab-king of Awadh in name, in reality, they were all too well aware that real power vested with the British. Man Singh's position was thus much more precarious than that of hereditary Rajput chiefs like Beni Madho of the Bainswara clan, whose claims to royalty were uncontested. Man Singh's family, on the contrary, acquired power through the favour of the Lucknow court and were 'state-created Rajahs'.[259] Bakhtawar Singh, the first raja of their family, was himself only a sepoy and thus they enjoyed no great and unshakeable claims to Hindu nobility.

In the hot summer of 1857 when Awadh was on the boil on account of nationalisms—both Hindu and Muslim—anti-British feelings,

---

[258]Iness, *Lucknow and Oude in the Mutiny*, p. 59.
[259]Ibid., p. 60.

and opportunistic anarchism, Man Singh was secretly advising the British through messengers. To the troops and the rebellious population he maintained appearances of being their ally. At his fort in Shahgunj, near Faizabad, Indian soldiers had revolted too, but had refrained from cutting and shooting down their English officers. They had assigned that job to the soldiers of another regiment that was marching from Azamgarh and was camping at Begumganj. A number of military officers had been asked by their troops to leave Faizabad in boats moored at the cantonment ghat. When they reached Begumganj, the hapless officers were either shot dead or drowned while attempting to escape. Colonel Goldley, who had been the commissioner, had moved his headquarters to Faizabad from Sultanpur in light of the disturbances, and had given Rs 1,000 to the Hanumangarhi priests for the care and protection of the British officers and families, was captured from his boat and led to the band of soldiers. 'I am an old man, will you disgrace yourselves by my murder?' he is said to have asked of them. Goldley was shot dead.

Days before he was killed, Colonel Goldley had released a prisoner who would turn out to be a most effective protector and ally of the British. 'At the beginning of the month Raja Man Singh, talukdar of Shahganj, was in confinement there. He had been arrested by order of the Chief Commissioner, in consequence of information telegraphed from Calcutta, which accorded with what had reached us at Lucknow.'[260] The information referred to here pertained to Man Singh's ostensible collusion with the rebel soldiers after he had been approached to lead them. Man Singh had stalled the soldiers by saying that he needed to first seek Nana Saheb of Kanpur's counsel.

At the beginning of the revolt, when news arrived of soldiers descending on Faizabad and Ayodhya from Azamgarh and other neighbouring districts, Man Singh had once again reached out to Colonel Goldley, and 'warned them that the troops would rise, and offered, if released, to give the Europeans shelter in his fort at Shahganj'.[261] Seeing the critical state of things, Colonel Goldley released him, and Man Singh at once commenced to put his fort in order and to raise levies or mercenaries. Perhaps this is equally telling of the limited nature of the revolt: that even in the tumult of anti-British frenzy, men were willing to fight as freelancers or levies for a sum of money.

---

[260]Carnegy, *Historical Sketch of Tehsil Fyzabad, Zillah Fyzabad*, p. 16.
[261]Ibid.

Soon after Man Singh's release from prison, the troops in Faizabad had revolted and Colonel Goldley and others were killed. The Faizabad cantonment was now 'free'. However, acting on instinct, some civil officers of the British East India Company had escaped to Man Singh's fort in Shahganj where they found refuge. But with the killings of the British, the rebellious troops had signalled their deadly hostility to their former employers. Acting in the interest of his own safety, Man Singh, who had sheltered the British fugitives so far, now wanted them to leave the fort. 'He, however, provided boats for them on the Gogra, to which they were escorted by night; and a party of Man Singh's levies accompanied them some way on their journey. They all reached the station of Dinapur in safety.'[262] After Faizabad's rebel troops had fled with the government treasure, he continued to help the British with information about the rebels' march and strength. Patrick Carnegy, who was in touch with Man Singh, positively assesses Man Singh's contribution: 'Raja Man Singh, with whom I was then in almost daily communication, kept me informed of their movements and of their want of ammunition; and wrote me that 500 match-lock men could wrest the treasure from them as they passed not far from Lucknow. I hoped that an attempt might have made been made to intercept them. Sir Henry Lawrence, however, decided against the measure.'[263] These soldiers later reached the Ganga at Kanpur and joined the local soldiery in the 'cruel destruction of the unhappy fugitives from the Cawnpur massacre'.[264]

MAN SINGH'S ADVOCACY FOR THE BRITISH

'The present time is worse than the former one. May God protect us!'

—Raja Man Singh in a letter to the talukdars of Awadh,
20 July 1857

With the benefit of hindsight and historical research, many historians have observed that the mutiny or the rebellion of 1857 was doomed from the start. It lacked a common goal, leadership and military organization. Therefore, it degenerated into anarchy and with the death and capture of

---

[262]Ibid., p. 17.

[263]Ibid.

[264]Ibid. For the massacre of the British at Kanpur, Nana Saheb was hanged along with others.

key rebel leaders like Beni Madho, Rani Laxmibai of Jhansi, Tatya Tope, Kunwar Singh, Maulvi Ahmad Ulla Shah and Begum Hazrat Mahal to name a few, it was quickly quelled by the British forces.

To Man Singh's credit, he had predicted the same while Awadh was in the throes of the revolt, in his British-backed appeal to the talukdars. A long letter[265] dated 20 July 1857 written by Man Singh is still perhaps the most comprehensive articulation of the reasons for the British success in putting down the revolt. It cited the 'misery and ruin' that 'Mahrattas [Marathas] and Mahomedans inflicted upon India in days gone by'. And added that the talukdars should 'wish for the same Government as abolished the tyrannical system of former days, and conferred comfort and peace on the people'. Because he believed in the innate flaw of the rebellion he warned his fellow chiefs that they 'can never hope to become rulers by merely assembling bands of armed followers in this time of anarchy, neither can the Telingas[266] ever achieve victory or success'.[267]

Then, closely following the structure of official British correspondence, Man Singh enumerated the reasons. He described the soldiers as unthinking machines who were incapable of fighting a war with strategy and planning. Man Singh wrote that though the soldiers:

> ...are well disciplined, and it is true that by their assistance the British conquered India, still, in reality, they were always kept like a machine which could move or fire a musket on the touch of a spring. They do not know how to fight, neither do they understand the art of war. The British officers kept this knowledge to themselves. Without those officers they are a machine without a spring, and in the time of need they will neither be able to move nor to fire.

He then went on to deride the basic character of soldiers. Citing their random acts of unjustified violence as proof of their monstrous unreliability, the letter said, 'They have plundered thousands of houses, and they consider every person's property to be their own. As for shame, every one knows they have none. The worst member of a family used to run away from his parents and enlist in the army.'[268]

---

[265]Iness, *Lucknow and Oude in the Mutiny*, p. 334.
[266]Telingas is a native term for sepoys.
[267]Iness, *Lucknow and Oude in the Mutiny*, p. 334.
[268]Ibid., p. 335.

Man Singh seemed to have forgotten his own personal background, which originated with his grandfather enlisting in the British-maintained Bengal Regular Cavalry.

But for Man Singh, who, in a sense, had everything to lose if the British were defeated, it was the fear of the rebels' next target that prevented him from siding with them. Man Singh was playing on precisely that insecurity when he wrote, 'First, we ought to consider that when they have thrown off the yoke of such a powerful Government from their shoulders, they are not likely to care much for us. Those who have butchered the children of their masters after eating their salt for ages, will never spare recent acquaintances like us.'[269]

In the concluding part of his argument against aiding the insurrection, Man Singh turned to the theme of religion and chose to present it in a way that indicates that he and many like him had come to view it in the same way as the British did. The tropes that Man Singh employed to label the Muslims as anti-Hindu are remarkably similar to how the British portrayed the rule of Muslim kings. As the rebellion was ultimately triggered by the rumour of cartridges greased with pig and cow fat, he addressed the issue of the rebellion being a war for religious freedom. Man Singh reckoned, 'We should indeed be surprised if any one was to say that we ought to take up the cause of our religion. The Telingas do not fight for religion. They do just the thing which our religion prohibits. They plunder and murder women and children, and no religion admits of such deeds... To become their ally is to take part in a sacrilegious deed.'[270]

The irony of this appeal against cruelty coming from one of the most detested nobles and the brother of the 'terror of Gonda', Raghubardayal Singh,[271] must not have been lost on the more than 200 or so talukdars of Awadh.

The barbarism of the soldiers established and the revolt declared irreligious, Man Singh now framed the most vital reasons for not supporting the rebellion. Man Singh, his father Darshan Singh and uncle Bakhtawar Singh all owed their wealth and power to the favour of the Awadh court. Past gratitude, however, never comes in the way of future success of men

---

[269]Ibid.

[270]Ibid., p. 336.

[271]For more on Man Singh's brother, see William Henry Sleeman, *A Journey through the Kingdom of Oude in 1849-1850*, London: R. Bentley, 1838.

like Man Singh, who had become chiefs and high officials because of their ability to please the rulers. The rebellion had shaken the roots of both the British East India Company as well as the relatively new foundations of state-created rajas such as Man Singh. As common Muslims and Hindus fought shoulder to shoulder, the spectre of a general insurrection against landlords haunted Man Singh. With these very real fears in mind, Man Singh raised the bogey of the return of Muslim rule in an attempt to persuade the talukdars to support the British. Addressing those talukdars who might still have been thinking of the rebellion as a war for their respective religion, Man Singh wrote:

> It is also surprising that people should aid and put into power those very Mussulmans who, on invading India, destroyed all our Hindoo temples, forcibly converted the natives to Mahomedanism, massacred whole cities, seized upon Hindoo females and made them concubines, prevented Brahmins from saying prayers, burnt their religious books, and levied taxes upon every Hindoo. They are those very Mussulmans who prided themselves on calling us infidels, and in subjecting us to all sorts of humiliation.

Harking back to the memory of past injustices done by Muslims rulers, Man Singh asserted, 'If any person will reflect on their former deeds, it will make his hair stand on end, cause such disgust that the very sight even of a Mahomedan will be abhorrent.'

Man Singh's assessment of Muslim rule was fairly exaggerated to the extent that he was voicing the views of the priestly and warrior classes. But in Awadh, Hindu–Muslim relations had been healthy and did not escape the notice of the British. Man Singh's litany of complaints against Muslim rule is neither supported by the general history of Awadh nor by his own history of being a recipient of nawabi favours. 'In matters of eating and drinking,' wrote C. A. Elliot, one of the first British settlement officers in Oudh, 'they [i.e., the Rajput converts to Islam] are as particular about their caste as any Brahmin. Many of them wear the Hindu dhoti and will greet a Hindu with the idolatrous salutation of "Ram Ram". Almost all keep a pundit to fix the auspicious moment of commencing any enterprise, or foretell the nature of its result, and they believe firmly in his predictions.'[272]

---

[272]John Pemble, *The Raj and the Indian Mutiny and the Kingdom of Oude—1801–1859*,

As his task was to win over as many talukdars to the British side as was possible, Man Singh was not bothered about the accuracy of his facts. In his desperation, Man Singh continued animatedly with the logic of past Muslim persecution while crediting the British for a Hindu revival. He wrote:

> What is more surprising still, is that the people should consider it a religious deed to kill and destroy those very persons who permitted the re-establishment of the decayed religion, and allowed all temples and places of worship to be rebuilt, and all religious ceremonies to be performed without any hindrance whatsoever.
>
> We should consider how much we suffered in the time of the Mahomedan kings in Oude.[273]

The British did aid in reviving Hinduism to some extent. As the vanquishers of Muslim nawabs of Bengal and Awadh, and as the de facto rulers of nineteenth-century India, they somewhat levelled the playing field between the largely Hindu subjects and their Muslim rulers.

Man Singh finally comes to the last section of the letter in which he credits James Outram, the British Resident at Lucknow, for the protection of Hanumangarhi in 1855. He conveniently overlooks the proclamation by Wajid Ali Shah prohibiting people from joining Maulvi Ameer Ali's march on Hanumangarhi.

Having put forth all possible reasons for the talukdars to consider supporting the British, Man Singh offered them the promise of a good old quid pro quo. He made a last appeal,

> In our opinion, to gain the favour of the British is to save religion; to annoy them is a violation of all things sacred... Those who have made it a profession to kill people can never hope for mercy... If all of you unite and seek for peace, I am sure the Government will remove all your doubts (of whatever kind), and something better will come out of the future. At any rate we cannot lose anything by the attempt.[274]

Man Singh's letter was the outcome of another written by the highest-ranking British official in Awadh at the time. Henry Lawrence, who had been appointed chief commissioner of Oude, assumed his post in February

---

New Delhi: Oxford University Press, 1960, p. 158.
[273]Iness, *Lucknow and Oude in the Mutiny*, p. 336.
[274]Ibid., 337–39.

1857, and had in a short time understood the worth of Man Singh as a collaborator. And it was to Man Singh that he turned for support during the first few months of the rebellion that started in May 1857. Man Singh first received Lawrence's letter dated 17 June 1857, and soon after he received another from Martin Gubbins, the financial commissioner, promising future prosperity. The letters read as follows:

My Dear Raja,

I have told your servants what I am ready to do for you. I regret I was not here last year as I should have prevented your estates being resumed. However, there is a good time to come. If you now do good service to government, you will find it to your own advantage, and you will become better off than you ever were.

You are too wise and clever to suppose that the present disturbance will not soon be settled, when the bad will be punished and the good rewarded.

your friend;
Lucknow
The 17th June 1857. (Sd) Henry M. Lawrence

Dear Raja Man Singh,

You have deserved well of the British government so far. Do yet more and earn for yourself the high reward which is held out.

Lucknow
Martin Gubbins
The 22nd June 1857
Financial Commissioner[275]

Notwithstanding these letters and their promises, when Man Singh, the staunch British supporter, felt the British could lose he was back to the rebel side.

AFTERMATH OF THE REVOLT: DURBAR OF 1866

By the end of 1858, the rebellion had ended in a destructive implosion. Begum Hazrat Mahal, Wajid Ali Shah's second wife and one of the main

---

[275]Carnegy, *Historical Sketch of Tehsil Fyzabad, Zillah Fyzabad*, p. 10.

leaders of the revolt, left to seek refuge in Nepal in February 1859, three years after her husband was dethroned and exiled to Calcutta. Maulvi Ahmad Ullah Shah died fighting a guerrilla war in Rohilkhand; Rana Beni Madho, Raja Devi Baksh and Raja Jia Lal were martyred—hanged to death. Lucknow looked like death itself. None of its palaces, buildings or even huts were spared the plunder, and none of its residents the hunger for revenge. The wrath of Scottish Highlanders, Punjabis, Sikhs and the Nepalese king Jung Bahadur's Gorkhas fell on men and women alike. In Delhi, Colonel Hodson[276] killed the young sons of Emperor Bahadur Shah Zafar, and the emperor himself was exiled to death in remote Burma. Nana Saheb's stronghold of Bithoor near Kanpur with its numerous temples was razed to the ground and set on fire. Its destruction was so complete that it took decades for the small town by the Ganga to revive itself. The talukdars of Awadh were the only class of people besides the merchants who were relieved that the 'deluge' had been swept away. With their lands and titles restored, the talukdars began to once again vie with each other for the patronage of the British. In 1860, Man Singh was made maharaja by the British and seven years later he was given the weighty title of 'Knight Commander of the Order of the Star of India' (KCSI). The talukdars paid for the entire extravaganza of the durbar and it also became a site for the old and intergenerational rivalry between the maharaja of Balrampur and the new maharaja of Ayodhya. The maharaja of Balrampur had been given the KCSI in the last durbar of 1866 at Agra. The talukdars now strove to outdo each other in ostentation; as a contemporary observer remarked, this 'must have rejuvenated the luxury industries as they competed in getting the finest and best of everything, from the best trappings of their elephants to the caps that adorned their heads'.[277]

According to an eyewitness account, 'the time and money spent on such seeming trifles was useful because the izzut (honour) of these men has been raised ten-fold. To be a Talookdar in Oude is with some to be better than a prince of the blood. These men made the most of a glorious opportunity to bask in the glow of their enhanced status while all Lucknow watched.'[278]

The most important purpose of the durbar was to establish the new

---

[276]Hodson raised a cavalry regiment during the revolt, which exists today as the 4th Horse Regiment in the Indian Army

[277]Veena Talwar Oldenberg, *The Making of Colonial Lucknow—1856–77*, Princeton: Princeton University Press, 1984, p. 253.

[278]Ibid., p. 254.

hierarchy firmly for the general populace: 'the men whom they supported during the rebellion—the talookdars and nawabs were now riding docilely behind the British Viceroy'.[279]

This new culture of a burlesque show of loyalty would come to define relations between the ruled and rulers for a long time, and arguably still does. An unnamed Indian observer of these durbars described it wryly:

> The relation between the ruler and the ruled is wholly artificial and superficial. Now loyalty means empty salaam-ing. It is shown in illuminations, explodes amidst fireworks and is eaten up in state banquets... Active loyalty is gone with the local prosperity, and hollow deeds are followed by hollow effects... For the loyalty is a huge sham which is not grounded in patriotism. Loyalty now is nothing but indirect selfishness.[280]

AYODHYA'S GROWTH AS A PILGRIM CENTRE

For Ayodhya, the loyalty of Man Singh and his rival from neighbouring Balrampur to the British can be argued to have been a blessing in disguise. If, and it is a very potent if, the Hindus with their Ayodhya-centric religious bearing had risen in revolt and joined the rebel soldiers, then the tide of the battle could have been turned against the British. If on the other hand, these parties had joined the insurrection and the British had won, it can be safely assumed that as in Bithoor, the British would have wreaked destruction on the ancient town in revenge.

But now, with Ayodhya under the Brahmin king Man Singh, its future as a Hindu religious centre looked bright. Most of the better-off Muslim families would soon migrate to Lucknow and other towns, and temple construction started in earnest after 1857.[281] The expansionist Ramanandi Bairagis, driven by their own Vaishnava fundamentalism, started laying claims to newer lands (lands remain a source of income) and in some cases, mosques.

Darshan Singh, Man Singh's father, had constructed a grand temple dedicated to Mahadeo in 1845. With the ascension of Man Singh, this temple acquired both his name and glory. In 1890, the Kingdom of Orchha in neighbouring Madhya Pradesh ordered the construction of Kanak Bhavan

---

[279]Ibid.

[280]Ibid., p.255.

[281]Lala Sitaram, *Ayodhya ka Itihas*, p. 136.

(Silver Mansion), a grand palace-temple for Lord Ram and his consort Sita. Stressing the continuity of the temple since the time of Ram, the official website of Kanak Bhavan states that:

> Its history dates back to Treta Yug when it was gifted by Ram's step-mother Kaikeyi to him and his consort Sita as a marriage gift. With the passage of time it fell to ruin, and was reconstructed and renovated many times. The first reconstruction was done by Ram's son Kusha in the beginning of Dwapar Yug, again by King Rishabdeo in middle of Dwapar, and Lord Krishna is said to have visited the ancient site in pre-Kali Yug era 614. In the current Yug called the 'Kali Yug', it was first built by Chandra Gupta Vikramaditya in Yudisthir era 2431, repaired & renovated by Samudra Gupta in 387 A.D. (Vikram Samvat 444), destroyed by Nawab S. Salarjung II Gazi in 1027 A.D. (V.S. 1084) and then finally reconstructed on the ruins & renovated in the present shape by H.H. Maharaja Sri Pratap Singh Ju Deo, G.C.S.I. [Knight Grand Commander of the Star of India], G.C.I.E. [Knight Grand Commander of the Order of the Indian Empire] of Orchha and Tikamgarh (Bundelkhand) and his Queen Maharani Vrisbhan Kunwari, and consecrated in 1891 A.D. (V.S. 1948) Vaishakh Shukl 6th, Guru Pushya [roughly the month of May].[282]

Man Singh did not live for long after the revolt had ended. In 1870, he and his two brothers all died in quick succession. Man Singh had only a daughter and a grandson, who was a minor. In contravention of the practice of primogeniture, which is also cited as one of the objects of the Ramayana, Man Singh, in his will, made his wife the caretaker of his estate until his daughter's son, Kunwar Pratap Narayan Singh, attained maturity. But Man Singh's wife seemed to have been a stickler for tradition and adopted the son of Man Singh's brother as her son so that he could be crowned the new king. However, armed with Man Singh's will, Pratap Narayan Singh moved the court and was decreed the rightful heir and declared king of Ayodhya by the British government's Privy Council in 1887.[283] Pratap Narayan Singh's reign lasted for twenty years during which time he mainly focused his energies on building a new British-style palace, the Raj Mahal, in Ayodhya.

---

[282] *Kanak Bhavan Temple* homepage <http://www.kanak-bhavan-temple.com/>.
[283] Lala Sitaram, *Ayodhya ka Itihas.*

RAMANANDI RECLAMATION OF AYODHYA

Hanumangarhi, over which hundreds of Muslims and Hindus had died, was no longer a flashpoint. However, the mosque (referred to as Babri Masjid hereafter) which had been used by Shah Ghulam Hussein as the launching pad for the attack on Hanumangarhi, had since then become a site of encroachment by Bairagis.

During the British fightback of 1857, the mahant of Hanumangarhi thought of a prudent strategy to lay claim to the Babri Masjid, which had come to be associated with the legend of being Ram's birthplace. Mahant Balram Das, encouraged by Man Singh's implicit support, and convinced that offence is the best defence, erected a rectangular brick-mortar platform outside the Babri mosque and called it the exact spot where Ram was born. This opportunistic encroachment came against the backdrop of the imminent and certain demise of nawabi rule. The Bairagis had not thought of claiming the Babri Masjid as Ram's birthplace in 1855 when they had temporarily overrun the mosque and killed scores of Muslims in and around it. But what they could not do then owing to the fear of the nawab, they did now, though in a limited way—by not occupying the mosque but only erecting a platform outside it.

On 30 November 1858, when the mutiny was all but over, the muttawali (caretaker) of Babri Masjid, Mohammad Asghar, had submitted a written complaint over the construction of the Chabutra (a raised platform or dais) to the deputy commissioner of Faizabad. On the same day, Syed Mohammad Khatib, the muezzin of Babri Masjid pleaded with government authorities about the intrusion in a detailed letter. The muezzin wrote:

In a recent incident one Nihang Sikh resident of Punjab Sikkhan, a government employee (sic) is creating riot on Janam Sthan Masjid situated in Oudh. Near Mehrab and Mimber, he has constructed, inside the case, an earth Chabutra measuring about four fingers by filling it with Kankars (concrete). Lighting arrangement 2303 has been made...and after raising the height of Chabutra about 1¼ yards a picture of an idol has been placed and after digging a pit near it, the Munder wall has been made Pucca. Fire has been lit there for light and Puja and Hom is continuing there. In whole of this Masjid 'Ram Ram' has been written with coal. Kindly do justice. It is an open tyranny and high handedness of the Hindus on Muslims. You are the master of both the parties since the Shahi era (sic) if any person constructs forcibly he would be punished by your honour. Kindly consider the fact that Masjid is a place of worship of the Muslims and not that of Hindus. Previously the symbol of Janamasthan had been there for hundreds of years and Hindus did Puja. Because of conspiracy of Shiv Ghulam Thandedar Oudh Government, the Bairagis constructed overnight a Chabutra up to height of one 'Balisht' until the orders of injunction were issued. At that time the Deputy Commissioner suspended the Thanedar and fine was imposed on Bairagis. Now the Chabootra has been raised to about 1¼ yards. Thus sheer high-handedness has been proved. Therefore it is requested that Murtaza Khan Kotwal City may be ordered that he himself visit the spot and inspect the new constructions and get them demolished (sic) and oust the Hindus from there; the symbol and the idol may be removed from there and writing on the walls be washed. Orders may be issued for the future (paper torn). Deemed necessary, so requested. Sd/- Syed Mohammad Khatib, Moazzim Masjid Babri sites in Oudh Dated November 30, 1858.[284]

Acting upon orders issued in response to the above complaint, a Sub-Inspector rank officer Sheetal Dubey, was finally able to remove the symbol and oust the intruding Nihang Sikh from the premises on December 10, 1858.[285]

After the rebellion was finally quelled, the British erected a wall around the mosque for its protection from further attacks by Hindus. The presence of black kasauti pillars inside the mosque and the growing legend that it was built on the ruins of a Hindu temple seem to have prodded the British to erect the wall so as to prevent future conflict.

The Allahabad High Court verdict of 2010 also deals with the erection of the wall but leaves out the period of its construction. All it says is that:

> It is not in dispute that the entire disputed area ABCD consist of two parts, (1) inner court, which included the disputed building and, (2) outer courtyard. This division of the disputed premises in the inner courtyard and outer courtyard came to exist in 1856-1857 when it is said that an iron-grilled wall was erected separating the

---

[284]Ayodhya Matter: Ram Janam Bhoomi- Babri Masjid Disputes (Special Full Bench Judgement) Allahabad High Court, Malhotra Law House, p. 2302 < http://www.ebc-india. com/downloads/rjbm/Justice_Sudhir_Agarwal/Judgment%20RJB-BM%20Vol-10.pdf>.
[285]Ibid., p. 2310.

disputed building along from the other constructed parts including the Chabutara called Ram Chabutara. The exact date or period is not on record nor could the parties throw any light thereon except that its existence has been noticed in P. Carnegi's Historical Sketch (supra) published in 1870 and that shows that it was constructed sometimes after 1855 and also admitted by Mohd. Asghar, defendant no.2 in Suit 1885 in his written statement.[286]

In Ayodhya, Ram's birthplace was already marked by a temple that had existed long before the 1855 conflagration. This was the Janamsthan Mandir (birthplace temple) situated just 40 metres north of the Babri Masjid. Patrick Carnegy, author of one of the most cited works on Ayodhya—*A Historical Sketch of Tahsil Fyzabad, District Fyzabad, Pargana Haveli-Oudh, 1870*—had recorded the Janamsthan temple to be 166 years old, which takes its origin to 1707, the year Aurangzeb died. According to local tradition, Carnegy found that it was built by a monk named Ramdas on land donated by Mir Masum Ali Mafidar.[287] In a later section we will see how this Janamsthan temple became an obstacle in the way of the VHP's propaganda of the Babri mosque having been built on the exact spot of Ram's birth. It was therefore first renamed as Sita Rasoi (Sita's kitchen) in 1991, and then finally demolished in July 1992, along with seven other old temples.

In 1857, the Babri Masjid was among several mosques that existed in Ayodhya. Graveyards spread in all directions as Muslims had come to revere Ayodhya as a sacred place for burial, and scores of cemeteries existed there. Devout Muslims in Ayodhya still recall with lament the legend that had a few more prophets been buried here it would have become as holy as Mecca itself. Significantly, Ayodhya is called 'Khurd Mecca' (mini Mecca) and 'Ayodhya Sharif' even now. But, notwithstanding the graveyards, Ayodhya was witnessing a Hindu-Ramanandi transformation of its landscape. It was being covered with temples, ashrams and dharamshalas. Many small-time Hindu chiefs, mainly from neighbouring regions, were building grand mansions that were used during annual pilgrimages.

Except for the construction of the Ram Chabutra at the site of the smaller platform which Hindus worshipped as the cradle of Ram during Tiefenthaler's visit in the 1760s, in the outer courtyard of the Babri Masjid, not much of note took place either at the masjid or at Hanumangarhi

---

[286]Ibid., pp. 2296–97.
[287]Carnegy, *Historical Sketch of Tahsil Fyzabad, District Fyzabad.*

between 1857–1858 and 1885.

In the rest of Ayodhya though, temples were being built at frenetic speed. Lala Sitaram, born in a well-established Kayasth family in Ayodhya in 1861, was Ayodhya's first modern historian who wrote at least two books on Ayodhya's history. He had grown up in an environment where the British were the supreme power, the nawabs had ceased to exist and the ideas of democracy and independence were still unborn. His book, *Ayodhya ka Itihas*, was first published in 1932 and, unsurprisingly, has nothing but words of praise for the British government. With regard to Ayodhya during their rule, Sitaram devotes a page that describes the transformation of Ram and his own birthplace.

> During the Muslim rule, Muslims were in a majority in Ayodhya. From Lakshman Ghat to Chakrateerth (two banks) on the Sarayu, many Muslim neighbourhoods came up and they still exist. During the rule of Awadh Nawabs, not only high Hindu officers, but kings from outside Awadh were also allowed to build temples in Ayodhya. With the advent of the British rule, Muslim influence diminished, and even though sometimes they are the cause of problems, largely, they have been reduced to penury and subsist through petty businesses.[288]

Sitaram credits the British for widening the narrow roads and making them 'pukka', for bringing the railway here and ensuring that all needs of pilgrims were taken care of. He adds, 'every day new temples come up in Ayodhya'. This is a common refrain still heard in Ayodhya today.

THE FATHER OF MODERN HINDI LITERATURE VISITS AYODHYA

In the summer of 1878, on the occasion of Ram Navami, or the day of Ram's return after exile, a special pilgrim got down at the newly built railway station of Ayodhya. The new station had been moved from the other side of the Sarayu to a site closer to Ayodhya. This station, which was built in 1874, has grown into a small hamlet in nearby Makkhapur village. Here, small mud houses stand where the platform once was, and old residents still point out its ticket window, the platform and an old wall, which continue to stand. The hamlet is fittingly now known as Tesaniya, a colloquial pronunciation of 'station'. After his visit, Bharatendu Harishchandra, the father of modern Hindi literature and theatre, described Ayodhya in what

---

[288]Lala Sitaram, *Ayodhya ka Itihas*, p. 136.

is considered to be the first-ever travelogue in Hindi. In a section titled 'Journey beyond Sarayu', Harishchandra, a well-heeled traveller, griped about the lack of drinking water at the stations on the way. He complained about the state of the hapless and overworked station staff who rebuked him when he asked for water, saying, 'Should we carry Dak [mail], light up the place, or give you water!' But thankful that he was in Ayodhya on Ram Navami, exhausted, he went to sleep and spent the next day in the company of the milling and sweaty crowds of pilgrims. At the time of his visit in 1878, it had been two decades since the revolt ended and the little development that Ayodhya had seen was in the form of a railway line meant to transport timber from the trans-Sarayu districts of Gonda and Basti. If there was any other visible development or improvement done at the behest of the British, it failed to impress him and is not mentioned in his short account of the day. He concluded his travelogue by saying that, 'the crowd is massive, the fair is poor and of unwashed hordes, people here are paupers'. Harishchandra correctly identified the adjective for the people of Awadh. The people, most of whom were farmers and farm labourers, had been reduced to penury and starvation after the annexation. Governor General Lord Canning's zeal to punish the peasantry for failing to support the British during the revolt had turned into the unchecked plunder and oppression of farmers and artisans.

Expensive goods made in England from Indian raw materials were being dumped back in the Indian market. As a result, domestic industries were destroyed, unemployment rose and when the weather gods failed in their duties—devastating droughts and deadly famines followed. The 1880 Famine Commission set up by the government concluded that the main reason for the widespread suffering was that the majority of people survived on agriculture. Awadh, which was called a 'nursery of fine soldiers' in early gazettes like the one by Walter Hamilton in 1828, was one of the most fertile provinces in India. In the decades after the revolt it grappled with food shortages and starvation deaths. Harishchandra's astute, if somewhat offensive, description of the people in the region of Ayodhya captures the suffering that an ordinary person went through on a daily basis. Between 1850 and 1875, 50 lakh people died and this figure trebled to 1.5 crore deaths between 1875 and 1900.

It was only the fast-growing pilgrim bazaar of Ayodhya that managed to escape the deprivations caused by droughts, famines and British taxation.

The annual fairs continued to be held and thousands of farmers from neighbouring districts continued to throng for a ritual dip in the Sarayu where they were administered rituals by the hundreds of pandas, or priests, who had come to dominate religious life.

As part of their administrative expansion, the British had deployed thousands of English soldiers as well as civilian officers. They had taken over the civil administration with the help of talukdars like the maharaja of Ayodhya. The British were running the courts, municipal boards, police services, revenue offices, hospitals, schools, railways and the dak. It was an unprecedented period of stability and peace, enforced by colonial rule. Ayodhya's religious bazaar was booming, as more pilgrims meant more business. Newer shrines meant more avenues to extract money from pilgrims, most of whom were poor farmers. By now, the Ram Chabutra or the small brick-mortar platform promoted by Ramanandi priests as Ram's birthplace at the Babri Masjid had become one of the most visited shrines in Ayodhya. Tiefenthaler[289] had noted the presence of a small platform which Hindus worshipped as the Bedi, or the Cradle. Since the middle of the eighteenth century, up to the conflagration in 1855, Hindus and Muslims seemed to have worshipped at the Bedi and the mosque respectively. Whether the Ram Chabutra was constructed over the spot where the Bedi existed is not known. Since 1855, and especially after the fall of the nawab's rule, the wall erected by the British had prevented any further encroachments by Hindus as well as any attempts by Muslims to remove the Ram Chabutra and the idols, etc., kept on it. However, with the gradual disempowerment of Muslims in the aftermath of 1857, Ramanandi Bairagis, driven by the promise of more donations, sought a legal way to expand their presence at the Ram Chabutra built outside the Babri Masjid.

BIRTH OF LEGAL DISPUTE OVER BABRI MASJID–RAM'S BIRTHPLACE
On 29 January 1885, Mahant Raghubar Das of the Janamsthan temple filed a civil suit in the court of Pandit Hari Kishan, district sub-judge of Faizabad. The relief asked for was to construct a temple over the aforementioned Chabutra which had charan paduka (feet impression) affixed to it. The prayer of Raghubar Das was that it would be a great comfort to pilgrims—who had to endure the harshness of the weather during the rains, the heat of summer and the cold of winter—if a building was built around the chabutra. He also claimed that as he owned the land, it was both his right

---

[289]According to Kunal Kishore, Tiefenthaler was the first person to mention the existence of the now demolished Babri mosque in Ayodhya.

and duty to take steps for the welfare of the pilgrims. As we have seen earlier, the defendant in the case was the muttawali of the Babri Masjid, Mohammad Asghar, who countered these claims by stating that Raghubar Das had no documentary proof of ownership of the said Chabutra and that the mosque was constructed by Emperor Babur. Mohammad Asghar's statement added that there was no Chabutra till 1856 and that it was built in 1857 and that Hindus had been allowed to worship there on the condition that no construction would be undertaken on it.

Pandit Hari Kishan, the sub-judge, rejected the plea of Raghubar Das and dismissed the suit. However, he acknowledged on the basis of gazettes mentioning the fact of the building of the Chabutra during the tumult of 1857,[290] that Hindus did own and possess the land of the Chabutra which was 17x21 feet, but as the Chabutra lay right outside the wall of the mosque, no construction of a Hindu orientation could be permitted in view of its potential for communal trouble.

This case also marks the very first time that the mahants of Ayodhya approached the court over matters of property. As we shall see later, in the twenty-first century there are hundreds of cases pending in various courts that pertain to land and property disputes in and around Ayodhya, some also involving murder and violence. The sacred land has also become very prized.

Undaunted by the dismissal of his suit, Mahant Raghubar Das filed an appeal against it in the court of F. E. A. Chamier, district judge, Faizabad, in March 1886. Chamier too dismissed the appeal after visiting the Babri Masjid on 17 March and included in his order a few words of sympathy for the claims of Mahant Raghubar Das of Janamsthan Mandir. He wrote, 'it is most unfortunate that a masjid should have been built on land specially held sacred by the Hindus, but as that event occurred 356 years ago, it is too late now to remedy the grievance. All that can be done is to maintain the parties in status quo.'[291]

Chamier also annulled his junior's order that the ownership and possession of the Chabutra was with the Hindus. In November that year, unsatisfied and unhappy that Chamier had deprived him of even the ownership and possession rights, Raghubar Das filed a second appeal against this in the higher court of Justice W. Young, judicial commissioner, Oudh.

---

[290]Carnegy, *A Historical Sketch of Tahsil Fyzabad, District Fyzabad.*.
[291]Sarvepalli Gopal, ed., *Anatomy of a Confrontation: Ayodhya and the Rise of Communal Politics in India*, New Delhi: Penguin Books India, 1991, p. 65.

But here too his appeal was crushed by Young who acknowledged the consistent efforts of Ramanandis to extend their various building activities. Young wrote, 'the Hindus seem to have got very limited rights of access to certain spots within the precincts adjoining the mosque and they have for a series of years been persistently trying to increase those rights and to erect buildings on two spots in the enclosure: (i) Sita ki Rasoi (ii) Ram Chandar ki Janam Bhumi'.[292]

Justice Young shared the wisdom and opinion of his judicial colleagues, Pandit Hari Kishan and Chamier. He found Raghubar Das's claims to be fit for dismissal.

A PREACHER'S TRYST WITH AYODHYA

By the late 1880s, Ayodhya had become a much bigger place of Hindu worship than it had ever been before. In addition to Darshan Singh's Mahadeo, or Shiva temple, which had existed there since 1845, the royal palace of his descendants was also being built. The shifting of their residence from nearby Shahganj was both symbolic and strategic. The fledgling dynasty hoped to benefit from the glory that the title of 'Lord of Ayodhya' bestowed. The British too were relieved to have a friendly ruling house for their administration of the districts that lay up north across the river, on the banks of the Sarayu. The annual religious fairs during the summer, monsoon and winter were drawing lakhs of devotees. Some pilgrims had even started using the railway to make the holy journey. Ayodhya had truly arrived as a pilgrimage site.

And all this while Faizabad, the site of much history and trouble for the British, had grown into a peaceful town, settling into the rhythm of the bazaar, the court and the cantonment. The British had come to enjoy a calm confidence about the stability of their new mode of administration which relied on the support of the talukdars and shunned any meddling with the lopsided and exploitative (for the peasant) status quo that existed between the peasantry and the landlords. One arena in which the British had been interfering, although cautiously, was religion. Churches that practised liberal tolerance towards other faiths had come into being since the time of the Mughals. With the horrors of the 1857 revolt now behind them, a new generation of British administrators were toying with the idea of providing a 'level playing field' for their Christian priesthood. The priests had

---

[292]Ibid., p. 66.

neither given up nor forgotten their role of 'saving' the barbaric Orientals from themselves. In fact, the Methodist and Wesleyan churches were already running several schools for boys and girls in towns like Banaras, Lucknow and even Faizabad. And it is through the accounts of the life of such a missionary that we are able to gather significant details about Ayodhya and Faizabad in the 1880s and 1890s.

In 1883, Joseph Alexander Elliot was posted to Faizabad, against his wishes, from Banaras where it had only been six months since he had settled in with his wife, Miss Shipham. Banaras being the 'strongest citadel of Hinduism', the missionary couple was quite aggrieved at having to leave the city.

Once in Faizabad, the India-born Irishman set about revitalizing his dwindling parish which was faring badly both in terms of followers and infrastructure. Padre Elliott set about working the official machinery and 'after many letters, and interviews with officials, and much weary waiting',[293] he managed to find a piece of land suitable for both preaching to Indians as well as his Anglo-Saxon coreligionists.

Being an ambitious man, Padre Elliott now set his sights on acquiring a spot in the middle of the Faizabad chowk (the centre of public life, usually situated in the main bazaar) from where he could preach. The importance of the chowk is best told in the priest's own words:

> The Chauk, in an Indian city, especially in the afternoons and at nights, presents a unique side of Indian life, and I felt that to get a preaching-place in that great quadrangle of the city of Faizabad was worth almost more to me than even a chapel in the city, because a chapel for some time would be very hard to fill, and then certain classes of natives would, from caste and religious prejudice, never enter it, whereas in the open air, from this iron pulpit, I should be able to catch and draw all classes.[294]

So, Elliott walked into the office of the chairman of the municipal board, and asked for a level playing field in religious preaching:

> ...in this city the Hindus have scores of temples and shrines on the thoroughfares, and so also the Mohammedans have their mosques, but

---

[293]A. W. Newboult, ed., *Padri Elliott of Faizabad: A Memorial*, London: Charles H. Kelly, 1906, p. 16.
[294]Ibid., p. 18.

we Christians, who are also a part of the community and pay our share
of the taxes, have not a yard of land nor any place of worship to call our
own. The request I want to place before you is a very modest one indeed.
All I ask for is a circle of land four feet in diameter nothing more.[295]

The chairman willingly agreed to this 'modest request'. But when the priest
told him that he wanted this preaching circle in the middle of the Faizabad
chowk, the 'chairman jumped as if a dynamite cartridge had exploded under
his chair'. Gradually, Elliott calmed the chairman down and laid out for him
a list of arguments that were to be used to convince the municipal board to
agree to this 'impossible' idea. The chairman, mentioned in Elliot's account
as only a certain 'Rai Sahib', was impressed by the arguments and asked the
pastor to send him a written application. He also told him to 'put in the
pathetic touches about the poor Christians who haven't a yard of land, and
no place of worship in this famous city...'[296]

The padre had offered to a shocked Rai Sahib certain ruses that he
was quite sure would be accepted by the municipal board, comprised as
it was of members who, in one way or another, owed their status to the
favour of the British government. A long account of the meeting is present
in the padre's memoirs but here it should suffice to say that after a long
animated discussion with the municipal board, the Rai Sahib assured the
members that even if the circle was denied to Padre Elliott nothing would
stop the Irishman in him from standing 'at the foot of the steps in front of
the great mosque of the city, on the west side of the Chauk', and preaching
from there. He then asked them dramatically, 'what will you Mohammedans
then say? And supposing he goes and stands in front of the Hindu temple,
and does the same there, then what will you Hindu gentlemen say? You
may complain, but you cannot do anything.'[297] According to the chairman,
the padre's case was a fait accompli, and the only solution was to give him
what he wanted. The padre was given his circle on which he built his
pulpit and started preaching every Monday and Friday.[298]

As mentioned earlier, the Elliotts were upset when the padre had been

---

[295]Ibid.

[296]Ibid., p. 19.

[297]Ibid., p. 24.

[298]The pulpit, which was flanked by two small water fountains, no longer exists. It was
demolished in the 1970s to 'make space'. Today, snack vendors do brisk business selling
their wares.

transferred to Faizabad from Banaras, the 'citadel of Hinduism'. They had expected to contribute to the cause of evangelization by bringing many idol-worshipping Hindus into the fold of Christianity in one of the most sacred places of the Hindu religion. Padre Elliott had expected the going to be easier in Faizabad and Ayodhya, but he was in for a rude surprise. He was born and brought up in British India and therefore had no problem in conversing with the natives, but no amount of friendly, alluring and persistent persuasion dented the faith of Hindus, as he found out in the most sought-after settings—the melas of Ayodhya. At mela-time Elliott and his staff pitched tents and lived and worked among the thousands of Hindu devotees who came there seeking both divine favour and a break from their work. Elliott wrote, 'The preaching occupied three hours at least in the morning and three in the evening. Numbers always came to the tent, and had private conversation with us regarding Christ and Christianity. Of a few we were hopeful.'[299] But despite spending massive amounts of money and deploying a large number of preaching staff at the melas, where close to 300,000 to 400,000 Hindus converged on Ayodhya, he met with little 'conversional' success. The padre, with practically unlimited resources at his disposal, arranged for tents, female staff, food and drink facilities, Hindi teachers and free literature. But nothing would entice the devout Hindu and the padre's earnest efforts came to naught on most occasions. Elliott recorded his failure after one such mela:

It makes one intensely sad to contemplate the small result following the amount of labour and money we put into these melas. Each mela costs about Rs. 35, and last November we threw sixteen preachers, four local preachers, and eight zanana teachers for work among the women, into it, and yet we get no visible results. It is one of the grandest opportunities we have in the whole year for addressing large and mixed Hindu audiences, and yet so little comes of it.[300]

Elliott then, quite understandably given his lack of understanding of Hinduism, blamed the Hindus for their rejection of Christ:

A ring of two or three hundred Hindus stood round us, silently observing the whole form of service, and amazed at its wonderful simplicity: no drums, no bells, no conch-shells, and, above all, no idol

---

[299]Newboult, ed., *Padri Elliott of Faizabad*, p. 267.
[300]Ibid. p. 267–68.

as a central object of worship! They could not take it in... Nothing less than a mighty outpouring of God's Spirit will convince this people of sin. They know not what sin really is; they have no true conception of it; hence they know not what true, real repentance is and salvation i.e. deliverance from the guilt, condemnation, and power of sin. Mukti (the Hindus' salvation) takes none of these things into consideration. The preacher has yet to come, another John the Baptist.[301]

In Ayodhya at least, Christianity could scarcely make a dent. Unlike in Faizabad, where the padre had been a little more successful, Ayodhya turned out to be another impregnable citadel of Hinduism. Even if Padre Elliott was disappointed by his failure to induce Hindus to embrace Christianity, he had the satisfaction of knowing that it was not from a lack of effort. Sometimes, these preaching campaigns took these brave missionaries to the doorsteps of the imposing temple of Hanumangarhi. Recounted in his memoirs, leavened with missionary humour, is one such episode which is reproduced here.

A PREACHER OUTSMARTS A HANUMANPUTRA

There existed, and to some extent still does, a category of monks among celibate Ramanandi Bairagis who fashion themselves after Hanuman, the monkey-god and Ram's war-winning general and deputy. They called themselves Hanumanputra, or the sons of Hanuman. Well-built, owing to their daily regimen of physical exercise, and besmeared with ashes, they carried themselves with an attitude of haughty human-monkeys. Padre Elliott witnessed an encounter between one such Hanumanputra and an open-air Christian preacher which ended with the former retreating thoroughly awed. It is important to reproduce it here at length as it shows that during the British Raj, a Christian preacher could not only give sermons at the foot of Hanumangarhi, the citadel of Hinduism in Ayodhya, but the public also approved of the ensuing duel of words and wit that finally ended in the preacher's victory. Elliott writes:

An old Baptist preacher Mr. McCumby, now dead, and a prince of Hindi out-door preachers was, on one occasion, preaching near the great Hanuman Garh temple, when one of these offsprings of

[301]Ibid.

Hanuman, a great, big, fat fellow besmeared with ashes, adorned with a cord of thick rope round his loins and his false hair done up in massive coils on his head, came up, with a great amount of 'side' and bombast, and ordered us off from his holy temple gates, and made himself a nuisance generally. We smiled; McCumby was a consummate master in debate, and knew the Ramayan as few of them did. He soon engaged the holy man clothed in ashes and a rope in conversation, and got a considerable amount of fun out of him for the crowd by cross-questioning. Finally he said, 'Come here, my son.' The man came up to him, looking rather defiant, and we all wondered what was going to happen next. 'Who are you?' inquired Mr. McCumby, 'I am a hanumanputra,' said the man, swelling his chest with pride. Mr. McCumby stepped up to his side, and, passing his hand slowly down his back, opened his eyes in mock astonishment, and exclaimed, '*Arre, laluwa ka punch nahin!*' (I say, the dear boy has lost his tail!). The effect on the crowd you can imagine. We had no more trouble from him.[302]

McCumby, whose knowledge of Hindi and the Hindu religion inspired awe in Padre Elliott, later died of cholera which he contracted in Ayodhya.

PLAGUE IN AYODHYA–FAIZABAD (1896–1897)

'The plague has at last come to Faizabad and Ajudhiya, apparently to stay. The death-rate has steadily risen. Panic has laid hold of the people, all classes of whom are flying in every direction, often leaving their dying and dead for the authorities to dispose of in any way they please,'[303] Padre Elliott recounts in his memoirs after a visit to Ayodhya during the plague epidemic in 1896. It was a special trip as he was accompanied by 'Rev. Gregory Mantle, Padri, Missionary, and Globe-trotter', who had 'arrived with all his luggage and a camera'.[304] Though a self-professed rationalist, Padre Elliott found himself playing the role of an ordinary panda while showing Mantle the different aspects of the temple town. On the way to Ayodhya in a horse cart, Elliott, 'filled in the intervals by magnifying the greatness and sacredness of the holy Ajudhiya till Mr. Gregory Mantle began to feel what he would have lost by missing

---

[302]Ibid., pp. 266–67.
[303]Ibid., p. 256.
[304]Ibid., p. 260.

a visit to it'.[305] Later, in a mocking tone, Elliott would enumerate in his memoirs the advantages that a visit to Ayodhya begets the visitor; he wrote:

> By this one visit Mr. Gregory Mantle purchased the salvation of all his ancestors. Through paying the fare for us both going there, he was assigned a passport to heaven with all his sons.... The mere sight of Ajudhiya absolves from all trivial sins, but a visit to it atones for the most heinous. The waters of its sacred river, the Sarju (Ghogra), wash away all sin.[306]

Mantle and Elliott visited Ayodhya in the wake of a particularly deadly bout of plague that had killed both devotees and priests. Upon entering Ayodhya, the padre and Mantle, his globetrotting guest, countenanced the effects of the deadly epidemic. They 'found the city empty and desolate of human beings, but the monkeys were all there. The people had fled, deserting their temples and gods. Indeed we found many of the temples closed. The priests were simply inconsolable.'[307]

Elliott and his companion found that the priests suspected the government's hand in bringing the plague to Ayodhya. The priests were despondent, they lamented to Elliott that 'they had done their best and tried everything, but the gods were immovable, and the people shamefully wicked to thus desert the place'.[308]

But, according to Elliott, the priests were being deceitful because when the plague had first broken out, 'the temples and shrines did a roaring trade'.[309] Prayer was no cure for plague. Ayodhya's population of '20,000 went down to 5,000'. By the time of Elliott's latest visit, 'there were hardly 4,000 left'.

Before bidding farewell to Mantle, Padre Elliott also took him on a quick 'plague-tour' of Faizabad's neighbourhoods. 'What most strongly impressed him,' writes Elliott about his guest, 'almost to awe, was the number of plague-stricken, deserted houses. In Reedganj nearly all the houses were forsaken, and across the doors where death had entered was printed on paper: "This is not to be opened or entered without orders," and on the

---

[305]Ibid., p. 262.
[306]Ibid., pp. 262–64.
[307]Ibid., p. 264.
[308]Ibid.
[309]Ibid., p. 259.

outside walls of other closed and forsaken houses was the blood-red sign of a rude cross.'[310]

Padre Elliott's accounts of Ayodhya and Faizabad are rare and invaluable as they illuminate the life in these twin towns in the late nineteenth and early twentieth centuries. His visits to Ayodhya are unique because hardly any other contemporary account of the place survives. Elliott's memoirs cannot be called objective, coloured and shaped as they were by his own racial and religious prejudice, but they do contain an outsider's perspective which is hard to come by, more so in Ayodhya's case. They portray a town breathing, dreaming, living and performing the Ramayana and its characters.

Before we return to the administration of Ayodhya's melas and to Ayodhya, it is worth learning about Padre Elliott's curious encounter with a woman seeking shelter in the ashram of a mahant.

PADRE ELLIOTT MEETS A DESTITUTE WIDOW

While taking Gregory Mantle around Ayodhya, the padre had decided to make one last stop. He had made several friends in the mahant community of Ayodhya and so he dropped by at the ashram of one such mahant. Elliott does not name the mahant; perhaps, all mahants and all of Ayodhya meant the same to him, one was representative of all and all were representative of one. Upon entering the monastery, the padre was greeted by the sight of a 'fine-looking, well-favoured, dignified little woman, apparently about twenty-one years of age',[311] sitting with the mahant. The padre in his ignorance had assumed that in Ayodhya, all Hindu mahants and their orders are celibate, so he disapprovingly enquired about the lady's presence. 'What's this, mahant... This is a new departure. I have always known you and your order as a brotherhood; whence, then, this daughter of virtue in fakir garb? Is this going to be a mixed order of yours in future?'

The mahant calmly told Elliott that in his order, marriage was in fact allowed. And the woman, Jamna Bai, was both an orphan and a widow. Her entire family had perished in a recent cholera outbreak.[312] She reached Ayodhya hoping for refuge in one of the temples, and after making acquaintance with a fakir of his order, whose skill was lying on a bed of nails, had come to the ashram of the mahant where she hoped to

---

[310]Ibid., p. 280.

[311]Ibid., p. 269.

[312]WHO: Cholera is an acute diarrhoeal disease that can kill within hours if left untreated.

stay and remain chaste and immersed in religion. The inquisitive padre, his curiosity aroused even more, now directly addressed Jamna Bai, 'tell me how you, a lone woman, came here for rest and shelter, and what keeps you here; and then I will tell you who I am, what my religion is, and how I and the Mahant became friends'. The lady fixed her stare on the two white men and answered, 'All that the *babaji* says is true. I am a Brahmani. I was betrothed when a child, and when a girl of eleven or twelve my *gowna* [marriage ceremony in which the bride is sent to the groom's house] took place. My husband was a bad, wicked man; he was very unkind to me. I used to come back and stay at my parents' house for months at a time. I had a son born to me when I was fifteen. My father died then; and in the year following my husband, my child, and my mother. They all died of cholera. Many in our village died that year of this awful *maran* [deadly disease]. I was left sorrow-stricken, broken-hearted, and forsaken. I was in a perilous position, because I was good-looking, young, and a woman. I was not brought up to work in the fields, labour I never did, beyond house work. My parents were gone, I had no protector, and I could not beg. I put in two awful years, fighting against temptations and evil men. I found I could only save and maintain my virtue and my womanhood by adopting the garb and life of a *sadhni*, which, after my slender means had run out, I did. But as there are no monasteries for women, I found shelter first in one temple and then in another; but the wickedness and evil intentions of priests and devotees, as well as of rich and well-to-do Hindus who came as worshippers, drove me from temple to temple, and I found them all equally bad. O sir! Men are wicked.'[313]

Jamna Bai had faced sexual advances from priests and devotees alike. She had fended them all off and now was sharing her agony with a benign-looking Christian padre who offered her assurance that 'not all men' were wicked. 'Well, I don't know about you white men, but the *kala admi*, the Hindus, they are all bad, sir, and the temples are the worst shelters on earth for a young, well-favoured woman. God only knows how I have had to resist and fight my way through,' she retorted, her eyes 'flashing fire'.[314]

In this very common story of harassment and ostracization of a 'family-less' woman in India there was one unexpected aspect: her absolute disgust with the educated Indian of the late nineteenth century. Elliott records it

---

[313] *Padri Elliott of Faizabad*, p. 273–74.
[314] Ibid., p. 274.

in detail. 'With a contemptuous toss of her head and a cynical curl of her lips, she clenched her fist tight and brought it down bang on her knee, exclaiming, "And the worst men are the educated men; the most unmitigated scoundrel of them all is the man educated in your English schools."'[315]

Jamna Bai may have hated 'brown sahibs' but she was courteous enough to enquire from the padre about his religion. He was only too happy to oblige. Counting and spreading the virtues of Christianity was after all his profession. The padre laid out for her the full spread of the gospel: that it teaches 'That all men and women are sinners alike' and that 'He [Jesus] wants to save you, and this [mahant], and all Ajudhiya. You talk about finding rest for your feet and your worn spirit, but oh daughter of virtue, you know nothing yet of the true rest and peace. All you have found is a worldly shelter from evil men. True rest and peace you will only find when you repent and turn in loving trust to Him and say, "Take me as I am".'[316]

His sermon delivered, the padre turned to his friend the mahant for approval, who was only too willing to provide it, 'Your's is a beautiful and true religion,' he reassured Elliott.[317] Jamna Bai, a broken soul, was hooked; in the padre's religion she saw her own salvation. She showed a keen interest in what it would entail if she were to become a disciple. The padre and his friend parted from the mahant and Jamna Bai, with her promising to visit him soon. The mahant happily agreeing that she would be better off with the padre than with him.

FAMINES, PLAGUES, MALARIA, MASS DEATHS AND BRITISH DENIAL

Between 1890 and 1900, nearly one million Indians died of plague while many more millions died of starvation. *The Lancet*, a reputed British medical journal, through its Indian special correspondent, concluded in its May 1901 issue that in the previous decade India's population had declined considerably. Though the journal considered a reduced birth rate to be one of the causes it concluded that, 'its influence cannot have been very great'. According to the journal, 'An enhanced mortality must be the chief factor. It is estimated that there were 20,000,000 more deaths than there should have been under ordinary circumstances, and if we put 1,000,000 deaths down to plague there remain 19,000,000 which can be attributed with

---

[315]Ibid.
[316]Ibid., pp. 276–77.
[317]Ibid., p. 277.

some reason either to actual starvation or to the diseases arising therefrom.'[318]

Ten million deaths from plague and nineteen million from starvation as an underlying reason, and yet the British were unwilling to accept that it was their rule and policies of taxation in India, and particularly in Awadh, that had caused such a large number of needless deaths.

Ayodhya, being chiefly a town of monks and mendicants, fared much better but most of the countryside reeled under bouts of plague, malaria and famines. The extent of British denial can be seen from the official correspondence between Sir Antony Macdonnell, lieutenant governor of the North-Western Provinces and Oudh, and William Digby, a writer, humanitarian and politician. Digby, the author of *Prosperous' British India*, quotes Macdonnell blaming the farmers and their customs for their plight, as we shall see soon. Unafraid to take digs at his government, he begins his book by saying, 'With the Hope, That the Facts herein recorded may lead to the amelioration of the condition of Many Millions of British Subjects who, on, every New Year's Day, enter upon a period which is certain, for their country as a whole, to be worse than the years already past.'[319]

S. S. Thorburn, a retired settlement officer who had studied peasants and their issues closely in the Punjab, had come to conclusions that directly indicted British rule for the depredations of the Indian farmer. Digby quotes Thorburn as follows: 'There was no general indebtedness in any village before 1871. Seasonal vicissitudes and the beginnings of debt stand in direct relationship one with the other. Indebtedness for small or careless holders begins with grain advances for food.'[320] He pointed out that the main reasons for indebtedness were:

(1) Fluctuation in yields;
(2) Loss of cattle—both usually consequences of seasonal vicissitudes;
(3) The morcellement [division of land or property into small portions] of holdings from the growth of the agricultural population without increase in certain production for each holder and his family; and
(4) The obligation, under the fixity principle, to pay land revenue, whether there be produce or not, where from to pay it.[321]

---

[318]William Digby, *'Prosperous' British India: A Revelarion from Official Records*, London: T. Fisher Unwin, 1901, pp. 137–38.

[319]Ibid., p. ix.

[320]Ibid., p. 325.

[321]Ibid.

The last reason—to pay land revenue tax whether there had been a good harvest or bad—led to rapid indebtedness of the peasantry as well as of the general population. Moneylenders who gained through bad harvests by providing loans also gained through good ones by having their loans repaid with added interest. Thorburn, after studying more than 700 farmers, noted that, permitting 'the profits of husbandry to pass to moneylenders is an intolerable revolution of an odious kind never yet known in India'.[322] He also found that only thirteen of the 742 peasant farmers recovered their freedom from moneylenders.

Sir Antony Macdonnell was much loved by the talukdars and shared their view that the poor are to be blamed for their poverty. Macdonnell was also the chairman of the Famine Commission that was constituted after the famine of 1897. But his view remained totally disconnected from the reality of peasant life in India. Macdonnell ascribed the deaths and the generally poor state of Indians to their 'recklessness in expenditure on festivals, and to the ruinous rates of interest he pays for loans'; he blamed the 'precariousness of the climate', the 'minute subdivision of holdings owing to the concentration of the people in the most fertile regions and their unwillingness to move to fresh lands only a short way off; and the insufficient facilities for irrigation'.[323] If blaming the farmer for their woes sounds familiar in contemporary India, it only underscores the largely unchanged feudal nature of the Indian state.

AYODHYA'S MELAS: MINEFIELDS OF DISEASES AND DEATH

Ayodhya is situated in one of the most fertile regions of north India. Fed by Himalayan rivers, its plains are well suited for year-long cultivation. Even today, the region remains agriculturally rich and is much contested over.[324] In the late nineteenth century an average farmer had next to no access to Awadh's natural wealth and resources. Crippled by British taxation and rapacious moneylenders, the peasant of Awadh found himself turning more and more to religion. Starved bodies with weak immunity were easy prey for malaria mosquitoes that flourished in the hastily built irrigation canals. Not a year passed without outbreaks of malaria, which was a disease of

---

[322]Ibid.
[323]Ibid., p. 323.
[324]Virendra Singh Rawat, 'UP govt to copy EC format to resolve 700,000 pending land dispute cases', *Business Standard*, 28 December 2017.

recent origin. Fever was common and became a chronic symptom in many villages. When villagers converged on Ayodhya during the annual fairs, they were sitting ducks for superstition and magical remedies. They sought refuge and remedy in god and godly cures.

The melas put a lot of pressure on the civic infrastructure of Ayodhya and a 'pilgrim tax' was thought of as a fair arrangement for its better administration. Pilgrim taxes were not popular though. In 1870, when half an anna (1 anna=1/16 of a rupee) was imposed at Ayodhya, the practice had to be suspended in the face of strong opposition by the town's prominent temples. It was altogether removed in 1875 by the maharaja of Balrampur[325] (Ayodhya's ruling house was then under the widow of Man Singh, while his daughter's son, the heir, was still a minor).

It was not until the 1900s that the Faizabad municipality decided to levy a tax on all visitors to Ayodhya. This time too, it was met with stiff opposition. The mendicants and ascetics, many of whom had taken eccentric vows, joined the protest. Historian Katherine Prior's study of taxation at pilgrim towns reveals that, 'Mendicants, many of whom had taken vows not to touch metal, were often troubled by pilgrim taxes and had to rely upon the charity of other pilgrims to get them through the toll barriers.'[326] These men of god still had it easy compared to the poverty-stricken farmers, thousands of whom could not pay the tax and participate in the mela. Barred from entering, they were often forced to perform their rituals and ablutions on the other bank of the Sarayu. A Municipal Taxation Committee formed in 1909 to review the tax concluded that pilgrims were harassed by the entry-tax at pilgrim centres like Ayodhya. It said, 'We had unanimous evidence of the strongest description from all the witnesses in Fyzabad, to the effect that thousands of pilgrims have been compelled, during the bathing fairs of the past year, to remain on the other side of the river.'[327]

Even those who had the money to pay to enter Ayodhya found the collection methods unnecessarily tedious and time-consuming. Gone were the days when they could leisurely go about their religio-entertainment tour. Now they had to haggle with temporary tax collectors who used the opportunity to extort whatever money they could from the gullible

---

[325]Katherine Prior, 'The British administration of Hinduism in North India, 1780–1900', Ph.D. diss., Cambridge: St Catherine's College, Cambridge University, 1990.
[326]Ibid., p. 232.
[327]Ibid., p. 233.

and illiterate public. The crowds and the waiting time at the collection points disturbed their experience of the mela. Unsurprisingly, this system of tax collection was dubbed 'unwieldy, costly and unjust' by the Municipal Taxation Committee of Faizabad in 1909.[328]

There is ample evidence to believe that the then maharaja of Ayodhya, Sir Kunwar Pratap Narayan Singh Mishra (KSCI), played a role in the subsequent improvements that followed in the administration of the annual melas. The maharaja was a personal friend of Lieutenant Governor Antony Macdonnell, and earlier, during the plague outbreak in the North-Western Provinces and Oude in the 1890s, had worked with a committee of prominent talukdars that tweaked the plague regulations to suit the upper-caste sensibilities of the Hindus. Besides the maharaja, other members of the 1890 committee were Raja Sir Muhammad Amir Hasan Khan, Rana Sir Shankar Bakhsh Singh, Nawab Agha Mehdi Hussain Khan, Nawab Mumtaz-ud-daula Faiyaz Ali Khan of Pasahu, Raja Tilsaddiq Rasul Khan, Raja Jagmohan Singh, Raja Jai Kishan Das, the Honourable Babu Sri Ram Rai Bahadur and Chaudhri Nasrat Ali. The committee's job was to temper some of the invasive regulations relating to plague control. For caste-conscious Hindus, the government's preventive measures like seizure of corpses, invasion of homes, segregation of patients[329] in special plague hospitals, and handling of women patients 'were worse than the disease itself'.[330] Most Hindus believed that worse than a case of plague in the family was the humiliation that followed 'from the implementation of the plague rules'.[331]

Though plague and plague control was a much bigger concern in more established pilgrim centres like Allahabad, Mathura and Haridwar, Ayodhya as a provincial pilgrimage site also received similar treatment. After the narrowly self-serving inputs of the 'respectable natives' like the king of Ayodhya and other talukdars, the plight of the poor Hindu remained largely unchanged. They were still being segregated in special hospitals and their huts burnt to the ground. The rich Hindus on the other hand were allowed the privilege of being segregated at home, and since they had the money, they could also 'erect hospitals for the exclusive use of one caste or sect'.[332] Thus with the intervention of the notables, led by the then maharaja of Ayodhya, native

---

[328]Ibid., p. 230.
[329]Ibid.
[330]Ibid., p. 217.
[331]Ibid.
[332]Ibid., p. 218.

elites won for themselves the same rights as Europeans afflicted by the plague. One change that had to be made for both rich and poor Hindus was regarding rules for women patients. Under the new rules, it was mandated that only female doctors could demand to examine women.

THE LODGING HOUSE ACT AND AYODHYA'S BLOOMING 'TEMPLE' INDUSTRY

Neither cholera nor plague outbreaks, smallpox, dysentery nor diarrhoea, nor even famines deterred pilgrims from undertaking insufferable journeys to Ayodhya to perform their religious duties. At least thrice a year, Ayodhya turned into a giant sea of humanity.

There was Ram Navami in summer, the Jhula or swing festival during August and the Kartik mela in the winter months. These melas drew hundreds of thousands of farmers who were on their seasonal breaks from sowing and harvesting. A majority of the visitors stayed in the open grounds and fields, but thousands of them also stayed in mandirs and ashrams, or temples and hermitages that were essentially lodging houses, with a crucial difference—they catered mainly to pilgrims.

When such a great number of people assembled in such unsanitary and unhygienic conditions, diseases were bound to spread. Between 1907 and 1913, nearly 600 people died from cholera alone in Faizabad and Ayodhya. In Banaras during this period more than 1,000 people perished. Significantly, in Haridwar, though a bigger place of pilgrimage than Ayodhya, the number of deaths was considerably less owing to the enforcement of sanitary and other regulations.[333]

The British emphasized sanitation, hygiene, methodical plans and execution. Their civic sense was outraged by the filth and excreta that defined pilgrim spots. On 24 August 1912, the British set up a three-member committee to find lasting solutions to the problem of annual outbreaks of cholera and plague 'at centres where Hindu and Muhammadan pilgrims congregate to worship'[334] in the United Provinces (a conglomeration of erstwhile kingdoms like Awadh, Banaras, Balrampur etc.)

Unaware pilgrims became carriers of disease when they travelled back to their homes. Railways had reduced travel time, but had also increased the chances of the spread of contagious diseases like cholera and plague.

---

[333]Report of the Pilgrim Committee—United Provinces, 1913.
[334]Ibid., p. 1.

The backdrop against which the committee was appointed at the suggestion of the British government was the severe and continuous outbreak of diseases, and the reasoning 'that large gatherings of pilgrims are responsible for much of the spread of infectious diseases in India'.[335] The committee was headed by Major J. C. Robertson, a sanitary commissioner with the government, and its three members were Lieutenant Colonel S. A. Harris, sanitary commissioner, United Provinces; G. F. Adams, an officer of the Indian Civil Service; and the lone Indian—Thakur Prithipal Singh, talukdar of Surajpur, Barabanki. In the winter months of 1912–1913, the committee toured many pilgrimage centres and fairs in the United Provinces. Besides the Hindu melas it also covered Muslim fairs like Makan in Kanpur and Pirankaliar near Roorki.[336] After the tour, the committee's report reinforced the view that large religious gatherings were responsible for the spread of diseases.

In Ayodhya's case the report of the committee found that the three annual fairs held there were responsible for the origin and intensification of cholera outbreaks in its surrounding districts. The committee's report covered the whole range of issues pertaining to pilgrimages, from the starting point of the journey to the issue of carriage vans used for pilgrims (usually goods trains were used for pilgrims who were stuffed inside carriages without much air, and no water or toilets). The old goods carriages (some of them are still in use today) had doors built towards the centre and during journeys, there was a constant struggle to get as close as possible to the only source of fresh air. One can't help but compare the scene with Holocaust images of Jews being transported like cattle to concentration camps. But that's where the similarity ends. Here, lakhs of mainly Hindu pilgrims were packed worse than animals, that too after paying for a ticket. When they reached their destination, they had to pay for entry to the holy place wherein awaited their village or family priests. Lodging at places like Ayodhya was another serious concern for the British government. To ensure that homes and lodging houses followed certain basic norms of sanitation and to regulate them, the Lodging House Act, 1882 and the earlier Sarais Act, 1867 had been put in place. But their enforcement was lax and many lodging houses in Ayodhya had managed to evade the rules under the guise of being temples. In the first assessment of its kind, the report noted that,

[335]Ibid., p. 2.
[336]Ibid.

'the keepers of the houses where pilgrims are put up are generally priests, and whatever fee or payment the pilgrim gives is called an offering in the name of religion, and not a consideration, direct or indirect, for lodging'.[337]

The report found that the pilgrims were supportive of the housekeeper in this, and 'prefer to do as the priests' [who was also the housekeeper in most cases] wish rather than tell an unpalatable truth in the Courts'.[338]

The committee, after thorough enquiries, came to the conclusion that 50 per cent of Ayodhya's houses 'are said to be used as lodging-houses' but were not licensed under either the Municipalities Act, 1900 or the Lodging House Act, 1882.[339] The reluctance to get their establishments licensed or registered for free stemmed from fear of government intrusion and scrutiny.

It is certain that if a similar committee of enquiry is constituted today, its findings wouldn't be very different, at least in Ayodhya. Although the management of crowds during fairs has improved, the stench of thousands of pilgrims defecating in the open for want of adequate latrines lingers in Ayodhya for days. Dysentry and bowel complaints remain as chronic a problem in Ayodhya's fairs today as they were a hundred years ago.

In fact the report's two-page note on Ayodhya sums up all the issues that have remained unresolved since then. Any visitor to Ayodhya cannot but remark on the pathetic state of its civic infrastructure—be it water supply, lack of a drainage system, unpaved lanes, dilapidated buildings, latrines, trenching, lodging houses or inadequate railway arrangements.

The report indicts Ayodhya as a 'pilgrim centre' with a 'long standing reputation as a distributor of cholera in these provinces and probably were information available, it would be found that it was spreading diseases everywhere throughout India'.

Among the Pilgrim Committee's most important recommendations for Ayodhya, the following are noteworthy for the fact that these recommendations remain valid and and are still not addressed.

The committee recommended:

- Creation of a water supply system for Faizabad–Ayodhya (cost: Rs 3,50,000) [$1,155,000],
- building a drainage system and paving lanes (cost: Rs 2,50,000) [$825,000],

---

[337]Ibid., p. 8.
[338]Ibid., p. 9.
[339]Ibid.

- erecting water-flushed latrines (cost: Rs 1,20,000) [$396,000], and
- building an Infectious Diseases Hospital (cost: Rs 24,000) [$79,200].[340]

British efficiency and priority was anything if not self-servingly shortsighted. Out of the four recommendations, the only one that was followed up was the hospital for infectious diseases. The other issues, though diminished to a certain extent, still remain the main concerns of voters and politicians alike. As we shall see later, Ayodhya's municipal budget now stands in crores of rupees. In 1913, the most expensive suggestion was creating a water-supply system at Rs 3,50,000, an amount which today is less than even the lowest budget heads marked 'protocol' and 'miscellaneous'. But in terms of civic infrastructure, Ayodhya is far behind in meeting the demands of increasing urbanization.

As the British grappled with widespread disease and death, there was also growing discontent among the peasants over unjust taxes and oppression by the talukdars. Before World War I, the talukdars had been illegally ejecting and extorting taxes and cesses from peasants at their will and pleasure. The greed of the talukdar had no limits and often his agents arrived to ask for a nazrana (an offering of cash or kind) soon after the death of a tenant. This was illegal under the Oudh Rent Act, but being a law unto themselves, the talukdars used the death of the tenant to evict his family from the land and replace them with one who was willing to pay a higher rent.

This brutal practice came to be known as 'Murdafaroshi' or the selling of corpses. The practice of nazrana or making gifts was a hangover from the nawabi time. It was what the revenue collectors paid to the ministers at the court to obtain rights to more lands. In the colonial period this practice was resorted to by talukdars to extort more money from their tenants by the threat of eviction. Typically, the rent-lease was for seven years but often the talukdars would demand a higher nazrana in return for letting the peasant-tenant remain on the land. Even in such cases some talukdars, in order to extract more money, transferred the land to a different peasant to demand a larger nazrana. This reduced some tenants to such desperation that they were forced to sell their daughters to older men looking for young brides. Among Hindus, the sale of daughters, or Kanya Vikray, is a crime punished with eternal hell. But impoverished peasants chose hell in the afterlife for the chance to survive by giving higher nazranas to continue cultivating their land.

---

[340]All amounts in dollars calculated based on currency valuation in 1947. No prior records of the Indian rupee's valuation exist. Ref: 'Busting the myth: Re 1 was not equal to $1 in 1947', *Money Control*, 16 August 2017.

Not satisfied with illegal nazranas and taxes, some landlords demanded additional cesses in the name of buying new cars, elephants, horses and even gramophones. The peasant had been reduced to a wish-fulfilling beast for the talukdars, who also collected taxes in the name of certain holy days and festivals. An instance was recorded of a landlord collecting 'dust-tax' for having to traverse dusty roads while touring his estates.[341]

Another source of strife which had not much to do with resentment against the British was the increasing assertion by so-called low-caste peasants who aspired to higher status within the Hindu caste system. Ayodhya was to become the centre of both these new movements in the 1920s. The last noteworthy development was the re-emergence of the centuries-old dispute between the socially liberal Ramanandis and the more orthodox Ramanujis. As we shall see in the following sections, Ayodhya became the stage where these intersecting movements played out.

AN AYODHYA-CENTRIC PEASANT AGITATION AGAINST TALUKDAR– BRITISH OPPRESSION

It is widely believed that in parts of the United Provinces, the peasant agitation of the 1920s had its roots in the mobilization of farmers by the Indian National Congress. However, the farmers of Awadh had also organized themselves under the leadership of a Fiji-returned indentured labourer. Baba Ramchandra was born in a poor Brahmin family in the Maratha kingdom of Gwalior in 1864. His birth name was Shridhar Balwant Jodhpurkar, which he changed to Ramchandra when enlisting for labour in Fiji. Ramchandra spent eleven years in Fiji (1905–1916), starting out as a plantation worker and gradually rising to the post of chief butler in a British business family's household. Towards the end of his time there, Ramchandra had started advocating for better facilities and more rights for Indian indentured labourers. During this period, he had been using the daily and sometimes weekly recital of Tulsidas's *Ramcharitmanas* to attract followers. When his arrest became imminent in Fiji, he fled to India and came to Banaras where he started working as a guard. Some time later, he claimed to have been instructed in a dream to quit working and go to Ayodhya to spread the word of the Ramayana. Ramchandra promptly gave up his job and moved to Kasaipur village about 100 kilometres from Ayodhya. There

---

[341]Leanne Bennett, *The Origins of the Peasant Agitation in Oudh: The Awakening of the Peasants*, Montreal: Concordia University, 1997.

began Ramchandra's political and social journey as a Ramayana-reciting leader of farmers. His notes, which are now preserved in Delhi's Nehru Memorial Museum and Library, reveal that every day after a light breakfast, he used to tie a voluminous copy of the Ramayana to his back and head out to do the rounds of neighbouring villages, returning home by nightfall. The austere and eccentric Ramayana-reciter had learnt some important lessons from his struggle in the Fiji islands. He had a macro picture of the British empire and its Raj in India. The time spent in Fiji had also exposed him to the importance of uniting both farmers and Hindus. Thus Ramchandra, working as a subaltern monk-cum-farmer mobilizer, stressed the role of peasants in creating awareness among themselves. Ramchandra, besides using couplets from Tulsidas's *Ramcharitmanas*, also deployed an idiom of the working class. He called the British empire a machine. He listed its components as: raja, maharaja, talukdar, mahajan, manager, district collector, patwari, village head, village guards, police, commissioner, governor and the head of all of them—the viceroy.

In 1917, the Awadh Kisan Sabha was formed under his leadership along with a few other notables of the region like Gaurishankar Mishra. Baba Ramchandra blamed talukdars and the British for the condition of the peasants. Like many others, he disparaged the talukdars as former criminals and traitors. Ramchandra's arrival in 1916 in Awadh coincided with World War I, which had begun two years earlier. The talukdars, to show their loyalty to the British crown, had liberally provided financial support by mercilessly extracting ladai chanda, or war tax, from their poor tenant-cultivators. Curiously, the Ayodhya maharaja's name doesn't feature in the list of talukdars who contributed to the war effort. But going by the other names from Faizabad, it is clear that it was the peasant who was paying for the glory of the British crown as well as for the talukdars' currying favour with the British governor in Allahabad, which was the new capital of United Provinces. Farmers were also lured to enlist in the army with the promise of waiving their rent as long as a family member was in military service.

This was the agrarian backdrop against which Baba Ramchandra had started mobilizing peasants against unjust taxation and eviction. He had tried to harmonize relations between the farmer and the talukdar but soon gave up that path because of the stubborn intransigence of the landowners. Now, he encouraged farmers to stop paying taxes and providing free labour. He egged them on to demand more rights over their lands, including the right to sink wells and dig tanks for irrigation of their fields.

'AYODHYA CHALO'

Besides uniting the peasants under the banner of the Awadh Kisan Sabha, Baba Ramchandra also has to his credit the still widely prevalent usage of the greeting 'Sitaram'. In his patchy notes, Ramchandra mentions that when he first moved to Kasaipur, it was the Urdu 'Salaam' that was used universally as a form of greeting. Gyan Pandey, in a brilliant essay on the peasant agitation of the 1920s, notes, 'as the movement developed, and his own popularity increased, it was enough for Ramchandra to raise the slogan "Sita Ram": the cry was promptly taken up in one village after another, and thus in a remarkably short space of time thousands would assemble to see him and hear his discourse'.[342]

Ramchandra wanted to forge a wider unity among the peasants of Awadh, and to do so he relied on the Ramayana-centric world of the people, most of whom were Hindu. He chose Ayodhya as the venue for a large farmers' meeting. Conducting a reconnaissance for a suitable spot from the top of the Hanumangarhi temple, Ramchandra wondered about the logistics required for accommodating thousands of people for a two-day-farmers' convention. On 21 and 22 December, in front of a lakh-strong congregation of the province's farmers, Ramchandra appeared in shackles tied to his neck, hands and feet. The symbolism of the farmer being chained was quickly grasped and spread to other areas very soon. The Congress, which had joined hands with Ramchandra's Awadh Kisan Sabha, too hoped to benefit from the mass strength of farmers.

GANDHIJI IN FAIZABAD

The December meeting of Awadh's farmers had come close on the heels of the launch of the anti-British Non-Cooperation Movement started under the leadership of South Africa-returned Mohandas Karamchand Gandhi. He had sounded the bugle of a non-violent movement in which Indians fighting for self-rule were boycotting foreign-made goods across the country. The December meeting in Ayodhya was the first meeting of the Awadh Kisan Sabha and had been wildly successful in terms of the turnout. Though it had ended peacefully, some farmers had understood the call of putting an end to atrocities by landlords as a call to direct action and

---

[342]Gyan Pandey, 'Peasant revolt and Indian nationalism: the peasant movement in Awadh, 1919–1922' in Ranajit Guha ed., *Subaltern Studies I: Writings on South Asian History and Society*, Delhi: Oxford University Press, 1982, p. 169.

had resorted to burning establishments owned by moneylenders in various towns of Awadh.

The farmer, for the first time since 1857, had burst onto the national scene with vengeance. But vengeance of a new nationalist and patronizing kind awaited them in the form of Gandhi's speech in Faizabad. Instead of offering them support, he chastised them announcing, 'You, the peasants should bear a little if the zamindar torments you. We do not want to fight the zamindars...[they] are also slaves and we do not want to trouble them.'[343]

A year after this denouncement by Gandhi, a farmers' protest turned violent again. On 5 February 1922, about 170 kilometres from Ayodhya, at the small village of Chauri Chaura, the police fired shots at a protesting crowd, killing three or four people. In retaliation, the mob burnt down the police station with at least twenty policemen inside. Following this, Gandhi called off the Non-Cooperation Movement on 7 February. Thousands of young Indians were enraged by Gandhi's unilateral withdrawal from the movement precisely when it was gathering momentum. Feeling betrayed, some of them like Ashfaqulla Khan and Ramprasad Bismil (both from the United Provinces) and others took to armed militancy against the British. The famous Kakori Train Robbery in 1925 was planned by these two men under the auspices of the Hindustan Republican Association. The young and inexperienced revolutionaries were no match for the organization and reach of the colonial government who deployed Scotland Yard to probe the case involving the loot of Rs 8,000. Nearly forty people were arrested from different parts of north and east India. Thirteen of them were convicted and given long jail sentences. Ashfaqulla Khan and Ramprasad Bismil were given the death sentence. On 19 December 1927, Khan was hanged in Faizabad central jail and Bismil in a jail in Gorakhpur. Every year on that day, a group of citizens mark their revolutionary sacrifice in Faizabad central jail.

The Kisan Sabha of Baba Ramchandra or the armed resistance of the likes of Ashfaqulla and Ramprasad did not fit into either Gandhi's or the Congress's scheme of how to carry on the national independence movement. The Congress party was an organization comprised largely of urban elites and rich landlords. To them, farmers were nothing more than a mass of people called to attend meetings, their numbers adding to the pressure created on the colonial government by the sophisticated oratory of Congress leaders. Baba Ramchandra was soon sidelined (permanently)

---

[343]Ibid., p. 153.

by the co-option of the peasant agitation by elite Congress leaders. Gandhi and the Congress wanted farmers moulded in their own ideas of non-violence and class hierarchy. They thought peasants could only be led, and not lead, not even in movements for their own freedom from oppressive taxes and talukdars' atrocities.

CASTE REFORMS AND SECTARIAN STRIFE IN AYODHYA

The farmers neither expected support nor did they receive any from the British and their allies, the talukdars. On the other hand, the jati reform samitis or caste reform committees relied heavily on British official literature for arguing their case for higher status in the Hindu caste hierarchy. This phenomenon thrived in Ayodhya, the geocultural hub of Ram-centric Vaishnavism in most of north India. Ayodhya was to become the centre of both these new movements in the 1920s. Interwoven with caste-reform movements was the intra-sectarian strife within Ramanandis and Ramanujis, the two Vaishnava sects.

In Ayodhya, the sectarian rift between the socially liberal Ramanandis and the puritan Ramanujis widened in the wake of a visit by Anantacharya, a Ramanuji mahant from the Totadri peeth in Tamil Nadu. The holy man refused to bow down to the idols of the deities in the Kanak Bhavan and Bara Sthan temples. He refused to drink the charanamrit (water with which the feet of the deity have been washed) at these temples and also avoided eating together with Ayodhya's Ramanandis.

These developments were brewing almost simultaneously in Ayodhya and it is almost impossible to understand them in isolation, although at first glance there weren't many similarities berween the peasant agitation, caste reform and the Ramanandi–Ramanuji conflict. At the same time, the different players shared much in common and their lives intersected at the common channels of the British government. Ayodhya's symbolism as a mobilizing platform for the province's Hindus and Muslims had been ably displayed by the Ramayana-reciting Baba Ramchandra. He used Ayodhya's mythical appeal as the capital of the just and kind Lord Ram to create unity among the various peasant classes.

The caste reform movements also relied greatly on the legitimizing power of Ram and Ayodhya. By tracing their origins to the Ramayana or other Vaishnava tropes, the Kurmis, Yadavas, Koeris and others sought to enhance their status in Hindu society. The castes of India were being categorized in utilitarian British writing as 'depressed', 'respectable', 'martial', 'criminal', 'priestly-knowledgeable' and 'untouchable'. In 1817, Francis Buchanan in his survey of the castes and communities of eastern India, had included communities from whom the upper-castes or the twice-born Dwijas were allowed 'to take water'. These communities were the Kayastha, Koiri, Kurmi, Kahar, Goala, Dhanuk (archers, palanquin bearers), Halwai (confectioner), Mali (gardener and vegetable-grower), Barai (betel-vine grower and seller) Sonar, Kandu (grain-parcher) and Gareri (goatherd). In 1894, the Kurmis were labelled as a 'depressed community', which barred them from entering the police service. A government forest official, Ramadin Sinha, resigned in protest. This was followed by a campaign of letters to the government urging it to rescind the label of 'depressed community'. In 1896, the government gave in to the campaign in another communiqué which said that 'his Honour [the governor] is...of the opinion that Kurmis constitute a respectable community which he would be reluctant to exclude from Government service'. This is how Kurmis became the first peasant community to organize themselves in order to win a Kshatriya identity for themselves.[344]

In their campaign for Ksathriyahood, caste reform leaders juxtaposed ancient glory with present disgrace; apparently, there had been a slow degradation of their community over centuries. Two clear prerequisites emerged from the movement for creating a new Kshatriya identity: a sympathetic theological patron who would certify the genealogical claims of descent from Lord Ram or Lord Krishna, and an identity that was based on the Vaishnava ideals of purity of food and drink.

William Pinch notes that 'the lives of Ramchandra and Krishna were frequently held up by jati reformers as the standard for morally correct attitudes and behaviour even at the risk of criticizing contemporary Vaishnava institutions'.[345]

Thus, extravagant temple rituals and weddings were criticized and members of the community encouraged to curtail their expenditure so that the money thus saved could be used for 'the betterment of the jati as a whole'.[346]

In Ayodhya, the Ramanandi Akharas, by now well established, were also going through what can be called a process of sectarian maturation.

---

[344]William R. Pinch, *Peasants and Monks in British India*, p. 55.
[345]Ibid., p. 58.
[346]Ibid.

Ayodhya had become a centre of the Ramanandi sect in Awadh, eastern Uttar Pradesh and bordering districts of Bihar. The Rasiks, or the followers of the subsect of Rasik Sampraday ('Sweet Devotion' to God), had become very influential, their Krishna bhakti-inspired motifs and traditions of 'love for God' firmly established in the temples of Kanak Bhavan, Bara Sthan and Laxman Qila. The Nagas of Hanumangarhi as well as the Tyagis had come to create their own spheres of influence in the region. But the age-old question of commensal relations and the debate over Ramanuja and Ramananda had still not been settled. It was about to re-emerge soon and jati reform movements were about to get involved in it.

The question of status within the Ramanandi Sampraday had been a matter of dispute since the time of the Galta conference in 1713. Two hundred years later, much had changed—the Shaiva Gosain armies were disbanded and many Shaiva monks had dissolved into the growing Vaishnava ascetic community of Nagas and Tyagis; the rule of the nawabs and peshwas had ended; and most significantly, British rule had enabled Indians to view themselves in a new manner.

The ideals of Vaishnavism, based on purity and morality, and of the Ramanandis of Ayodhya, based on the socially liberal philosophy of Ramanand, had acquired the approval and sanction of the Christian rulers. But within the sect itself, the question of equality had never been decisively settled. Also left unsettled was the question of Ramanand's own descent—whether he was a spiritual descendant of Ramanauj or whether he was forced to form his own sect because he had been excommunicated for breaking the rules of commensality.

All these matters came to the fore in Ayodhya against the backdrop of Baba Ramchandra's peasant agitation and the pathetic state of India's masses, who were plagued by a continuous outbreak of deadly diseases across most of north and central India. The religious life—which was practically all life in Ayodhya—was dominated by Ramanandi centres such as Laxman Qila, Kanak Bhavan, Bara Sthan and the Hanumangarhi temple. There were other temples and akharas but they looked to these temples for guidance in sectarian matters. A small Ramanuji enclave also thrived (which exists till today) near Vibhishan Kund (pond), situated at some distance from the Ramanandi centres.

CLASH OVER COMMENSALITY

Almost two centuries after the Vaishnava revival began in Ayodhya, the sectarian fault line over equal status arose once again. The trigger for it was the 1918–1919 visit of Anantachari. As we have seen, owing to his own sense of superior Shri Vaishnava lineage, Anantachari neither bowed to the deities in Kanak Bhavan and Bara Sthan nor did he drink the holy charanamrit. He gave sermons denigrating the Ramanandis and refused to share meals with the leading Ramanandis of Ayodhya of that time.

His actions incensed the Ramanandi community to such an extent that some of them threw away their kanthis (a necklace made of tulsi or basil plants worn by Ramanandis). Soon after Anantachari's visit, there came another Shri Vaishnava-Ramanuji saint from the Vatakalai temple in Mysore. Though he accepted the charanamrit and paid obeisance at Kanak Bhavan and Bara Sthan, he too, refused to eat with the Ramanandis.

The third immediate cause for Ramanandi resentment was Balramchari, a South Indian Sanskrit teacher who refused to teach pupils who were not 'branded with the Sri-Vaishana Ramanuji markings of a disc and conch'.[347] The Ramanandi tattoos were a bow and arrow. This particular teacher also gave sermons in which he asserted the greatness of Ramanuji mantras over Ramanandi mantras of initiation.

Against this repeated humiliation by the Ramanujis, a meeting of Ramanandis was called at the Hanumangarhi by Bhagavadacharya, a priest of the Bara Sthan temple, a Rasik centre of Ayodhya. At this meeting, Shri Ramanandi Vaishnava Mahamandal, an organization to bring together the Ramanandis was founded with the support of Sitaram Das, the mahant of Hanumangarhi, and Ramdas, the mahant of Barabhai Dariyam tyagis.[348]

Bhagavadacharya (who called the meeting) was an orphan whose caste origin is unclear.[349] His claim of being a Brahmin was dismissed by his opponents who claimed he was of low caste. Before he came to Ayodhya, Bhagavadacharya, unlike most other Ramanandis, had studied English, and later, the commentary on the Vedas by Dayanand Saraswati in Calcutta. His knowledge of theology as well as English served to fuel his 'unlimited' ambition and resolution. Now, with the help of the recently formed Shri Ramanandi Vaishnava Mahamandal, he set about writing a new genealogy of Ramanand. The new genealogy, which contained no link with Ramanuja,

---

[347]Peter van der Veer, *Gods on Earth: The Management of Religious Experience and Identity in a North Indian Pilgrimage Centre*, New York: Bloomsbury Academic, 1988, p. 103.
[348]Ibid.
[349]Ibid.

was then conveniently 'found' by another Ramanandi monk as he was flipping through a book bought in Ayodhya.

Armed with this new genealogy, Bhagavadacharya invited the Ramanujis to a shastharth (debate on religious interpretation)[350] during the kumbh at Ujjain in 1921. Meanwhile, according to Peter van der Veer, a Dutch anthropologist whose work on Ayodhya is considered pioneering, Bhagavadacharya had recoursed to writing and publishing fake Ramanuji books which contained derogatory references to Ram. Van der Veer writes that Bhagavadacharya had 'already created a suitable atmosphere for the split between Ramanujis and Ramanandis by publishing books under the name of Ramanujis in which devotion to Ram and the Ram mantra were ridiculed'.[351]

During the Ujjain Kumbh of 1921, the stage was set for an open debate in Sanskrit between the Ramanujis and Ramanandis. Bhagavadacharya, having acquired the reputation of a defender of Ramanandi pride, was also confident of emerging the victor, as the jury of the contest was composed of sympathetic mahants belonging to Ramanandi akharas.

Unsurprisingly, the Ramanuji faction lost and the Ramanandis declared themselves independent of the Ramanuji Shri Vaishnavas.

But contrary to expectations, Bhagavadacharya and other rebel Ramanandis, though successful in giving Ramanandis a proud identity, were not able to bring about any dramatic transformation in sectarian relations back home in Ayodhya. In the course of his study in the 1980s, Veer found that 'during the 1920s and 1930s there were regular discussions in Ayodhya between the two parties and the topic is still an emotional one'. The topic has lost much of its importance now but has by no means disappeared. Caste concerns among the Ramanandis have only gone underground, camouflaged by poltical correctness.

To understand this in full detail, reproduced below is an account of caste dynamics captured by van der Veer. It traces the experience of one Lakshmandas, a Ramanandi mahant, whom Veer interviewed in the 1980s.

Veer's interviewee was Lakshmandas, whose story follows the pattern of many Ramanandi mahants', as I have found out in my research for this book.[352] Born in UP in a Brahmin family, he was brought to Ayodhya by a

---

[350]Ibid.

[351]Ibid., p. 104.

[352]Interview with Mahant Gyan Das, Hanumangarhi, Ayodhya.

Ramanuji preacher who also became his guru. The guru was a householder, and Lakshmandas studied Sanskrit and philosophy till the age of twenty.

In 1943, nearly two decades after the Ujjain Kumbh in which the Ramanandis declared themselves a separate sect over commensal relations with Ramanujis, Lakshmandas experienced Ramanuji discrimination first-hand. He recounted to van der Veer that until then he had never eaten nor drunk at his guru's house. However, one time when he was very thirsty, he asked his guru for some water. Lakshmandas was a Ramanandi in his beliefs, and the guru knew that. According to the story narrated by Lakshmandas, his 'guru gave him a water pot, but when he came outside and walked to the well he saw that it was the pot used when going to the latrine, which was never cleaned. The guru knew that he was of high caste birth, but since he was a Ramanandi he thought him so low that he did not give him the brass water pot normally used for guests.'[353]

After this humiliation, Lakshmandas left his guru and found a Ramanandi teacher to continue learning Sanskrit. Van der Veer interviewed Lakshmandas in the 1980s, nearly four decades after this incident, and found Lakshmandas, a strict Brahmin sadhu, still rankled by the memory of it. Veer deduced from this encounter that 'even a sadhu of high caste (such as Lakshmandas) was seen by Ramanujis as inferior, simply because he belonged to the Ramanandi community'.

However, the possibility that van der Veer leaves out of his anthropological study is that Ramanandis were traditionally considered to belong to the lower non-Brahmin castes, and Lakshmandas was perhaps not a high-caste Brahmin and as his guru knew that, he could not have given him the same pot that was used in his kitchen.

BHAGAVADACHARYA: A RAMANANDI REBEL

Prior to the debate at the Ujjain Kumbh in 1921, Bhagavadacharya, like a proverbial rebel, had first defeated Ramanoharprasad, the mahant of Bara Sthan, who was also his guru, in a debate that took place in Hanumangarhi in 1919. His guru, being more conservative, had disagreed with his disciple's public disavowal of Ramanuj and had challenged him to a debate. Bhagavadacharya won that debate but was thrown out of Bara Sthan. He had subsequently won Ramanandi independence from Ramanujis.

But not all Ramanandis shared Bhagavadacharya and his supporters'

---

[353]Veer, *Gods on Earth*, p. 105.

angst against Ramanuji discrimination. In fact, one of them, Swami Dharnidharacharya, 'was so impressed with the philosophical and moral discourses' of Anantachari, the Ramanuji Totadri leader who had incensed others like Bhagavadacharya, that Dharnidharacharya became his disciple and was given the name of Dharnidhar Ramanujdas.

It is worth recounting Dharnidharacharya's story as it is narrated in *Shri Awadhavamshiya Kshatriya Martandah,* which traced the origin of those who claimed descent from Lord Ram. The booklet is no longer in circulation and is not available in the few bookstores that line Ayodhya's main street.

In the wake of the visit of the south India Ramanuji leader, radical Ramanandis hardened their position under Bhagavadacharya's leadership. The 1921 Ujjain Kumbh and the Ramanandi triumph over Ramanujis over the question of guru-lineage had riled the hearts of many like Dharnidharacharya in Ayodhya. With meticulous effort the Ramanandis had conjured up a new genealogy of Ramanand from which Ramanuja was completely omitted. The response of Dharnidharacharya, himself a Sanskrit scholar of repute, consisted of marshalling other antiquated and ancient textual evidence, predating perhaps the documents put forth by his rivals. He cited as proof of Ramanuj's precedence over Ramanand, Sanskrit hymns composed by ancient seers (rishis) well before the advent of either Ramanand or Ramanuja. The texts put forth by him 'shared in common the prediction that the four main divisions of Vaishnava sampraday or chatuh sampraday would be founded by Vishnuswami, Madhavacharya, Ramanujacharya, and Nimbarakacharya'.[354]

All these assertions proved futile in halting the Ramanandi takeover of Ayodhya. Disappointed and embittered by defeat, Dharnidharacharya left for a long pilgrimage across the subcontinent hoping to put some time and distance between him and the happenings at Ayodhya.

In 1924, he returned to Ayodhya and settled in Uttar Totadri Math situated in the then serene setting of Vibhishan's pond. From thereon Dharnidhar Ramanujdas or Dharnidharacharya would become famous for his scholarship as Swami Dharnidharacharya. His return home was in a way also a return to his own Varma-Kshatriya roots. He would soon attract the attention of reformist Kshatriya ideologues belonging to communities such as the Kurmis and Kushvahas. By 1930, Dharnidharacharya had published the history of Bihar-kurmis who called themselves Awadh Vamshiya Kshatriyas.

Summing up, Ramanuji espousal of reformist Kshatriya movements

---

[354]Ibid.

didn't mean that Ramanandis opposed caste reform. It only signals to their socially liberal, and therefore, more indifferent attitude to caste matters; after all, it was the Ramanandis' core beliefs around caste that had led to the split in Ujjain. Pinch notes, 'not only was an institutionalised Vaishnava discourse inherent in the dialogue of social change, certain Vaishnava monks were willing and able to act as intellectuals on behalf of agricultural and artisan communities'.

Caste reform movements sprang up across India in the last and first decades of the nineteenth and twentieth centuries respectively. They were all rooted and expressed in Vaishnava mores of dignity of labour and the Vaishnava idea of a 'personal god'. By linking their origins to the dynastic genealogies of Lord Ram and Krishna, who are asserted to be historical figures as well as gods, the Kshatriya reform movements both gained from and gave legitimacy to Ayodhya as the centre of the Vaishnava-Kshatriya universe. In the early twentieth century the endorsement of Kshatriya reform allowed the caste-conscious, vanquished Ramanujis a degree of political and intellectual expression besides a chance to remain relevant in an overwhelmingly Ramanandi Ayodhya.

William Pinch concludes in his study, 'the ideological need for a birthplace of Ramchandra can also be understood as symptomatic of the historiography of Kshatriya ancestries grounded in a Vaishnava discourse. In other words, at some point claims of genealogical descent from God demand the physical presence of the remains of God.' Thus, it is persistently stated by those who believe in Ram's historicity, 'if Ayodhya exists, then the birthplace where Ram was born must be located within it'.

While in Ayodhya, the Ramanandis and Ramanujis were engaged in their own Sampraday matters over caste rules and lineage, the nationalists of the country had been dwelling on issues such as self-rule, equal rights to employment and British oppression. Whether they were of Gandhi's non-violent kind or of Ashfaqulla and Ramprasad's revolutionary breed, India was gradually waking up to demand its freedom from the imperial government. Also awakening—and helped by the British-filtered view of their own history—were Hindu and Muslim communalists. They, of course, thought of themselves not as communalists but nationalists. A methodical rewriting of the subcontinent's history emerged as the master narrative, subsuming within it the individual, and often much more nuanced, Hindu–Muslim narratives.[355] In the decades to come, Ayodhya would begin to emerge as the actual place where 'God was born as Ramchandra'.[356]

PARTITION, COMMUNALISM AND THE BRITISH

Although the rift between the fringe elements of Hindus and Muslims was not a British creation, the diffusion of communal hatred in colonial India was aided and abetted by British policy and practice. The conflicts over Hindi and Urdu, cow slaughter, and later, separate electorates, suited the British, as in their assessment these would prevent the repetition of the 1857 revolt and help them maintain their stranglehold on India. They had never really forgotten the lessons from the revolt and it continued to shape their policies, ultimately resulting in the partition of the subcontinent on religious lines.

Unlike Banaras and Kanpur, two major cities of the United Provinces, Ayodhya experienced very little communal violence in the decades after 1857 and until 1934, when a major conflagration over cow slaughter took place across towns in Awadh and UP. The last violent conflict over a place of worship in Ayodhya was the 1855 Hanumangarhi conflict. In 1934, it was once again the Bairagis of Hanumangarhi who attacked the Babri Masjid over rumours of cow slaughter in a nearby village. But this time, the colonial police took prompt action, chased off the Bairagis and later imposed fines on the Hindus of Ayodhya to pay for repairs to the damaged domes of the mosque. The bricks used in the repair work were made in a kiln that was owned by the family of Haji Mehboob, a prominent Muslim landlord in Ayodhya and a vocal opponent of the VHP.

Two years later in 1936, the British governor of the United Provinces enacted the Muslim Waqf Act. The Babri Masjid and the surrounding graveyard were recorded as the property of the Sunni Central Waqf Board. The Ram Chabutra, which had been erected after 1855, continued to remain open to worship by Hindus. Soon after, Shias alleged that the mosque was a Shia property erected by Mir Baqi, a Shia in the service of Emperor Babur. The claim was investigated and dismissed and the Babri Masjid was declared a Sunni Waqf property in the official gazette of February 1944.

---

[355]Gyan Pandey, *The Construction of Communalism in North India*, New Delhi: Oxford University Press, 1990.
[356]Gyanendra Pandey, 'Modes of history writing: new Hindu history of Ayodhya', *Economic and Political Weekly* Vol. 29, No. 25 18 June 1994, pp. 1523–28.

No objection to this was raised by either the mahants of the adjacent Janamsthan temple or by the Bairagis of Hanumangarhi who had attacked the mosque in 1934. But the Shia Central Board went to court against this order in 1945. Their claim was again dismissed in an open court on 23 March 1946 by Faizabad's civil judge, Akhtar Ahsan. (In 2017, the UP Shia Waqf Board petitioned the Supreme Court of India challenging this order. Their appeal remained pending at the time of writing this book.)

The same day that the Shia claim was dismissed in 1946, the Cabinet Mission arrived in Bombay to devise an early settlement of India's independence. The mission comprised three cabinet ministers of the British government—Lord Pethick-Lawrence, Sir Stafford Cripps and A.V. Alexander. Their task was to get both the Congress and the Muslim League to agree to the plan of a united India with states grouped together on religious and cultural lines. But with the Congress opposed to any such grouping of states and the Muslim League adamant on separate states for Muslims, the Cabinet Mission failed miserably in its task.

The Muslim League raised the threat of Hindu domination if the separate state of Pakistan was not granted to Muslims and declared 16 August 1946 as Direct Action Day. Bengal, the only province where the Muslim League was in power, witnessed large-scale riots. The worst of them took place in Calcutta, its capital, and the massacre of Hindus and Muslims that took place there is now remembered as the 'Great Calcutta Killings'. In its wake, the possibility of a united India died too, and the secular elements in the Congress, including Jawaharlal Nehru, were to remain helpless observers as communal frenzy engulfed large parts of western, northern and eastern India.

If communal frenzy in the lead up to Partition had spared Ayodhya it was because the Muslim population had dwindled considerably since 1857. Over the last hundred years it had slowly transformed into a Ramanandi centre. Its graveyards, though still existing, were not used as much as before. By the time of Independence in 1947, Ayodhya's Ramanandi takeover was absolute. Ramanandi Vaishnavism had originated and survived through its ability to assimilate and co-opt the 'good practices' of other sects and religions, be it the socially liberal approach towards caste or the replication of the akhara system of Shaivas. After the subsectarian dispute between Ramanujis and Ramanandis was over, the Ramanandis had all but muddled the distinction between themselves and the self-acclaimed 'purer' Ramanujis. Following the lead of Bhagavadacharya, other Ramanandis too had started affixing 'acharya' after their names. Their largest temple, the Hanumangarhi, was firmly established and attracted the highest number of pilgrims. The Ram Chabutra outside the Babri Masjid, believed to mark the exact place of Ram's birth, also drew a large number of pilgrims, as did other Rasik centres like Kanak Bhavan and Dashrath Mahal or the Bara Sthan. A string of temples like Kaushalya Bhavan and the Janamsthan Mandir (located near the Babri Masjid) also fell on the pilgrim's path but were in no way a match for the Hanumangarhi or even the temple of Devkali, the reigning goddess of Ayodhya. The Ramanujis were confined to the edge of the sacred boundary of Ayodhya at Vibhishan Kund. Asharfi Bhavan, Uttar Totadri Peeth, Shri Venkatesh temple and a temple built by a Rana queen of Nepal were some of the Ramanuji establishments that formed the community. The boundary remains marked by the temple of Mattgajendra (Mangenda in the local dialect).

BOOK II

Chapter 8

INDEPENDENCE AND ITS AFTERMATH

When India became independent on 15 August 1947, Ayodhya witnessed nothing out of the ordinary. In Faizabad, Congress leaders made perfunctory speeches, the tricolour was hoisted and the day came to an end. Later in 1947, some Bairagis and members of the Hindu Mahasabha, the Hindu counterpart of the Muslim League, gathered in Ayodhya and vowed to capture the Babri Masjid by force. The mahant of Hanumangarhi, Sitaram Das, and others also tried to impose restrictions on Muslims offering namaz in the mosque.[357]

Amidst this communalized atmosphere, the chief minister of the United Provinces, Congress's Govind Ballabh Pant, a masterful tactician and a known sympathizer of the communal Hindu Mahasabha, changed the official Congress candidate at the last minute in the June 1948 by-election for the Faizabad seat. This had become necessary to defeat the socialist leader Acharya Narendra Dev, Pant's rival and someone who enjoyed Nehru's confidence more than Pant. Narendra Dev was the leader of the Congress Socialist Party, which had remained in the Congress as a separate faction since its formation in 1934.

In 1948, Narendra Dev had resigned along with thirteen other legislators of his party, thus necessitating by-elections. Pant, who had become chief minister through fortunate circumstances, now needed to prove once again that he was in control of the Congress in UP. The candidate that Pant nominated for the Faizabad seat was Baba Raghav Das, a Gandhian sadhu from Deoria in eastern UP. Das led a communally vitriolic campaign against Narendra Dev, who was a local as well as a socialist leader of national stature. He received substantial support from student volunteers who 'were

---

[357]Krishna Jha and Dhirendra Jha, *Ayodhya: The Dark Night: The Secret History of Rama's Appearance in Babri Masjid*, New Delhi: HarperCollins India, 2012.

a mainstay of his campaign to retain his assembly seat'. Caste-based parties played (and still play) a key role in elections in Uttar Pradesh, and Ayodhya–Faizabad was also subject to their influence. The Kayastha Party had thrown its weight behind Pant's candidate, Baba Raghav Das. Following the age-old dictum of 'the enemy of my enemy is my friend', the Khattri Party lent its support to Narendra Dev despite his leftist leanings and the fact that he had alienated many people by his public atheism and lack of regard for the overt religiosity of the Bairagis and Hindu Mahasabhaites.[358] Baba Raghav Das and his backer, Pant, campaigned extensively in Ayodhya and Faizabad. Pant made full use of the religious zeal of the people of Ayodhya and the lack of it in Narendra Dev, even pointing out that Dev, though a Hindu, did not follow certain religious practices. Besides attacking Narendra Dev for his socialist leanings, Baba Raghav Das's campaign also appealed to orthodox Hindus by distributing tulsi leaves.[359]

The polling took place in June and the results were announced a month later in July 1948. Acharya Narendra Dev lost by 1,000 or so votes to Baba Raghav Das. This was the first time that Ayodhya's religiosity was harnessed in a democratic election.

COMMUNALISM ON THE RISE

Authors Dhirendra Jha and Krishna Jha, in their meticulously researched book, *Ayodhya: The Dark Night,* note the importance of the Ayodhya victory for Hindu communalists, especially the Hindu Mahasabha. They write that the victory 'had set a useful precedent for the Hindu Mahasabha and had shown militant Hindu communalists that gains could be achieved by exploiting religious sensibilities for popular mobilisation in Ayodhya'.[360] The Hindu Mahasabha would never be able to make a mark in electoral politics but this victory had signalled that communalists had a powerful sympathizer in G. B. Pant, the UP chief minister, and this realization would spur them to conceive of another plan to capture the Babri Masjid. However, in July 1948, the Hindu Mahasabha was banned and its leaders imprisoned following Mahatma Gandhi's assassination and their suspected role in it. It is not known if Gandhi's last words, 'Hai Ram', had moved them enough to

---

[358]Ibid., p. 183.
[359]Harold. A Gould, *Grass Roots Politics in India: Century of Political Evolution in Faizabad District*, London: Oxford & IBH Publishing Co. Pvt. Ltd., 1995.
[360]Jha and Jha, *Ayodhya: The Dark Night*, p. 44.

regret their role, if any. But their dedication to 'free' the holy places of Ram (Ayodhya), Shiva (Banaras) and Krishna (Mathura) remained undiminished. One of the Hindu Mahasabha leaders, the head of the Gorakshpeeth in Gorakhpur, Mahant Digvijay Nath,[361] charged up by the victory of Mahasabha-backed Baba Raghav Das in Ayodhya, emerging from jail in September 1948 in Delhi, said:

> I am fully convinced that no government can kill Hindu feeling... the recent by-elections to the UP Legislative Assembly have clearly demonstrated how deep is the Hindu feeling engrained in the masses; so much so that to win the elections the Congress leaders had to appeal to the Hindu feeling of the voters. I, therefore, call upon all the Hindus of the province not to lose heart. It is through trial and tribulations that success is achieved...[362]

Less than a year later in June 1949, the ban on the Hindu Mahasabha was lifted. Two months later the Mahasabha renewed its commitment to the restoration of Hindu places of worship. In its resolution dated 14 August 1949, the Mahasabha used the government decision to rebuild the Somnatha temple in Gujarat as an example to be emulated. The resolution said:

> The meeting endorsed the demand of the All India Working Committee of the Hindu Mahasabha for the restoration of the temples of Shri Vishwanathji at Kashi, Shri Ram Janma Bhumi at Ayodhya and Shri Krishna Mandir at Mathura which were converted into mosques in the Mughal times and the remains of which are still there.
>
> This meeting reminds the government that the same policy in respect of these temples should be pursued as has been pursued by the central government in the restoration and erection of the temple of Shri Somnath in Saurashtra.[363]

Pursuant to this resolution the Mahasabha scaled up its mobilization of Bairagis and the general Hindu public in Ayodhya. In 1949, its local leaders had formed the All India Ramayan Mahasabha in Ayodhya and under

---

[361]In 2017, the mahant/head of the Gorakshpeeth, Adityanath, was sworn in as the chief minister of Uttar Pradesh.

[362]Jha and Jha, *Ayodhya: The Dark Night*, p. 44.

[363]Ibid., p. 47.

its aegis, in October 1949, they organized a nine-day recital of Tulsidas's *Ramcharitmanas* in Hanumangarhi. The recital was attended by a massive gathering of white-clad Ramanandis, lay devotees, Mahant Digvijay Nath, Swami Karpatriji, its UP president, Baba Raghav Das, Hindu Mahasabha's local leaders—Ramchandra Paramhans of the Digambar Akhara, Gopal Singh Visharad and a little-known activist, Abhiram Das, of Nirvani Akhara, Hanumangarhi.

On the ninth day, after the recital had ended, the Hindu Mahasabha leader Mahant Digvijay Nath and others addressed a public meeting in which they announced the plan for a similar recital to be held a month later. This was to be held at the Ram Chabutra outside the Babri Masjid and would start on 24 November. The purpose of the recital was to pray for a miracle by which the idol of Ram Lalla placed at the Chabutra would move inside the Babri Masjid because, the Hindu Mahasabha leaders insisted, that was the original place of birth of Lord Ram.[364] Like the previous recital, this one also ended after nine days on 4 December, but the idol of Ram Lalla had not chosen to move inside the mosque.

RAM LALLA IDOL 'APPEARS' INSIDE BABRI MASJID

Bhaye prakat kripala Deen Dayala

(There appeared the kind God himself)

Almost three weeks later, on behalf of Ram Lalla, the miracle was performed by a group of Bairagis led by Abhiram Das, a young Naga of the Nirmohi Akhara. On the night of 22–23 December 1949, this band of men scaled the wall of the Babri Masjid after overpowering the lone sentry posted outside, beat up the muezzin, and placed an idol of infant Ram below the central dome of the masjid.[365]

As we have seen earlier, Krishna Jha and Dhirendra Jha[366] have strongly and persuasively tried to establish the role of the Hindu Mahasabha leaders in the conspiracy to place the idol of the infant Ram in the Babri Masjid. In the absence of equally robust historical evidence to counter it, the merits of their arguments cannot be easily challenged. A stunning claim made in a book launched on 20 September 2018 by the RSS Chief Mohan Bhagwat

---

[364]Ibid., Testimony of Bhaskar Das.
[365]Ibid.
[366]Ibid.

and BJP president Amit Shah added a new twist. According to the book, the then RSS chief M. S. Golwalkar was present in Ayodhya a day before the idol was planted inside the Babri Masjid.[367] The same book claims that Sher Singh, a sentry posted outside Babri Masjid, opened the locks and allowed the band of Bairagis to enter the mosque.[368] It also cursorily mentions that Nanaji Deshmukh, a doyen of the RSS considered to be an architect of the Ram Janmabhoomi movement along with Morepant Pingle, was present in Ayodhya on 22 December 1949.[369] The implications of these facts, if they are true, cannot be overstated. It could also be argued that in the time to come the RSS is likely to be more open to take credit for its role in the Ram temple movement. The RSS was then considered the youth wing of the much more established Hindu Mahasabha.[370]

The First Information Report (FIR) lodged by Constable Mata Prasad on 23 December 1949 at the local police station in Ayodhya named Abhiram Das and two others, Ram Shukla Das and Sudarshan Das. The rest were described as '50 to 60 other persons, names and addresses not known of thana Ayodhya'.[371]

Interestingly, the FIR was lodged some time during the day but district magistrate Krishna Kumar Karanakar Nair had already received information about the events of the night on his daily morning walk. Mata Prasad had stated in the FIR that he reached the mosque at 9 a.m. In Faizabad, at a distance of a few kilometres, Nair had sent a radio message to the three topmost government officials in Lucknow by 10.30 a.m. The radio message to the chief minister, the chief secretary and the home secretary said:

A few Hindus entered Babri Masjid at night when the masjid was deserted and installed a deity there. DM and SP and force at spot. Situation under control. Police picket of 15 persons was on duty at night but did not apparently act.[372]

---

[367]Hemant Sharma, *Yuddh mein Ayodhya*, New Delhi: Prabhat Paperbacks, 2018, p. 282.

[368]Ibid., p. 277.

[369]Ibid., p. 438.

[370]Smriti Kak Ramachandran, 'RSS-Hindu Mahasabha had a tumultuous relationship: Sangh ideologue', *Hindustan Times*, 14 September 2016.

[371]A. G. Noorani, ed., *The Babri Masjid Question, 1523–2003: A Matter of National Honour*, New Delhi: Tulika Books, 2004, p. 210.

[372]Radhika Iyengar, 'Babri Masjid-Ram Janmabhoomi: here's what happened 1934 onwards', *Indian Express*, 24 April 2017.

K. K. K. Nair was stating the truth when he said that the situation was under control. But it was only a half truth.[373] The situation was under *his* control, as it was he who had been part of the plan since its inception. He was also ably assisted by his wife, Shakuntala Nair, who led the singing of bhajans and kirtan outside the entrance to the Babri mosque, effectively creating a deterrent against forcibly dislodging the idol from the mosque. Nehru learnt of the incident the next day and gave directions that were expressly clear: the idol needed to be removed and the mosque restored to its original state prior to 23 December.

Three days later on 26 December 1949, Nair explained to his superiors in Lucknow why he had not taken any preventive action to avert the incident. He wrote that he had no prior information about it and nothing of this nature was suggested by the last Crime Investigation Department (CID) report he received on 22 December. This was not the case, as we shall see shortly. Nair, who was a master of half-truths, stated one more reason for his unpreparedness. He wrote, 'Neither through official nor through non-official channels have we ever received any report of such a move with the exception that during naumi path [nine-day Ramayana recital] there was a rumour that the mosque would be entered on Poornmashi Day, but that attempt was not made.'[374]

As the district magistrate, Nair ideally ought to have been aware of the various incidents of desecration of graveyards and the razing of a small mosque called the Kanati Masjid (kanat means tarpaulins of canvas which are installed on special days for the benefit of offering namaz) located close to the Babri Masjid.[375] Along with these incidents, reports of Muslims being stopped from entering the Babri Masjid were published by *AAJ*, a local daily, on 10 December 1949. Besides newspaper reports about the atmosphere that prevailed in Ayodhya, Nair had also received direct information from Akshay Brahmachari, a leading Gandhian and secretary of the Faizabad District Congress. Brahmachari had been an outspoken critic of the Hindu Mahasabha and other communalists. After learning about the destruction of the Kanati mosque, he visited the site on 13 November. Subsequently, he petitioned the city magistrate Gurudutt Singh to prevent any breach of peace. As no action seemed forthcoming from Gurudutt Singh, he met

---

[373]Jha and Jha, *Ayodhya: The Dark Nght*, pp. 26–27.
[374]Ibid., p. 62.
[375]Ibid., pp. 62–63, 81–83.

Nair and apprised him of the situation. Two days later he was assaulted inside his house by three men who appeared to know the details of his meeting with Nair.[376] These details form part of the memorandum that Brahmachari submitted to Lal Bahadur Shastri, the home minister of the United Provinces, in January 1950.[377]

K. K. K. NAIR: A 'DEVOUT' DM

In July 1949, Nair had arranged for a request by the Hindus of Ayodhya to build a temple at the Ram Chabutra to be sent to the chief minister's office. And even though Nair had got his protégé Gurudutt Singh, the city magistrate, to send a favourable 'go-ahead' report, nothing had come of this plan. The city magistrate's reply in October had stated that 'there is nothing in the way and permission can be given as Hindu population is very keen to have a nice temple at the place where Bhagvan Ramchandra Ji was born, the land where temple is to be erected is of Nazul (government land)'.[378]

Until 10 October 1949 (the day when the city magistrate sent his reply), it was the Ram Chabutra which was considered and universally accepted to be Lord Ram's birthplace. But the capture of the Babri Masjid had caught the fancy of many men like Nair. He also had the support of Mahant Digvijay Nath and his friend, the Mahasabha's local leader, Gopal Singh Visharad. The role that Nair played in ensuring that the idol remained inside the mosque after it was forcibly implanted was crucial. Without him and his carefully worded replies to his superiors, the idol would have been removed and the masjid restored to its previous state. But Nair warded off pressure from Lucknow by citing reasons of law and order and by maintaining that the issue was an emotional one, which needed to be handled with great sensitivity. By advising against the removal of the idol, Nair was buying time to mobilize people from surrounding areas to congregate at the mosque where Bhagwan had appeared. In Lucknow, the chief minister was coming under increasing pressure from Nehru, who urged Pant to immediately remove the idol from the mosque. But based on Nair's advice, Pant placated Nehru and assured him that the situation was being taken care of.

---

[376]Ibid., p. 63.
[377]Radhika Iyengar, 'Babri Masjid-Ram Janmabhoomi: Here's what happened 1934 onwards', *Indian Express*, 24 April 2017.
[378]Jha and Jha, *Ayodhya: The Dark Night*, p. 56.

Nearly a week had passed since the idol was placed. Nair knew better than anybody that the situation could easily go out of control and cause more bloodshed, in which case the idol would most likely have to be removed. A legal device to maintain the present status quo needed to be deployed quickly. Although it would have been easy for him as the district magistrate of Faizabad to get the Babri Masjid transferred into the government's custody, or 'attached',[379] as it was now a disputed property, he still had to zero down on a trustworthy receiver.[380] Nair's hunt for a reliable receiver ended in Babu Priya Dutt Ram, who was the chairman of the Faizabad-cum-Ayodhya Municipal Board and came from a Kayastha political family. Like Nair and his deputy, the city magistrate Guru Dutt Singh, Priya Dutt Ram was also a sympathizer of the Hindu Mahasabha.[381]

On 29 December 1949, the Babri Masjid was attached and Priya Dutt Ram was appointed its receiver. Nair had succeeded in his plan of capturing the Babri Masjid[382]—for all practical purposes it now stood converted into a temple. But one last thing needed to be done: Nair needed to ensure that the right of worship was given to Hindus, along with this he needed to secure legal protection against the removal of the idol by the district administration in the future.

One afternoon in April 2017, I met Aasharam Pandey. In his early nineties, his tall figure seemed shrunken as he sat on a string cot under the shade of mango trees at his son's house in Haidergarh police station range, near Ayodhya. Pandey was a government driver in 1949, and remembers K. K. K. Nair with pride and respect. According to Pandey, it was Nair who had given him the job. A devout Brahmin, he maintains the standard story that is prevalent in Ayodhya. 'It was all managed by K. K. Babu and Shakuntala Devi. I was there too.' He recalls how fair-complexioned Nair was and makes sure that I take down the full form of K. K. K.—Krishna Kumar Karanakar. But besides broadly repeating what is already known and even published in booklets like *Ram Janambhoomi ka Raqt Ranjit Itihas*,

---

[379]Section 145 of the Criminal Procedure Code (CrPc) 1989 empowers the district magistrate to bring into the government's control and supervision any property which is under dispute.

[380]A receiver is sometimes appointed by the court to preserve property during litigation between two parties who appear to have an equal right to use the property but who are unwilling to acknowledge each other's interest.

[381]Jha and Jha, *Ayodhya: The Dark Night*, p. 89.

[382]Ibid., pp. 26–27.

Pandey is unable to shed more light on Nair's role. To him, it seems there was no element of subterfuge. 'Bairagis installed the idol and Nair sahib made sure that they were not removed, that's all!' he told me, as his son's curiosity seemed to be turning into suspicion.

On 24 December 1949, the day after the idol was placed inside the Babri Masjid, the Hindu Mahasabha began its national session in Calcutta. The events at Ayodhya, naturally, featured in the deliberations. The organization's newly elected president, N. B. Khare, represented the hardliners in the Mahasabha and used the occasion to attack their two main adversaries—the Congress and Muslims. The Calcutta session of the Hindu Mahasabha ended on 26 December with new hope and energy, fuelled in no small measure by their success at Ayodhya. They also felt that it was the right time to amplify that success by providing the local leadership with some artillery support in the form of the big leaders of the Mahasabha.

Nair had concealed the involvement of the Mahasabha leaders in his official communication to Lucknow. He had not mentioned it in his radio message nor was it recorded in the FIR lodged on 23 December. Therefore, there was no apprehension of the law in his mind when the Hindu Mahasabha's vice president, V. G. Deshpande, reached Ayodhya on 16 January 1950. He was received ceremoniously by the district secretary of the Mahasabha, Ramchandra Das Paramhans. As Deshpande drove in to Ayodhya with Mahant Digvijay Nath, he was given a rousing welcome by the town's Bairagis, sadhus and lay devotees amidst pro-Mahasabha and pro-Ram Janmabhoomi slogans. Deshpande's visit galvanized the motley group of sadhus, Ramanujis, Bairagis and even the Arya Samajis into a united pro-temple stand. Nobody wanted the idol removed and it was towards achieving this aim that a key functionary of the Mahasabha was missing from his side. Gopal Singh Visharad was busy filing a suit in the court of Faizabad civil judge, Thakur Bir Singh. Visharad wanted the court to grant him and other Hindus the right to worship the idol of Ram Lalla. He also wanted the court to issue an order restraining the defendants (the imam and muttawali of the Babri Masjid, the district magistrate, superintendent of police and additional city magistrate of Faizabad) from removing the idol. Civil Judge Singh had been persuaded by Nair to cooperate in the name of Lord Ram and Singh did so by granting the two orders.

The mosque's transformation into a temple was almost complete now as Muslims lost the right to worship at the place they had prayed in for the last four centuries. Hindu pilgrims to Ayodhya had already started worshipping the idol of Ram Lalla from outside, and the donations that were pouring in had not failed to attract the notice of the mahants of Ayodhya's notoriously competitive Ramanandi akharas. Though the Ram Lalla idol remained locked inside the mosque, the various akharas soon started squabbling among themselves for control and ownership of the new temple.

For the Mahasabha this infighting was a big setback, but they were given a reason to rejoice when the chargesheet for the crime of trespass was filed on 1 February 1950. The chargesheet was filed on the basis of the FIR of 23 December, in which Abul Barkat, a police constable, was named as one of the nine prosecution witnesses. He had been on duty outside the Babri Masjid and was unaware of the trespass till daybreak, when as per their plan, Abhiram Das and others had lit a lamp and started chanting prayers accompanied by the sound of bells, conches and cymbals.

Abul Barkat had reached the post after the 'few Hindus' had already hid themselves inside the mosque. As a result he was completely taken aback when he saw the idol and the group of Bairagis inside. His statement to the magistrate was based on what he saw, and in a curious and absurd way, it vindicated the Mahasabha's propaganda of god's magical appearance inside the mosque. Abul Barkat told the magistrate that:

> ...he saw a flash of divine light inside the Babri masjid. Gradually that light became golden and in that he saw the figure of a very beautiful godlike child of four or five years the like of which he had never seen in his life. The sight sent him into a trance, and when he recovered his senses he found that the lock on the main gate (of the mosque) was lying broken and a huge crowd of Hindus had entered the building and were performing the aarti of the idol placed on a Singhasan and reciting: Bhaye prakat kripala Deen Dayala.[383]

Though this statement pleased the Mahasabhaites, it was soon clear to them that the conflict over donations at the new Ram's birthplace shrine was not going to end soon. The struggle for control of the shrine between various mahants and local grandees paid to the Mahasabha's hope of using the temple issue to derive political mileage.

Even so, the Nairs gained political success soon afterwards. Shakuntala Nair became a Hindu Mahasabha Member of Parliament from neighbouring Gonda in 1952. K. K. K. Nair became a Member of Parliament in 1967

---

[383]Ibid, p. 76.

on a Jan Sangh (an offshoot of the Hindu Mahasabha and the parent
party of the BJP) ticket from Bahraich. He also amassed huge tracts of
land in and around Faizabad during his nine-month tenure as the district
magistrate there.[384]

AMRITLAL NAGAR IN AYODHYA: PULP HISTORY LEGITIMIZED

Nearly eighty years after Bharatendu Harishchandra visited Ayodhya, in
1957, another Hindi writer who would be called the heir to Bharatendu's
legacy came to Ayodhya. Amritlal Nagar's *Gadar ke Phool* (*Flowers of Chaos*),
is a book based on his tour of Awadh a hundred years after the revolt
of 1857. He visited all the main centres of the revolt and endeavoured
to collect stories, legends and other memories of India's 'first war of
independence'. In some places he met witnesses who claimed they had
been alive at the time of the revolt. In Faizabad and Ayodhya, despite much
effort, he failed to find a survivor or even substantive information about the
revolt. Nagar's meeting with an aloof mahant in Hanumangarhi also proved
useless as the mahant showed no interest in history, not even the history
of Hanumangarhi itself. Instead, the mahant rebuked Nagar for asking
questions relating to historical facts.[385] On realizing that 'not much water
can be found in the desert of asceticism', Nagar returned to Faizabad where
he met two prominent citizens of the town. In 1957, Babu Priya Dutt Ram,
the chairman of the municipal board, was still the court-appointed receiver
of the Babri Masjid. The second man that Nagar met was Akhtar, editor
and publisher of the local Urdu daily, *Akhtar*. Babu Priya Dutt Ram could
not provide much information about the 1857 revolt except to share how
the matter was never discussed in their family because the elders feared that
the children might also be contaminated by a feeling of rebellion against
the British. Babu Priya Dutt Ram's family's aversion to discuss the revolt is
understandable—the family had risen to prominence through British favour.

With Akhtar, a suave editor and publisher, Nagar had a more lively
discussion on Ayodhya's importance as a religious place for Muslims. Akhtar
told Nagar that Muslims believed 'the first son of Adam lies buried in a grave
behind Mani Prabat. Therefore not just for Muslims, Ayodhya is important
for all of humanity.' Nagar, an agnostic, countered Akhtar's hypothesis with
his own theory of how the Dargah of Sheesh Paigambar (Adam's son in

---

[384]Ibid.

[385] Amritlal Nagar, *Gadar ke Phool*, New Delhi: Rajpal & Sons, 2012. p. 57.

Islam) came to exist in Ram's Ayodhya. Nagar told him, 'Since you are talking about Hazrat Sheesh, I am reminded of the Hindu God Shesh. Lakshman, Ramchandra's younger brother is believed to be an incarnation of Shesh Nag [King of Snakes], the seat of Vishnu. Is it not possible that there existed a temple of God Shesh in Ayodhya which the Muslims started calling Hazrat Sheesh? The names are very similar.'[386]

Nagar's time in Ayodhya proved to be largely fruitless as far as collecting material regarding 1857 was concerned. But he did record the existence of a booklet titled *Janmasthan ka Rakt Ranjit Itihas* (*The Blood-soaked History of the Birthplace*).

Nagar couldn't meet Ram Gopal Pandey 'Sharad', the author of this work, but later received a written note on the events in Ayodhya during 1857. Sharad sent Nagar a detailed description of the rebellion in Ayodhya and the united stand that locals took against the British.

The booklet is history written in a staccato style. It presents a collage of facts and names put together in such a way that it becomes impossible to ascertain fact from fiction, from legend, from history. 'Sharad' had created a new history of Ayodhya which Nagar reproduced without verifying. Some of those tales are now enshrined as truths. The book survives, though in a truncated form, in a booklet that is sold on Ayodhya's streets. *Shri Ram Janmabhoomi ka Rakt Ranjit Itihas* is a recension of the original *Janmasthan ka Rakt Ranjit Itihas* by Ram Gopal Pandey 'Sharad'. A translation of the recension *Shri Ram Janmabhoomi ka Rakt Ranjit Itihas* (*The Blood-soaked History of Shri Ram's Birthplace*) is openly sold outside the disputed site of the Ram Janmabhoomi–Babri Masjid. It has been authored by Ranjana Sarvesh Mishra and contains a foreword by Jamejaya Sharan, president of the Ram Janmabhoomi Mandir Nirman Samiti. In his foreword Sharan describes the book as a repository of the brave men who died on 30 October 1990 and in December 1992.

The original 'street' version of history by 'Sharad' also survives in the 'guided' tours in Ayodhya. The guides tell pilgrims and tourists about two holy men, Ameer Ali and Baba Ramchandra, who fought against the British. Baba Ramchandra was the leader of the rebel Bairagis of Hanumangarhi and Ameer Ali was his 'right-hand' man. Ameer Ali had persuaded the Muslims to 'return' the birthplace of Ram, over which Babur had constructed his mosque, to the Hindus. But, continues the

---

[386]Ibid., p. 61.

guide (as well as the booklet by 'Sharad') 'because of British policy of divide and rule it could not be done. Both Ameer Ali and Ramchandra were hanged from a tamarind tree on 18 March 1858.' The rest of the booklet goes on to enumerate the dozens of battles that Hindus had waged to regain the birthplace of Lord Ram.

If Amritlal Nagar had met Ram Gopal Pandey, the author of this 'pulp' history booklet, perhaps he would have discovered his involvement in the 'capture' of the Babri Masjid. Just a year earlier in 1956, Ram Gopal Pandey, who was the editor and publisher of *Virakta*, rival of the Urdu daily *Akhtar*, had published in a banner headline on the front page the news of the acquittal of Abhiram Das and others in the case lodged against them for their alleged crime of trespassing the mosque. The headline read 'Janmabhoomi ki Shandaar Vijay' (Glorious Triumph of the Birthplace). Ram Gopal Pandey had been a Hindu Mahasabha member too, but by 1953 had fallen out with other Mahasabhaites like the former city magistrate Guru Dutt Singh, Gopal Singh Visharad and Ramchandra Paramhans. Sometime after 1950, these three men had set up an organization to fight the Muslims' claim over the mosque and to create favourable public opinion by holding birthplace-related events in Ayodhya. Pandey, whose newspaper had played the role of a mouthpiece for the Mahasabha so far, now fell out over the large amount of donations that the new organization, Shri Ram Janmabhoomi Seva Samriti, was receiving. Vexed by the feeling of having been left out, Pandey started publishing detailed reports about the siphoning away of donations by Visharad, who subsequently filed a defamation suit against Pandey. The suit was dismissed. Following this episode, the unity of the Bairagis and Mahasabhaites soon came to an end. The akharas subsequently filed legal cases claiming ownership of Ram's birthplace. The cases remain pending to date, but Ram Gopal Pandey's attempt at creating a new 'miraculous' version of the 1949 trespassing by Abhiram and others has transformed from pulp history to a widely believed 'real' history of Ram's birthplace.

LEGAL WAR OVER BABRI MASJID AND RAM JANMABHOOMI

Abhiram Das, the burly Bairagi who led the band of men and implanted the idol inside the Babri Masjid, belonged to the Nirvani Akhara of Hanumangarhi. In later years Abhiram Das took to calling himself 'Ram Janmabhoomi Uddharak', or the one who saved or salvaged Ram's birthplace. The Digambar Akhara was represented by Ramchandra

Paramhans who, as a local Mahasabha leader, was one of the key actors in the idol implantation episode in 1949.[387] The three akharas have remained at loggerheads over the Ram Janmabhoomi till today.

The first one to independently go to court was Ramchandra Paramhans. In December 1950, he pleaded in the court that neither the Muslim defendants nor the government nor the Sunni Waqf Board had any right to interfere or obstruct his worship of the Ram idol placed inside the Babri Masjid. As we have seen earlier, at that time the masjid along with the idol had been attached and Babu Priya Dutt Ram, the chairman of the Faizabad-cum-Ayodhya Municipal Board, had been acting as the receiver under the order of the deputy commissioner of Faizabad.

Almost a decade later in December 1959, the Nirmohi Akhara reclaimed its right over the management of the worship of the Ram Lalla idol and the Babri Masjid. The suit was filed on behalf of the then head of the akhara, Mahant Raghunath Das. In a way, the Nirmohi Akhara was the oldest litigant in the dispute; its plea to construct a birthplace temple over the Ram Chabutra dated back to 1885.

When the Sunni Waqf Board of Uttar Pradesh filed its suit in December 1961, it added each of the plaintiffs in preceding suits to the list of defendants, which also included the state of UP and its agents. The Sunni Waqf Board named all those it believed had impinged on the sanctity of the Babri Masjid as the defendants. Besides Gopal Singh Visharad, Nirmohi Akhara, Digambar Akhara, the state of UP, the offices of the district magistrate and the superintendent of police of Faizabad, the suit also named the receiver, Babu Priya Dutt Ram, Abhiram Das, the All India Hindu Mahasabha, the All India Arya Samaj (the Arya Samaj had supported the Mahasabha in 1949–1950 in the matter) and six other individuals.

Its plea was to have the mosque (and the attached graveyard) restored to Muslims and the idol and other articles of worship that were placed in the mosque removed. The Sunni Waqf Board's action was delayed by eleven years but the earlier two suits by the Nirmohi and Digambar Akharas were pending along with lakhs of others in the understaffed and overburdened lower courts. Ayodhya and Faizabad fall under the jurisdiction of the Allahabad High Court, which is the largest High Court in India. Its pendency of cases even now stands at approximately seven lakh cases.

Subsequent to the Sunni Central Waqf Board case in 1961, the dispute

---

[387]Jha, and Jha, *Ayodhya: The Dark Night.*

faded into the background. And along with the dispute the crusaders of Ram Janmabhoomi, who had become victims of their own greed, also faded away from people's minds. In any case, the birth of a new temple was not unprecedented in Ayodhya, where every square foot of land was marked holy by priests. Festivals and melas continued to draw huge numbers of pilgrims. The Ramanandis, Vaishnav Nagas, Bairagis, Shiva devotees in the month of Sawan, Ramanujis, Rasiks, Tyagis, Muslim fakirs and the occasional Buddhist, Sikh and Jain devotee went uninterruptedly about their religious business.

AYODHYA: 1960–1980

By 1960, rising unemployment and struggling socialism along with the comprehensive loss of the Mahasabha's ideology to the Congress' electoral machine, had pushed Ayodhya to the margins of the national conscience. Ayodhya would remain on the margins for three decades between 1950 to the mid-1980s. However, the voters of Ayodhya continued to patronize Hindu nationalist leaders like Baba Raghav Das of the Congress, the Hindu Mahasabha and later, its offshoot, the Bharatiya Jan Sangh, and still later in the 1980s, the progeny of the Jan Sangh, the Bharatiya Janata Party.

But after the victory of Baba Raghav Das of the INC in the Faizabad by-election of 1948, the Congress continued to hold the seat till 1974 when the Bharatiya Jan Sangh's Bed Prakash Agarwal won the Ayodhya (so renamed in 1962) legislative assembly seat by a narrow margin of 283 votes. The Jan Sangh, founded in 1951, had exercised considerable hold over the voters of the Ayodhya constituency and with this victory it achieved a long-standing, and so far unfulfilled, goal. But this victory too was shortlived. In the next election to the UP assembly held in 1977, the Jan Sangh lost the seat to the Congress's Nirmal Khatri. The way Ayodhya's politics played out during this period was a reflection of what was generally taking place in north Indian politics.

In the 1977 elections, held after the Emergency ended on 21 March 1977, Uttar Pradesh was swept by the pantheonic Janata Party. With twenty contestants, Ayodhya held the distinction of being the seat with the highest number of candidates. Swayed by the Janata Party wave, Ayodhya too elected its candidate: Jai Shankar Pandey.

Chapter 9

THE RAM JANMABHOOMI MOVEMENT

The VHP, which was formed in 1964, took two decades to launch an Ayodhya-specific campaign to mobilize Hindus. The Ram Janmabhoomi Mukti Yagna Samiti (the committee to perform the ritual for the liberation of Ram's birthplace) was formed in July 1984. The decision to form this samiti was taken at the first Dharma Sansad (parliament of religion) held in April 1984 in Delhi's Vigyan Bhavan, a government-owned auditorium. Vigyan means science in Hindi. Whether or not the organizers and those who attended the Dharma Sansad even gave a thought to the name of the venue, it didn't stop them from concluding at the end of the meeting that Ram's birthplace needed to be liberated. But from whom?

Those who attended the Dharma Sansad represented the multitude of Hindu sects and traditions. A total of 558 religious scholars, monks and gurus participated in the meeting. Together they represented seventy-six sects and traditions. From Ayodhya, Ramchandra Paramhans, a member of the original team from 1949, was present as well. Besides Ayodhya's Ram Janmabhoomi–Babri Masjid shrine, Kashi's Vishwanath and Mathura's Krishna Janmabhoomi temples were also to be liberated, the Sansad had decided. The Dharam Sansad had the support of Gulzarilal Nanda, a former trade union organizer, seasoned Congressman and two-time interim prime minister. In 1967, Indira Gandhi had eased Nanda out along with a few other leaders whom she perceived as threats to her hold on the Congress. Nanda, a committed cow protection campaigner and Hindi zealot, had since then nursed a grievance against Mrs Gandhi. Another slighted Congressman was Dau Dayal Khanna, a maverick leader from Moradabad and a former minister in the UP government. Dau Dayal became the head of the Ram Janmabhoomi Mukti Yagna Samiti.

To oppose this mobilization by the VHP for 're-claiming' Hindu temples, Muslims also formed the Tahaffuz-i-Masjid Committee (committee for the protection of mosques). Both sides held press conferences and sought the support of the press, and through them, the public. The first press release by the samiti was signed by both Khanna and Ashok Singhal, general secretary of the VHP. Only English language newspapers tried to present both sides objectively. The samiti launched its maiden campaign as a march from Sitamarhi in Bihar (considered to be Sita's birthplace) to Delhi. The march was called the Ram-Janki Yatra and Ayodhya and Lucknow were going to be prominent stops during the march. The yatra received lukewarm support from non-upper caste Hindus. The marchers for the cause of liberating Ram's birthplace were given government support by the Congress's UP chief minister, Narayan Dutt Tiwari. This support was in the form of medical teams to accompany the marchers and other logistical arrangements. When the yatra reached Ayodhya on 7 October 1984, it consisted of at least 2,000 people. Local newspapers ran the news with prominent photos on front pages.

The procession consisted of some trucks, one of them carrying decorated portraits of Ram and Sita. From Ayodhya and Faizabad, the yatra reached Lucknow, where a massive crowd awaited. After addressing a rally, its leaders met the chief minister and presented a memorandum asking for an ordinance that would 'return' the three temples in Mathura, Kashi and Ayodhya to the Hindus. Worship continued in these three temples, but the 'return', to a large number of VHP supporters, meant the construction of grand temples at these three holy places. But the first step as part of an incremental campaign was to open the locks of the Ram Lalla shrine inside the Babri Masjid so that Hindus could worship there. Some of the slogans raised in Ayodhya also sought the blessings of Hanumangarhi's Bairagis by invoking Bajrang Bali (a name for the monkey-god Hanuman):

Bajrang Bali ki hai lalkar, Tala kholegi sarkar

(Bajrang Bali demands, the government must open the locks)

Bajrang ne lalkara hai, Tala khulne wala hai

(Bajrang Bali declares, the lock is going to open soon)

Before the yatra could reach Delhi and petition Prime Minister Indira Gandhi, who it appeared was growing close to certain Hindu godmen, her life was cut short. On 31 October 1984, Mrs Gandhi's Sikh bodyguards gunned her down as revenge for the Indian army storming the Sikh extremist J. S. Bhindranwale's base at the Golden Temple, Harmandir Sahib, in Amritsar. In the aftermath of her death, it was as if life had gone out of the Sangh Parivar's free Hindu temples movement. Some of the slogans that were raised in the yatra did gave away the larger future designs of the Sangh Parivar:

Hindu bahulya shakti ko tolo
Janmabhoomi ka tala kholo

(Realize the strength of Hindu power
Open the locks of Janmabhoomi)

The following slogan that survives to this day (twenty-six years after the demolition of the Babri Masjid) was first used in the yatra. It directly attacked the Muslims of India for the acts of Mughal emperors.

Babur ki santano se badla
Le ke rahenge, le ke rahenge

(From the children of Babur
We will extract revenge)

The slogans were not historically correct but they were rhetorically sound. Islam in India dated back to the seventh century when it first entered through Malabar on its western coast. In Awadh, too, Islam had been practised at least since the eleventh or twelfth century CE.

The yatra had failed to get popular support in the wake of the countrywide wave of sympathy generated after Indira Gandhi's murder but even so, at least in Uttar Pradesh, the Ram Janki Yatra had showcased the wide range of support it had attracted. Retired judges, students, middle-class housewives, government officers and politicians along with a retired director general of police of UP, S. C. Dixit, had endorsed the demand for the liberation of Hindu temples from 'Babur's children' and joined in the essentially anti-Muslim campaign of the VHP.

Although the yatra had failed, Ayodhya, almost overnight, became the stage of the RSS's plans to capture political power by creating a Hindu vote bank. On 2 April 1984, the Bajrang Dal, a militant youth wing, was formally launched inside the premises of Ayodhya's Digambar Akhara, and Vinay Katiyar was made its founder-convener.

Responding to the growing focus on Ayodhya, the Congress government in UP started the first major development project at Ayodhya in 1984–1985. Chief Minister Sripati Mishra sanctioned the construction of Ram ki Pairi, a bathing channel with ghats on the lines of Har ki Pauri in Haridwar. Water from the Sarayu was diverted into a culvert to the artificial bathing ghats. But like many well-initialized but pathetically executed government schemes, Ram ki Pairi today symbolizes the poor state of civic infrastructure in Ayodhya. The bathing tanks are choked with refuse throughout the year except when they are cleaned sporadically for visits by top government ministers and important dignitaries.

RAJIV GANDHI GOVERNMENT HIT BY TURBULENCE

In 1985, the Supreme Court of India passed the famous Shah Bano judgement allowing Shah Bano, an elderly divorced Muslim woman from Indore, the right to financial maintenance from her husband. The All India Muslim Personal Law Board took to the streets to oppose this decision. Earlier in the year, a new government led by Prime Minister Rajiv Gandhi was hit by turbulence when Vishwanath Pratap Singh, the then finance minister, quit the party. V. P. Singh was believed to possess confidential information about corruption at the highest levels of government. Rajiv had won an absolute majority in the general election that was held in December 1984, two months after the killing of his mother Indira Gandhi. With V. P. Singh's resignation in protest against alleged corruption by people close to Rajiv, the Gandhi name was marred by stories of favouritism and bribery. A novice in politics, Rajiv had allowed himself to be influenced by a small coterie made up of long-time friends, sycophants and hubris-ridden politicians like his uncle, Arun Nehru.

When Rajiv Gandhi saw millions of Muslims protesting the Shah Bano judgement in much of India and particularly in Bihar, he wavered and, on the advice of Arun Nehru, went against his own best instincts to nullify the Supreme Court verdict through an Act of Parliament.[388] The Muslim orthodoxy was pleased and hailed the decision. While the Muslim clergy was protesting judicial encroachment on what they called their fundamental right to live by the Sharia, their Hindu counterparts, the RSS and its brother organizations (and later a sister one too—the Durga Vahini), were protesting against Rajiv's decision in the Shah Bano case. The Parliament was to enact the Muslim Women (Protection of Rights on Divorce) Act in the monsoon session (typically held during the months of July–August)

---

[388] Ajaz Ashraf, 'Arif Mohammad Khan on Shah Bano case: "Najma Heptullah was key influence on Rajiv Gandhi"', *Scroll.in*, 30 May 2015.

of 1986. In order to pre-empt (or what he believed would be pre-empting) the backlash from a large number of Hindus, the Rajiv government was advised to appease them as well.[389]

On 19 January 1986, Vishva Hindu Parishad's functionaries and VHP-enlisted religious leaders held a conference in Lucknow from where they served a fatwa, or an ultimatum, to the Uttar Pradesh chief minister, Vir Bahadur Singh who had become CM by defeating his predecessor N. D. Tiwari in the game of musical chairs for the coveted post. The VHP's ultimatum was clear—if the government did not unlock the Babri Masjid and 'liberate Ram Lalla', the VHP would forcibly do so themselves. The fact that the Babri Masjid was under lock and key at the orders of the court did not matter to them. Vir Bahadur Singh, a veteran politician who was known to be a VHP sympathizer, consulted Arun Nehru, Rajiv's confidant and adviser.

To sabotage the VHP's campaign, it was decided by the Congress leadership in Delhi and Lucknow that it would be better to risk sabotaging communal harmony in the country than risk losing Hindu votes. Of course, Rajiv and his coterie had calculated that by appeasing Hindu communalists they would negate the impression that they were anti-Hindu.

'HEAVENS WILL NOT FALL'

A young lawyer, Umesh Chandra Pandey, who was not a party to the dispute, petitioned the court of District (Civil Judge) K. M. Pandey demanding permission to perform puja of the Ram Lalla idol placed inside the Babri mosque. As the file of the dispute was with the High Court bench in Lucknow and the case had at least four other parties, the district judge could not even have admitted Pandey's petition. Therefore, it was duly rejected on 28 January 1986. Undeterred, Pandey, who was acting at the behest of higher powers, now appealed to the higher court of District Judge Krishna Mohan Pande. District Judge Pande overruled the wise decision of his subordinate, and based on the assurances regarding law and order made by the district magistrate and the senior superintendent of police of Faizabad, ordered the opening of the locks which had been placed in December 1949.

'Government works at its own pace' is an aphorism that is true for

---

[389]'Role of Arun Nehru, Rajiv in opening masjid ignored', *The Hindu*, 25 November 2009.

most if not all levels of the government, and it usually signifies a snail's pace. But, on 1 February 1986, within an hour of Pande's order at 4.15 p.m. to open the Ram Lalla shrine inside Babri for worship by Hindu devotees,[390] the Faizabad DM and SSP along with their lock-opening party joined the state-run Doordarshan and All India Radio crew who were already present at the Babri Masjid. The administration had acted at lightning speed but the keys to the heavy iron locks placed more than three decades ago could not be found. Armed with the court's order, it was decided to break open the locks. The state-run TV and radio broadcast the news amid celebration by Hindus outside the Babri Masjid. On that day in Ayodhya, in ways that were not apparent then, much more had been broken. To begin with, the judge, K. M. Pande, had broken with established practice by ordering the lock to be opened without hearing out the Muslim party and the three Hindu parties. At a deeper and still unseen level, the prime minister of the country had allowed a violation of established judicial practice. Almost everybody, including the VHP, was caught by surprise.

In 1986, the Sunni Central Waqf Board filed a contempt case against the opening of the locks; which is 'still pending', according to Zafaryab Jilani, who filed the case on behalf of the Sunni Waqf Board. Outside the Babri Masjid in Ayodhya, scenes of Hindus celebrating reminded people of 23 December 1949. 'It was like déjà vu,' according to Majnu, a seventy-seven-year-old Ayodhya resident. Govind Tiwari, his friend since childhood, agreed, 'We could not believe it happened so suddenly.'

The day was celebrated as 'Victory Day' by Hindus, who sang, danced and chanted Ram's name till late in the evening. The Muslim neighbourhoods sullenly ignored them and huddled into a winter sleep. That same morning, Pope John Paul II had arrived in India on a fourteen-day state visit. He was personally received by Prime Minister Rajiv Gandhi and President Zail Singh at the airport. If Rajiv had dreamt of being applauded for the opening of the locks, he was mistaken. According to a *New York Times* report, on the eve of the Pope's visit, a crowd of Hindus, estimated by the police at 6,000, marched through the streets of New Delhi chanting anti-Pope slogans. The next day, 2 February 1986, the VHP organized a public meeting in Ayodhya, in which it asked for the formation of a trust to construct a 'grand temple' at Ram's birthplace. Hashim Ansari, the old,

---

[390]Ayodhya Matter: Ram Janam Bhoomi-Babri Masjid Disputes (Special Full Bench Judgement) Allahabad High Court, Malhotra Law House.

dark and toothless man who was to become the 'face of the Muslim side'[391] in Ayodhya, was also busy on that day as he was organizing telegrams of complaints to be wired to the president and prime minister. On 3 February 1986, Hashim Ansari followed up his telegrams by going to the High Court against the Faizabad district judge's order. The High Court admitted his plea and passed a stay order to maintain the status quo that had held since 1949. Subsequently the Allahabad High Court also transferred all the cases related to the dispute to the bench at Lucknow.

Faizabad District Judge K. M. Pande had declared that the 'heavens will not fall' while justifying his order to open the locks. But it was soon clear that the chained, restrained, closeted beast of religious communalism had descended on Uttar Pradesh's densely populated towns and villages. Riots broke out across UP following 'victory' celebrations organized at the behest of the VHP. Muslims responded violently to the provocation. It seemed that the country was getting engulfed in communal fires spreading as far as Kashmir and Gujarat. According to contemporary media reports, communal violence peaked in the state during Vir Bahadur Singh's first three years as chief minister of Uttar Pradesh. In all, 181 people were killed in riots that occurred in at least 37 districts of the state in the wake of the opening of the locks of the disputed Ram Janambhoomi–Babri Masjid.[392]

The assurances of the DM and SSP, based on which the Faizabad district judge had given his orders, lay dead like the victims of the communal violence. Later, still unmindful of the effects of his maleficent order, Pandey wrote in his autobiography, *Voice of Conscience*:

> ...when the order was passed, a Black Monkey was sitting for the whole day on the roof of the Court room holding the flag post. Thousands of people of Faizabad and Ayodhya offered him groundnuts and fruits. Strangely, the monkey did not touch any of the offerings. The District Magistrate and SSP escorted me to the bungalow. The monkey was present in the verandah of my bungalow; I was surprised to see him. I just saluted him, taking him to be some Divine Power.[393]

---

[391]'Hashim Ansari, face of Babri suit, no more', *Tribune India*, 21 July 2016.
[392]Dilip Awasthi, 'Uttar Pradesh Chief Minister Bir Bahadur Singh completes record 970 days in office', *India Today*, 31 May 1988.
[393]Aviral Virk, 'Ayodhya part 2: did a divine monkey unlock Babri Masjid?', *The Quint*, 11 November, 2017 and K. M. Pandey, *Voice of Conscience*, Lucknow: Deen Dayal Upadhyay Prakashan, 1996.

Pandey's absurdity fitted quite well into the pattern of the development of the dispute. The forcible planting of the idol of Ram Lalla inside the mosque too had been hailed as a 'miracle' by the Hindu Mahasabha in 1949–1950. 'The opening of the locks was an example of a judicial order that was against us,' says Khaliq Khan, a prominent Muslim activist in Faizabad. He is a man with a wry sense of humour, 'It was a government miracle in 1986, otherwise how is it possible that the locks that were placed in 1949 were on Babri Masjid, a mosque, but when they were opened our masjid had become a temple and we were not even heard before the district judge took his decision? Should we also not have got the right to worship there?'[394]

1986–1989: RAM AS A POLITICAL WEAPON

In response to the opening of the locks, Muslims under the leadership of Syed Shahabuddin, a former diplomat turned politician, formed the Babri Masjid Action Committee (BMAC) on 15 February 1986. The day before had been observed as a Black Day by Muslims across India. Religion invaded politics in true earnest in 1986. In July, Hindu–Muslim riots in Ahmedabad killed nearly sixty people during the traditional Rath Yatra as it passed through Muslim neighbourhoods. Hindus shouted anti-Muslim slogans and when Muslims retaliated with stones, large-scale violence erupted. Later that year, unimpeded by the killings, the VHP-backed Ram Janmabhoomi Mukti Samiti set up the Ram Janmabhoomi Trust and demanded that the government transfer the property rights of the Babri Masjid and the idols placed inside it to the trust for its plan to build a 'grand temple'.

The war over who the owner of the disputed site was had now begun. VHP's mobilization was met with counter-campaigns by Muslim groups. Between 1986 and 1989, Uttar Pradesh, a state where a majority of India's Muslims live alongside Hindus, saw internecine bloodshed. Its major towns like Meerut, Moradabad, Allahabad, Banaras, Kanpur, Lucknow and Rampur burnt in the communal fires, which were being stoked by Hindu extremists on one side and Muslims on the other. Meerut's most famous doctor, the Padma Shri awardee Hakim Saifuddin Ahmed, who had also been a physician to President Zail Singh and other presidents before him, was quoted by *India Today* as blaming the two committees for

---

[394]Interview with the author.

'most of the hatred between the two communities. It has become so bad that if two buffaloes get into a fight, one will be labelled Hindu and the other Muslim'. Ayodhya was still surviving without any major incident of communal violence, but peace was tenuous in the small town.

Rajiv Gandhi had got the locks opened at the behest of Arun Nehru and Uttar Pradesh Chief Minister Vir Bahadur Singh in 1986.[395] By 1987, Nehru had turned against his cousin and joined Rajiv's bête noire, Vishwanath Pratap Singh.[396] Politically, Rajiv Gandhi had played directly into the hands of the RSS and the VHP, and of the Muslim orthodoxy led by men like the Shahi Imam of the Jama Masjid.[397] Progressive Muslim leaders in the Congress like Arif Mohammad Khan were sidelined for opposing the government's decision to nullify the Shah Bano judgement through an Act of Parliament.[398] RSS-led propaganda preceding the opening of the locks had successfully evoked the suffering of Ram Lalla, the pre-eminent God for billions of mainly Vaishnava Hindus. After the locks were opened, the VHP and the RSS went on the offensive and sharpened their propaganda of Hindu persecution, as did Muslim organizations.[399] And as we shall see later, the persecution of the idol of Ram Lalla had also worked magically to consolidate the great divided Hindu society into a unified vote bank. The VHP had enlisted the services of a wide range of godmen from across the country. They spoke the language of religion and Hindu pride. The image of a Ram idol jailed inside the Babri Masjid seared itself in the minds of Hindus.[400] In the carefully crafted hysteria it was easily overlooked that the gods are supposed to help mortals and not the other way around.

At this time, there were other developments that fuelled religious fervour in the country. One such phenomenon took place in 1987, when the state-run broadcaster, Doordarshan, started airing a televised version of Tulsidas's Ramayana. In a country where large sections of people were relatively

---

[395]'The misunderstood Nehru', *Rediff.com*, 26 July 2013.

[396]Inder Malhotra, 'Rear view: How Rajiv had a great fall', *Indian Express*, 5 January 2015.

[397]Ramesh Thakur, 'Ayodhya and the politics of India's secularism: A double-standards discourse', South Asia: Responses to the Ayodhya Crisis, *Asian Survey*, Vol. 33, No. 7, July 1993, p. 655.

[398]'I want to surrender to the BJP', *Rediff.com*, 24 February 2004.

[399]Dilip Awasthi, 'Hindu, Muslim organisations stage massive shows of strength in New Delhi and Ayodhya', *India Today*, 30 April 1987.

[400]Erik Reenberg Sand, *Rituals between Religion and Politics. The Case of VHP's 2001-2002 Ayodhya-campaign*, Tore Ahlbäck, ed., *Ritualistics*, Åbo, Finland: Donner Institute for Research in Religious and Cultural History, 2002, p. 162–76..

media illiterate and uneducated, the television set became a holy medium and object. Before watching the show which was aired every Sunday, some Hindus reportedly first bathed, worshipped their TV sets with flowers and incense, and then sat down to receive the *Ramayan*, the audio-visual version of their favourite epic created by film director Ramanand Sagar. For many Hindus who had remained aloof from the Ram Janmabhoomi movement, the airing of the TV series was not just entertaining but strongly persuasive. In a strange way, the fictional televised images of Ram and Ayodhya turned the abstraction of 'Ram Lalla enslaved in a Mosque' into something real and palpable. To some extent technology aided the process of commodification of religious and cultural mores; specifically Ramayanic mores. Other TV series like *Buniyaad*, based on the Partition, and *Nukkad*, on the struggles of the working classes, had been aired before, and along with *Ramayan*. But, for millions of Indians, it was *Ramayan* that became their first ever audio-video special effects experience. Ayodhya and its divine characters came alive, as did Ayodhya the place.

In July 1988, the final episode of the TV series *Ramayan* was aired by Doordarshan. It had captured the public mind and instilled a tendency to suspend disbelief. The disbelief stayed suspended until long after the series had ended. The actors who played Ram and Sita found themselves mobbed in public, their photographs were added to a mélange of idols and images that adorn a corner of every religious Hindu's home. Differences of education and class were temporarily put on hold as Hindus across class and caste turned into a homogenized audience feeding from the same religio-cultural pool.

1989: AYODHYA AS A RALLYING POINT

The year 1986 had been the first marker of the Indian state's surrender to both Hindu and Muslim fundamentalism through the opening of the locks at the Ram Lalla shrine and the Shah Bano case. In 1989, religious fundamentalist groups upped the ante. It was also the year when the Rajiv Gandhi-led Congress government would suffer a series of setbacks on both domestic and international fronts. The Bofors scandal,[401] V. P. Singh's anti-

---

[401]On 18 March 1986, India signed a Rs 1,437-crore deal with Swedish arms manufacturer A. B. Bofors for the supply of 400 155mm Howitzer guns for the Army. A year later, on 16 April 1987, a Swedish radio channel alleged that the company had bribed top Indian politicians and defence personnel to secure the contract. The scandal rocked the Rajiv Gandhi-led government in the late 1980s. On 22 January 1990, the Central

corruption campaign and the loss of Indian lives in the LTTE conflict in Sri
Lanka coupled with the growing anti-Hindu violence in Kashmir painted
Rajiv's government as being indifferent to Hindus. The VHP, confident that
it had the support of the Hindu majority, now pressed further for the
complete liberation of the Ram Lalla idol and his birthplace.

On 1 April 1989, the VHP declared that on 20 September it would
host a ceremony to lay the foundation stone for a 'grand Ram temple' at
the Babri Masjid in Ayodhya. They presented it as a logical next step—why
should 'our Ram remain inside a mosque' was the simple argument. The
All India Babri Action Committee responded with declarations of 'March
to Ayodhya' as well as a rally in Ayodhya in August and October, to stop
the proposed plans of the VHP.

Contemporary observers described it as a full-blown campaign of hatred
by communalists on both sides. Though Ayodhya remained peaceful, a feeling
of being helpless spectators was creeping in among the town's people. 'What
could we do, the whole country was talking about us; not only talking,
Hindus and Muslims were killing each other in the name of Ayodhya.
Nobody wanted to know what we thought,' Mahant Satyendra Das, head
priest of the Ram Janmabhoomi shrine, told me in an interview in 2016.
The VHP's mobilization drive pegged Ayodhya as the physical location
that united Hindus, but it was their hearts and minds that the VHP and
BJP corroded with vitriolic speeches. In 1989, the first visible attempts at
the construction of a Ram temple were started. It began in January with
a call to collect 'Ram Shilas' (bricks embossed with the name 'Ram') and
Rs 1.25 from every Hindu from the more than six lakh villages in India
(the number of villages has gone down since then). The call was given
by the VHP-propped Dharam Sansad, setting 30 September as the date
when these bricks would be ceremonially consecrated before being taken
to Ayodhya. Here they would be used in the Shilanyas (foundation-laying
ceremony), which would start on 9 November and end on 10 November
1989. The vast Hindu diaspora spread over North America, Europe, Asia
and Africa too sent in a large number of bricks through friends, family
and cargo mail.

India's judiciary, with one ear always to the ground, refused to stop the

---

Bureau of Investigation (CBI) lodged an FIR against the then president of Bofors Martin
Ardbo, alleged middleman Win Chadda and the Hinduja brothers for criminal conspiracy,
cheating and forgery. See 'What is the Bofors scam case?', *Indian Express*, 3 February 2018.

processions being taken across the country for the consecration of Ram Shilas. On the appeal to stop the processions for fear of violence, which was filed by V. M. Tarkunde, the Supreme Court held on 27 October 1989 that the respective state governments were responsible for communal violence that often accompanied these processions. It was a failure of law and order, the court held.[402]

From 5 November onwards, the Ram Shilas started arriving in Ayodhya accompanied by Bajrang Dal volunteers for protection. The town's Muslims watched them with the same curiosity as the numerous other Hindu residents. Ayodhya was suddenly churning the entire country and this amused many cynics among the locals. 'You will make the temple while our masjid is still there, will you make it on top of it?' Basheer would tease his neighbour, Rajkumar Yadav. And the response would be equally strong, 'Your mosque has been there for five hundred years, now it's our turn, why are you troubled?'[403]

Devraha Baba, a short, stoutly built sadhu, enjoyed a massive following in Hindi-speaking north India. He was associated with Ayodhya and was respected by both the VHP and the 'secular' camp led by the Congress. He used to meet and greet visitors and disciples from atop his machan; in that sense he was literally above party politics and religious divides. He was a fakir who did only his own bidding and had maintained a semblance of neutrality as a saint. Sensing that Devraha Baba might be able to persuade the VHP to postpone the Shilanyas, Rajiv Gandhi was advised by Arun Nehru and others to get the Baba's support. But when Rajiv's emissaries—UP Chief Minister N. D. Tiwari and Home Minister Buta Singh—met the Baba with this request, they were disappointed. The VHP had already convinced him to support their peaceful campaign for a Ram temple.

In 2017, journalist Ajay Singh wrote that Buta Singh, a Congress minister, had arranged a meeting between Devraha Baba and Rajiv Gandhi.[404] It was at this meeting that Devraha Baba told Rajiv, 'Bachcha, ho jane do' (Son, let it happen) and just like that, Rajiv had allowed the Shilanyas to take place. After that, Rajiv Gandhi went to Faizabad and launched the 1989 election campaign days before the Shilanyas was to take place. At Faizabad,

---

[402]'Rama Janma Bhoomi', *Inderprastha Vishva Hindu Parishad* <http://vhpdelhi.org/ Content.aspx?Page=20; https://sabrangindia.in/in-fact/babri-librehan>.

[403]Interview with Rajkumar Yadav, Ayodhya.

[404]Ajay Singh, 'Ram Mandir in Ayodhya: How Rajiv Gandhi obeying Deoraha Baba opened the floodgate of trouble', *Firstpost*, 25 December 2015.

Rajiv invoked Ram and famously announced that if elected, the Congress would establish 'Ram Rajya'.

Meanwhile, on 7 November, the Allahabad High Court dealt a legal blow to the VHP's plans by declaring that the site chosen for the proposed Shilanyas was part of the 'disputed land', and therefore, no changes could be made there by allowing the foundation stone to be laid. But the VHP was ready to defy the court's orders through 'satyagraha', the form of protest popularized during the freedom movement by Mahatma Gandhi.

Mahant Avaidyanath, the pre-eminent saint among the VHP's line-up and and the head of the Gorakshpeeth in Gorakhpur, was the next target of the government's attempts to postpone the Shilanyas ahead of the elections. A government plane was sent to fly him from Gorakhpur to Lucknow. Discussions between UP Chief Minister N. D. Tiwari, Union Home Minister Buta Singh, and Mahant Avaidyanath began:

> N. D. Tiwari: The plot where they want to do the Shilanyas has been declared disputed by the High Court. Our request is that you change the location of the Shilanyas.
>
> Avaidyanath: We cannot accept that. The High Court's orders are not applicable to us. If the government creates obstacles in our way, we have only two options, the Shilanyas or Satyagraha. We have come to Ayodhya ready for Satyagraha.[405]

The government, having realized that the VHP would not hesitate to escalate the situation, now looked for a face-saver. Old British-era maps that had became yellow and frayed were pulled out once again and it was 'discovered' that in fact, the site for the Shilanyas did not fall in the disputed land. The Shilanyas could now be performed, the solicitor general of the government of UP informed Mahant Avaidyanath.

VHP WINS AGAIN: FOUNDATION STONE LAID
On 9 November, the Bhoomi puja or ceremony to consecrate the ground for the Shilanyas, was performed with traditional rituals. On 10 November the VHP brought forward Kameshwar Chaupal, a Harijan (as Dalits were then called) to lay the first Ram Shila. VHP supporters erupted in joy across Ayodhya. The air was pierced with cries of 'Jai Shri Ram', 'Bharat mein rehna hai, Jai Shri Ram kehna hai' and 'Mandir wahin banayenge'.

---

[405]Gopal Sharma, *Karseva se Karseva Tak*, Jaipur: Rajasthan Patrika Limited, 1993, p. 34.

More than 200 saints participated in the Shilanyas. The time fixed for the Shilanyas was around 1 p.m. At the appointed hour, Hindus across the country participated in ceremonies organized by the BJP and the VHP to mark the holy hour. They did so by offering flowers and consecrated water while facing towards Ayodhya.

That evening the VHP gave a call for temple construction to start the next morning. Under the orders of Chief Minister N. D. Tiwari, the district magistrate of Faizabad refused permission for the construction citing court orders. The VHP complied and its supporters were asked to reassemble at Allahabad between 25–27 January 1990. The next date of temple construction would be decided then. The VHP was ecstatic with its success. In three years it had forced the Congress on the back foot twice. First, it had succeeded in opening the locks and had organized the Shilanyas. It had also galvanized a large section of upper-caste Hindus, other backward classes, Dalits and tribals. The BJP had come out in the open with its Palampur Resolution of June 1989, drafted by its new president, L. K. Advani. It had called upon 'the Rajiv government to adopt the same positive approach in respect to Ayodhya that the Nehru government did with Somnatha. The sentiments of the people must be respected and Janamsthan must be handed over to the Hindus—if possible through a negotiated settlement or else by legislation. Litigation is certainly no answer.'[406] The BJP was poised to take advantage of the VHP's success. On the other side, the Congress too was trying to garner credit for the opening of the locks and the Shilanyas. Meanwhile in Ayodhya, Ram Lalla's idol was still being worshipped inside the Babri Masjid, oblivious to the gathering storm of communal politics outside its old but still strong walls.

1989: RISE OF THE BHARATIYA JANATA PARTY

Until 1989, it was the VHP and its army of godmen who had been calling for a government that belonged to Hindus and worked in the interest of Hindu religion. When Rajiv Gandhi launched the 1989 election campaign with the promise of 'Ram Rajya', Ayodhya and Ram came to dominate the political discourse. In the last week of November 1989, nearly 300 million Indians voted to elect '525 members of the Lok Sabha, India's pre-

---

[406]Christophe Jaffrelot, *The Hindu Nationalist Movement and Indian Politics: 1925 to the 1990s: Strategies of Identity-building, Implantation and Mobilisation*, London: C. Hurst & Co, 1996, p. 382.

eminent national legislative body'.[407] The Congress's tally of more than 400 MPs fell to 197, V. P. Singh's Janata Dal, a conglomeration of disgruntled Congressmen and others, won 141 seats. The BJP, an offshoot of the Jan Sangh which was formed in 1980, won 85 seats. This was attributed to the Ram Janmabhoomi movement, which the BJP had officially come to support in 1989. In the last general election in 1984, the BJP had won only 2 seats in the Lok Sabha. However, significantly, and this is something which observers often overlook, it had been the runner-up in several dozen seats.

From the Faizabad Lok Sabha constituency, it was Mitrasen Yadav, a firebrand Yadav leader, who won the seat on a Communist Party of India ticket. Congress's Nirmal Khatri stood second while the Bahujan Samaj Party, a new outfit that claimed to represent the Dalits, came third.[408]

Interestingly, the BJP did not put up a candidate from the Faizabad constituency, which included Ayodhya. Evidently, it wasn't sure of even a fighting chance; therefore it chose to play safe. A loss in the seat would have given the opposition the best stick to beat them with. Thus, the BJP for all its support to the Ram temple movement did not contest from the one seat that mattered the most. It is an irony that was lost in the celebration of its 85-seat win.

An interesting aside is worth mentioning here. While at the national level, the BJP and the Congress were vehemently opposed to each other's politics, in Ayodhya, their respective candidates had joined forces. 'The synergy was evident in the common poll slogan: "*Ek vote Lallu ko, ek vote Panja ko*" (one vote to Lallu, another to the hand symbol).'[409] Lallu Singh, the BJP candidate for the state assembly elections, lost to Jai Shankar Pande of the Janata Party.

Assembly elections in Uttar Pradesh coincided with the 1989 general elections. Notwithstanding its success in winning 85 Lok Sabha seats, the BJP could win just 57 seats in the UP legislative assembly elections.

With a weakened Congress and non-existent BJP, it was Mulayam Singh

[407]'The 1989 Indian national elections: A retrospective analysis', *International Foundation for Electoral Systems* <http://www.ifes.org/publications/1989-indian-national-elections-retrospective-analysis>.

[408]*Statistical Report on General Elections, 1989 to the Ninth Lok Sabha,* Vol. I, New Delhi: Election Commission of India, 1990 <http://eci.nic.in/eci_main/StatisticalReports/LS_1989/Vol_I_LS_89.pdf>.

[409]Dhirendra K. Jha, 'In UP, Congress plays communal card', *Open Magazine*, 15 September 2012.

Yadav, then in the Janata Dal (Secular), who became the first non-Congress chief minister of Uttar Pradesh since Charan Singh in 1970. A key difference was that Yadav had never been in the Congress unlike the Jat leader from western UP. In Delhi too, a non-Congress government appeared to be an achievable possibility to non-Congress parties. In a remarkable move of opportunistic politics, barely a month after the Shilanyas were performed in front of the Ram Janmabhoomi–Babri Masjid complex, the avowedly secular V. P. Singh of the Janata Dal was sworn in as India's seventh prime minister on 2 December 1989. The V. P. Singh government was formed with the support of the BJP and the Left parties. An anti-Congressis sentiment had united communist comrades and RSS-backed Ram bhakts.

1990: MANDAL, RAM MANDIR AND BABRI MASJID

Though the BJP's plan of building a grand Ram temple had been rejected by the voters of Ayodhya, it continued to obsess over them. Throughout Ayodhya's history, its fate had been decided by events that had taken place out of turn and by rulers who had little to do with it.

In continuation with this historic pattern, yet another meeting of the VHP's contingent of saints was held at Allahabad on 25 January 1990. The holy men enlisted by the VHP decided that now that the foundation stone had been laid, construction of a Ram temple should begin as soon as possible, and the date that they chose was less than a month away—14 February.

On the assurance of the new prime minister, V. P. Singh,[410] that he would resolve the dispute over the Babri Masjid and Ram temple in four months, the VHP-backed saints postponed their plans till the next meeting which was to be held in Haridwar.

Between the January meeting and the upcoming one in June, a crucial legal development took place in the Babri Masjid-Ram Janmabhoomi dispute. On 25 May 1990, a special bench of the Allahabad High Court framed the issues under consideration. A total of forty-three issues were framed by the court; several of them were outside the scope of law and fell under the 'grey areas of history, mythology and religion'.[411] A majority of those issues would remain undecided until 2010, when a three-judge bench of the same High Court delivered its 'historic' judgement. A number

---

[410]J. Venkatesan, 'V. P. Singh regime withdrew ordinance on Ayodhya', *The Hindu*, 6 June 2003.
[411]Manoj Mitta, 'Anatomy of a confrontation', *Times of India*, 25 June 1990.

of issues related to the antiquity of Ram worship at the disputed site, the nature of the pillars present inside the mosque and whether the site was the birthplace of Lord Ram. One of the issues proposed by the Hindu Mahasabha, one of the oldest parties in the dispute, asked the court to decide 'whether the division of India was unauthorized and unconstitutional'. The judges declined to admit this issue as it was not under their domain. The counsel of the VHP was unsuccessful in convincing the court to drop the issue pertaining to the disputed site being Ram's birthplace. However, based on his pleas, the court subsequently added issues concerning Islamic scriptures. One of the issues that the court added was 'whether the pillars inside and outside the building in question contain images of Hindu gods and goddesses? If the finding is in the affirmative, whether on that account the building in question cannot have the character of mosque under the tenets of Islam?'[412]

During the month of June, Haridwar, an important site of Shaiva worship, was teeming with Hindu tourists heading up to the mountains to visit some of the holiest shrines in north India. By June, the four-month period requested by Prime Minister V. P. Singh had passed, and there was no solution in sight. Therefore, the saints and godmen met in Haridwar, and decided in a meeting held on 23–24 June that their next date for temple construction would be 30 October 1990. This meeting was also significant because it was here that the now notorious word, 'karseva', was used by the assembly of VHP-affiliated saints for the very first time.[413] In Sanskrit, karseva means service with one's hands. In a couple of years, this word would come to symbolize fanatic zeal, devotion, the VHP, Babri, Ayodhya, swords, riots and Hindu militancy. It would carry many meanings within it that were revealed or changed as the situation demanded. Karsevaks would mean terror for Muslims, misguided youth to the progressive liberal Hindu, militant Hindu activists to the non-violent Hindu, defenders of Hindu pride to most Hindus, and specifically in the context of the Haridwar meeting where it was first used—liberators of the Ram Lalla idol incarcerated in Ayodhya. Responding to the issues framed by the Allahabad High Court, the assembly of godmen—and a few godwomen too—clarified that matters of faith would not be decided by the court, and said that 'there would

---

[412]Ibid.
[413]Ibid.

be no compromise on the location of the proposed Ram temple'.[414] The Ram Lalla idol would remain where it was (under the central dome of the Babri Masjid) and the temple would be built *there*.

On 1 August, the saints met again in Mathura, believed to be the birthplace of Krishna. The day was aptly named, 'Sant Sankalp Divas' (day of resolve). Here it was decided that Shri Ram Jyoti Week would be marked between 12 and 18 October. The Ram Jyoti Week was like an Olympic torch marshalling Hindus across the country to enlist as karsevaks. The first lamps were lit by sparking fire through Arni Manthan (creating sparks using a wooden hand drill). The Arni Manthan ceremony in Ayodhya was accompanied by shouts of 'Jai Shri Ram' that grew louder as the smoke from wood rubbing against wood gave way to flames leaping out from the pile of twigs used as kindling. From there this 'fire', called Shri Ram Jyoti, was taken to Banaras and Mathura. The plan was to use the symbolism of Ram Jyoti to mobilize karsevaks for 'temple construction' in Ayodhya. This 'fire' would eventually cover five lakh villages and towns. RSS and VHP volunteers were asked to ensure that on Diwali, which fell on 18 October, marking the end of Shri Ram Jyoti Week, Hindu families would light their diyas with the Shri Ram Jyoti that had been carried from Ayodhya.[415]

A week later on 7 August, V. P. Singh announced the implementation of the Mandal Commission's report. In 1980, the Mandal Commission had recommended that 27 per cent of jobs in the central administration and public corporations be reserved for Other Backward Classes (OBCs). With this move V. P. Singh threatened to neutralize Devi Lal, a Jat leader, and a minister in Singh's government till a few days ago. As other observers have pointed out, with this measure he could be sure of undermining Devi Lal's rural base and of fomenting caste divisions in the Hindu community from which the BJP was attempting to create a vote bank. In Ayodhya, the reaction to the decision to implement the Mandal Commission's report was on predictable lines. While the Brahmins and Rajputs labelled it anti-Hindu, and even anti-Constitutional, the large majority of people hoped that it would provide them much-needed government jobs. The reaction of the RSS was visceral. Its mouthpiece, the *Organiser*, called it an attempt to divide Hindus on 'forward, backward and Harijan lines'.[416] For the BJP

---

[414]Sharma, *Karseva se Karseva Tak*, p. 40.

[415]Ibid.

[416]Jaffrelot, *The Making of Hindu Nationalist India*, p. 415.

to oppose reservations in the name of OBCs, who constitute more than half of India's population, was politically unthinkable; and so was supporting it, as that would have alienated some of its traditional voters among the upper castes.

The only way out was to support reservation in principle, and based on economic criteria. In the meantime, the BJP hoped to find a legitimate cause to topple the V. P. Singh government.

Ever since the BJP had passed its politically rewarding 1989 Palampur resolution and openly backed the RSS and VHP position on the Ram temple issue, L. K. Advani, the powerful president of the BJP, had emerged as one of the sharpest political minds. Under his leadership, the BJP had increased its tally to eighty-five MPs from just two in 1984. The V. P. Singh-led National Front government depended on the BJP for survival and Advani was acutely aware of the power that he and his party had come to wield in a short time. Although he refused to be interviewed for this book, his autobiography, *My Country My Life*, provides an interesting sidelight to those hectic times. According to Advani's account, he wanted to explore 'every possibility of an amicable solution while ensuring survival of the National Front government'.[417] Knowing that V. P. Singh's position as prime minister was on a sticky wicket after he had failed to find a solution to the Mandir–Masjid dispute in the stipulated time of four months, Advani took 'an important initiative' by offering a solution which he thought would be acceptable to Muslim leaders.

Advani's solution was that he 'would personally request leaders of the VHP to relinquish their demand on the Hindu shrines in Mathura and Varanasi if the Muslim claim over the Ramjanambhoomi was voluntarily withdrawn, paving the way for the construction of the Ram temple'.[418] Muslim leaders had no faith in such patronizing offers and rejected it summarily. Advani was 'deeply disappointed'.

Advani's disappointment did not last long. On 12 September, he called a press conference at the BJP's national headquarters in Delhi and announced his decision to 'undertake a 10,000-kilometre-long Rath Yatra, starting from Somnatha on 25 September and reaching Ayodhya on 30 October to join the kar seva'.[419] It was an electrifying time. The Yatra united lakhs of Hindus

---

[417]L. K. Advani, *My Country My Life*, New Delhi: Rupa Publications, 2008, p. 371.
[418]Ibid.
[419]Ibid., p. 374.

who were now told by the local coordinators of the RSS and VHP to prepare for karseva in Ayodhya on 30 October. The Rath Yatra was a barely concealed early mobilization campaign plan for the next general election, which the BJP hoped would soon become necessary.

FROM SOMNATHA TO AYODHYA: BLOOD AND FIRE

As planned, Advani began his Rath Yatra on 25 September 1990 from Somnatha on the western coast of India in the state of Gujarat. The rebuilding of Somnatha temple had also been the original inspiration for the Mahasabhaites to 'capture Babri Masjid' in 1949.[420] Other than Advani, out of the several BJP and RSS functionaries who were present that day, the only notable person who is still alive is India's prime minister, Narendra Modi. The wheels of Advani's customized Toyota truck slowly turned to the chants of 'Jai Shri Ram' and 'Saugandh Ram ki khaate hain, Hum Mandir wahin banayenge' (In the name of Ram, we resolve: We shall build the temple there—at Ramjanambhoomi) [Advani's translation].

The slogan reflected the attitude of the proponents of the Ram temple. Convinced of Ram's efficacy as glue to unite Hindus by its political success in the 1989 elections, the RSS, VHP and BJP had consistently expanded their demands. In 1984 and until 1986 their demand to get the locks opened was exemplified in this slogan: 'Aage badho, zor se bolo, Janmabhoomi ka tala kholo' (Move forward, say it out loud, unlock the Janmabhoomi).

In 1990, with the national government surviving on their support, the RSS-led 'Ram Bhakts' had hardened their stance; so had ordinary Hindus and Muslims. Communalization, which had hitherto been limited to certain pockets, was now spreading like a virus. The Ram Jyoti lit from the fires produced at Ayodhya was being taken out in processions through provincial capitals, towns and hamlets. In many places, these processions triggered violence when they forced their way into Muslim neighbourhoods.[421]

Advani's Rath Yatra too seemed to be either followed or preceded by communal violence wherever it went. In Gujarat, violence began soon after Advani's Toyota-Rath Yatra left Somnatha. Forty-one people were killed in communal rioting in Ahmedabad, Bapunagar, Baroda and Ankleshwar.[422]

---

[420]Jha and Jha, *Ayodhya A Dark Night*, p. 36.
[421]Jaffrelot, *The Hindu Nationalist Movement and Indian Politics*, p. 419.
[422]Jaffrelot, 'Myth of moderation', *Indian Express*, 12 May 2014 and Jaffrelot, 'Refining the "Moderation Thesis" regarding "Radical Parties"', The Jana Sangh and the BJP between Hindu Nationalism and Coalition Politics in India, 2010 <hal-01069458>.

After covering Madhya Pradesh, Rajasthan, Andhra Pradesh, Karnataka, Gujarat, Maharashtra and Delhi, when the Rath Yatra reached Bihar— which was then ruled by the Janata Dal's firebrand chief minister, Lalu Prasad Yadav—it was grounded and Advani detained by the Bihar police in Samastipur. Ayodhya with its minuscule population of Muslims remained peaceful although communal slogans were raised there and in Faizabad. In Advani's detention, the BJP found the legitimate cause that it had hoped for and withdrew support from V. P. Singh's National Front government. Meanwhile, the countrywide bandhs against his detention by Sangh Parivar activists not only brought life in the country to a halt, but also fanned communal violence. 'In Gujarat violence was widespread; communal riots erupted in 26 different localities, leading to about 100—fatalities between September 1 and November 20, 1990'.[423]

Meanwhile, the proposed plan of the RSS, VHP and BJP to do 'karseva' at Ayodhya, or in other words demolish the mosque to make way for a new temple, had turned Ayodhya into a town under siege. Mulayam Singh Yadav, derisively called 'Mullah Mulayam', 'a fake Yadav' and a 'fake Hindu' by karsevaks, had declared Ayodhya a 'no-karsevak' zone. In the days leading up to 30 October, the day on which karseva was to be done, he had arrogantly asserted that 'Parinda bhi par nahin maar sakta' (Not even a bird can flap its wings) near the Ram Janmabhoomi–Babri Masjid site. But securing Ayodhya, which is accessible through fields, river, rail and at least three road routes, had proved to be impossible. Karsevaks travelling from Hindi and non-Hindi states were gushing, trickling and sneaking into Ayodhya. The UP government hadn't even been able to stop the VHP's general secretary, Ashok Singhal, who reached Ayodhya on 28 October in disguise, dressed in shirt and trousers instead of his usual dhoti-kurta and tilak on his forehead. His presence raised the morale of the karsevaks 'to the heights of Mount Kailash', to borrow a simile from Valmiki's Ramayana. Thousands of karsevaks had arrived a couple of days early and many of them were camping in the bigger ashrams like the Digambar Akhara and Maniram Das ki Chavni. Thousands more were making their way on foot, spending the day hiding in Hindu-dominated villages and moving only in the dark of night. Near Ayodhya, karsevaks were waiting on the banks of the Sarayu, having taken the Gorakhpur route. By the night of 29 October, all entry points to Ayodhya were choked with karsevaks, mostly men, and

---

[423]Jaffrelot, *The Hindu Nationalist Movement and Indian Politics*, p. 420.

some women too. They were beseeching the police to let them join those already inside Ayodhya.

In the weeks before 30 October, the VHP had muddled its real position by the occasional softening of stance. In late September the VHP was reported to have dramatically reduced its demands to merely the removal of the stone inscriptions believed to have been installed by Mir Baqi. In the same statement, Ashok Singhal was quoted as saying that more than 15 lakh people would reach Ayodhya ready for a fight to the finish for the sake of Ram Janmabhoomi.

Rankled by communal killings in the name of Ayodhya, at least one attempt was made by its residents to make their views heard. The Janata Dal MLA from Ayodhya, Jai Shankar Pande, travelled to Delhi along with social activists and prominent citizens to petition the prime minister, but their trip ultimately proved futile as it did not stop the influx of thousands of karsevaks into Ayodhya. Their grouse was a fundamental one: nobody had asked them what they wanted.

On 19 October, prior to the BJP's withdrawal of support to his government, V. P. Singh had enacted an ordinance to acquire the disputed structure of Babri Masjid-Ramjanmabhoomi and the surrounding land totalling 2.5 acres. The Babri Masjid Action Committee and other Muslim organizations called a 'Bharat Bandh' on 30 October to protest this ordinance. Fearing a Muslim backlash and sensing the lukewarm response of the VHP, V. P. Singh withdrew the ordinance on 21 October and soon after that the BJP withdrew its support. This further emboldened the karsevaks.

The morning of 30 October in Ayodhya dawned with tense anticipation for the police and the administration. The UP government had deployed dozens of extra officers (for many of them it was their first visit to Ayodhya) to manage the nearly 28,000 personnel belonging to hundreds of companies of the Indo-Tibetan Border Police (ITBP), the Border Security Force (BSF), Central Reserve Police Force (CRPF), state police and UP's notoriously anti-Muslim Provincial Armed Constabulary.[424] Many of their officers were staying in the sprawling Birla Dharamshala in Ayodhya. V. P. Singh was still the prime minister. How divided the country was over the VHP's and

---

[424]Farzand Ahmed, 'Meerut: As politicians fan communal passions, trigger-happy PAC display anti-Muslim bias', *India Today*, 9 November 1998 and Dilip Awasthi, 'Provincial Armed Constabulary faces flak for controversial role in Meerut riots', *India Today*, 30 June 1987.

BJP's karseva is reflected in news reports of a tiff between V. P. Singh and his pro-temple wife Sitadevi, who wanted him to support the construction of a Ram temple.[425]

On 30 October, karsevaks pushed their way towards the Ram Janmabhoomi–Babri Masjid complex from all directions. At the Sarayu Bridge, in defiance of a curfew and shoot-at-sight orders, nearly 40,000 karsevaks jostled with the security forces to let them enter the town.

The security forces were under orders from Chief Minister Mulayam Singh Yadav to protect the mosque at any cost. Before the security forces finally opened fire, their patience was tested several times by unruly crowds.

A man bearing the appearance of a sadhu (old, long haired and bearded) hijacked an empty bus and drove towards the disputed site running over police pickets and barricades. A short while earlier, a retired director general of UP police and VHP leader, S. C. Dixit, had addressed a rapturous crowd of karsevaks using a megaphone provided by the police. Soon after, dozens of karsevaks had attacked the Babri Masjid with pickaxes and iron bars. On the main road that passed through Ayodhya, stone-throwing by hundreds of karsevaks caused many injuries to security forces. The firing and lathi charge by the police at the Sarayu Bridge prevented a complete breakdown of the security lockdown.

During the course of 30 October, the dilemma of firing at largely unarmed crowds faced by the average policemen was made worse for those who were Hindu. The karsevaks were cajoling the men in uniform by chanting:

Hindu-Hindu bhai bhai
Beech mein vardi kahan se aayi

(Hindus are brothers,
Let the uniform not divide us)

The UP police, particularly the Provincial Armed Constabulary, had acquired notoriety for the brutal and targeted killings of Muslims during riots in the preceding years. Swayed by the chanting of karsevaks and the exhortations by a former director general of police, the mainly Hindu policemen sympathetic to karsevaks[426] did not stop them. The hijacking of

---

[425] Arvind Kumar Singh, *Ayodhya Vivaad: Ek Patrakar Ki Diary*, Delhi: Shilpayan, 2010.

[426] Anand Patwardhan, dir., *Ram ke Naam*, 1992; and Hemant Sharma, *Ayodhya ka Chashmdeed*, New Delhi: Prabhat Prakashan, 2018, p. 415.

the bus and the breakdown of the security perimeter around the masjid-temple complex was a result of the police's predicament in dealing with a mob that was acting in Ram's name. The karsevaks destroyed the wall separating the Ram Chabutra and the Babri Masjid, many of them climbed atop its domes, and in their zeal to free 'Ram Lalla', started hammering them down. Some of them persuaded the police to open the locks of the temple inside the mosque,[427] which the karsevaks surrounded in their frenzied state, singing bhajans.

Besides taking up Mulayam's dare that 'not even a bird can flap its wings', so far, the karsevaks had fulfilled the first half of the promise in their slogan—'Ram Lalla hum aayenge, Mandir wahin banayenge' (Infant Ram, we will come, we will build the temple there). The karsevaks had made their point by causing damage to the boundary wall of the mosque and by planting saffron flags on top of the domes. The state police had refrained from firing at the karsevaks atop the domes, who were being joined by more every minute. It was only when an Indian Air Force helicopter appeared in the sky that both the police and karsevaks relented. A Border Security Force man fired at the men on the domes, after which the karsevaks scattered and curfew could eventually be reimposed. A saffron flag flew atop the central dome of Babri Masjid-Ram Janmabhoomi till late in the evening. A monkey which was sitting on the dome had appeared to the devout policemen to be Hanuman himself guarding the flag, and so they had desisted from removing it. After the monkey came down of its own accord, the flag was removed by policemen.[428]

The karsevaks were triumphant with their achievements for the day. Despite Mulayam's orders and some incidents of firing by the police, they had planted the saffron flag on Babur's mosque, 'the symbol of their ancestors' slavery'. According to VHP supporters, the day's death toll was in 'hundreds'. But according to government figures, six karsevaks had died in the firing at Sarayu Bridge and near Hanumangarhi.[429] Innocent villagers who had come for the annual circumambulation, or parikrama, were also caught in the crossfire. VHP leader Ashok Singhal's photograph holding a bloodied handkerchief to his head made it to the front pages of most English and

---

[427]Sharma, *Karseva se Karseva Tak*, p. 73.

[428]Ibid., p. 75.

[429]Jaffrelot, *The Hindu Nationalist Movement in India*, New York: Columbia University Press, 1993.

Hindi newspapers. Rumours of vindictive and hostile ITBP and CRPF personnel gained currency among the believers.[430] The neighbourhoods around Digambar Akhara and Maniram Das ki Chavni became liberated zones where police couldn't enter. Ram bhakts added a new slogan to their repertoire: 'Ayodhya hui hamari hai, ab Mathura ki bari hai' (Ayodhya belongs to us, now it is Mathura's turn).

The attack on the mosque was also being felt by Prime Minister V. P. Singh. He was close to Syed Shahabuddin, his Janata Dal colleague and one of the tallest leaders of the Babri Masjid Action Committee (BMAC), who was considered a role model by the Muslim community. Shahabuddin was well versed in Islamic scripture as well as English literature. One of the many educated Muslims in Faizabad who looked up to Shahabuddin was Khaliq Ahmed Khan. 'Shahabuddin used to trust me,' Khaliq told me. On 30 October, much confusion prevailed about the extent of the damage to the mosque. According to Khan, he told Syed Shahabuddin on the phone that a physical inspection must be done at the Ram Janmabhoomi–Babri Masjid. 'Syed Sahab told V. P. Singh and gave him my name and number,' recalls Khan, sitting in the drawing room of his Faizabad home. The government machinery moved fast: the city magistrate telephoned Khaliq Khan to arrange his visit to Ayodhya in the middle of a curfew. Eventually, it was a delegation of five persons including Yunus Siddiqui, the local representative of BMAC, that reached the Babri Masjid around 9 p.m. Khaliq recounts the night's events:

> The DM of Faizabad at that time was Mr. R. S. Srivastava; we used to joke with him calling him RSS. He was already present at the mosque. On inspection we found out that the mob had destroyed the wall-railing structure that separated the mosque from Nirmohi Akhara's Ram Chabutra. It had also tried to break the dome but besides minor damage it was intact. That night, the local daily *Jan Morcha* was asked by the district administration to delay its edition.[431]

At 11 p.m. the delegation of five Muslims announced to television cameras and reporters that the damage to the mosque was 'not serious'.

Khaliq continued, 'We also gave it in writing. I wrote that it was "mamooli nuksaan" (minor damage). Many Muslims and non-Muslims were

---

[430]Sharma, *Karseva se Karseva Tak*.pp. 93–94.
[431]In an interview with the author, November 2017.

upset by this statement, but we reported what we saw. We believed that the main outcome of the day was that if the government had the will, the administration could protect the mosque and maintain law and order'. It was also the beginning of Khaliq Khan's serious engagement with the Ayodhya dispute. In 2017, he was still the nominee of a party, Laulana Mehfoozur Rahman, named in the title suit, as well as the convener of the Faizabad Hilal Committee.

2 NOVEMBER 1990

Most of the karsevaks had been driven away from the Babri Masjid-Ram Janmabhoomi complex to the further side of the main road that runs through Ayodhya. Outside the barricades at the entry points, devotees camped along the banks of the Sarayu alongside sadhus, a number of them ascetics who had ventured out of their remote hermitages to witness what they believed was a historic moment. On the bridge over the Sarayu too, Sadhus built small yagya-kunds, or sacrificial fire pits, where they did ritualistic prayers for those karsevaks who died in the firing.[432] When they led a public chanting of Aum in protest, a number of policemen present to secure the bridge also joined the karsevaks and sadhus in reciting one of the most sacred and primeval sounds for millions of Hindus, Buddhists and Jains. The Ramayana was being recited by hundreds of priests, giving the appearance of a massive religious congregation to the entire scene. Inside Ayodhya, chaos and confusion prevailed and only mahants like Nritya Gopal Das and Ramchandra Das Paramhans were able to keep the anarchy of thousands of karsevaks in check. On 1 November, Ashok Singhal, Swami Vamdev, Nritya Gopal Das and others decided to resume 'karseva' the next day. On 2 November, the karsevaks, led by Ramchandra Paramhans, moved in a large and dense column towards Hanumangarhi; the Babri Masjid lay behind it 500 metres away.

Having learnt its lesson from the 30 October incident, the state administration was better prepared this time. An additional district magistrate, one of the several that the UP government had deputed to Faizabad–Ayodhya, was deployed near today's Shaheed Gali in Ayodhya on that day. Speaking to me at his home in a Delhi suburb on the condition of anonymity, he recounted that day: 'It was getting a little cold, the autumn heat was giving way, but fans were still needed in the day and a half-sweater had to be

---

[432]Hemant Sharma, *Ayodhya ka Chashmdeed*, p. 428.

worn in the evenings'.

This young officer had been posted in Agra but since September 1990, he had been stationed in Faizabad district as part of the Mulayam government's effort to create and enforce a security lockdown in Ayodhya. Now retired, the former Indian Administrative Service (IAS) officer appeared to be still affected by that day. As his son joined us, he continued, 'There were only central forces deployed on that day. I was in charge of two companies of CRPF (nearly 200 men).' Shortly after he took his position near the Hanumangarhi, the karsevaks had started moving towards his position. The massive crowd of thousands was aggressive and started pelting stones; in response, he recalled, nearly forty-five tear gas shells were fired to chase them away, 'but the wind was blowing in our direction', he said, laughing. They also had information that some of the karsevaks were carrying country-made handguns. Faced with an aggressive and violent mob the CRPF men opened fire after one of their officers suffered a head injury inflicted by a large stone.

Speaking to various eyewitnesses and availing other accounts of that day, it appears that bullets were fired by some elements who had mingled in the crowd of karsevaks. The CRPF and BSF personnel responded with equal force and fired from the top of houses and temples.

By the end of that day, sixteen (fifteen according to other accounts, including an official statement by the government in Parliament, twelve according to the *Jan Morcha* report 3 November 1990) dead bodies underwent post-mortems. Two brothers, Sharad Kothari and Ram Kumar Kothari, lay dead in a heap outside an old building.

Later, in a bid to derive more political mileage out of their deaths, all sixteen casualties were celebrated as martyrs and their ashes taken around in brass urns throughout the country. The VHP also launched a campaign of mass communication through video cassettes and audio tapes. Eventually, its claims of mass murders by central paramilitary forces numbering in 'hundreds' were proven to be false. Months later in an investigation by *Frontline* magazine, many of those claimed dead by the VHP turned out to be alive.[433]

After 2 November, the young officer who had allowed the firing became a marked man. 'A reward was announced to kill me. I travelled under false names, my family suffered.' Mulayam Singh Yadav became a messiah for Muslims while he and other senior and junior officers were openly villainized

---

[433]S. P. Singh and Venkitesh Ramakrishnan, 'When the "dead" came back', *Frontline*, Vol. 8, 24 May 1991.

by the VHP. Now living a quiet life, the retired government servant still loathes talking about that day and its consequences. 'All I can say is that I was doing my duty as a government officer with fairness.'

On 3 November 1990, Swami Vamdev, another VHP-enlisted godman, called off the karseva in Ayodhya. In Faizabad, wives of state government officers and army officers took out a protest march against the 'massacre of Hindus'. Had Shakuntala Nair been alive, she would have approved of the action by the officers' wives.

It wasn't the first time that women had come out on the streets of Faizabad. A women's march was taken out on 20 October 1990 by the National Federation of Indian Women. An organization with communist origins, it had organized a massive peace rally of women who had assembled from different states. By 7 November 1990 most karsevaks had left Ayodhya. The same day in Delhi, V. P. Singh's minority government, which had so far continued to function, collapsed. V. P. Singh resigned as prime minister the same day. Mandir politics had defeated his mandal politics. Singh was outdone by his rival Chandra Shekhar, who became the prime minister with Congress support. In Uttar Pradesh, Mulayam Singh Yadav was secure in his position as chief minister with the support of the Chandra Shekhar-led Janata Dal (Socialist) faction of the old Janata Dal. Chandra Shekhar, a Thakur leader from Uttar Pradesh, was sworn in as prime minister on 20 November 1990.

Until November 1990, Ayodhya had never witnessed violence on this scale. The last reported incident of communal violence dated back to 1934 when the Babri Masjid had been attacked by Hindus over rumours of cow slaughter in a neighbouring village. As noted earlier, the British government had then imposed a fine on Ayodhya's Hindus for damaging the walls of the mosque and the inscriptions said to have been put up by Mir Baqi in 1528. 'We were more used to mahants and their supporters fighting with each other over disputed temples and lands, and those were occasional incidents. We had never seen so many people before except during the melas. The firing scarred us as it was in our holy town that the blood of innocent Hindus was shed. People became both scared and angry with the government,' Ajay Gupta, a local businessman, recalled. The deaths of the sixteen karsevaks were to become a tool in the hands of the RSS, VHP and BJP. The VHP was quick to launch nationwide mass media campaigns pegged around the 'martyrs of Ayodhya'. A BJP MP, J. K. Jain, arranged for the production of a video cassette entitled *Pran Jau,*

Par Vachan Na Jai (At The Cost of Our Lives, Our Promise Will be Kept) which showed the events of the two days, and used cinematic techniques to portray the karsevaks as innocent and helpless, while security personnel belonging to central paramilitary forces were made to appear as brutal and vindictive, as 'they were firing indiscriminately on unarmed Ram Bhakts'.[434] The video declared the firing in Ayodhya 'worse than the massacre of Indians by British General Dyer at Jallianwala Bagh in Amritsar in 1919' and sought to portray the incident as the seventy-seventh war over Ram's birthplace.[435] This helped them perpetuate the myth of a continuous Hindu struggle to reclaim the Ram Janmabhoomi from Muslim rulers. Besides this, the VHP also produced other cassettes with similar themes.[436] The purpose of the video was to indoctrinate Hindu masses with the VHP's version of events and history. Most Indians in the late 1980s and 1990s had almost no prior electronic media exposure (except the airing of the *Ramayan* to some extent). Women especially were moved by images of a cherubic boy Ram incarcerated in a 'jail' (Babri Masjid). Gory visuals of the dead bodies of karsevaks, accompanied by a voiceover which openly castigated the UP state government and central paramilitary forces, enraged the average viewer who quickly became a convert to the cause of the VHP. Some of the more popular videos produced at the behest of the VHP were *Bhay Prakat Kripala* (Appeared the Kind God), which portrayed the magical appearance of the Ram Lalla idol inside the Babri Masjid in 1949; *Ram ji ki Sena Chali* (March of Ram's Army), which showed the mobilization of karsevaks for the cause of the Ram temple; and *Ram Rajya ki aur Chalein* (Let's go for Ram's Rule), a video used extensively in the 1991 UP assembly and national elections, that sought to persuade people to vote in favour of those who would bring in Ram Rajya.

MANDIR–MASJID TRUMPS MANDAL

The collapse of V. P. Singh's government was a direct fallout of his decision to implement the Mandal Commission report which recommended reservation for OBCs. It was after he played the caste card that the Advani-led BJP had created the Rath Yatra campaign to 'unite all Hindus'. After the firing at Ayodhya, the triumvirate of the RSS, VHP and BJP, along with

---

[434]Jaffrelot, *The Hindu Nationalist Movement in India*, pp. 420–26.
[435]Ibid.
[436]Pradip K. Datta, 'VHP's Ram at Ayodhya: reincarnation through ideology and organisation', *Economic and Political Weekly*, Vol. 26, No. 44, 2 November 1991, pp. 2517–26.

the Bajrang Dal and the student's wing of the RSS, the Akhil Bharatiya Vidyarthi Parishad (ABVP), began to work in tandem to further consolidate the feeling of 'Hinduness'. Brijesh Sahu, no more a VHP supporter, was a leading mobilizer of karsevaks in Karawal Nagar in Delhi in 1990. According to him, 'we really believed in everything that was being told to us by the big leaders, and saints. When they said, Pehle Hindu, Uske Peeche Jaat [first comes your identity as a Hindu and then comes your caste], we felt finally we are going to end the discrimination on the lines of caste, we were truly exhilarated by that hope.' Sahu was not the only one. The video campaigns, complemented by the on-ground presence of RSS coordinators, were largely successful in convincing OBCs that the need of the hour was to unite all Hindus. The growing anti-Pandit violence in Kashmir was often cited as an example of Hindus being persecuted 'in their own country' and so were other issues like the Uniform Civil Code. In the late eighties and early nineties Hindus in Kashmir were targeted by fundamentalist Islamic militant groups due to which many of them had to leave the state forever. According to media reports, 'different accounts give different statistics of the total number of Kashmiri Pandits who fled their homes for their life in the 1990s. While some say around 1,00,000 of them had left the valley, others suggest figures as high as 1,50,000 to 1,90,000. A report by the Jammu and Kashmir government says as many as 219 people from this community were killed in the region between 1989 and 2004.'[437]

1991–1992: A TURNING POINT FOR AYODHYA

To his credit, though Chandra Shekhar's short-lived government had inherited the bloody baggage of karsevaks' deaths, he was successful in bringing the VHP and the Babri Masjid Action Committee (BMAC) to the same table for a dialogue. Meanwhile, the legal cases remained undecided in the Allahabad High Court. Since 1986, the VHP had openly demanded that Muslims 'shift' the Babri Masjid elsewhere because, they argued, the 'birthplace of Ram' could not be changed and reiterated that under no circumstance would the Ram Lalla idol be moved. This is when differences over what constituted history arose between the two groups. The debate became more polarized when questions were raised about the historicity of Ram and the Ramayana by the BMAC representatives, who also argued

---

[437]'Exodus of Kashmiri Pandits: What happened on January 19, 26 years ago?', *India Today*, 19 January 2016.

that there was no evidence to show that today's Ayodhya is in fact the one mentioned in Valmiki's Ramayana. The negotiations collapsed in the absence of a sincere intention to resolve the dispute.

The VHP wanted the BMAC to apologize for questioning the historicity of Ayodhya. (The question of historicity remains unsettled.) A compromise formula based on Muslims surrendering the disputed site to Hindus in return for Hindus surrendering their claims over any other mosque-temple, came closest to being acceptable to the BJP and VHP. However, the Muslims were as divided as the Hindus. The hardliners among them argued that even if they were to overlook the crime of the 1949 trespass of the mosque, they could not simply 'give away' the mosque, as it was a Wakf property. The nature of any property under the Wakf could not be changed or converted. In the aftermath of the October–November 1990 firing in Ayodhya, RSS and BJP leaders coined a new term for their opponents—pseudo-secularists. The country, including its urban middle class, was now debating the pros and cons of building a temple at the disputed site. Hindus, by and large, came to blame the 'stubbornness of Muslims' for the continuation of the dispute.[438] Though attempts at negotiations continued to be made, nothing came off of them. Ram Lalla remained inside the Babri Masjid, and outside, the bitterness between the two communities was brewing into a communal toxin. Chandra Shekhar resigned as prime minister on 6 March 1991 after the Congress withdrew its support. Rajiv Gandhi, recovering from the anti-Congress mandate of the 1989 election, hoped to gain in the new elections which were scheduled to be held two months later in May.

In April 1991, the RSS, VHP and BJP together held the biggest rally ever at Delhi's Boat Club,[439] on the grounds lying between Raisina Hill and India Gate. It was so well attended that, as the saying in Ayodhya goes, 'there was no space for even a sesame seed'.

This was perhaps the turning point in Ayodhya's as well as India's modern history. By stigmatizing and vilifying Muslims, who constitute more than 10 per cent of the population, the Sangh Parivar had used the symbolism of a mosque—Ayodhya's Babri Masjid—to unite Hindus in the name of Ram. Its multimedia and multilevel propaganda had freely deployed multiple anachronisms harking to the golden era of Ram Rajya. Now, from the

---

[438]Sharique N. Siddiquie, 'Ayodhya: The justified injustice', *Zee News*, 5 August 2011.
[439]Shahnaz Anklesaria Aiyar, 'VHP gains strength with each passing day, poised to play key role in coming polls', *India Today*, 30 April 1991.

power centre of the country, its battery of saints and godwomen gunned for electoral democracy itself.

His voice choking with tears, Acharya Dharmendra, a VHP-backed godman first introduced the nearly three-lakh strong crowd of 'Ram bhakts', to the grieving family of the two Kothari brothers who had become the face of the 1990 'Martyrs of Ayodhya'. Subsequently, many of the nearly 1,000 saints, godwomen like Sadhvi Rithambara and Uma Bharti, all hues of godmen, RSS and VHP leaders and BJP stalwarts addressed the crowd. Each one of them exhorted the participants to act on religious lines and used the presence of the family of the 'Martyrs of Ayodhya' to manipulate their emotions against all other non-BJP parties.[440] However, before the rally, the BJP had dismissed charges that it was a 'single point party', and after the rally it strove to 'maintain a secular image'.[441]

At the rally, one speaker after another made speeches that ended with an appeal to vote for the BJP. Satyanand Giri said, 'This is not about a majority (in Parliament) but Ram Rajya,' V. H. Dalmia equated the firings of 1990 to the Jallianwala Bagh massacre, and Sadhvi Rithambara incited the crowd to snatch the seat of power from politicians. The erstwhile queen of Gwalior, Vijayraje Scindia, piously stated, 'Those assembled here are like the vanar sena (monkey army) of my Ram.' She went on to condemn forty-four years of misrule and asked for the ouster of 'such people from power'.[442]

Ayodhya's leading mahant, Nritya Gopal Das, equated the Ram temple's construction to the construction of a Hindu nation. The rally was a grand success. Elections were due a month later in May 1991.

The main themes of the speakers were built around the following points:

- Do you wish to live in a country dominated by the aulaad [descendants] of Aurangzeb, who burnt his father in oil? Or do you want to live in a land ruled by the men of Ram, who fought valiantly to save their brother at the cost of their lives?
- The men who buried Saint Xavier and destroyed Aurangzeb should now eliminate Mulayam and all those he panders to.
- Why should Hindus give in to those who want to overpower them with their multiple breeding and anti-national views?[443]

---

[440]Gopal Sharma, *Kar Seva se Kar Seva Tak*, p. 138.
[441]Ibid.
[442]Ibid., p. 139.
[443]Aiyar, 'VHP gains strength with each passing day'.

The rally's main purpose was summed up in the three main points which emerged from various speeches. These were:

• Every Hindu should rise to 'liberate' and 'reconstruct' the three temples allegedly destroyed by Muslim invaders—in Ayodhya, Mathura and Varanasi.

• Every Hindu should use his vote to destroy the dastardly oppressor of all Hindus, Mulayam Singh Yadav and 'the gang of three'—V. P. Singh, Rajiv Gandhi and Chandra Shekhar—who caved in to Muslim pressure and stalled the reclamation of the Ayodhya temple.

And,

• The only way to herald Ram Rajya was to vote for the BJP.[444]

On 21 May 1991, Rajiv Gandhi was assassinated by the LTTE, a Tamil guerrilla group fighting against the Sri Lankan government for a separate state, and against whom Rajiv had sent Indian troops in his previous stint as prime minister. This tragic assassination is believed to have won the Congress more seats than was widely expected before his killing. However, in Ayodhya, the BJP won both the assembly and the Lok Sabha seats. The BJP's long-time local leader, Lallu Singh, was elected as MLA, and Vinay Katiyar, the founding president of the Bajrang Dal, won the Faizabad Lok Sabha seat. In the UP assembly elections which were held at the same time as the national elections, the BJP won 221 out of 419 seats. Kalyan Singh, a leader of the numerically important Lodhi community, was sworn in as the chief minister on 24 June 1991. Soon after taking oath, he visited the Ram Janmabhoomi–Babri Masjid site along with his ministers and the new BJP president, Murli Manohar Joshi. All of them, ignoring the fact that the dispute was pending in the court, resolved to build the Ram temple at the site of the Babri Masjid.[445]

> As chief minister, Kalyan Singh turned the cry of 'Ram Lalla hum ayenge, Mandir wahin banayenge', into the topmost priority of the state government. Photos from that day show the new Chief Minister, BJP's senior leader M. M. Joshi among others, standing outside the Ram Lalla shrine inside the mosque, holding their hands outstretched above their heads in jubilation. Also seen in the photograph is the then

---

[444]Ibid.
[445]Gopal Sharma, *Karseva se Karseva Tak*.

chief priest of the Ram Janmabhoomi temple, Pujari Lal Das. Lal Das, a Bairagi with Marxist leanings, was a vocal critic of the VHP. He also believed that the VHP was behind attacks on his life. In March 1992, Lal Das was removed as the chief priest by the state government. Less than a year after Babri Masjid's demolition he was shot dead by unknown assailants on November 16, 1993.[446]

After Rajiv Gandhi's death, the Congress formed a minority government under the leadership of a reclusive and religious-minded P. V. Narasimha Rao. It was a time of rapid change in India and Rao oversaw unprecedented and enduring developments in the country. Today, he is remembered mainly for taking the Indian economy towards economic liberalization as well as for being the prime minister who allegedly slept through the afternoon on 6 December 1992 when thousands of karsevaks destroyed the Babri Masjid in the presence of thousands of security personnel.

---

[446] Arvind Kumar Singh, *Ayodhya Vivaad Ek Patrakar ki Diary*, p. 111.

Chapter 10

COUNTDOWN TO 6 DECEMBER 1992

The VHP and the BJP government in Uttar Pradesh considered the Babri Masjid-Ram Janmabhoomi issue as essentially a religious dispute which could only be solved by the construction of the Ram temple at the exact place where the mosque stood. To both, the fact that the title suit was pending in the courts was an unavoidable technical and procedural obstacle. However, at the new prime minister Narasimha Rao's initiative, half-hearted efforts to resolve the dispute through dialogue took place sporadically. Meanwhile in Ayodhya, the UP government began a methodical process of 'building a Ram temple'.

In violation of prevailing legal status quo in the title suit—which had made slow progress—the Kalyan Singh government first cut down security at the mosque. By the end of July 1991, it had removed checkposts on the roads leading to the disputed site, and under pressure from its local MP, Vinay Katiyar, it also removed the iron railing around the Babri Masjid. Just a few months earlier, in October–November 1990, in order to protect the mosque, UP's Mulayam Singh government had turned Ayodhya into a fortress. Now, where karsevaks had been killed, the fortress was being reengineered to allow greater access to karsevaks.

Like all generalizations, an oversimplification about the socio-economic and demographic profile of most karsevaks is likely to be flawed. They were motivated by different aspects of the movement; most of them hailed from urban and semi-urban areas, were often unemployed or poorly employed and showed a 'taste for adventure'.[447] Given the late development of Ayodhya as a pilgrim centre, it was not surprising that most Hindus had never been to Ayodhya. In a way Ayodhya had been brought to them only through technology and media exposure. To them the slogan of 'Mandir wahin

---

[447]Jaffrelot, *The Hindu Nationalist Movement in India*, p. 428.

banayenge' carried an emotional and religious appeal which was dramatically enhanced by the VHP's 1990s campaigns pegged at the 'Martyrs of Ayodhya'. The VHP had been successful in doing away with the complexities involved in the case with actionable slogans like the one mentioned above. They had convinced Hindus that it was indeed Ram's birthplace and that Babur destroyed a Ram temple and built a mosque over it.

Many Hindus also believed that by building a grand Ram temple, they would take revenge on Muslims, or as the VHP called them, 'Babur's children'. In 1991–92, a new slogan had become very popular very quickly:

Jab Katue Kaate Jaayenge
Tab Ram-Ram Chillayenge

(When they are being chopped,
Muslims will shout Ram-Ram)[448]

Unlike this slogan, which directly incited violence, 'Mandir wahin banayenge' was considered a logical, creative, and even constructive assertion. Of course, nobody really knew for sure how this temple would be built.

PREPARING FOR DEMOLITION

The Ram Janmabhoomi–Babri Masjid complex was surrounded on three sides by Hindu temples, which had been built on graveyards. Like other temples in Ayodhya, these temples also functioned as houses in which people lived, and sometimes ran shops that sold religious items. The VHP's demand was that this undisputed land should be given on a permanent lease to the Ram Janmabhoomi Trust. It was the VHP-led Ram Janmabhoomi movement that had brought the BJP to power, and now it was anxious to see the construction of the Ram temple without further delay. On 18 and 19 September 1991, the RSS's top leaders, H. V. Sheshadri and Morepant Pingle, surveyed the area around the Ram Janmabhoomi–Babri Masjid in the presence of the VHP's Ashok Singhal.

The Uttar Pradesh government transferred 2.77 acres of land before the VHP's deadline of 31 October 1991. Soon after, with the demolition of temples around the disputed structure, the first step towards building the Ram temple was taken. The land where the old temple-houses had stood had been given to the VHP's Ram Janmabhoomi Trust with the stated aim

---

[448]A. G. Norrani, 'How Advani went Scot-free', *Frontline*, Vol. 21, No. 2, 17–30 January 2004.

of 'promoting tourism'. By 18 October, Sankat Mochan Temple, Lomash Ashram, Gopal Bhavan, Keshav Das Temple and Churakarm Temple were turned to rubble by karsevaks, as BJP MP Vinay Katiyar supervised the operation.[449]

On 29 October 1991, the VHP and RSS organized a Bajrang Rudra Yajna in Ayodhya to honour the karsevaks who had died in 1990. By now, karsevaks were virtually running Ayodhya. On 31 October when central minister Subodh Kant Sahay visited the disputed site along with six other leaders of the National Integration Council, they were heckled by karsevaks. On the same day, some karsevaks again attacked the Babri Masjid, damaged its outer wall, and hoisted a saffron flag inside the mosque.[450] Under pressure from the BJP's central leadership, Kalyan Singh publicly criticized this action of the karsevaks, but defiant 'VHP sadhus defended it'.

In an attempt to justify the abusive heckling of members of the National Integration Council, Vinay Katiyar claimed that one of its members, M. J. Akbar, had entered the Ram Janmabhoomi shrine wearing sandals. This led to a huge protest in the UP Assembly. More than sixty-five MLAs were suspended for their unruly behaviour.[451]

By March 1991, the UP government had done away with all pretenses. It gave over 42 acres of land acquired for Ram Katha Kunj to the Ram Janmabhoomi Trust. In defiance of the court-ordered injunction against any construction at and around the disputed site, the state PWD (Public Works Department) was constructing a brick wall or 'Ram-Deewar' around the Babri Masjid-Ram Janmabhoomi. [452]

On 22 March, bulldozers hired by the tourism department destroyed Abhi Ram Mandap, Char Bhaiyon ka Mandir, Sumitra Bhavan, Ganesh Ashram, VHP's exhibition gallery, Sakshi Gopal Temple, the house of Falahari Baba and several shops. 'It was clear to us now that our strategy was to clear a staging ground for the attack on Babri Masjid,' said a former member of the Ayodhya unit of the BJP who did not wish to be named. The plan was well thought out. By July 1991, a large area facing the mosque was cleared of temples, buildings, mazaars (mausoleums) and graves using government bulldozers. The destroyed buildings were some of the oldest in Ayodhya

---

[449]Sharma, *Karseva se Karseva Tak*, pp. 152–55.

[450]Ibid., p. 155.

[451]Ibid., p. 156.

[452]Ibid.

and contained stone artefacts, statues and other antiquities, which were carefully stored in a separate area.

5 JULY 1992

A year later, under the Kalyan Singh government's watch, and in violation of the court's orders, VHP's sants started preparations for the construction of the temple. The area they chose for it lay between the Babri Masjid and around the courtyard of the newly built Ram Deewar. At 8.30 a.m., the VHP's Acharya Giriraj Kishore, Dau Dayal Khanna and Uma Bharti, who was now an MP, ceremonially started the construction of a concrete platform on which the Singh Dwar (lion gate) of the proposed temple was to be erected. The ceremony consisted of breaking a few bricks with a small hammer and trowelling some mortar on the ground. The concrete platform was a large one spanning 80 feet long, 133 feet wide and 6 feet thick. This was to be the base of the proposed Singh Dwar and the Nritya Mandap or dance hall. The design of the temple was based on scriptures and in accordance with the architecture of Hindu temples. VHP's Ashok Singhal thought the day was 'historic', but soon, the day descended into chaos. Unwilling to be kept out of offering karseva at the holy site, the assembled karsevaks started throwing gravel and stones at the site and at the 'VIPs' who were present there. Many VHP leaders were injured by the rain of gravel. Finally the mahant of the nearby Chauburzi (four armed) Hanuman Temple mounted his horse and restrained the karsevaks by beating them with his staff.

In order to prevent the recurrence of similar indiscipline, the VHP announced a plan that addressed the wishes of those who wanted to participate in the holy task of building the Ram temple. For the first two months, only karsevaks from the eleven districts around Faizabad were asked to do voluntary work at the site.

Ayodhya was now frantic with excitement. Songs that both incited hatred against Muslims and inspired karsevaks blared from loudspeakers in the holy town. Wild and sudden chanting of 'Jai Shri Ram' by bands of roving karsevaks became the norm and local shopkeepers made a killing selling stoles, bandanas and shawls printed with 'Ram' and 'Jai Shri Ram' on them. The whole town seemed euphoric and obsessed with one thing alone—participating in the construction of the Ram temple.

11 JULY 1992

In the presence of thousands of charged up karsevaks, Shankarrao Chauhan, minister for home affairs, visited the disputed site. Accompanied by Vinay Katiyar, he prayed at the Ram Lalla idol. Outside, the crowds raised 'home minister go back' slogans. The central minister left, feeling concerned both for himself and the safety of the mosque. In a meeting with the press he vented his anger which had built up during the day.[453] He decried the state government's reduction of the security of the mosque and announced that five companies of paramilitary forces were to be deployed for its safety. He added that even the CCTV cameras installed around the disputed site were inadequate and not in working condition. His analysis would turn out to be a portent for later events.

Meanwhile, the digging and levelling operations were causing outrage in Parliament. Karseva became a dreaded word that meant destruction of the mosque followed by construction of the temple. For the supporters of karseva, the VHP and its army of saints, it was not just about the mosque and the temple, it was about destroying the 'symbol of slavery' and building a new 'national identity'.

DEMOLITION IN SLOW MOTION

The Babri Masjid was situated on high ground. It had a steep slope on the west—the side facing Mecca which is always at the rear of a mosque, a gradient on the north and south, and level ground on the east, which is the entrance of the mosque.

The temples that were demolished stood on the eastern side. As would become evident later, these temples had to be demolished to create an open area where a large number of karsevaks could assemble. The ground on the eastern side of the mosque was dug more than on the other sides. The extracted mud was then dumped around the north and south sides, mainly along the perimeter wall of the mosque.

Because of the digging of the level ground on the eastern side, a depression of 12 feet was created (therefore in photographs of the mosque's demolition, it appears to be elevated on the front). When the rains arrived in July, the depression was filled with water; how much of it seeped into the foundations of the mosque is not known. Whether the structure was weakened by the seepage of water into the foundation is not known either. In any case it was to be the last monsoon for the mosque that had survived

---

[453] Arvind Kumar Singh, *Ayodhya Vivaad Ek Patrakar ki Diary*, p. 68.

400 (if not more) rainy seasons.

So far, Kalyan Singh, a belligerent Ram bhakt himself, was keeping his promise to BJP supporters even in violation of the court's orders.[454] On 23 November 1992, the Supreme Court warned the UP government through its counsel, K. K. Venugopal, for violations of court orders in Ayodhya.[455]

Between October 1991 and November 1992, the Kalyan Singh-led Uttar Pradesh government filed ten affidavits in the High Court and the Supreme Court. All of them contained the same assurance that his government was committed to the protection of the 'Ram Janmabhoomi structure'. Outside the court, VHP and BJP leaders mobilized their cadres, karsevaks and supporters. The meetings between Hindu and Muslim delegations to try to resolve the dispute through dialogue also continued from the beginning of September to almost the end of November. Apart from feeding media headlines nothing much came out of these meetings between the Babri Masjid Action Committee and the Vishva Hindu Parishad.

CONGRESS FAILS TO PREVENT THE DEMOLITION

The Congress government led by P.V. Narasimha Rao was repeatedly urged to take immediate action to ensure that the karsevaks did not destroy the mosque

Rao was in secret backchannel talks with a number of BJP, RSS, VHP, and Hindu religious leaders, and has been indicted for poor judgement in repoing faith in their assurances about the mosque's safety.[456] Some of the warnings came from Rao's own ministers—prominent among them, his rival, Arjun Singh, the then minister for human resource development. Besides, Rao was being regularly updated by Intelligence Bureau officers posted in Ayodhya as well as those who were tracking leaders of the RSS, VHP and BJP. But some of the loudest, most unambiguous and public warnings that the structure would be demolished were given by the VHP and BJP themselves. On 1 December 1992, BJP President Murli Manohar Joshi appealed to people in Mathura 'to assemble in Ayodhya in large numbers

---

[454]P.V. Narsimha Rao, *Ayodhya: 6 December 1992*, New Delhi: Penguin Books, 2006, p. 111 and Manoj Mitta, 'Supreme Court judges face some awkward questions over Babri Masjid demolition', *India Today*, 15 November 1993.

[455]P.V. Narsimha Rao, *Ayodhya: 6 December 1992*, p. 111.

[456]Vinay Sitapati, *Half-Lion: How P. V. Narasimha Rao Transformed India*, New Delhi: Penguin Books, 2016, pp. 254, 251.

for Karseva and to demolish the so-called Babri Masjid'. The same day in Kanpur, Advani was clarifying to supporters that 'Karseva did not mean bhajans and kirtans... That karseva would be performed with bricks and shovels.'[457] A month earlier, V. H. Dalmia, one of the most senior leaders of the VHP, had finally cleared all doubts about the scope of the karseva: 'the Ram Janmabhoomi temple would be constructed in the same way it was demolished by Babur'.[458]

One of the ways that Rao, as prime minister, could have prevented the demolition was by using Article 356 of the Constitution of India to impose President's Rule in Uttar Pradesh. But behind Rao's deliberate and catastrophic inaction lay the reasons of his government's survival as well as his overestimation of his abilities as a tactician and strategist.

The P. V. Narasimha Rao-led Congress government formed in 1991 was perhaps the weakest Congress government in India's history. There had been crises of leadership in the past as well, but the Congress had never run a government which didn't have its own majority in Parliament. For instance, though the vacuum in the wake of Nehru's demise triggered a power struggle and a brief period of instability following Prime Minister Lal Bahadur Shastri's sudden death in Tashkent, it had quickly ceased with Indira Gandhi becoming the prime minister. Later on, the Emergency and the failure of the Janata Party to lead a stable government had only strengthened Indira's grip on Indian politics until her death in 1984. Rajiv Gandhi's massive majority of 432 seats in Parliament had ensured that his government survived for the full term of five years even though its public image had suffered unprecedented damage.

However, Rajiv's killing had not given the Congress a clear majority as was the case with Indira's assassination. In 1992, the Congress government was battling one crisis after another. The Rao government's decision to liberalize the Indian economy in 1991 had yet to bear fruit; meanwhile Kashmir was in flames and the Congress had lost major strongholds like Madhya Pradesh, Rajasthan and Uttar Pradesh.

The other significant reason for Rao's indecisiveness over the Ram temple dispute lay in the realm of the Congress's internal politics. Narasimha

---

[457]See Ranjit Bhushan, 'Pile of evidence', *Outlook*, 22 September 1997; 'The Sardar trapped', *Outlook*, 18 December 2000 and Jyoti Sharma, *Secularism and Ayodhya Politics in India*, New Delhi: Deep and Deep Publications Pvt. Ltd., 2007, p. 444.
[458]A. G. Noorani, 'Silent spectator', *Frontline*, Vol. 23, Issue 10, 20 May–2 June 2006.

Rao was not a towering personality who commanded respect and loyalty from Congress leaders, many of whom were envious and saw him as an opportunist who had raced ahead. This made the job of imposing President's Rule in Uttar Pradesh a tricky one. A government fighting for survival could not have mustered the courage and conviction to protect the rule of law, especially when Hindu masses seemed to favour the VHP's proposed karseva. The fear of a Hindu backlash had become the Congress's weakness at least since 1986, when Rajiv Gandhi had 'managed' to get the locks of the Babri Masjid-Ram Janmabhoomi opened. The rule of law was virtually non-existent in the weeks preceding 6 December 1992. Laws were being broken openly by godmen, godwomen and politicians who made hate speeches on a daily basis. In their speeches, they also warned the Congress government against imposing President's Rule by threatening violence and anarchy if it were to do so. And it did not help that Kalyan Singh was unconcerned about losing the chief ministership.

Rao, in his posthumously published book, *Ayodhya: 6 December 1992*, sought to explain why President's Rule was not imposed in UP. A large part of his argument pertains to the repeated assurances that the UP government had given to the National Integration Council, to the central government, and most importantly, to the Allahabad High Court as well as the Supreme Court of India. In court, the UP government's counsel would file solemn affidavits promising to uphold the rule of law. But outside court, Kalyan Singh had publicly sworn that between the Ram temple and his government, he would support the temple. The most violent warnings came from the two fringes of the VHP and BJP. On 23 November, Sadhvi Rithambara addressed a rally of Hindus in Nagpur; she seemed to be voicing the thoughts of the RSS when she warned the Congress government against imposing President's Rule. In Faizabad, Vinay Katiyar threatened to throw the rubble of the Babri Masjid into the Sarayu River if any attempts were made to remove the Ram Lalla idol. Three days earlier Katiyar had made an assurance that the Babri Masjid would be protected as long as the idol was inside it.

In the end, the mosque, and with it, India's communal harmony were destroyed at the altar of political expediency. Narasimha Rao and Kalyan Singh both held the highest public offices in their respective capacities as prime minister of India and chief minister of Uttar Pradesh, but protecting the Ram Janmabhoomi–Babri Masjid seemed to be a lose-lose proposition for them. It was unsurprising therefore, that while Kalyan Singh acted to support the demolition, Rao remained inert towards it—achieving the same end, political mileage.[459]

FINAL COUNTDOWN

On 5 December, Gita Jayanti (another VHP contribution to the list of Hindu festivals) was marked in Ayodhya by a dress rehearsal of the next day's karseva, which was officially professed to be a symbolic offering of sand from the Sarayu on the concrete platform built for the VHP-proposed temple in July. By now Ayodhya was teeming with more than one lakh karsevaks, a large number of them women. 'The whole town used to stink all the time,' recalled a retired teacher, S. K. Upadhyay. The government had made temporary toilets but there were not enough of them. The little town was packed to its gills and, faced with the unending influx of people who wanted to participate in the 'holy work of building the Ram temple', the VHP sent out appeals telling people to go back to their homes. Most Muslim families had sent their women and children to places of safety elsewhere.

Among the karsevaks who were present in Ayodhya, confusion still prevailed owing to contradictory statements from their leaders. Most of them wished to do something 'meaningful' and not just bring fistfuls of sand. A day earlier in a rally in Lucknow, BJP's Atal Bihari Vajpayee indulged in creative interpretation of the Supreme Court's order permitting only 'peaceful karseva that included a congregation of people singing devotional songs and doing a symbolic worship'. Vajpayee said in lucid Hindi and with his trademark flourish, 'for the karsevaks to be able to do bhajan and kirtan, the ground filled with sharp stones [would] have to be cleared'.[460]

The 200 companies of the central paramilitary forces dispatched by the centre were camped outside Ayodhya. They were to move in when the state government asked them to. They never did. Advani, who was in Lucknow on 5 December, drove to Ayodhya at night and took part in a meeting held at Vinay Katiyar's house.

---

[459]Kumar Anshuman, 'Home ministry had a plan to prevent Babri demolition, but PM Rao didn't allow it', *The Print*, 6 December 2017 and 'Babri demolition had Narasimha Rao govt's backing: ex-BJP MP Vedanti', *Deccan Chronicle*, 20 May 2017.
[460]'Atal Bihari Vajpayee speech at Ayodhya', *Kraft News*, 16 December 2014 <https://www.youtube.com/watch?v=3rGW7GF1qCY> and 'There are sharp stones there, the ground has to be levelled', *Outlook*, 7 December 2009.

6 DECEMBER 1992—PART ONE: DEMOLITION OF BABRI MASJID AND RAM CHABUTRA

On 6 December, the winter sky was overcast and the air dark and cold. The huge stage erected in the Ram Katha Kunj about 200 metres to the east of the Babri Masjid was filled with saints, mahants and politicians. Instead of narrow roads that led to the disputed site, now there was an 8-feet wide road. Two years ago in 1990 the karsevaks' accommodation had been arranged in Manram Das ki Chavni, but now they were assembled at Ram Katha Kunj. While earlier, karsevaks could only enter from two narrow lanes, now they were free to march towards the disputed mosque from all sides. The so called security wall, Ram Deewar, was never completed by the UP government. It was not even built in the north of the mosque. In the past, karsevaks had to walk almost a kilometre for food, but this year both food and stay were provided for at Ram Katha Kunj.[461] Buildings with a view of the mosque like the Janamsthan Sita Rasoi and Manas Bhawan, were also occupied by those eager to witness the proceedings away from the dust and din being raised at ground zero—the concrete platform, which was ringed off with wooden poles. Policemen and RSS volunteers were on duty to control the karsevaks and maintain order.

Besides UP's Provincial Armed Constabulary, a couple of companies of CRPF men were also guarding the entry and exit gates as well as the outer periphery of the disputed area. Till 10.15 a.m. there was order and the massive crowd assembled in front of the VIP stage had responded in the affirmative to the commencement of a symbolic karseva. But soon after, a short and athletic man was seen on top of the left dome. When he unfurled a saffron flag the day began to unravel. By noon, peaceful and disciplined karsevaks had turned violent. The CRPF and state police who were deployed to guard the mosque melted away after a few minutes of stone-throwing by the karsevaks. As soon as the mosque's outer fence was breached, members of the press became the target of violent mobs. Manas Bhawan, which was the 'press gallery' arranged by the VHP, was also targeted. Cameras were broken, reels snatched out of pockets and bags; those who resisted were beaten up.

Dozens of shovels, iron bars and thick ropes were brought in jeeps and distributed. Overpowered by hysteria, people clambered on top of the domes of the 'symbol of slavery', while the more focused and purposeful

---

[461]Hemant Sharma, *Ayodhya ka Chashmdeed*, p. 163

karsevaks started digging up the foundations of the mosque from all sides. At the same time, columns of smoke arose in the distance. The attack on Muslim neighbourhoods, mosques and mazaars had begun. The house of Haji Mehboob, a local landlord, became the refuge for many of those Muslims who had stayed back in Ayodhya despite clear danger to them. Luckily, Mehboob's house was situated opposite a police station, and though the karsevaks managed to set it on fire, its occupants were saved.

In Ayodhya, some Muslims had completely failed to see the threat from karsevaks and had hobnobbed with them despite warnings from friends and family members; at least one such 'karsevak-friendly' Muslim man was killed by other karsevaks in Ayodhya. A local landlord, Nawab Tahir Hussain Sahab, whose family had lived in Ayodhya for more than 300 years, was burnt alive inside his house. His wife, Aliya Begum, had survived by hiding in the bushes behind the house. Ten days later when the police came to take stock of Shikwana, the neighbourhood where the elderly couple lived, Aliya Begum beseeched them to take her eyewitness account; but they refused saying that she wasn't present at the spot.[462] Technically, the police were right. 'It is true that I didn't see anything but I could hear them shouting, "Maro, kato, luto, phoonk do phoonk do" (Kill him, cut him, loot, burn burn) as I hid in the bushes under the window at the back of the house... I will swear on anything you say, the Quran, the Ramayana,' seventy-year-old Aliya Begum pleaded with the police.[463]

By 5 p.m. the last dome of the Babri Masjid disappeared against the setting winter sun. The crowds cheered and jeered unaware of the fact that they had also destroyed the Ram Chabutra located within the compound of the mosque. Since its presence was recorded for the first time by the Jesuit missionary Joseph Tiefenthaler in the 1760s, the Ram Chabutra had been continuously worshipped for more than 200 years. In their hysteria, the Ram bhakts had pulverized the shrine so that it was indiscernible from the fallen debris. Almost at the same time as the dust began to settle, a still and silent darkness fell on the Muslim quarters of the town. In complete contrast, temples, Hindu homes and the streets of Ramkots and Hindu areas in Ayodhya came alight with furious celebrations and the lighting of diyas.

More than fifty Muslims who had taken shelter in the police station

---

[462] Ashis Nandy, et al., *Creating a Nationality: The Ramjanmabhumi Movement and Fear of the Self*, New Delhi: Oxford University Press, 1998, p. 190.
[463] Ibid., p. 200.

when Mehboob's house was being burnt worried about those among them who were missing. Never before had they felt alien and scared in their own town. Haji Mehboob had admitted that firearms were used in defence when karsevak mobs attacked his house. 'I had my men and we were prepared with guns and more. That's how we survived otherwise Ayodhya would have been made free of Muslims on 6 December.' Haji Mehboob had stayed back with his wife and children; his wife, who studied in Bombay's J. J. School of Art, refused to leave Ayodhya without him. 'She is my biggest pillar of strength...but yes I sometimes do regret coming back from Bombay.' So why did he come back, I asked him. 'This might be Ram's birthplace. At the same time, it is definitely my birthplace and those of my ancestors,' Haji Mehboob replied.

In the targeted killing and destruction of Muslim homes, local Hindus had acted as guides for the karsevaks. But Hindus had also saved Muslims by passing them off as Hindus and hiding them inside their homes. Zubair, then a six-year-old boy, was almost thrown into a bonfire made out of furniture, beds, etc., from his own house when a Hindu friend of his father's intervened and told the karsevaks that Zubair was his son.[464]

By midnight, despite the imposition of President's Rule, Ayodhya was under 'karsevak raj' and men, women and children were busy levelling the debris of the mosque to build the 'grand temple' that they had dreamt of. Many karsevaks were contemplating going back with the souvenirs of bricks and other pieces of masonry that they had extricated from the rubble of the Babri Masjid. The mood was festive and triumphant: most of the tens of thousands of Ram bhakts who had assembled in Ayodhya were unaware of the politics behind the demolition. They had come to participate in what they sincerely believed to be the sacred work of building a Ram temple. From the evening of 6 December to the morning of 8 December, men, women, the elderly and children stood in long human chains and passed on buckets and trays of debris and later took part in the levelling of the remaining debris (not all of it could be removed) so that the idol of Ram Lalla could be replaced at the same spot over which a few hours ago had stood the central dome of the Babri Masjid. By the next morning victorious karsevaks had coined a new slogan:

---

[464]Ibid., p. 201.

Jai Shri Ram!
Ho Gaya Kaam

(Long live Shri Ram!
The work is done.)

At least thirteen Muslims were killed in Ayodhya, many of them burnt alive. In all, 134 homes belonging to Muslims were burnt down, leaving their occupants homeless.[465] Only those Muslim homes that were adjacent to Hindu homes survived; local Hindus were afraid that the fire might spread to their homes too. Mahant Nritya Gopal Das and Acharya Dharmendra, known for his hate speeches, blamed the Muslims for burning their own homes to 'claim compensation from the government'.[466] The police, who had stood by during the day, now egged the arsonist karsevaks on. Babu Khan, owner of Lala Tailors in the older part of Ayodhya, recalled that the police told those who were destroying his father's shop to give them some wood to burn for the night. 'They didn't even leave a spoon undamaged.' Today, Babu Khan is a peace activist and also dabbles in local politics.

The idol of Ram Lalla, which had been removed before the domes collapsed into rubble, although restored to the same spot before the sun had set, was homeless too.

Mahant Satyendra Das, the head priest of the disputed Babri Masjid-Ram Lalla shrine in Ayodhya, maintains what he said the day after the demolition: 'They have broken our temple not a mosque. For the last forty years Muslims didn't even visit the mosque. It was a temple, and now Ram Lalla is sitting on the rubble, under the open sky unprotected from the cold.' Das also recounted that the donation box, brass bells and other items got buried under the debris.[467] 'Many of them started breaking the walls in the sanctum sanctorum and I feared for the idol itself but managed to save it,' he said. Satyendra Das is one of the very few priests in Ayodhya who remain apolitical and regretful of the demolition.

'DEATH TO JOURNALISTS'
Media, particularly the foreign press, and Indian English-language

---

[465]Ibid., pp. 197–98.
[466]Ibid., p.202 .
[467]Arvind Kumar Singh, *Ayodha Vivaad: Ek Patrakar ki Diary*, p. 29.

newspapers, magazines and video magazines like *Newstrack*, were considered hostile by the karsevaks and their ideologues in the RSS, VHP, and to some extent, by leaders of the BJP. Most of the Hindi media, on the other hand, were considered to be friendly and supporters of the Ram temple. There were exceptions like the local daily *Jan Morcha*, *Amar Ujala* and a few others but largely, Hindi newspapers, often owned by Hindu business families, acted as mouthpieces of the VHP and BJP. Because of their abject bias towards the RSS, VHP and BJP, the Hindi media had come to be pejoratively called 'Hindu Media' while the English media earned itself titles such as anti-national, anti-Hindu, anti-Ram, communist and pseudo-secular.

On 6 December 1992, as karsevaks attacked the Babri Mosque, they also turned their wrath on members of the English press who they considered to be 'Ram Virodhi', or opposed to Ram. Foreign correspondents covering the issue became the first targets of their wrath. Jeff Penberthy, *Time* magazine's South Asia Bureau chief, was present in Ayodhya's Manas Bhawan but escaped the attack because of the rapport he had built with Bajrang Dal activists. Penberthy's colleague, Anita Pratap, was also with him. The duo's name had reappeared in relation to the demolition when Lalu Prasad Yadav, the former chief minister of Bihar, publicly asked for their eyewitness accounts. Lalu thought they had survived by disguising themselves as karsevaks. Later, Penberthy wrote a detailed account of what he saw that day. His report is available on the website countercurrents.org. According to Penberthy, it was a well-coordinated operation that began with a single shot fired from a pistol. He writes, 'a man in a suit jacket waded into the crowd below us and fired a pistol held high above his head—like a signal'. Soon after that the attack—on the disputed structure as well as journalists—began. 'The cry "patrakar murdabad" or "death to journalists" had gone up, and gangs were seeking out the journalists,' he wrote. Penberthy was still safe on the terrace of Manas Bhawan, though below him journalists were being assaulted. From his vantage point he saw Peter Heinlein (a *Voice of America* reporter, who now covers the White House), who had been 'knocked unconscious' by the blow of an iron rod, being helped by his friend, Edward A. Gargen of the *New York Times*.

He saw Dieter Ludwig, a photographer, 'wisely hightail' it away from the rocks being thrown at him. Chris Kremmer of the Australian Broadcasting Corporation fled for his life down the lane behind the mosque towards the river, passing formations of the PAC whom he later said were sitting in the fields 'looking terrified'. Kremmer's account of senior government officials in their suits and ties, along with their wives, 'lounging under a shamiana like senators and their consorts watching a Roman spectacle' is also confirmed by the footage recorded by the *Newstrack* team. The officers appeared to be overseeing the demolition while drinking tea, at least in the beginning.

Penberthy believed that he was spared 'because of cricket', Sachin Tendulkar to be precise. After asking him a few questions, a Bajrang Dal youth frisked him, made him chant 'Jai Shri Ram' and put the red Ram-printed bandana on his head. Penberthy wrote:

> But India is India, the wait was long and the talk soon turned to cricket. And I immediately ingratiated myself by having picked up early on the potential of an emerging Indian batsman named Sachin Tendulkar, the new Don Bradman. I was made—and immediately labelled Alan Border, to whom I bear a slight physical resemblance.

This brief camaraderie developed in the morning later saved him, when Penberthy had gone down to see injured karsevaks who were being given first aid in a nearby temple. On the road leading to the under-destruction mosque, an agitated middle-aged man rushed up and shouted to his face, 'Are you a Hindu?' 'Once again, good luck and cricket saved me. A young man also down from the roof recognized "Alan Border" and hustled me back to the shelter of the Manas Bhawan building,' Penberthy wrote.[468]

Los Angeles Times correspondent Bob Drogin's account[469] of the assault on journalists is not the same. His report dated 8 December 1992 details the utter desperation to which the journalists had been reduced. It is also a good read for scribes, photographers and radio and TV journalists who might find themselves in hostile situations. Among the women reporters who were attacked that day was Sarah Brezinsky, a young American freelance photographer. She had been chased by scores of sword-wielding men and was saved when by sheer chance she ran into a room full of women in a nearby dharamshala. Once inside the women protected her by rolling her in a carpet. They 'sat on her while an old woman stood guard at the wooden door, refusing time after time to let attackers in'.

Indian journalists were not spared either. Video magazine *Newstrack*'s

---

[468]Jeff Penberthy, 'What I saw at Babri Masjid', *Asian Age*, 17 September 2004 <https://www.countercurrents.org/comm-penberthy170904.htm>.

[469]Bob Drogin, 'Documentary: scrambling for safety amid a merciless mob: no one was spared as Hindu militants stormed a mosque in India. "No camera!" they screamed before attacking journalists', *LA Times*, 8 December 1992.

Mrityunjay Jha and his cameraman were saved by the police who locked them in a room inside Manas Bhawan. Among the most badly injured in the attack was the photographer of *Rashtriya Sahara*, a Hindi daily which did not always toe the VHP's line. He remained bedridden for eight months and had to undergo multiple surgeries.[470] *Voice of America*'s Peter Lienhemn too had to get stitches on his head after it was split open by karsevaks. Delhi-based journalist Ruchira Gupta's shirt was ripped open by the Ram bhakts before they tried to strangulate her. Pablo Bartholomew, a photographer, was thrown over a dirty lavatory and beaten till he started bleeding. Bartholomew had a narrow escape that day. Praveen Jain, also a photographer, witnessed journalists being asked to pull down their pants to allow the mob to verify if they were Hindus or Muslims. Pranesh K., an editor with *Newstrack*, also was saved by police in the nick of time. But perhaps nobody was as brutally targeted as Suman Gupta of the local daily *Jan Morcha*. A popular Hindi daily, *Jan Morcha* had consistently reported on the Ram Janmabhoomi movement like other outlets but it had not toed the VHP or BJP's line and had found itself as the main media adversary of the karsevaks, the sants and the VHP. Gupta was beaten, stripped, abused and almost stuffed into the boot of a car by karsevaks.[471]

Thanks to the presence of mind of the *Newstrack* team, there is a videotaped record of the controlled anarchy that accompanied the well-coordinated attack on the Babri Masjid. The footage shows karsevaks talking about the demolition and then the actual execution of their plan on the predetermined day. Ironically, in the interests of public law and order, India's censor board banned the broadcast of that *Newstrack* report. But several months later, on the appeal of the *Newstrack* team, Justice B. Lentin of the Film Certification Appellate Tribunal, a statutory body, allowed its broadcast, commenting that the entire country should watch it. The entire country never got to see it; the episode is available on YouTube.

The international repercussions of the destruction of the mosque were felt most severely in India's neighbourhood. The revenge for Hindus destroying the medieval mosque in India was taken out on the Hindus of Pakistan. Hindu temples were burnt and Hindus were killed in Bangladesh as well. In Lahore, a temple built by Motilal Nehru, the Congress leader and

---

[470]Shuchi Bansal, 'Ayodhya: For the first time, the media faced right-wing frenzy', *Livemint*, 3 December 2012.
[471]Joeanna Rebello, 'Behind the byline', *Times of India*, 20 September 2015.

founder of the Nehru-Gandhi dynasty, was demolished. The Organisation of Islamic Cooperation, which represents fifty countries with more than a billion Muslims, condemned the Indian government. Its secretary general, Hamid-al-Gabid, issued a statement saying, 'the entire Islamic world was shocked by the heinous and premeditated crime against an Islamic symbol of value, not the Muslims in India alone, but to Muslims everywhere'.[472] Shekhar Gupta, one of India's well-known journalists, writing about it in 2011, noted, 'India has rarely found itself so vulnerable and humiliated amongst the international community. Its liberal, secular credentials stood severely eroded as the karsevaks rubbed the nation's nose in the debris of Babri Masjid.'[473]

In India itself, more than 1,000 people died in the week following the demolition. The communal fire triggered by the demolition in Ayodhya affected all major towns of north and west India. But no other town burnt in religious fury to the extent that Bombay did. In the first quarter of 1993, two rounds of deadly riots left hundreds dead, and were followed by so-called revenge bombings by the Dawood Ibrahim faction of the underworld. The role of Pakistan's Inter-Services Intelligence was later revealed, which showed that alienation created by the destruction of the mosque had become a weapon in the hands of India's neighbour.[474] Stories of humanity prevailing even during the insanity of communal violence were the only honourable exceptions. But they were merely faint flickers and fading sidelights in the darkness of curfewed nights when hutments were set on fire, men killed, women raped and children speared. In Ayodhya, only two mosques remained unharmed, which laid hollow the claim often made by proponents of the Ram temple that their movement was not against Muslims or their mosques but only limited to the one built by Babur at the place where Lord Ram was believed to have been born.[475] Acharya Dharmendra, known for wearing silk kurtas and for his carefully styled hair, had justified the attacks on Muslims and mosques in Ayodhya saying 'this was the only way in which Ayodhya could become a Vatican for the Hindus'.[476]

---

[472]Edward A. Gargan, 'Hindu militants destroy mosque, setting off a new crisis in India', *New York Times*, 7 December 1992.

[473]Shekhar Gupta, 'Masjid demolition 1992: How the world reacted', *India Today*, 5 December 2011.

[474]'ISI pressured Dawood to carry out Mumbai blasts', *Rediff.com*, 22 December 2002.

[475]Nandy, et al., *Creating a Nationality*, p. 197.

[476]Ibid., p. 197.

The Shiv Sena was the first political party to welcome the demolition. Widely held to be more radical than the BJP, Shiv Sainiks participated in large numbers in the demolition and arson. The party's patriarch and founder Bal Thackeray said, 'They have done nothing wrong.' 'They' being the karsevaks, of course, many of whom were Shiv Sainiks. Shiv Sena's Uttar Pradesh president, Pawan Pandey, was photographed with a horde of karsevaks posing with the broken stone inscription believed to have been put up by Mir Baqi at the time of the mosque's construction. Speaking during the riots that killed more than 900 Muslims and Hindus, Thackeray added, 'Hereafter we Hindus will not tolerate any nonsense from any quarter. We have to be respected and must be respected. Enough is enough.'[477]

The BJP played down the demolition and dismissed criticism that they had willy-nilly violated the Constitution. S. S. Bhandari, the BJP vice president, flanked by Narendra Modi, then an RSS functionary, insisted that it was only a simple 'crime' committed by a mob. L. K. Advani and BJP president M. M. Joshi explained to reporters that the destruction was the result of 'pent-up anger of Hindus' at the appeasement of Muslims since Independence.

Through the 1980s, this sense of Hindu persecution vis-à-vis 'Muslim appeasement' was systematically spread through godmen and media propaganda among Hindus. It was amplified where it existed and created where it did not exist.

After the demolition, at the time of his arrest, L. K. Advani, accompanied by his wife, spoke in the same vein of 'Hindu persecution' and indulged in 'whataboutery' about the destruction of Hindu temples in Kashmir (without mentioning the mass killing of Kashmiri Pandits).

After nearly three months, in February 1993, Ayodhya began limping back to normalcy. But most Muslim families either did not return or maintained a second base outside Ayodhya. Haji Mehboob was charged with cases of murder and other IPC sections pertaining to possession of arms and explosives. In a revealing side story of 6 and 7 December, Mehboob recounted the transformation of the police from 'dancing and singing' with karsevaks into a professional force as soon as President's Rule was imposed. Of course, he added, 'the additional motivation for the police was that the karsevaks who wanted to kill us had threatened to even set the police

[477]Mrittunjoy Kumar Jha, 'Newstrack December 1992', 3 December 2014, 39:27 onwards <https://www.youtube.com/watch?v=cxVxFS81EKU>.

station on fire if we were not handed over to them'. This apparently made
Prem Narayan Shukla, the station house officer, very angry and according
to Mehboob, he told the karsevaks to back off or he would shoot all of
them dead. Mehboob remembers his exact words, "If you have drunk your
mother's milk, come and attack...'"

Mahant Gyan Das was the only important Ramanandi mahant who had
not supported the VHP. After the demolition, Gyan Das visited the under-
construction makeshift temple with armed guards and received darshan of
the Ram Lalla idol. 'It had a huge moat behind it, it would have fallen
anyway but these people demolished it. I could not stop them but I did not
support the demolition either. People were carried away by Ram bhakti,'
he said to me, twenty-five years after the demolition of the Babri mosque.

Gyan Das was not the only one who disapproved of the demolition.
'It wasn't like Muslims had tried to stop us from worshipping there or that
there was a Muslim force protecting the mosque. It was collective foolishness.
We were all taken in by the hysteria,' offered Ramdeen, a young man at
that time, who now ferries people in his cycle rickshaw for a living. He
was born in a family of labourers on the other side of the Sarayu. When
the temple movement had just started to grow in the late 1980s, he used
to work at a dhaba. 'I was moved by the zeal of karsevaks who used to
leave their homes and come here,' he said. 'If your neighbour ransacks and
burns your house down, will you return to live there?,' he asked. There
are many people in Ayodhya who are ready to tell their stories about 6
December 1992, but Ramdeen was not one of them. 'I have forgotten much
of it, what is left in my memory is not worth talking about,' he insisted.

Chapter 11

AYODHYA LEFT BEHIND, INDIA MOVES ON

In the aftermath of the demolition, the RSS was banned by the Government of India for the second time since Independence (the first time was in 1948 in the wake of Mahatma Gandhi's assassination). It also emerged that Prime Minister P. V. Narasimha Rao and the RSS and its offshoots like the VHP, BJP, Bajrang Dal and various godmen had played the cynical politics of majority appeasement. Prime Minister Rao ignored the calls for his resignation, and on 16 December 1992, constituted a one-man commission of enquiry under a retired judge of the Andhra Pradesh High Court. Justice M. S. Liberhan would take nearly seventeen years to submit his report in 2009.

On 7 January 1993, Rao succeeded in getting Parliament to enact the Acquisition of Certain Area at Ayodhya Act, 1993. The Act empowered the government to acquire a total of 67.03 acres of land, which included the disputed Ram Janmabhoomi–Babri Masjid site. As a result, all pending suits over ownership of the land stood to be aborted. On the day of the enactment of the Act, the government also, through a presidential reference under Article 143(1) of the Constitution, asked the Supreme Court to decide whether 'there was a pre-existing temple on the disputed site before the mosque came into existence'.[478] The 'Statement of Objects and Reasons' of the Act, which was laid in Parliament two days later, said:

> ...as it is necessary to maintain communal harmony and the spirit of common brotherhood amongst the people of India, it was considered necessary to acquire the site of the structure and suitable adjacent land for setting up a complex which could be developed in a planned

---

[478]Nani Palkhivala, 'Muslim India' in Noorani, ed., *The Babri Masjid Question—Vol 2*, New Delhi: Tulika Books, 2004, pp. 248–49 and 250–51.

manner wherein a Rama temple, a mosque, amenities for pilgrims, a library museum and other suitable facilities can be set up.[479]

'AYODHYA IS A STORM THAT WILL PASS'

Prime Minister Rao's enactment of the Act to acquire land surrounding the disputed site in Ayodhya was challenged by Dr M. Ismail Faruqui and others in the Supreme Court of India. Their petition also questioned the validity of Rao's Presidential reference under Article 143 (1) of the Indian Constitution. Prime Minister Rao had sent to the apex court for answer a single-point presidential reference on the Ayodhya dispute.

The Court rejected the Presidential Reference, upheld the acquisition of certain areas in and around the disputed site, and validated worship by Hindus by maintaining the status quo as it existed on 7 January 1993.[480] The Supreme Court also ordered one day's imprisonment for Kalyan Singh for 'a smaller contempt committed by him at Ayodhya five months prior to the demolition when he had allowed a platform to be constructed despite the status quo order'.[481]

As we will see later, the Sunni Central Waqf Board questioned this particular judgement of the Supreme Court in February 2018. On 27 September 2018, twenty four years later, India's highest court rejected its demand that questions settled in the 1994 Dr M. Ismail Faruqui vs Union of India case should be examined by a larger Constitution bench. While rejecting the appeal for referral the three-judge bench ruled by majority that, 'we again make it clear that questionable observations made in Ismail Faruqui's case as noted above were made in context of land acquisition'. More crucially, for the main title suit over the disputed site, Chief Justice Dipak Misra and Justice Ashok Bhushan also said the observations made in the Faruqui case 'were neither relevant for deciding the suits nor relevant for deciding these appeals'.[482]

One of the sticking points of this judgement pertain to whether or not a mosque is integral to worship under Islam. 'The order in Dr M Ismail

---

[479]V. Venkatesan, 'Against the law', *Frontline*, Vol. 19, Issue 4, 16 February–1 March 2002.
[480]'Dr. M. Ismail Faruqui Etc, Mohd. ... vs Union Of India And Others on 24 October, 1994', *Indian Kanoon* <https://indiankanoon.org/doc/37494799/>.
[481]Manoj Mitta, 'When even the Supreme Court let down the nation', *The Wire*, 6 December 2017.
[482]Valay Singh, 'Ayodhya case: The SC ruling makes no difference to the title suit', *Economic Times*, 29 September 2018.

Faruqui Etc. vs Union Of India And Others (October 24, 1994), passed a little less than two years after the Babri Masjid was demolished, said that a mosque was not an "essential part of the practice of the religion of Islam" and hence, "its acquisition (by the state) is not prohibited by the provisions in the Constitution of India".[483]

Back in 1994, the five-judge Constitution bench of the Supreme Court headed by Chief Justice M. N. Venkatachaliah ruled unanimously that the abortion of the pending title suits was 'unconstitutional' and 'unfair' to Muslims. Significantly, the court approved the acquisition of the disputed site as well as adjoining land. By a majority, the court ruled that the acquisition of 67.03 acres was necessary to ensure that in the event that the Muslim parties were found to be the owners of the disputed site, they would be able to access the site. The court also upheld the reasoning in the Act that if the Muslim parties won the case the Hindu owners of adjacent and surrounding properties might deprive the Muslims of access to the site.

Between 2 February 1986, the day the locks were opened, and 6 December 1992, the day of the demolition, Hindus had enjoyed full access to worship the Ram Lalla idol kept inside the Babri Masjid.

The Act, however, had a provision curtailing the earlier rights of worship to a reasonable and appropriate distance (as it exists today) and barred Hindus from enlarging the 'scope of the practice of worship'.[484] The majority judgement upheld this provision which confined the worship, saying it 'appears to be reasonable and just in view of the fact that the miscreants who demolished the mosque are suspected to be persons professing to practise the Hindu religion. The Hindu community must, therefore, bear the cross on its chest, for the misdeed of the miscreants reasonably suspected to belong to their religious fold.'[485]

Justice S. P. Bharucha, writing the minority judgement for himself and Justice A. P. Ahmadi, appeared to call the Narasimha Rao government's bluff of asking the court to decide whether or not a temple existed prior to the mosque. He wrote:

---

[483]Ananthakrishnan G., 'In Ayodhya case, a question recalled: Is mosque central to prayer in Islam?', *Indian Express*, 19 March 2018.

[484]'Dr. M. Ismail Faruqui Etc, Mohd. ... vs Union Of India And Others on 24 October, 1994'.

[485]Ibid.

...it is clear that the Central Government does not propose to settle the dispute in terms of the Court's opinion. It proposes to use the Court's opinion as a springboard for negotiations... It leaves us no doubt that even in the circumstance that this Court opines that no Hindu temple or Hindu religious structure existed on the disputed site before the disputed structure was built thereon, there is no certainty that the mosque will be rebuilt.[486]

In the concluding words of his minority judgement, Justice Bharucha underscored the transience of the decades old Ayodhya dispute and justified returning the presidential reference unanswered. He wrote:

...but this opinion is intended to create a public climate for negotiations and the criticism would find the public ear, to say nothing of the fact that it would impair this Court's credibility. Ayodhya is a storm that will pass. The dignity and honour of the Supreme Court cannot be compromised because of it.[487]

The court's returning of the presidential reference was both lauded, for the same reasons as cited by Bharucha so articulately, and criticized for prolonging the dispute by choosing to duck and leave the ball instead of playing it, to use an analogy from cricket. If the Supreme Court of India was unable to answer the question, then who would, the critics reasoned. A more fundamental criticism expressed the disappointment of Muslims with the majority ruling that allowed Hindus the right to worship the Ram Lalla idol at all. While justifying their ruling, Justice J. S. Verma had argued that the Muslims had not prayed at the disputed Ram Janmabhoomi–Babri Masjid since 23 December 1949, so their worship which had not existed after that, could not be curtailed. The criticism of this argument was best articulated by one of India's leading laywers, Soli Sorabjee, who wrote:

The majority judgement overlooks that the reason why the worship in the mosque had come to a standstill was the surreptitious entry into the mosque and the placing of idols in a clandestine manner... The real issue was not whether Hindus are offering worship in a reduced form but whether worship and puja of idols by one community should at all be permitted after the dastardly act of destruction...[488]

---

[486]Ibid.
[487]Ibid.
[488]Soli Sorabjee, 'Minorities: national and international protection, Minorities Council of

Sorabjee's critique continues to resonate as by allowing the right of worship for Hindus, the majority judgement (J. S. Verma, J. Ray and M. N. Venkatachaliah) of the Supreme Court supported 'a situation which was the outcome of an act of national shame'. As Khaliq Khan, the Muslim activist in Ayodhya, pertinently asked, 'according to the court, it meant that anybody can first encroach upon any mosque, install an idol, then destroy the mosque, and still keep enjoying his worship there. Are we equal citizens or not?'

However, the 2018 ruling by the Supreme Court implies that now the main 'title suit over the disputed site will have to be heard purely as a property dispute devoid of any religious connotations. It is for this reason that Muslim parties in the case are now hopeful that the litigation will be decided soon and in their favour.'[489]

Narasimha Rao's long-standing confidant, P.V. R. K. Prasad, revealed in his book, *Asalemi Jarigindante* (*What Actually Happened*), that Rao had been called the 'first BJP prime minister of India' by a Congress MP. According to Prasad's memoirs, Narasimha Rao's concern after the demolition of the mosque was to get a temple constructed in its place with the consent of both Muslims and Hindus. Towards this end he asked Prasad to lead a 'secretive' and covert mission to enlist non-VHP-aligned saints and seers. Prominent among those that Rao believed would be part of a new trust were:

> The heads of Adwaita, Dwaita and Visishtadwaita Peethams, Sankaracharyas of Sringeri, Kanchi, Dwaraka, and Puri, Tamilnadu Jiyars and Andhra Jiyyangars, heads of Vaishnava Mutts all belonging to the Ramanuja tradition in the North, heads of Udipi and Uttaradi Mutts belonging to the Dwaita tradition, Gurujis of Vallabhacharya, Gowdiya and Chaitanya traditions, and Mahants of Ayodhya and other Hindu organisations.[490]

This grand plan did not remain a secret for very long, and the RSS, BJP and VHP opposed it vehemently. The many saints that Rao wished to collaborate with declined to be a part of any initiative that excluded the VHP-affiliated godmen and saints.

India', New Delhi: 1995 in Noorani, ed, *The Babri Masjid Question*—*Vol. 2*, p. 272.

[489]Valay Singh, 'Ayodhya case: The SC ruling makes no difference to the title suit'.

[490]A. G. Noorani, 'Ayodhya and Narasimha Rao', *Frontline*, 5 April 2013.

Narasimha Rao's strategy 'to checkmate the BJP from monopolizing Lord Ram'[491] failed miserably as he could not get support from either Hindus or Muslims.

Ayodhya and 'Ram' were monopolized by the RSS and its affiliates like the VHP and BJP. The identification of one with the other came to be complete in the wake of the demolition. As noted earlier, in March 1993, the former head priest of the Ram Lalla shrine in the Babri Masjid, Mahant Lal Das, who had consistently opposed the RSS and VHP, was shot dead by unknown assailants. His killing, which remains unsolved, perpetuated the climate of fear in the temple town. Also living in fear in the months after the demolition were leaders of the Ram temple movement like Ashok Singhal, V. H. Dalmia, Uma Bharti and Vinay Katiyar. Ashok Singhal's security was so stringent that even 'while enjoying the winter sun' in his house he used to be surrounded by at least four gun-toting personal security officers.

POLITICAL AFTERMATH: 'THE AYODHYA CARD'

Politically, the BJP did not benefit dramatically from the demolition in the short term. After the dismissal of the Kalyan Singh government on 6 December 1992, assembly elections were held in the middle of 1993. Though the BJP won the highest number of seats it could not form the government in Uttar Pradesh. Mulayam Singh Yadav, who had founded the Samajwadi Party in 1992, first allied with the Bahujan Samaj Party and ruled with the support of the Janata Dal and the Congress. Meanwhile, Ayodhya remained alive as a communally polarizing issue. But the great number of claims that the RSS, BJP and VHP had made with regard to the construction of a Hindu vote bank turned out to be hollow and false. The Ayodhya movement had raised the consciousness of Hindu–dom but the barriers of caste had not been scaled. Though the BJP retained the Ayodhya assembly seat till 2012, it could form a government only once in the decade that followed the demolition.

After 1993, the next elections in Uttar Pradesh were held in 1997. The intervening four-year period saw the state being ruled by Mulayam Singh Yadav, Mayawati and the President of India. In 1997, Kalyan Singh formed the government with the support of the Bahujan Samaj Party. In November 1999, he was removed by the BJP leadership after the BJP's Lok Sabha tally in UP fell from 57 in 1998 to 29 in 1999. For his public avowal to not fire at the karsevaks under any circumstance, Kalyan Singh

---

[491]Ibid.

had been hailed as one of the heroes of the demolition. The day he was sacked as chief minister, he visited Ayodhya to hold a press conference to send a message of defiance to the BJP top brass in Delhi. Playing the martyr he invoked Ram-centric political symbolism and appeared to equate his future with the construction of a Ram temple at Ram Lalla's makeshift temple. On 9 November 1999, Kalyan Singh said, 'the BJP is not doing the right thing by just forgetting about the Ram temple. I am committed to ensuring construction of the temple and it is my cherished dream to see the Ram temple in its magnificence before I die... I know that I would be punished for saying what I am saying about the Ram temple but I stand committed to the cause of the temple.'[492] His commitment did not come in the way of his launching the next election campaign from a different shrine near Banaras though.

In 2003, when Mayawati's government fell after the BJP withdrew its support, she too used the 'Ayodhya card' to take the higher moral stand. On 28 August 2003, having been ousted from office, she told reporters that she had refused BJP's demand to bury the Babri demolition cases and that they had wanted the Ram temple to be built so it could be 'used during the next Lok Sabha polls' which were to be held a year later in 2004.[493]

From the Muslim card, Hindu card, Sikh card, to several caste cards, Indian politics had invented and established the usefulness of the emotive appeal of a 'Ram temple in Ayodhya' and created a new 'Ayodhya card'. Ahead of assembly elections in three Hindi-speaking states as well as the parliamentary elections in 2019, both the BJP and the Congress, a self-professed secular party, are trying to revive the emotive appeal of this issue. The BJP and its large family of organizations like VHP, Bajrang Dal, and of course the RSS have been making consistent 'noises' in public that now that Supreme Court has cleared the last hurdle of referring the Ismail Faruqui judgement to a larger bench, the temple will be built soon. The Congress too has sought to cover itself in the glory of Ram by portraying its president Rahul Gandhi, the great-grandson of Jawaharlal Nehru, as 'Ram Bhakt Pandit Rahul Gandhi' in posters in a rally in Chitrakoot in Madhya Pradesh. The party also launched the Ram Van Gaman Path Yatra from Ayodhya 'amid chanting of shlokas and bhajans' to 'trace the route

---

[492]Sharad Pradhan, 'Ram Prakash Gupta to replace Kalyan Singh', *Rediff.com*, 9 November 1999.

[493]Sutapa Mukerjee and Bhavdeeo Kang, 'Dark room tactics', *Outlook*, 8 September 2003.

taken by Lord Ram on [his] way to exile'.[494]

Like most cards, Ayodhya had two sides to it—the pro-temple or the BJP side, and the closeted pro-temple side of the rest of the major political parties like the Congress. The promises of rebuilding the mosque had been forgotten even before Narasimha Rao's term ended in 1996.[495] Therefore, there was never a clear 'pro-rebuilding Babri' side to the 'Ayodhya card'. A third side of the Ayodhya card, which was never electorally tested, had emerged from the realm of common sense, brotherhood and rationality—of sanity and peace and it found the support of mainly peace activists, the secular public, communists, socialists, academics, atheists, patriots and a few spiritually inclined godmen.

Nationally, the decade of 1991–2000 turned out to be one that would change Indian society forever. The near-shutdown of the economy in 1991 was overcome by opening India's markets to the global economy and by doing away with stringent licensing, notoriously known as the License-Permit Raj. Narasimha Rao's first significant decision was to salvage the economy. The next year, India was hit by the 'Ayodhya storm' and the sense of alienation among Muslims gave India its first major serial blasts in Bombay even as Kashmir's insurgent flames leapt higher and wider. The Mandal Commission's report on the Backward Classes remained a matter of contention and gradually caste-based reservations, which reflected the ancient inequalities in Hindu society, overpowered the magic realism of the RSS and its affiliates who galvanized Hindus by invoking Ram and his incarceration in a jail. 'Babri Masjid, the so-called symbol of slavery was destroyed, so many of them stopped coming to Ayodhya. It was natural. More people join in setting a house on fire than in putting it out,' offered Shambhunath Pande, an Ayodhya resident.

India after Ayodhya has found new distractions like satellite TV shows and programmes. Sachin Tendulkar's success drove the youth to pick up the bat and practise their strokes while the titles of Miss Universe and Miss World brought home by Sushmita Sen and Aishwarya Rai presented a world of possibilities for urban and educated Indians. If the Ayodhya movement illustrated the effects of videos on a population that had never

---

[494]Milind Ghatwal, 'Congress begins Ram Van Gaman Path yatra from Chitrakoot', *Indian Express*, 3 October 2018.

[495]Sitapati, *Half-Lion*, p. 249; Zoya Hasan, *Congress after Indira: Policy, Power, Political Change (1984-2009)*, New Delhi: Oxford University Press, 2014 and 'Rao defends inaction on Ayodhya', *Rediff.com*, 30 April 2001.

seen a TV set before, the power of satellite television was attested when lakhs of people rushed to feed milk to the idols of Ganesha. In Ayodhya, besides the royal family and a few rich landlords, it was the mahants of prominent temples who first enjoyed the visible fruits of liberalization like satellite TV and new cars. Ayodhya gradually returned to its routine of annual fairs and festivals.

In 1996, Narasimha Rao's minority government would end in disgrace for its involvement in multiple financial scams. But the most defining aspect of the 1990s was the public perception that increased flows of foreign direct investment had created high economic growth and employment.

Between 1996 and 1999, India had a spate of four prime ministers. On two occasions, Atal Bihari Vajpayee, the 'liberal' and 'soft Hindutva' face of the BJP, was sworn in but lost the vote of confidence in Parliament. Finally, stability arrived in the country in the form of a new 'religion'—'the coalition dharma' or 'religion of coalition'—a BJP coinage for the pulls and tugs of running the National Democratic Alliance (NDA) in which the BJP was the single largest party.

Though the construction of the Ram temple was one of the stated agendas in the BJP manifesto, it was compelled by 'coalition dharma' to abandon it from the government's priorities. Out of the thirteen parties that comprised the NDA, only the Shiv Sena shared the BJP's obsession over the Ram temple. In its strategy to ensure the coalition's survival and appease its base of karsevaks and upper-caste Hindus, the Vajpayee government resorted to the shock and awe tactic of nuclear explosions.[496] In May 1998, just two months after the government was formed, a series of five nuclear explosions were conducted in the desert of Pokhran in Rajasthan. This sent most of the country, irrespective of caste, class and religion, into a 'web of delight' as it propelled India into the select club of nuclear powers. Ayodhya remained as much on the mind of the BJP as on the mind of the godmen, saints and ordinary karsevaks of the RSS-affiliated groups like the VHP and Bajrang Dal. Many observers thought that the government had gone for the lowest hanging fruit instead of dealing with the issues of 'a Ram temple in Ayodhya, a uniform civil code, and repeal of Article 370'.[497]

---

[496]Rita Manchanda, 'Militarised Hindu nationalism and the mass media: shaping a Hindutva public discourse', *Journal of South Asian Studies*, 2002, Vol. 25, No. 3, pp. 301–20.
[497]Sunil Narola, 'Pokhran-II: What led to the 53-kiloton bombshell?', *Outlook*, 25 May

The excitement over Pokhran II, as the nuclear tests were called, wore off gradually after the costly victory in the Kargil war. After Kargil, jingoistic nationalism would fade away, but before too long, efforts would renew to revive temple politics.

AYODHYA: 2002–2012

In Ayodhya, the VHP resorted to using similar pressure tactics on the NDA government as it had done in the past with previous governments. It also realized that because the BJP was bound by the coalition dharma of power it would desist from upholding Hindu dharma by the construction of the Ram temple.

Ramchandra Paramhans, who was perhaps older than even the idol of Ram Lalla and those of his brothers (installed soon after the demolition), renewed the campaign for temple construction by calling for a shiladan divas or donation of bricks on 14 March 2002. Karsevaks were mobilized from across the country, particularly from states like Rajasthan, Madhya Pradesh, Andhra Pradesh and Gujarat, among others. It was the first time that the BJP was in power at the centre and in the states of Gujarat and Madhya Pradesh. In UP, Chief Minister Rajnath Singh's government had given way to President's Rule before the impending elections. But despite Paramhans's public appeals to Prime Minister Vajpayee, whom he called 'a supporter of the temple movement', the central government displayed no overt zeal in supporting the shiladan.

On 27 February 2002, karsevaks returning from Ayodhya had a scuffle with some Muslim men at Godhra station in Gujarat. More than fifty karsevaks were burnt to death reportedly by a 'Muslim mob'. The riots that followed left more than 2,000 Muslims and hundreds of Hindus dead in Gujarat. In the five years of BJP rule in UP, three chief ministers had been changed but the party had failed to create any positive movement towards the construction of the Ram temple. The call for shiladan for the construction of the temple had given the VHP occasion to flex its muscles and force the BJP-led NDA to receive the two carved slabs of consecrated stone in a symbolic gesture. The stone slabs were meant to be the foundation stones of the proposed Ram temple. The BJP government's rule had ended on 8 March 2002, just a week before the proposed shiladan ceremony on 15 March, and the state was under President's Rule. The disputed area was

1998.

under the Supreme Court's protection, and according to the Acquisition of Certain Area Act at Ayodhya, 1993,[498] the commissioner of Faizabad was not authorized to receive any 'foreign' objects in his capacity as the 'receiver' appointed by the Supreme Court. The media (mainly Hindi dailies) had once again exaggerated the number of VHP activists who had reached Ayodhya despite rail and road blockades. The actual numbers were not more than a few hundred people. Riots in Gujarat continued unabated, which adversely affected the mobilization plan as families refused to send their men out of fear of a repetition of the Godhra attack. At the centre, the BJP was reluctant to jeopardize its government by doing anything that might rile its 'secular' allies like the Telugu Desam Party.

In Ayodhya, Ashwini Kumar Pandey had cleared his higher secondary examination the year before, in 2001. A well-built youth, who wears the janeu (sacred thread), he was charged up in anticipation of the shiladan called by Paramhans who had acquired the halo of a fakir since 1992. Pandey had come from Faizabad on 14 March and was staying at a relative's house so that he too could finally participate in the 'struggle' for the Ram temple. The stories of 'Hindus destroying the Babri mosque' with their bare hands had always both fascinated and saddened him. 'I wished I was old enough in 1992 so I could have taken part in the historic movement.'[499] In 2002, he had believed his wish to 'be of service to Ram Lalla' was going to be fulfilled with shiladan. On 15 March, Pandey walked with the crowd that accompanied the creaky handcarts carrying the two 'shilas'. Amidst 'Vedic chanting' by priests and cries of 'Ram Lalla hum aaye hain, Mandir wahin banayenge', the stone slabs were brought to the VHP-run 'workshop', where stones are said to have been carved since 1990. Unknown to Pandey and other VHP activists—some of whom had travelled from far-off states like Orissa—the commissioner of Faizabad, Anil Kumar Gupta, had informed Paramhans and Faizabad MP Vinay Katiyar about two things: he would not be able to 'receive the shilas' nor would he allow them to place the shilas inside the acquired land.

A few days earlier, Paramhans had given the government a few anxious moments by threatening 'self-immolation' in public if he was stopped from

---

[498]'The acquisition of certain area at Ayodhya Act, 1993', 3 April 1993 <https://indiacode.nic.in/bitstream/123456789/1915/1/199333.pdf>.
[499]Interview with the author.

carrying out shiladan and starting the construction of the Ram temple.[500]
On 15 March, after the commissioner's categorical refusal, Paramhans, now
ninety-two years old, did not make any such attempt. Instead, a 'face-saver'
deal was worked out in conjunction with the Vajpayee-led NDA government.
Under this face-saving scheme,[501] Shatrughan Singh, an official from the
Ayodhya cell in the Prime Minister's Office, flew down and ceremonially
'received' the two stone slabs. Pandey recalls the day with undisguised disgust
and peppers his account with expletives. 'We were made a fool out of... I
could not believe that these senior mahants and politicians are such frauds...
when I learnt that Paramhansji has secretly handed over the shilas to an
official from Delhi...I felt cheated and fooled.'[502] He joined the throng of
activists who in 2002 called themselves Ramsevaks (instead of karsevaks)
and began shouting abuses at and heckling Ashok Singhal and other VHP
officials. All this was happening inside the Digambar Akhara, a monastery
of the Ramanandi Bairagis. The angry crowd also charged Paramhans with
making a fool of the Hindus. 'If this was the fraud that they wanted to
play on the Hindus, they shouldn't have called us,' said a Ramsevak from
Maharashtra, quoted in the *Times of India*.[503] Another sidelight of the failed
shiladan reflected the vast change that had taken place in India since 1992.
A VHP saint, while addressing the Ram bhakts, pointed to the large number
of tribals among them as 'Hanuman's army'. As we have seen earlier in
the book, in 1991, Vijayraje Scindia too had called the sea of karsevaks in
Delhi, 'Vanar sena (monkey army) of my Ram'. But the repeated reference
to Hanuman's monkeys riled an educated young graduate from the Kondh
tribe in Orissa. While the saint was still speaking, he stood up and told
him, 'if you can wear a gold watch, fly in a plane and all your disciples
are twenty-first century Ram bhakts with mobile phones, why must we
remain monkeys?'[504]

For the first time, in 2002, the VHP and BJP's 'Ayodhya card' was

---

[500]J. P. Shukla, 'The VHP had unflinching faith in the Paramhans', *The Hindu*, 1 August
2003 and Anjali Mody, 'Central emissary receives "shila"; Ayodhya breathes easy', *The
Hindu*, 16 March 2002.

[501]Ibid.

[502]Interview with the author.

[503]Atul Chandra, 'Shila daan concludes peacefully in Ayodhya', *Times of India*, 16 March
2002.

[504]Shikha Trivedi, *Ayodhya: A Place Without War (More News is Good News)*. New Delhi:
HarperCollins India, 2016, p. 184.

exposed to their own supporters. To salvage his reputation as a firebrand leader Paramhans and his bhakts had given a casteist-Hindu spin to the face-saving scheme of Shatrughan Singh flying in from Delhi. According to this version, still prevalent in Ayodhya,[505] 'at the last minute Paramhans declared that as a Brahmin he cannot hand over the holy foundation stones to the commissioner, Anil Kumar Gupta, a Baniya. And therefore Shatrughan Singh, a Kshatriya and who had once been the commissioner of Faizabad, was "summoned" from Delhi.'[506] If true, it exposes the casteist nature of the movement even more than it would if it had been just a spin to salvage Paramhans's reputation. More so because in 1989 when Paramhans had led the Shilanyas outside the outer courtyard of the Ram Janmabhoomi–Babri Masjid structure, the first brick had been laid by Kameshwar Chaupal, a Dalit from Bihar, and this had been used by the VHP and BJP as proof of their belief in 'Hindu first, caste later'. In 2002, few people remembered this.

Another side story of the 2002 shiladan episode relates to the resurfacing of traditional rivalries between the mahants of different temples and akharas. Till 6 December 1992, mahants like Gyan Das of Hanumangarhi Temple, who had been opposed to the VHP and BJP-led Ram temple movement, had refrained from doing anything to impede the movement. They had simply remained passive. By 2002, the meteoric rise of local VHP-saints like Paramhans and Nritya Gopal Das had created resentment and jealousy over 'supremacy' in the religious town. In 2001, Mahant Nritya Gopal Das was attacked by a rival mahant when he allegedly tried to 'grab' his temple.

Therefore, when Paramhans gave the local administration the slip and deposited one of the shilas in the compound of Dashrath Mahal 'Bada Sthan' near the Ram Janmabhoomi complex, this angered the then mahant of 'Bada Sthan', who threatened to dump the 'shila' in the drain in his compound. His ire had been provoked because Paramhans had neither taken him into confidence before leaving the shila in his temple nor had he done so after the incident. There was also the very real possibility of his prestigious temple getting involved in the dispute. But most of all, it was the fear of the takeover of his temple by the VHP-propped Ram Janmabhoomi Trust.[507] The temple attracts a lot of pilgrims, as it is believed

---

[505]Interview with the author.

[506]Anjali Mody, 'Central emissary receives "shila"; Ayodhya breathes easy', .

[507]Manjari Katju, *Vishwa Hindu Parishad and Indian Politics*, Hyderabad: OrientBlackswan, 2003, pp. 72–102.

to have been built at the site where Ram's father Dasharatha lived, therefore its name Dashrath Mahal.

Faced with the scenario of a consecrated foundation stone ending up in the sewage of Ayodhya, the administration removed it from there and placed it in the government's treasury office in Faizabad. The BJP and VHP cut a sorry figure in the whole episode. 'We realized that as long as they did not have power they used Ram temple to get power but once they got power, they worshipped power alone,'[508] said a shopkeeper in the Haridwari bazaar area of Ayodhya. Meanwhile in Gujarat, the 'revenge-riots' triggered by the Godhra incident in February 2002 continued.

Three days before the Godhra incident on 27 February 2002, Gujarat's recently appointed chief minister, Narendra Modi, had won his first-ever election from Rajkot constituency. In the UP elections that were held a few months later in 2002, 'the RSS increasingly managed the BJP's affairs... It appointed three senior pracharaks including Narendra Modi to oversee the 2002 Assembly elections.... The RSS backed militant leaders like Adityanath and Varun Gandhi...it encouraged the BJP to make Vinay Katiyar its UP state President. Katiyar after becoming the President duly re-affirmed his party's commitment to building a temple in Ayodhya.'[509]

The BJP also raised the spectre of the state being under threat from Islamic terrorism and Pakistan in its efforts to transduce the Ram-centric Hindutva into a broader nationalist Hindutva. The effort failed, as the voter in UP was seized more by the absence of basic civil amenities like roads, electricity and law and order.

The BJP did better than the Congress but its vote share dropped to 20 per cent from 32 per cent in 1996. It won 88 seats, the Bahujan Samaj Party did slightly better at 98 seats, while the Samajwadi Party got 143 seats and was the single largest party. Mayawati became the chief minister with the BJP's support and remained in the post till 29 August 2003 when their alliance broke up over what Mayawati termed the BJP's demand to 'withdraw' the cases[510] against their leaders in the Babri demolition case. During Mayawati's tenure, Ayodhya, like the rest of the state remained by and large peaceful. After her ouster, Mulayam Singh Yadav once again

---

[508]Interview with the author.

[509]Amrita Basu, *Violent Conjunctures in Democratic India* (Cambridge Studies in Contentious Politics), Cambridge: Cambridge University Press, 2015, p. 225.

[510]Sutapa Mukerjee, Bhavdeeo Kang, 'Dark room tactics'.

replaced Mayawati with the support of the BJP and a rebel faction of her Bahujan Samaj Party.

ASI EXCAVATIONS: 2002–2003

It had been ten years since the idol of Ram Lalla had been forced out of the confines of vaulted thick walls, beautiful mosaic flooring and carved pillars into a tent atop the debris of its previous home. The demolition was done in Ram's name because the devotees wanted to 'free him' from captivity in Babur's mosque. Ever since 6 December 1992, the same Ram Lalla idol and the idols of his three brothers were subjected to the elements: harsh heat, monsoon rains and bitter cold.

In December 2002, efforts to settle the dispute took a decisive scientific turn when the special full bench of the Allahabad High Court, Lucknow, asked the ASI to get the disputed area surveyed by Ground Penetrating Radar (GPR). The court had passed this order to ascertain whether there was any temple or structure that had been demolished when the mosque was constructed on the disputed site. In essence, the ASI was asked to establish what the Supreme Court had declined to do in 1994 when it returned the presidential reference to determine whether a temple existed on the disputed site. The ASI handed the job of conducting the GPR survey to Tojo-Vikas International, a Delhi-based firm, which carried it out between 30 December 2002 and 17 January 2003.

Saroj, an elderly woman who runs a small tea stall near the disputed area remembers the time as one of a flurry of activity, 'It was after the mela time and winter months are "off-season" for us. Hardly anybody comes then, but after many years we saw convoys of vehicles coming and going through the security post. Later we heard that they are using underground satellite to find out what was there.'

The GPR survey covered an area of less than one acre (3,900 square metres) by dividing it into a 1x1 metre grid. GPR surveys are usually done before carrying out underground construction work, such as building dams and correcting or repairing structural problems in bridges. In India, the court-ordered GPR survey in Ayodhya was the first instance of it being used for the purpose of archaeology. The results of the GPR survey were inconclusive, and Tojo-Vikas International cautioned that the 184 anomalies it found have 'to be confirmed by systematic ground truthing, such as provided by archaeological trenching'.[511]

The court now ordered the ASI to start a new round of excavations and submit its report within a month. This was unique in the ASI's history: never before had a court ordered an excavation to establish a specific fact.

It was also unique because both independent historians like Irfan Habib who had opposed the VHP and pro-temple archaeologists like B. B. Lal criticized the proposed excavation. While Habib alleged prejudice, Lal was more upset about the ASI redigging the site to establish what he thought he had already done. He reportedly claimed that, in the face of such unprofessionalism, he had no option but to sit on a hunger strike outside the ASI.[512] He did not.

In Ayodhya, people received the news with mixed feelings. Most of them echoed what Ramchandra Paramhans said about excavation plans, 'An excavation is not required. Hindus believe that Lord Rama was born there and that is good enough.' However, the VHP welcomed the move as it suited its strategy of providing its arguments the cover of scientifically gathered evidence. It was also expected that it would cover up the demolition of not only the Ram Janmabhoomi–Babri Masjid but also of the other temples around it. The VHP is said to have surmised that if the excavation proved (which it did in the minds of some Hindus) that there was a temple at the spot prior to the mosque, then the demolition of the Babri Masjid was justified. In order to allay fears of bias by the ASI, which was under the central government headed by Atal Bihari Vajpayee, the court had allowed litigants, their lawyers or their nominees in the dispute, independent witnesses and observers to be present during the excavations. Among them was Khaliq Khan, the nominee of Maulana Mahfoozur Rahman, a plaintiff in the title suit since 1989. Khan recalls, 'Of course, none of us had any knowledge about excavation or archaeology, but we learnt on the job as it were and pointed out the ASI's dubious recordings.'[513] During the course of the excavations, which lasted for five months, Khaliq and other Muslim parties would go on to file objections against the manner in which the excavations were being conducted, and also alleged suppression of artefacts and other items found.

---

[511]Josy Joseph, 'Tojo-Vikas: "Surveying for truth in Ayodhya"', *Rediff.com*, 11 March 2003.

[512]Poornima Joshi and Ranjit Bhushan, 'Notes from the underground', *Outlook*, 17 March 2003.

[513]Interview with author.

EXCAVATION DISALLOWED UNDER THE CENTRAL DOME

In 1949, the Allahabad High Court had barred the ASI from conducting excavations at the spot where the Ram Lalla idol was placed—the central dome of the Babri Masjid.

According to the court, the nerve centre of the cataclysmic dispute, the 'wahin' of 'Mandir wahin banayenge', the exact spot where Ram was allegedly born, was to remain out of the purview of the new excavation. The court order stated, 'it is made clear that the archaeologists (excavators) shall not disturb any area where the idol of Shri Ram Lalla is existing and approximately 10 feet around it and they shall not affect the worship of Shri Ram Lalla and thus, status quo as regards his Puja and worshippers' right of Darshan shall be maintained'.[514]

On 13 March 2003, the ASI team started the excavation, a slow and delicate process that required patience and skill. It necessitated digging up the ground under the supervision of excavators. These new excavations at Ayodhya had a clearly defined objective—to establish whether a temple existed prior to the mosque. In a way the team knew what they were looking for.

During the course of every excavation, the ground is usually dug in rectangular and square sizes of varying lengths. The supervisor of a trench keeps a daily record of objects and items found in the course of the excavation. The supervisor also records the progress of the excavation by noting the depth of the digging that has been done every day. In this way a sequential timeline of the excavation is recorded without room for subjective extrapolation or interpretation later. Therefore, the daily diary or daily register of any excavation is considered of crucial importance, as it contains raw and unprocessed data. B. B. Lal was the first archaeologist to claim[515] that there was strong evidence in the form of pillar bases that suggested the existence of a temple at the disputed site. But Lal's excavation diaries had not been shared and this was considered by other archaeologists and historians as an attempt to conceal the true nature of his findings in

---

[514]ORDER IN O.O.S. No. 4 of 1989, Sunni Central Board of Wakf Vs. Sri Gopal Singh Visharad Connected with O.O.S. No. 1 of 1989, O.O.S. No. 3 of 1989, ANDO.O.S. No. 5 of 1989, p. 19 <http://elegalix.allahabadhighcourt.in/elegalix/ayodhyafiles/hondvsj-ann-3.pdf>.

[515]'Was there a temple under Babri Masjid?', *Economic and Political Weekly*, < https://www.epw.in/engage/article/was-there-temple-under-babri-masjid-enter-ayodhya-excavation-site-through-interactive>.

the excavations done by him between 1977 and 1978.

In the 2003 excavation, the maintenance of a daily register was made mandatory and the findings at the end of every day were 'signed off' by court-appointed watchdogs like Khaliq Khan and witnesses like Dr Jaya Menon and Dr Supriya Verma. Among the more than 1,300 objects that were found from the ninety trenches laid by the ASI, a 'Fuji Non-TV Zoom lens' was also recorded. This was presumably broken by karsevaks on 6 December 1992, and remained buried in the rubble. At the request of the ASI, the excavation had been extended from one month to five months with the permission of the court. The first ninety days, from 12 March to 12 June, had been spectacularly frustrating for the ASI team led by Dr B. R. Mani.

The entire area was still covered with the debris of the 'mosque-structure', as Advani and other VHP and BJP leaders used to call it.

Despite the levelling done by karsevaks in 1992, a 1-metre-thick layer of rubble covered the raised platform at the centre on which the Ram Lalla shrine was situated. Concerned about the manner in which excavations were done and fearing manipulation of the daily findings, Muslim parties filed eleven written complaints to the court-appointed observers between 21 May 2003 and 27 July 2003. The court replaced the team leader B. R. Mani with Hari Manjhi, another ASI officer, but Mani continued as an excavator.

The ASI submitted its final report to the Allahabad High Court on 23 August 2003. Ten days earlier, Dr S. P. Gupta, the leading VHP-linked archaeologist, shared with the press an unauthorized and unofficial preview of the soon-to-be submitted report. The 'striking similarities' between his version and that of the ASI would go on to confirm the suspicions of Muslim parties and non-VHP experts like Irfan Habib and Shereen Ratnagar.

The full ASI report is a voluminous document comprising ten chapters, including the summary of results. On page 19 of the final report, the ASI gives the details of the anomalies found in the GPR survey. The GPR survey had indicated a total of 184 anomalies at the disputed site and had specified the depth for each anomaly. In its excavations, the ASI could confirm 39 anomalies at the specified depth, and 74 anomalies could not be confirmed despite digging up to the required depth. According to the ASI report 'In view of the importance of the structures found at the upper levels than the depths indicated in GPR Survey, another 27 anomalies could not be located. It was not possible to verify the remaining 44 anomalies as their location restricted the probing due to either non availability of sufficient space like raised platform or the presence of gangways, barricades, pathways and trees etc. for conducting the excavation.'[516]

One of the findings of the 2002–2003 excavations pertained to the period when Ayodhya first came to be inhabited. It was in line with the rich archaeological treasure in the entire region of Awadh: the ASI used the Carbon-14 (14C) dating technique and found that its ancient remains go back 'to the middle of the 13th century BC'.[517] The earlier antiquity of the site determined by Professor B. B. Lal in 1976–1977 had 'revealed that the first occupation of Ayodhya could be ascribed to the early seventh century BC'.[518] The antiquity of Ayodhya had never been the bone of contention; it was the interpretation of this antiquity and the development of Ayodhya as a centre of Ram worship that was under dispute. That Ayodhya came to be inhabited in the thirteenth century BCE is one of the few undisputed conclusions from the ASI report related to the antiquity of the site.

The most contentious assertion of the report was that excavations found remnants of a 'circular shrine'-like structure, as well as fifty pillar bases running in the north-south direction along the length of the Babri Masjid. It also concluded that a construction for public use remained under existence for four centuries between 1200–1600 CE. Thus, the ASI in its five-page summary of the 308-page report concluded that, 'There is sufficient proof of existence of a massive and monumental structure having a minimum dimension of 50mx30m in north-south and east-west directions respectively, just below the disputed structure.'[519] A careful reading of the daily register and the ASI report makes it clear that most of the trenches that were laid did not go deeper than the pile of debris of the destroyed Babri Masjid. Besides, most of the trenches were covered with pieces of animal bones and shards of glazed pottery.[520]

Given the history of the dispute, reactions to the ASI report were on expected lines. The VHP and the BJP welcomed it saying that it confirmed what they had been saying all along. The Muslim parties in the dispute called it a questionable and self-contradictory report. Non-VHP historians raised doubts over the reliability of the report, as the ASI did not explain the

[516]B. R. Mani, et al., 'Cuttings' in *ASI Report 2002-03 Ayodhya Excavation*, p. 19.

[517]Meenakshi Jain, *Rama and Ayodhya*, p. 207.

[518]Ibid., p. 169.

[519]*ASI Report 2002-03 Ayodhya Excavation*, p. 270.

[520]Kannan Srinivasan, 'The ASI report', *The Hindu*, 14 October 2003.

presence of the fifty pillar bases across different structural levels. Allegations and denials flew thick and fast between the two groups, reminding people of the 1990s when scholars on both sides of the divide had engaged in public debates over the archaeology and history of the Babri Masjid-Ram Janmabhoomi.

Unperturbed by any scientific doubts, the supporters of the VHP turned the 308-page report into a ten-word chant:

ASI ne diya pramaan
Ayodhya mein hi hain Shri Ram

(ASI has given proof
Shri Ram is in Ayodhya)

In the wake of its report, the reputation and credibility of the Archaeological Survey of India, a 143-year-old institution, was compromised and communalized. [521]

The BJP-led NDA government at the centre welcomed the completion of the report. The BJP and VHP added it in its quiver as further 'proof' of the Ram temple. In Ayodhya, Banwari Das was amused, 'I could have told them that there was a temple beneath Babri Masjid,' he told me fourteen years later. He runs a small shop near the Naya Ghat that sells religious books and magazines. 'By the time of this khudaai (excavation) we realized that Ram temple won't be built any time soon, at least not till BJP gets full majority,' he added. A full majority at the centre would come for the BJP nearly twelve years later, in 2014.

The BJP-led NDA lost the 2004 parliamentary election to the United Progressive Alliance, led by the Congress. As we have seen earlier in the book, in 1989, Rajiv Gandhi had launched his election campaign fom Ayodhya and promised to bring Ram Rajya. In 2004, Prime Minister Atal Bihari Vajpayee too came to Ayodhya to launch his election campaign under the pretext of inaugurating a new railway bridge over the Sarayu. But the BJP's 'India Shining' election campaign turned out to be a lead balloon. After 2004, the BJP remained the second largest party and continued to hold power in some states in the Hindi-speaking areas of north India. In Uttar Pradesh, the Mulayam Singh government formed after the BJP

---

[521]Jyotsna Singh, 'Experts split on Ayodhya findings', *BBC*, 26 August 2003 and Sushil Srivastava, 'The ASI Report—a review', *Frontline*, Vol. 20, No. 22, 25 October–07 November 2003.

withdrew support to Mayawati, completed its full term with the outside support of the BJP in 2007.

The NDA government's reign was marked by deadly terrorist attacks covering a wide geography of the country. Jammu and Kashmir, Ahmedabad, Mumbai, Dhemaji and Delhi were targeted by terrorists linked to Pakistan-based terrorist groups in one way or another. The blast in Dhemaji was triggered by a local militant group, the United Liberation Front of Assam (ULFA) on 15 August 2004, India's Independence Day. The most daring of them all was the December 2001 attack by Lashkar-e-Taiba terrorists on the Indian Parliament. The terror attacks continued after the UPA took power under the leadership of Dr Manmohan Singh, a noted economist and the finance minister credited with India's economic liberalization of 1991. The ASI report, and the bitterness in its wake, was quickly forgotten in Ayodhya. Locals here had always been more concerned about the lack of development of their town and a deep disenchantment with the VHP was slowly setting in. The Ram Janmabhoomi–Babri Masjid site was placed under a stringent security grid. Local pilgrims and those from outside continued to throng the site, as much out of curiosity as out of devotion. Most residents of Ayodhya had never made a big fuss about Ram's birthplace in any case, to them every inch of Ayodhya was sacred and holy. A natural indifference towards the disputed temple hung over the town, as Ayodhya began to fade into oblivion in the national consciousness.

On 5 July 2005, Ayodhya would be back in the national discourse. A group of five men armed with grenades and automatic assault rifles attacked the Ram Janmabhoomi–Babri Masjid shrine. No terror group claimed responsibility but security agencies blamed the attack on the Lashkar-e-Taiba. The local driver who ferried the five assailants narrowly escaped when the explosive device planted in his jeep was detonated to distract state police personnel who were guarding the outer perimeter of the disputed compound. Santi Devi, a shopkeeper, was injured and later succumbed to her injuries. Another bystander also died in the blast. The terrorists were engaged at the outer periphery of the disputed shrine. A gunfight ensued in which grenades were lobbed by the terrorists in the direction of the makeshift temple of Ram Lalla. CRPF personnel killed the five terrorists in the encounter which lasted for more than an hour. During this time, the pilgrims at the site were safely evacuated. Though the terrorists failed in their mission to destroy the makeshift temple, they were successful in reviving the Ayodhya issue to some extent. Following the attack, L. K. Advani said that Ayodhya had been attacked because it was 'a symbol of cultural nationalism'.[522] The BJP called for nationwide protests and Advani visited the disputed shrine the very next day accompanied by Kalyan Singh. The protests drew a 'patchy' response except in Delhi where BJP supporters shouted anti-Pakistan slogans. In Ranchi, Hindu–Muslim clashes occurred and six people were reportedly injured.[523]

Markets and other establishments remained shut in Ayodhya and panic reigned. 'It was the first time Ayodhya—the place without war—had been attacked by a group armed with modern weapons, it was a shock to us as we thought that these things happen only in big cities or Kashmir,' Mohan Lal Verma, a trader in Ayodhya, said.

The day after the attack, the Allahabad High Court overturned L. K. Advani's acquittal by a lower court in the violence that followed the Babri Masjid's demolition. The High Court ruled that 'he should stand trial for his alleged role in the violence'.[524]

In the years after the attack, normal life in the temple town would become dominated by the government's threat perception related to its security. If the Babri Masjid signified a symbol of enslavement by Muslim rulers, now the makeshift temple on the mosque's ruins stood for a symbol of Hindu nationalism. Between 2006 and 2010, Ayodhya was quieter than it had been in the last two decades. The sounds of the stones being carved (for use in the VHP-proposed Ram temple) had been growing faint at the VHP-run karyashala or workshop, which now had only a solitary artisan at work while the heavy stone-cutting machines gathered rust. Except tourists and their guides hardly anybody ventured there, even though the karyashala remained a part of the pilgrim-tourist bazaar of Ayodhya.

The occasional group of sloganeering karsevaks were often met with sneers from exasperated locals like Raghunath Das. 'I used to tell them to go back and use their time constructively and do social work in their own hometowns or villages. This is Ram's Ayodhya, Hanuman's Ayodhya we don't need you to waste your life,' he recalls, sitting at a tea shop near the road leading up to the Ram Janmabhoomi shrine.

It was in the name of religion that Ayodhya had been tossed into a violent storm, now when it seemed over, it was in religion that the town immersed

---

[522]'Hindus protest at Ayodhya attack', *BBC*, 6 July 2005.
[523]Ibid.
[524]Ibid.

itself. Peace, stability and predictability was what the people longed for.

In the wake of the terror attack, the town was turned into one of India's most densely paramilitarized zones (and remains so). It was the price that people paid for the calm oblivion that Ayodhya enjoyed until 2010, when once again, the country was reminded that the Ayodhya dispute is neither dead nor forgotten.

2010: ALLAHABAD HIGH COURT'S 'ONE BY THREE' VERDICT

On 30 September 2010, the Allahabad High Court passed its verdict on the Ram Janmabhoomi–Babri Masjid dispute. Ahead of the day of the judgement, the central government had asked all state governments and security agencies to maintain strict vigil in view of anticipated violence over the verdict. Ayodhya was especially sensitive, although after 1992 there had been no communal violence there. The Mayawati government in Uttar Pradesh, elected with a thumping majority in 2007, took no chances and turned Faizabad–Ayodhya into temporary garrisons. The army at the Dogra Regimental Centre in Faizabad was also on alert. Sufi, a young Muslim businessman from Ayodhya, remembers the time when Mayawati had earned genuine admiration for her even-handed suppression of all hues of criminal elements. 'She had deployed so much force that nobody could even squeak here,' he said. A day before the verdict, security agencies conducted a flag march—an exercise consisting of platoons of police walking though the town in anti-riot gear. The idea was to send a message to possible troublemakers what they would face if they attempted to break law and order. On the day of the verdict, markets remained shut, as did many other establishments in the town. Most of the state was under a virtual lockdown as all major cities were heavily barricaded and vehicles were being checked at entry and exit points.

The court had to decide on many questions, but most of them were subsumed by the one question that mattered and which was the moot legal point of contention: to whom did the 2.7 acres of disputed land belong? Many of the questions that the court had to settle related to history, myths and legends. For instance, in an answer to one such question, the court declared that the spot under the central dome of the Babri Masjid where Ram Lalla was forcibly implanted was in fact the birthplace of God-king Ram 'according to the faith and beliefs of Hindus'.[525] Two judges out of

---

[525]Allahabad High Court Judgement, para 4570, Malhotra Law House, 2010, p. 2876 <http://elegalix.allahabadhighcourt.in/elegalix/ayodhyafiles/honsaj-gist.pdf>.

the three-judge bench of the Allahabad High Court also ruled that the Babri Masjid was 'constructed as a mosque by or under orders of Babar. It was actually built by Mir Baqi or someone else is not much material'.[526] However, the three-judge bench of the High Court did not answer the moot question of the ownership of the land till the idol was placed on it in 1949.

Instead, the three judge-bench, S. U. Khan, Sudhir Agarwal and Dharam Veer Sharma—ordered a three-way equal division of the 2.77 acres between the deity Shri Ram Lalla Virajmaan (considered a juridicial entity), the Sunni Central Waqf Board and the Nirmohi Akhara. Justice Sharma dissented with the one-third formula as he believed that Hindus 'had exclusive rights to the entire site'.[527] The court granted the deity Shri Ram Lalla Virajmaan rights over the spot where it was located. Nirmohi Akhara, the oldest litigant in the dispute, was given rights over the Ram Chabutra and Sita Rasoi, and the remaining land went to the Sunni Central Waqf Board even as the Board's suit for title and ownership was dismissed by the court.

The verdict had skirted the main issue of ownership of the land. Expectedly, the Sunni Central Waqf Board felt that not only had they been deprived of the land where the Babri Masjid stood till 6 December 1992, but that the verdict had legitimized the forcible placement of the Ram Lalla idol in the mosque in 1949 as well as its destruction in 1992. The 8,000-page judgement contained three different summaries by the three judges. All three judges agreed that Ram Lalla Virajmaan, the deity, should be allotted the land it presently occupies.

Justice Khan in his summary underscored that both Hindus and Muslims had been using the same compound for worship. Justice Agarwal held that the inner courtyard of the building belonged to both Hindus and Muslims. However, Justice Khan dissented from the findings of Justice Agarwal and Justice Sharma in which they asserted that a temple was demolished to build the mosque. Justice Sharma also dissented from his brother judges in their conclusion that the 'disputed' structure (Babri Masjid) was indeed a mosque. He ruled that, 'the disputed building was constructed by Babar... against the tenets of Islam. Thus, it cannot have the character of mosque.'[528]

---

[526]'Text of Allahabad high court order on Ayodhya dispute', *Times of India*, 30 September 2010.
[527]'How the three judges ruled', *Telegraph India*, 1 October 2010.
[528]Ayodhya Matter, Ram Janambhoomi-Babri Masjid Disputes Special Full Bench Judgment, Allahabad High Court (Lucknow Bench), Malhotra Law House.

However, the 2010 High Court verdict did not settle the dispute even though Hindu parties had together received two-thirds of the land that included the area under the central dome, Ram Chabutra and the Sita Rasoi. Though the BJP welcomed the verdict, Mahant Nritya Gopal Das, president of the Ram Janmabhoomi Trust, declared that they would appeal against it in the Supreme Court. 'We want all the land and not only a part of it,' was the refrain of the Nirmohi Akhara. The Sunni Central Waqf Board also appealed against the one-third formula.[529]

After the announcement of the verdict, confusion had prevailed in the newsrooms of local and national news channels. Was it a Hindu win or a Muslim win? Confusion had also prevailed among Ayodhya's Hindus who were initially unsure whether to welcome the verdict or to oppose it. Using common sense, some of them asserted that since one-third of the land, which is presently occupied by the deity Shri Ram Lalla Virajmaan had been given to the deity by the court and another one-third to the Nirmohi Akhara, the dispute could now be resolved and the Ram temple built. Many of them were following the news on TV, and distributed sweets once it was clear that there was no threat of the removal of the Ram Lalla idol. Ramanandi monks and priests were soon out of their temples and ashrams celebrating in Ayodhya's congested lanes.

Hashim Ansari, who was a representative of the Muslim side and was the oldest Ayodhya-based litigant in the case after the death of Ramchandra Paramhans in 2003, summed up the disappointment caused by the verdict, 'With what hope should we go to Supreme Court now?' he reacted. In Pakistan too, the verdict was closely followed in the media and among Islamic clerics who shared the opinion of many Indians that the verdict was more 'political' than 'legal'. No violence was reported against the verdict either in India or in Pakistan.[530]

For devout Hindus, the verdict had rekindled hopes of the construction of a Ram temple; for Muslims too, even though they considered the verdict unfair to them, there was a resolution in sight. 'At least they would build the temple and stop bothering us is what I thought,' Mohammad Nasir, a local, recalled. But residents of Ayodhya were surprised once again when

---

[529]Nikhil Kanekal, 'SC stays Allahabad HC order on disputed site in Ayodhya', *Livemint,* 9 May 2011.

[530]Hamid Mir, 'How the Ayodhya verdict plays out in Pakistan', *Rediff.com,* 1 October 2010.

the parties went to the Supreme Court to protest the verdict. Influenced by propaganda which blamed fundamentalist Muslims for blocking the construction of the Ram temple, Hindus now held Muslims responsible for the delay and continuation of the dispute. But facts belied their belief.

Aggrieved by the High Court's judicial intervention which awarded neither relief nor closure, fourteen appeals were filed in the Supreme Court against the 2010 judgement. Six of those appeals were by Muslim parties, the remaining eight by Hindus.[531] Khaliq Khan, the nominee of Maulana Mahfoozur Rahman, a party in the case, said to me, 'The Vishva Hindu Parishad and its supporters blame the Muslim parties for not allowing the construction of the temple. Why don't they mention that out of the five appeals against the land being given to Shri Ram Lalla Viraajman, three have been filed by Hindu organizations or individuals?'

When the Supreme Court heard the appeals against the judgement in 2011 it made remarks critical of the High Court verdict, calling it 'strange'. The parties' unity against the verdict also did not escape the attention of the two-judge bench of the Supreme Court. On 9 May 2011, one of the judges, Justice S. Rafat Alam, remarked, 'At least on one issue, all of you are unanimous.' Crucially, the court agreed that 'a new dimension has been given by the High Court as the decree of partition was not sought by the parties. It was not prayed for by anyone. It has to be stayed.' The court continued in its stay order, 'How can a decree of partition be passed when none of the parties had prayed for it? It is strange. Such kind of decrees cannot be allowed to be in operation. It is a difficult situation now. The position is that the High Court has created a litany of legislation.'[532] After these damning observations on the Allahabad High Court's verdict, the Supreme Court of India stayed the HC order. The situation at the disputed site remained unchanged.

In the two decades since the demolition of the Babri Masjid and the riots that followed it, the RSS's Ram-centric mobilization of Hindus had diffused into a wider spectrum which no longer focused on the Ram temple alone. A number of dramatic terror attacks that were linked to Pakistan-based terror groups along with the growing global identification of terror with Islamic fundamentalism had helped the Hindu nationalist

---

[531]Valay Singh, 'Ram mandir: Why is SC passing the buck?', *DailyO*, 22 March 2017.
[532]J. Venkatesan, 'Supreme Court stays Allahabad High Court verdict on Ayodhya', *The Hindu*, 9 May 2011.

groups and parties like the RSS-VHP and BJP to project a larger fault line between 'us' Hindus and 'them' Muslims. The 'symbol of slavery', the Babri Masjid, having been demolished, old communal cards of 'cow slaughter', 'forced conversions by Muslims' who posed a demographic challenge to Hindus, terrorism and the bogey of 'love jihad' have been in play at least since 2006 in Uttar Pradesh.[533]

In Ayodhya, the minuscule population of Muslims and the presence of thousands of police and paramilitary forces as well as multiple intelligence agencies had almost negated the likelihood of communal flare-ups, but in neighbouring Faizabad, which has nearly 28.32 per cent Muslims (of a total population of over 2.5 lakhs), riots are more easily triggered. Faizabad was the founding capital of the Awadh dynasty, and most of the present city came into existence after the capital had been moved to Lucknow in the late eighteenth century. However, because the Queen Mother of Nawab Asaf-ud-daulah lived here till her death in 1816, various palaces, mausoleums and gardens built during and after her lifetime, mark the city. Thus, in many ways, Faizabad retains its identity as a 'Muslim city'. To local Hindus and Muslims Faizabad has always symbolized the now virtually extinct (or at least invisible) Ganga–Jamuni Tehzeeb (a syncretic Hindu–Muslim culture that flourished in the plains of the rivers Yamuna and Ganga) that evokes both romanticism and scorn, depending on who you are talking to.

THE ADVENT OF NARENDRA MODI

In February 2012, Mayawati lost the UP assembly elections to Mulayam Singh Yadav's Samajwadi Party (SP), which had become an established regional party since 1990. Crucially, the BJP's Lallu Singh who had held the Ayodhya–Faizabad assembly seat ever since 1991, lost the election to Tej Narain Pandey, a young SP candidate. Unlike previous elections, the 2012 fray was fought on the plank of development. People liked Lallu Singh for his humility but virtually nothing had improved in the town on his watch in the last two decades. One of the independent candidates in the polls was a eunuch, Gulshan Bindu, a migrant from Janakpur (Sita's mythical home). One of Bindu's campaign slogans was 'Na Muslim Na Hindu, Abki Gulshan Bindu (Not Hindu not Muslim, let's go for Gulshan Bindu)', projecting her identity to urge voters to rise above religion. The slogans were also evocative

---

[533]Subhash Gatade, 'How Yogi Adityanath wants to do a Modi?', *Communalism Watch*, 5–6 January 2007.

of the history of Faizabad (as of most medieval kingdoms in India), where eunuchs were once a powerful group who enjoyed unmatched power and access. 'The men of Ayodhya–Faizabad have never done anything for this place,' Bindu would castigate her male opponents and promise development of the town. Her presence as a candidate had surprisingly not evoked the derision that accompanies attempts by the marginalized eunuch community to enter electoral politics. Though Bindu lost the election she secured more than 10 per cent of the votes and stood fourth, ahead of the official Congress candidate. It was perhaps a vindication of the intrinsic tolerance of the locals who are steeped in tales of eunuchs being an integral part of Ramayana folkore and the Muslim nawabs. The respect accorded to the 'sakhis' or 'friends of Sita' in the 'Sweet Devotion' tradition of Ramanandis also helped Bindu overcome the aversion that society usually has for eunuchs.

The BJP was rattled by the results of the election. It had won only 47 of the 398 seats in the state. The party needed to infuse new vigour in its cadres ahead of the upcoming 2014 general elections. And to do so it had to re-energize its agenda of Hindu identity. Events in Ayodhya–Faizabad were to soon give it a platform to play on the anti-Hindu image of Mulayam Singh Yadav and his party which had appointed his son Akhilesh Yadav as the chief minister.

On the night of 21–22 September 2012, idols from the Faizabad temple of 'Badi Devkali', a local deity, were stolen. Idol thefts are not uncommon in this part of India and almost every year a few such incidents are reported. Devkali is considered to be the kuldevi or clan goddess of Lord Ram, and therefore the temple, of great importance to Hindus in the region, attracts thousands of pilgrims during the nine-day Durga Puja festival. The incident of theft of the idols was used by BJP leaders like Yogi Adityanath, who was then an MP from neighbouring Gorakhpur, as a ruse to issue threats of mass agitations against the Samajwadi party government.[534] A few months before this incident, tensions had increased in the district over a dispute regarding the construction of a compound wall which was adjacent to a temple. The atmosphere of communal harmony that had lasted for the past several years now stood vitiated.

On 22 October 2012, the idol-thieves were caught and found to be part of an organized racket that deals in the illegal sale of antiquities.[535]

---

[534]Ibid
[535]Ibid.

They were all Hindus (two were Brahmins and two from the OBCs), but by then it was already too late.[536]

On 24 October 2012, during the Durga Puja procession, violence erupted against Muslims and their businesses in Faizabad. A prominent mosque in the Faizabad chowk was vandalized and property worth crores was destroyed.[537] Two people were killed, a Hindu and a Muslim, and several were injured. According to eyewitness accounts and independent fact-finding teams, the violence was planned and organized. It soon spread to neighbouring towns and villages. Later, Chief Minister Akhilesh Yadav distributed compensation totalling Rs 1 crore to victims of the riot.

In 2012, at thirty-eight, Akhilesh Yadav was India's youngest chief minister. In 1984, when the VHP first launched its movement to 'liberate' the Ram Lalla idol from the Babri Masjid, Yadav was ten years old, growing up in the thick of the turbulent Mandir–Masjid years. His transition into adulthood was marked by the realization that he was the son of Mulayam Singh Yadav, derisively called 'Mullah Mulayam' by millions of Hindus.

It was the SP-founder's image of being partisan towards Muslims at the cost of Hindus that was now helping the RSS-linked outfits to smear his rule with bloody communal riots. Akhilesh Yadav had taken oath as the chief minister barely six months ago on 15 March 2012.

In the first seven months of his tenure the state witnessed six major riots including the one at Faizabad. By the time the country went to the polls in May–June 2014, Uttar Pradesh was scarred by the riots like the victim of a pellet-gun blast. At least 116 people were killed in nearly 430 incidents of Hindu versus Muslim violence. In many of these, it was found that several backward castes like Pasis, Rajbhars and Nishads had participated in large numbers from the Hindu side. Through a systematic integration of caste and community folk heroes and legends—like Bijli Pasi of the Pasis, King Suheldev of Rajbhars, Valmiki, the author of the Ramayana for the Balmiki community, and King Nishad Guha of the Ramayana for the Nishads—into the larger Hindu cultural identity, the RSS and VHP had begun the process of turning these communities in favour of the BJP. The school and college run by the VHP in Ayodhya contributed to this process by imparting lessons in repackaged history to youth from these communities.

---

[536]Scharada Dubey, 'Sabre rattling', *India Legal Live*, 19 December 2014.
[537]Omar Rashid, 'Faizabad violence was well-planned and targets had been selected', *The Hindu*, 1 November 2012.

The advent of Prime Minister Narendra Modi on the electoral stage in UP only served to hasten the consolidation of these disparate castes with distinct histories of Brahmin subjugation into a Hindu vote bank. Modi catalyzed this process because his appeal rested on the trident of governance, development and an aggressive Hindu nationalism. The twilight years of the decade-long rule of the Congress-led UPA were marked by the ugly unravelling of scams, the perception that it was the most corrupt government in India's history and that it put the interests of 'vote bank' politics before the interests of the country.

On 5 May 2014, Modi held a campaign rally in Faizabad in which he repeatedly invoked Ram's name. 'It is Ram Rajya where even a poor washerman gets justice,' Modi said, making a direct reference to an episode in the *Ramcharitmanas* in which a washerman refused to accept his wife who defied his order and went to her mother's home. Ignoring his wife's explanations the washerman is said to have told her, 'I am not a fool like Ram who took Sita back even after she had spent so much time in Lanka.' Ram happened to hear this remark and as an example of his sensitiveness to the views of his people towards his rule, banished Sita to the forest.

Nowhere in his speech did Modi refer to the Ram temple or even the demolition. Wary of the caste mix of the Faizabad constituency, he didn't even greet the crowd with a 'Jai Shri Ram', a signature greeting of the region. Modi attacked the governments of 'Mother–Son' (Sonia Gandhi–Rahul Gandhi), 'Father–Son' (Mulayam Yadav–Akhilesh Yadav) and 'Behenji' (Mayawati) for 'ruining' and 'destroying' the country, and promised 'from the land of Shri Ram' that he would 'fight corruption throughout my life'.[538] Like in the rest of north India, in UP too, the BJP swept the election and won 71 of the state's 80 seats. From Faizabad–Ayodhya, its five-term former MLA Lallu Singh was elected as a member of the Lok Sabha with a margin of over 2 lakh votes.

On 16 May 2014, the results of the elections were announced. Even before the day had ended, the VHP's headquarters in Ayodhya was celebrating the return of 'Hindutva' amidst deafening cries of 'Modi Modi Modi' and 'Jai Shri Ram'. 'The Ram temple will be built now', the crowd echoed in one voice. Mahant Satyendra Das, the head priest of the Ram Lalla shrine at the Ram Janmabhoomi–Babri Masjid site, was not swayed by the BJP's

---

[538]Arunav Sinha and Arshad Afzal Khan, 'Narendra Modi invokes Lord Ram at Faizabad rally, EC seeks report', *Times of India*, 5 May 2014.

success. 'I have seen so many elections where my lord Ram has been used as a polling agent by the BJP and other parties, if the temple will be built, it will be through the court's order and not by any government. Of course, as prime minister [Modi] can try to create consensus between Hindus and Muslims, but will he?' Das noted at the time.[539]

6 DECEMBER 2014

The VHP had been celebrating 6 December 2014, the anniversary of the demolition, as Shaurya Diwas (day of bravery), but local members of Yogi Adityanath's outfit, Hindu Yuva Vahini, decided to mark it that year as Bhagwa Diwas (saffron day) and asked all Hindu homes in the town to fly saffron flags. At the last minute, this plan was shot down by the state party leaders in Lucknow, and the VHP observed muted celebrations in view of the BJP government's emphasis on 'development'. Faizabad and Ayodhya's Muslims had been mourning 6 December every year as Yaum-e-Gham (day of sorrow). Amidst tight security and tensions both the camps held their small functions and gave speeches, as they had done for the last twenty-two years. 'We celebrate this day so that our children know its importance,' VHP leaders were quoted as saying, and Haji Mehboob, a member of the Babri Masjid Action Committee, echoed the sentiment. 'Future generations should know that on this day rule of mob won in our country, and Muslims were butchered along with their mosque,' he said.

---

[539]Interview with Mahant Satyendra Das.

Chapter 12

AYODHYA NOW

Ayodhya's religious boundary is marked nearly a kilometre before one reaches the town by an ornamented concrete gate built by the Akhilesh Yadav government. The gate stands at the crossroads of the Ayodhya–Faizabad road and Parikrama Marg, which pilgrims use to circumambulate the holy town at least twice a year.

As one heads out towards Ayodhya leaving the incessant honking and hubbub of two-wheeler and three-wheeler traffic behind, a short spell of relative calm and quiet ensues. On either side of the Faizabad–Ayodhya road, stand a few landmarks like the Saket P. G. College, the Dargah of Badi Bua, the premises of the 63rd Battalion of the CRPF, Parag Dairy Restaurant run by the state-run milk cooperative, and once inside Ayodhya, the localities of Tedhi Bazaar, Kaziana and the Sri Ram Hospital (built on the recommendations of the Pilgrim Committee Report 1913). One of the oldest temples in Ayodhya, Kshireshwar Mahadev, is located just past the hospital. At the tri-junction near it, one road leads to the railway station and the other towards Ayodhya. The tri-junction is a bustling place. Medical stores, a tempo stand and a few paan shops that also stock Hindi adult magazines do good business here. This is also the point where the district administration erects barricades to stop the entry of vehicles during fairs and festivals. In a town dominated by temples, akharas, ascetics and monks, religion permeates every sphere of public and private life.

Ayodhya Census, 2011[540]

Town	Population	Hindu	Muslim	Christian	Sikh	Buddhist	Jain	Others	Not Stated
Ayodhya	55,890	93.23%	6.19%	0.09%	0.14%	0.12%	0.10%	0.01%	0.12%

---

[540]'Ayodhya population census 2011' *Census 2011* <http://www.census2011.co.in/data/town/801109-ayodhya.html>,

At tea shops or in homes, religion dominates the discourse and primarily defines the day-to-day activities of its citizens. After all, for centuries the main business of the town has been religion. During the Sultanate period (1200–1500 CE), Ayodhya was discovered by Muslim fakirs and Sufis, who were quick to settle here and continued as residents until the time of the mutiny of 1857. Today, its graveyards and at least forty-five mosques[541] stand as testimony to the importance of this place for Muslims, some of whom, as we've seen, know it as Khurd Mecca (mini Mecca) and Ayodhya Sharif.

'Sitaram, Sitaram, Sitaram!..Bolo Sitaa-raam-sita-raam-sitaa-raam!'

The names of the divine couple are continuously chanted in Ayodhya. From small temples—some of them smaller than a telephone booth—to the fort-like temple of Hanumangarhi that straddles the town's skyline, the chanting of holy words greets visitors as far as half a kilometre away on a quiet day. Hanumangarhi stands at the entrance of Ramkot, the mythical fort of Lord Ram, and is considered the holiest part of the town. Among the many places of worship that lie inside Ramkot, the Ram Janmabhoomi–Babri Masjid shrine, Dashrath Mahal (Bada Sthan) and Kanak Bhavan, are the ones that receive the highest number of footfall in Ayodhya's religious bazaar.

Hanumangarhi stands on a 200-feet-high hillock that juts out abruptly. It is surrounded by residences of its important mahants, and shops line the three roads converging at its footsteps. It attracts the highest number of devotees and can justifiably be called the centre of Ayodhya's religious life. A narrow road starting from Hanumangarhi and cutting across the main street has come to be called Shaheed Gali since 1990. It was here that karsevaks mobilized by the RSS and its affiliated groups were killed in clashes with the police and paramilitary forces. On the right side of this road are the places of later origin—the Birla Dharamshala Temple, the palace of the king of Ayodhya, Digambar Akhara and Maniram Das ki Chavni and its various establishments. At some distance beyond the railway line lies Vidya Kund, whose history is connected with the Galta conference of 1713; Khaki Chowk, the seat of the Tyagis; the local police station; and behind it, the grave of Nuh or Noah, which according to local legend, grows in length every year.

A few hours in Ayodhya does not reveal the long history and pedigree of the place. The main road that cuts across town and joins the Lucknow–Gorakhpur highway near the river is dotted with crumbling buildings and

---

[541] RTI reply from Office of the Municipal Corporation of Ayodhya, 9 August 2017.

other physical attributes of many tier-3 and tier-4 towns. Most buildings have not been painted for years, not for want of money but because they are stuck in lawsuits. In this holy town, which draws attention for the many challenges it has thrown to India's laws and the Constitution, the court is an unavoidable part of life. Lawyer Deen Dayal Upadhya, a resident of Ayodhya, calls it the 'curse of the katchehri' (katchehri means court in Hindi). 'Most buildings that are more than eighty years old are mixed in lawsuits. There are as many as four claimants in at least half of the cases,' he says. After religion it is the judiciary and its peripheral services that are quite profitable in Ayodhya.

Officially, there are 7,000 houses[542] and only 101 temples[543] in Ayodhya. But in reality, almost every second building is a temple-house. A temple-house is a residential building with a temple in it, sometimes with a hired priest, provided the family can afford one. The priest performs the rituals and takes care of the temple and the deity installed in it. During festivals and fairs these temple-houses turn into lodging homes. The owner can evade taxes if the property has the facade of a temple.

Mahant Satyendra Das lives on Shaheed Gali in an ashram called Satyadham Mandir, with his extended family. Satyendra Das's living quarters are cramped but offer him a level of privacy and convenience. A set of two and a half rooms on the first floor of the building is all the space he has. The ground floor has a big hall, which is used as a temple-cum-living space. The rooms around the courtyard are occupied by members of his extended family. Since March 1992, which is when he was appointed by the government as the head priest of the Ram Janmabhoomi temple, Satyendra Das's life has followed a fixed pattern.

After waking up early in the morning and completing his ablutions he settles down for his daily study of the scriptures. Around 10.30 a.m. he leaves for the makeshift temple of Ram Lalla. The ritual of offering food to the deity is conducted under his supervision. After spending some time at the shrine, he returns home by 5 p.m. 'It is both a job and an honour for me to take care of Ram Lalla. It is the world's best job,' he says. Bespectacled, with a flowing white beard, Satyendra Das is different from the other mahants in Ayodhya with his mild manners and soft-spoken

---

[542]'Population of Ayodhya', *Nagar Nigam Ayodhya* <http://nagarnigamayodhya.in/pages/en/newtopmenu/ayodhya-city/en-population-in-ayodhya>.

[543]RTI reply from Office of the Municipal Corporation of Ayodhya, 9 August 2017.

demeanour. Ayodhya's mahants are usually animated and boisterous, but Das, who remains aloof from the street life of Ayodhya, is more inclined towards spirituality. At the same time, the spiritual side of him doesn't prevent him from being one of the main voices of Ayodhya—he is a much sought-after spokesperson and regularly features in news reports about the town and the Ram Janmabhoomi–Babri Masjid issue. Das doesn't tire of repeating his stated position—that 'only the Supreme Court can decide the case, but Ram Lalla will not move from that spot'.

Satyendra Das was a disciple of Abhiram Das, the man who placed the idol inside the Babri Masjid in 1949. Two other famous disciples of Abhiram Das also remain involved in the affairs of Ayodhya. Baba Dharam Das, a priest attached to the Hanumangarhi temple, inherited the property of Abhiram Das and continues to stay in the same quarters. He is also a party in the legal case. His stock has risen considerably since Adityanath became the state's chief minister.[544] The third disciple, Ram Vilas Vedanti, turned into a VHP ideologue and became a Member of Parliament in 1996. In 2017, after the Supreme Court advised both parties to resolve the dispute through dialogue, Vedanti managed to garner media attention by telling the press that it was he who had brought down the Babri Masjid.[545] Vedanti continues to remain in media headlines with his frequent and controversial statements with regard to the dispute.

Mahant Nritya Gopal Das, a top cat among the powerful mahants of Ayodhya, remains at the centre of its intrigues and machinations. His headquarters lie outside Ramkot but his influence extends up to Lucknow and the national capital, Delhi, and to capitals of other states where the BJP is in power.

As head of the VHP-backed Ram Janmabhoomi Trust, Nritya Gopal Das remains a key figure in the Ram Janmabhoomi–Babri Masjid issue. He is the head of the Maniram Das ki Chavni Trust—the largest and the richest in Ayodhya. Besides its proximity to the VHP and BJP-backed Ram Janmabhoomi movement, the trust is known for the network of temples, dharamshalas and hospitals that it funds and supports. Nritya Gopal Das, usually found in only a janeu (sacred thread) and a loincloth, is a burly

---

[544] Anoop Kumar, 'Ayodhya seekers demand Ayodhya instead of Faizabad', *Patrika*, 5 April 2018.

[545] 'Who incited mob to raze Babri Masjid? Former BJP MP Ram Vilas Vedanti says he did it, not Advani', *India Today*, 21 April 2017.

and gruff man. Outside his quarters on the first floor of a massive marble temple, four CRPF guards are permanently present to protect the powerful and controversial mahant.

Interestingly, the Maniram Das ki Chavni, or Choti Chavni, finds no mention in any of the gazettes during the British period. Its geographical location underlines its secondary role as a place for Ramanandi monks in Ayodhya. The holy of holies is the area of Ramkot and the ghats of the Sarayu—none of which are close to the opulent complex, built with the VHP's support during the turbulent years of the Ram temple movement.

To pilgrims, Hanumangarhi is the sun of the solar system of Ayodhya. Its well-recorded history, along with the appeal of the power of Hanuman, draws lakhs of pilgrims each year. During the reign of the nawabs of Awadh, Hanumangarhi was granted vast tracts of land in and around Ayodhya. It has four pattis, or sections—Jaipuri, Sagariya, Ujjaini and Basantiya. All monks affiliated to Hanumangarhi belong to the Nirvani Akhara. Though Hanumangarhi retains supremacy in Ramanandi affairs and the religious life of Ayodhya, it is the Digambar Akhara (to which Ramchandra Paramhans belonged) that has grown to become the largest akhara in the country. A great number of Digambar Akhara branches opened up after 1992 due to the crucial role played by its head, Ramchandra Das Paramhans, who also remained the head of the Ram Janmabhoomi Trust till his death in August 2003. As authors Dhirendra Jha and Krishan Jha establish in their book,[546] Ramchandra Paramhans was part of the original team that conspired to place the Ram Lalla idol inside the Babri Masjid in 1949. The Nirvani Akhara is also the oldest litigant in the legal dispute around Ram's birthplace. The three main akharas—Nirmohi, Nirvni and Digambar—are further divided into sub-akharas, also called khalsas. Hanumangarhi, the seat of Nirvani Akhara, has seven khalsas or sub-divisions, Nirmohi has nine and the Digambar Akhara has two.[547]

Although Nirmohi Akhara's main deity is also Hanuman, its followers favour the more aggressive form of the monkey-god. Nirmohi Akhara is present in several Indian states but its main centres are in Ujjain, Vrindavan, Govardhan, Puri, Nasik, Ayodhya, Haridwar, Prayag [Allahabad] and Chitrakoot.[548] Its followers abound in Delhi, western Uttar Pradesh,

---

[546]Jha and Jha, *Ayodhya: The Dark Night*, pp. 5–7.
[547]Interview with Mahant Gyan Das.
[548]Interview with Mahant Ram Das, Nirmohi Akhara.

Rajasthan and Haryana. They can be recognized by the sign of three arrows placed on a bow. Along with calling themselves Ramanandis they also worship Baba Shyam Khatu, whose origin is traced to the Mahabharata. Stickers printed with the slogan 'Haare ka Sahara, Baba Shyam Hamara' (The Saviour of the Weak is our Baba Shyam) are pasted on many cars in north India. 'They are all adherents of Nirmohi Akhara,' says Mahant Ram Das, the akhara's spokesperson. The 2010 Allahabad High Court judgement in the title suit of the Ram Janmabhoomi–Babri Masjid gave one-third of the 2.7 acres of land to Nirmohi Akhara. As mentioned earlier, the rest of the land was divided between the deity Shri Ram Lalla Virajmaan and the Sunni Waqf Board.

Mahants Gyan Das, Nritya Gopal Das and Ram Das represent the three largest akharas in the Vaishnava tradition. Gyan Das belongs to the Nirvani Akhara, Nritya Gopal Das to the Digambar Akhara tradition (though as head of Maniram Das ki Chavni he is independent of Digambar Akhara which is headed by Mahant Suresh Das), and Mahant Ram Das to the Nirmohi Akhara.

In a reflection of the intrinsic rivalry between mahants, in April 2017, the Nirvani Akhara got involved in a intra-akhara dispute over who should be the legal representative in the legal dispute. Mahant Ram Das's status as the legal representative is now contested by his rival Mahant Dinendra Das.[549]

On a spring afternoon in 2017, Mahant Gyan Das was seated on a wooden bed dressed in the Ramanandi attire of a single piece of white unstitched cloth wrapped around his chest and reaching down to his knees, leaving his shoulders bare. Sitting cross-legged, he was performing his daily ritual of mala jaap, or counting 5,300 rudraksh beads in his rosary. His quick nod to the state police guard was the signal for me to enter the covered veranda outside his living quarters. As the head of the most important of the four divisions or pattis of Hanumangarhi, he is arguably the most powerful mahant in Ayodhya. His story encapsulates both the harsh reality and the potential for self-furtherment in the Ramanandi Akhara tradition.

Born in a poor Mishra Brahmin family in Gorakhpur district, Gyan Das was brought to Ayodhya by his older brother who left him as a chela (disciple) with Baba Shyam Das, who was attached with the Hanumangarhi. He doesn't remember the exact year he came to the temple town but it

---

[549]Anoop Kumar, 'Before the Supreme Court's verdict on the Ram Temple, a big controversy arose in the Nirmohi Akhara', *Patrika*, 17 April 2018.

must have been in 1963–1964 when he was eleven years old.

In 1987, he became the mahant of the Sagariya Patti. Today, he is one of the most powerful of the mahants in Hanumangarhi and by implication, in all Ayodhya. His proximity to the Congress and the Samajwadi Party is well known.

A few years after Gyan Das's arrival, the 'secular mahant' Yugal Kishore Shastri, then a child displaced by poverty, reached Ayodhya wrapped in only a towel.[550] Known for his anti-communal and pro-secularist position, Yugal Kishore Shastri, like Gyan Das, is a self-made personality. In 1968, he took shelter in Maniram Das ki Chavni in return for labour. From there, Shastri traversed the full spectrum of sects and ideologies. From the monastery of Digambar Akhara to becoming a Rasik (a follower of Rasik Sampraday, a Ramanandi sub-sect) and then an RSS pracharak, Shastri is today known as Ayodhya's spokesperson of secularism, and has been given labels like 'secularism's sentinel' for his active campaign against the VHP.[551] Shastri's critics though, consider him opportunistic and greedy.

Shastri, Gyan Das and many other ascetics and monks are not the only ones who have found refuge in the holy town. Ayodhya's allure as a sanctuary for escaping the material world is now clouded by its reputation to attract criminals of all kinds who find easy and safe shelter in its numerous temples and ashrams. Although the garb of a monk or mendicant has been intrinsically misused for a long time, as scores of villainous characters disguised as 'babas' in countless Bollywood films portray, the derision that the sadhu community evokes from locals in Ayodhya is startling. On the main Naya Ghat road in Ayodhya, Aakash Maurya, a street vendor selling fried snacks, voices his disgust with 'Baba log' without prodding. 'They are the vilest people in this town. There is not one sin that the sadhus here don't indulge in.' He says there is nothing godly about them and alleges that they have been involved with murders and get drunk and womanize. The underlying reason for the bitterness is the fact that a large number of houses and shops are the property of one or the other temple or akhara. And though it is hard to prove it, the livelihood of a large number of people like Aakash depend on being on the right side of the babas. Ayodhya's younger monks are even less popular. Being young and from the dominant group, they

---

[550]Scharada Dubey, *Portraits from Ayodhya: Living India's Contradictions*, New Delhi: Tranquebar Press, 2012, p. 38.

[551]Interview with Mahant Gyan Das.

adopt a swaggering arrogance rather than the humility expected of holy men. Of course, the silent majority of monks and ascetics still enjoy respect and evoke devotion. But since there are so many of them in this town, 'it is natural that the stink caused by a few bad apples hides the fragrance of the good ones,' said Mahant Gyan Das.[552]

In present-day Ayodhya, the dominant group is the 'Baba-Bairagi log', a catch-all term for Ramanandis, Ramanujis and other ascetics. Every second person is a Das and every third person a Sharan, 'Das' and 'Sharan' being the honorifics associated with the Bairagis and Rasiks respectively.

DEATH OF A RAMANANDI WRESTLER: 1 MARCH 2017

A palanquin with a wooden box open to view on one side came hurtling down the street on the shoulders of Bairagis of the Hanumangarhi. In front of it walked Mahant Gyan Das and his posse of disciples and guards. Ahead of both of them walked two umbrella bearers, a liveried band of musicians and policemen. Inside the box, (known among among sadhus as a Viman or aircraft) sitting cross-legged and upright was the body of Harishankar Das, who had passed away the previous night. Das was popularly known as 'Pahalwan Baba' (Wrestler Monk), a Naga Bairagi of the Nirvani Akhara of Hanumangarhi. In 1972, he had won the Hind Kesari, the highest title in wrestling in India. Gyan Das was his disciple in wrestling.

In Ayodhya, ascetics take special care to obliterate their lives before joining an akhara or starting as a disciple of a guru. Most of them answer questions about their origins with vague replies of a philosophical nature. Perhaps for many of them, their life really begins as Ramanandi or Ramanuji ascetics or priests. In death, after having lived well, the community of Bairagis and householders come together to make the last journey a memorable one. Only asectics are given a 'water-burial in the sitting position'. It distinguishes them from the Hindu laity who are cremated (or buried in some sects). The band played on their pipes, drums and cymbals, the well-known song:

Maarne wala hai Bhagwan
Bachane wala hai Bhagwan

(God is the one who kills
God is the one who saves)

Pahalwan Baba was being carried to the Sarayu River to the musical

---

[552]Ibid.

rendering of the Bairagis' motto of leading a life without fear. Gyan Das walked in sporting his usual blue Crocs, with a thin white shawl tucked under his arms to stop it from falling. He was joined by nearly 200 people on this 2-kilometre walk to the Naya Ghat. As the box-like palanquin swayed on the shoulders of his disciples and well-wishers, Pahalwan Baba's head bobbed from side to side. Upon seeing his body being carried to the river, people bowed their heads and uttered prayers. It was a sombre moment when the permanent chaos of Ayodhya's streets appeared to be frozen for a moment. A group of sadhus played a simple beat on their cymbals, which was drowned in the collective chanting of 'Ram Naam Satya Hai' (the name of Ram is the only truth).

The procession reached Tulsi Park where the palanquin bearers were about to overtake Mahant Gyan Das who trotted faster while his disciples told the bearers to slow down. 'What's the hurry?' someone asked.

The palanquin was decorated like a small shrine. Pahalwan Baba's body was wrapped in a saffron shawl with 'Jai Shri Ram' printed on it. The old sadhus with their cymbals broke into a dance as the procession reached closer to the river. The palanquin, which had been put down a few times for people to pay their respects to the deceased baba, was brought down one more time with a thud. Pahalwan Baba's head moved as though there was a spring beneath it. At the dried riverbed, Gyan Das pointed to an empty spot where the palanquin was placed. Gyan Das perched himself on a wooden bed used by local pandas for rituals. The sadhu's body was lifted and given a ritual dip in the Sarayu. He was then brought back to the bank where one of his female disciples was also present to pay her respects for the last time. Some Bairagis were distributing twigs of the tulsi plant, for the custom during cremations of throwing the twigs in the pyre. Here the twigs were thrown at the body of Pahalwan Baba.

According to their sub-sect, Ramanandi ascetics wear different tilaks on their foreheads, but after they die, all of them sport the Lashkari tilak on their foreheads. The Lashkari sub-sect among Ramanandis was started when Balanand of Galta decided to arm themselves against repeated attacks by Shaiva sanyasis in the early eighteenth century. The mark is done in the simple way of a soldier by smearing sandalwood pasted on one's forehead. Pahalwan Baba's forehead was smeared with sandalwood powder by more than one disciple. The tulsi twigs were thrown; people bowed their heads with folded hands and moved to make space for each other. Others raised slogans of 'Hind Kesari Pahalwan Baba ki Jai'. An old friend of the dead sadhu approached, walking with the help of a stick, and was ushered inside the circle of men to pay his respects. Gyan Das added a touch of humour by loudly commenting, 'He is also preparing to go, let him see Pahalwan Baba.' The band, which had been playing softly so far, now picked up tempo, belting out the new foot-tapping version of 'Raghupati Raghav Raja Ram'. Meanwhile, a boat glided up to the bank. In it were three muscular young Bairaigis. One of them, with a shaved head and prominent red tilak on his forehead, was better built than the other two and looked spectacular in his red loincloth. He seemed to be enjoying the attention he was getting. Gyan Das was philosophically discussing 'death' with the small crowd that had gathered around him. He said, 'Soon it will be my turn to go.' Brij Bhushan Sharan Singh, a Member of Parliament from neighbouring Kaiserganj, and also president of the Wrestling Federation of India, arrived and paid his respect to Pahalwan Baba. Singh is a wrestler himself. He has been an accused in more than forty criminal cases, including one 'related to giving shelter to members of the Dawood Ibrahim gang'.[553] On the day of Babri Masjid's demolition, 'Singh was allegedly in Ayodhya and provoked the VHP kar sevaks to demolish' it.[554]

Another MP of the BJP and an influential leader of the Kurmi community, Jagdambika Pal, arrived, walking hurriedly straight to the body, which was still in the sitting position. Pal bowed his head and placed flower petals at the feet of Pahalwan Baba.

The darshan by VIPs over, the body was now transferred to the boat. It was not in the sitting position any more but lying down. After reaching the centre of the wide course of the Sarayu, the boat stopped. The man in the red loincloth was helped by two others in lifting the body and dropping it in the water; heavy stones tied to the body as anchors made it disappear in the water. At the shore Gyan Das and the two politicians sung praises of Pahalwan Baba to the media. The crowd gradually moved away. Gyan Das and other VIPs also left in their convoy of cars.

Bairagis have been giving water-burials to their dead for centuries. It is an honour that few householders receive in Ayodhya. 'If you have lived like a sadhu, if you deserve it only then you will be given this honour by

[553]Amita Verma, 'Uttar Pradesh criminal MPs a headache for Narendra Modi', *Deccan Chronicle*, 20 May 2014.
[554]'Brij Bhushan shares space with Advani and Dawood in CBI files', *Times of India*, 4 May 2014.

your friends and followers,' Gyan Das said later. He himself is more than seventy years old and later that evening he appeared to be in a pensive mood. 'I have transferred all my rights, the abbotship of Sagariya Patti to Mahant Sanjay Das, so that when I die there is no dispute between my disciples,' he says without being prompted.

Changing the subject, I ask him what God meant to him. 'Look, I am not well read but I am well taught. People come and ask me to bless them so that they find a job, or their children get married or something else. I tell them: Pray to Hanumanji, I cannot pray for you. As far as God is concerned, to me God-matter is the electricity in this wire,' he pointed to a cable on the wall. 'You feed it in an AC it gives cold air, you use it in a heater it creates heat. People have turned religion into business; there are mobile applications to remember prayers. But if we don't devote time and effort ourselves to God and his worship why will God help us.'

SARAYU AND NAGESHWARNATH

Fifty-seven kilometres from Ayodhya in Prahlad Patti village, Jagdambika Prasad Mishra woke up at daybreak, a little earlier than usual. The spring sun rose fast and by the time he reached Ayodhya, his cotton shirt was soaked in sweat. The purpose of his solo trip was to take a dip in the Sarayu River. After joining him at the tempo stop near Hotel Shan-e-Awadh in Faizabad, we exchanged pleasantries and sat back in our sweat-drenched shirts. Mishra was a relatively well-off man compared to most of the people of Awadh. Besides owning some land, he had been able to educate his two sons well. His sons are involved in a small business which he 'doesn't fully understand' and that allows him to stay at home and look after his wife. The sons are married and live separately.

Mishra is a regular at Ayodhya. He comes at least twice a month to bathe in the Sarayu, pray at the temple of Nageshwarnath and at Hanumangarhi. Unlike the 'package tour' pilgrims who come from other parts of the world, he cannot be lured by either the guides or the pandas. A Brahmin, he doesn't need another to offer worship. While he took his ceremonial bath in the river, I was drawn to voices speaking in Tamil. A family of four adults and two children had just had their ritual bath in the river and were drying themselves. As one of the young sons seemed idle, I approached him.

'Do you speak English?'

'No.'

'A little bit of Hindi?'

'No.'

'Tamil?'

'Yes!'

'Where in Tamil Nadu?'

'Chennai!'

'Good good.... How do you manage? No Hindi, no English?'

'Guide! Guide!'

Meanwhile, Mishra who had come out of the water, was drying himself with the thin cotton towel he had brought along in a small plastic bag. Behind him, standing in ankle-deep water, dozens of devotees were holding on to the tails of young calves as part of a ritual called gau dan (cow donation). This ritual of donating a cow or a calf is believed to ease one's crossing of the Vaitarini River which divides the earth and hell, and in which Yama, the god of death, is said to live. All souls have to cross the Vaitarini and it is believed that those who perform this ritual are saved from sinking in this river of the dead.

As he was buttoning up his shirt, Mishra suggested, 'Let's go to Nageshwarnath.' It is interesting that devotees often address their favourite gods by just the first name without attaching a formal 'shri' in the beginning or 'ji' at the end. It is an informal and personal relationship which doesn't rest on the use of honorifics that are unfailingly used when addressing godmen, pujaris of temples and priests of monasteries. After the darshan at Nageshwarnath we head back to the main road. Before we said goodbye to each other near Hanumangarhi, I asked him if he would visit the temple of Hanuman, 'No, not today, I am in a hurry.'

'And, do you go to Ram Janmabhoomi?' I asked.

'Never,' replied Mishra.

Jagdambika Mishra believes that Ram was born in Ayodhya. But like many others in and around Ayodhya, he refuses to obsess about the makeshift temple at the Ram Janmabhoomi–Babri Masjid complex. To him all of Ayodhya is sacred, 'People go where there is a crowd but I have been coming here since I was a child. This fuss over one temple doesn't attract me,' he said. Even during the massive mobilization of karsevaks on December 1992, Jagdambika had abstained from any direct participation out of reasons of personal safety. 'There were free buses to take us from the village to Ayodhya. I also came along with others but we were wise enough to stay out of any possible harm. Those who had come from other parts of India were more charged up. We just enjoyed the tamasha and went back home,' he said, laughing. And leaving it at that, we parted ways. His cynicism about the VHP-led mobilization lingered on in the mind. To many locals like him, the Ram temple movement had discredited itself even before the mosque had been demolished. But since 1992, the disillusionment of the locals has become entrenched. Mishra was certainly a more urbane man. But he was also casteist. He had derided the pandas at the ghat, insinuating their low-birth origins. He had also scoffed at the pandas administering rituals. 'You saw that panda who wanted to extort Rs 10 out of me for putting a tika on my forehead? He looked like he hadn't had a bath for ten days,' he had said before going on to blame the huge population of Dalits and the lack of unity among higher castes for the sorry state of 'Hindu society'. Prejudice and piety are conjoined twins.

A VISIT TO RAM'S BIRTHPLACE

The monsoon months in Ayodhya are teeming with pilgrims. Between Diwali (marking Ram's return from exile) in October–November and Ram Navami (celebrated as the day when Ram was born) in March–April, Ayodhya is relatively less crowded. The same is true for the months of May and June and later for December and January. This doesn't mean that no pilgrims visit, they do. Pilgrims from near and far come to Ayodhya as part of organized 'packaged tours', which include other pilgrimages like Banaras, Gaya and Naimisharanya. But compared to the rest of the year, Ayodhya is a calmer place. The contrast can sometimes be pleasantly unnerving.

During these months the Ram Janmabhoomi–Babri Masjid complex draws even fewer tourists. It is more apt to call them tourists because, as a local guide put it, 'people go there out of curiosity and not to pray'. When I reached there around 9 a.m. on one such day during the off-season, most of the shops on the way were either shut or just opening. 'First, you should pray at Hanumangarhi,' hollered a young boy. Ignoring his instruction I continued towards the disputed site.

In the peak months the narrow road which is lined with shops selling books, idols, religious CDs and other such items is packed with visitors. A popular and timeless music video of Tulsidas's *Ramcharitmanas* by Sanjo Baghel, a Jabalpur-based artist, which is usually played in a loop, was also missing, and so was the queue of people clamouring to see the 'Ram Janmabhoomi, where Hindus destroyed the Babri Masjid'.

In the frisking booth, there was only one guard instead of the usual pair. Ahead of me, a CRPF trooper was getting his wallet checked. Upon finding two mobile phone SIM cards in it, the guard told him to produce his identification card, which the trooper did; his SIM cards were then deposited.

The Ram Janmabhoomi complex is one of the most secure sites in India, 'not even a pen or its cap' is allowed inside the cordoned-off area which is why there are hardly any photographs of the makeshift temple that sits on the debris of the Babri Masjid.

With the hope of scribbling some notes I had carried one of those cheap pens that are given away during conferences but had to drop it in the plastic dustbin placed there to collect objects like paan, gutkas, matchboxes, pens, cigarettes, diaries, keychains, buttons and bidis. A locker room outside can be used to store bags and mobile phones along with other valuables. However, tourists are advised to leave their belongings in their hotel rooms or with somebody they know.

The road leading to the next booth was virtually empty, a posse of policemen waited at the end of the road, looking relaxed, even languid. The omnipresent monkeys were alert as it was their breakfast time. These are daring and skilled monkeys, known for snatching food from even the pockets of visitors. Taking no chances, I covered the bulge of the packet of prasad and walked hurriedly, carefully avoiding eye contact with the tailed terrorists of Ayodhya. At the barricade, there is a board marked 'VIP route'. The road beyond it is open only for visiting VIPs—VIP in most of India is an undefined 'open' category. Guests of senior officials in the administration as well as those of the CRPF and senior army officers in the Faizabad cantonment are regularly allowed to use this route. High-level government officers from the neighbouring districts, the state capital Lucknow, senior officers of local banks, basically 'anybody who is somebody' can wrangle the privilege of jumping the queue. The VIP route saves the trouble of walking through the circuitous 'gangway', which reminds one of being in an iron cage and which I was about to enter at last. But first, another booth and another round of frisking. Two young policemen were present in the booth to check visitors at the entrance of the zoo-like enclosure. Having entered the 'gangway' after walking along the Ram Deewar built during Kalyan Singh's regime in 1991–1992, I reached the third checkpost where a grumpy guard enquired brusquely, 'any SIM cards, pen drive in the wallet?' I thrust my wallet at him in response. This seemed to have aggravated his grumpiness because he refused to check it and waved me out.

The security checks are painful and time-consuming but necessary. As mentioned earlier, in 2005, the Ram Janmabhoomi–Babri Masjid complex was attacked by five heavily armed terrorists believed to belong to the Lashkar-e-Taiba. All five were killed before they could cause damage to the ground zero of Hindutva and trigger another communal inferno. Since then an additional iron fence has been erected around the existing fence and security is strict to the point of being paranoid. But no other attack has taken place after that. In June 2016, the Indian government released a graphic book describing the heroic counter-attack by CRPF personnel. It is called *Ayodhya ke Shoorveer* (*The Bravehearts of Ayodhya*).

On both sides of the iron 'gangway' monkeys roamed freely, trying to extricate food from careless visitors. Soon after the third checkpost, on the right-hand side lies a well that is maintained by the State Bank of Baroda. The wall of the well is painted white and on it is painted 'Sita Koop' (Sita's Well)—presumably the well from which Sita is believed to have drawn water to cook and for other purposes. Unseen from the cage but within a stone's throw stands the Janamsthan Sita Rasoi temple. It was from the terrace of this temple that officers of the district administration oversaw the beginning of the demolition while sipping tea.[555]

On the Sita Koop, a big electric motor is fixed to supply water for the needs of hundreds of security personnel deployed for the shrine's security. Two armed guards are stationed under the tin shed that covers the well. The three checkposts allowed me to catch up with some other tourists and devotees. A family walked ahead with one of the men carrying his son in his arms. He was accompanied by other elderly people. From their dialect it seemed they could be from the Malwa region of Madhya Pradesh. The man with his son confirmed that they are from Madhya Pradesh and then complained about the inconveniences of getting a darshan of Ram Lalla, 'So much trouble for only a darshan, I had not known it was like this', he grumbled.

A little further, a young man was giving a guided tour to a much older dhoti-clad companion, who was barely able to walk. Abutting the Sita Koop is an open area in which lie a concrete platform and a small pond filled with green water. The young man told the old man, 'The platform was built by the Congress government during Rajiv Gandhi's time.' In a 2003 Archaeological Survey of India map the platform is marked Shankar Chabutra. Continuing with his tour, he pointed to a dilapidated

---

[555]Shuchi Bansal, 'Ayodhya: For the first time, the media faced right-wing frenzy'.

building in the distance and informed his curious companion, 'that is Sita Rasoi, from where the terrorists tried to throw a grenade'. Local guides are not allowed inside the Ram Janmabhoomi–Babri Masjid complex. Besides security concerns, the guides also slow down the movement of people which is exactly what was happening now. The young man was testing the patience of the CRPF female guards who ordered him to stop his commentary and hurry along the iron passage that turned left.

This is where one gets the first real glimpse of the off-white waterproofed canvas tent that houses the idols of Ram and his brothers. The 'gangway' turns left and runs parallel to the mound on which the shrine is located. Now the tent is clearly visible, and at a distance of roughly 40 metres. A canine squad was patrolling on this occasion and the dogs were drawing considerable attention while we waited for the imminent darshan of the idols. This passage is heavily guarded with armed guards on both sides of the passage as well as inside it. The passage runs along the length of the destroyed mosque and has a clear view of the tent that sits in its place instead.

The exact spot from where one can get a clear view of the idols is about 4 feet in size. Outside the passage there is a donation box. A pujari, sometimes two pujaris, are deployed here to accept offerings from devotees, keep half and return the rest. This takes less than half a minute, and on a crowded day less than ten seconds, in which time you are expected to pray to the deity and move on. Those who try to linger in order to savour the sight are sternly asked by the guards to 'keep moving'. 'The Ram Chabutra used to be here,' the young man informed his enthusiastic older companion as we exit the passage and came out into the open area. The feeling of exiting the 'gangway' is similar to the relief of coming out of an airless room.

The last stretch out of the disputed complex is a 500-metre walk in the acquired land. The side of the road is strewn with the rubbles of the several temples that were broken under the Kalyan Singh-led BJP government in 1991.

Further in the distance lie the remnants of the Kuber Tila, another Ayodhya mound whose origins are now untraceable. The Hindus claim it as being part of the sacred territory of Ramkot, or Ram's fort, while the few remaining Muslims of Ayodhya insist that on the Kuber Tila was a mazaar of a Sufi saint where pregnant women used to pray. These Hindu and Muslim claims have been accommodated together in the legend of the hanging of Baba Ramchandra and Ameer Ali during the revolt of 1857. This version was immortalized by Ram Gopal Pandey 'Sharad', author of *Ayodhya's Blood-soaked History* and editor of *Virakta*. As it is situated inside the acquired land, the Kuber Tila is out of bounds for the common public, as is the grave of Musa Ashikan, which is said to lie close to it. The Buddhists believe that like other mounds in Ayodhya, Kuber Tila too is of Budhist origin.

On the final stretch of the exit route, the sight of a grand building greets visitors all of a sudden. Topped by a conical structure made of precious-looking stone is the building of the Sri Aurobindo Ashram. It is a tranquil place and is very unlike the rest of the temples and ashrams in Ayodhya. It almost feels out of place. Here, the teachings of the Mother and Sri Aurobindo of Pondicherry are preached and practised by the followers of the sect. The ashram was founded by Sri Ramakrishna, who discovered Sri Aurobindo's teachings while he was living in Ayodhya in the 1940s. Like many spiritual seekers he had escaped marriage by running away from his home. He joined the ashram in Pondicherry in 1945.

After dedicating this ashram and adding to Ayodhya's religious and spiritual diversity, he passed away in 1998. Right after the boundary of this establishment lies a street lined with shops selling all kinds of souvenirs and idols of Ganesh, miniature Shivlings, framed photos of Ram parivar (Ram, Sita, Lakshman, Bharat, Shatrughan and Hanuman), sandalwood, janeu and other items.

CDs of the demolition of the Babri Masjid, and booklets of a new recension of *Ayodhya's Blood-soaked History* written by Ram Milan Tiwari were being hawked by young boys and men. The CDs and booklets are quite popular and never fail to attract the attention of pilgrims. The CDs are also continuously and loudly played by shopkeepers to attract customers. The noise of the demolition is a visual representation of the booklet, with the addition of dramatic commentary and background music. The film seems more like an exercise in propaganda to incite those like us who had just received darshan of Ram Lalla. However, both the film and the booklet fail to mention that the karsevaks also destroyed the Ram Chabutra[556] on 6 December 1992. The movie opens with a young man shouting in a hoarse voice:

---

[556] Arvind Lavakare, 'Ayodhya's original sinners: Part I', *Rediff.com*, 19 December 2000.

Jis Hindu ka khoon na khaule, khoon nahin wo paani hai

(The blood of a Hindu which doesn't boil, isn't blood but water)

Jo Ram ke Kaam na aaye, wo bekar jawani hai

(Youth not in the service of Ram is youth wasted)

The first sentence appeared to imply that those who don't share the outrage of karsevaks also deserve their blood to be shed like water—they can be killed or removed from the path towards building a Ram temple. The second slogan was used to exhort young men—and some women too—to join the Ram Janmabhoomi movement between 1986 and 1992. These slogans are used less frequently now as the movement for a Ram temple is no longer the single point of the BJP's agenda. But it remains one of its trump cards.

The film repeats VHP-approved statistics such as '3.75 lakh Hindus were martyred for the cause of the Ram temple', and 'seventy-six religious wars have been waged on Muslims by Hindus, now Hindus are ready for the seventy-seventh battle'.[557] The figure of 3.75 lakh is absurd and has no basis whatsoever, but to its credit the VHP has turned puerile propaganda into popular history. Even so, most of the tourists prefer watching parts of the movie for free. Many of them do pick up copies of the *Blood-soaked History of Shri Ram's Birthplace* and the CD for their neighbours and families. The fact that these CDs and booklets are continuously sold outside the disputed site, under the ever-present and watchful eyes of multiple intelligence agencies, is proof that there is tacit approval from them. But most people, like the two middle-aged women resting their age-worn knees at a tea shack just behind the shops, didn't seem to be bothered by the high-decibel propaganda. 'What is the benefit of darshan if one has to suffer so much,' one of them said aloud, addressing nobody in particular. Just then, her tea arrived and the man who served it also gave her the answer, 'When Ram Lalla himself is in pain, why should we not be!'

For most of the tourist-pilgrims who come on organized package tours, it is their only visit to Ayodhya. They have ticked it off their list. Similarly, most residents of Ayodhya stay away from the Ram Janmabhoomi temple, and not only because of the hassles involved in getting a darshan of Ram

---

[557]Vijaya Pushkarna, '"Construction of Ram mandir will start in 2018": VHP Joint Gen Sec', *The Week*, 10 September 2017.

Lalla. To them, 'Ram is Ayodhya and all of Ayodhya is his birthplace'. But Sonu, the tea-bearer, was perhaps expressing the pain of Ayodhya's common people 'who suffer the pain that Ram Lalla suffers'.

'It is difficult for us too,' Sonu said, as for many years now they have been living under a security lockdown much like the idols of Ram Lalla and his brothers. 'Terror is a real and ever-present threat here,' he added. All the covert and overt intelligence agencies of the state and central government are deployed in Ayodhya. Ayodhya is a potential target for terrorists and any incident there can trigger communal convulsions across the country. It used to be said in the 1990s and in the first half of the following decade that 'a small ripple in Ayodhya can cause a storm in India'. While that might seem far-fetched today, the town remains a dormant volcano capable of causing eruptions in the entire country. The Ram Janmabhoomi–Babri Masjid complex is the magma chamber of this volcano.

HANUMAN'S BIRTHDAY CELEBRATIONS

On 28 October 2016, two days before Diwali, Mahant Gyan Das was sitting with his rope-sized rosary counting the 5,300 beads in it. Later that night, as the clock struck twelve Hanuman's birthday would be celebrated by his diehard devotees. Gyan Das's authority has prevailed over Ayodhya for the last two decades. As we have seen, his power flows from being the virtual custodian of Hanumangarhi. A centre of Vaishnava Nagas of the Ani (also called Nirvani) Akhara, Hanumangarhi has been the most well-established temple since at least the time of the 1855 conflict.

Urged repeatedly by Mahant Gyan Das to witness the Hanuman Jayanti celebrations, I reached the temple a little before midnight to find it packed with pilgrims. Pilgrims jostled to get in front of the gold-plated doors under the watchful eyes of the four mahants of Hanumangarhi. The gaddi, or the seat of the gaddi nashin, a titular head of the akhara, remained vacant, presumably out of respect for the deity. Various mahants and some godwomen, sat on the raised veranda that runs around the shrine. Mahant Ram Das, the gaddi nashin, hurled abuses at those who had dared to invade the 'enclosure meant for saints' and pushed them back.

Like toothpicks stuffed in a box, men, women and children waited for midnight. On the unwalled terrace of the temple and on the verandas, people sat reading the Ramayana and the Hanuman Chalisa.

On the terrace, three friends in their early twenties read the Hanuman Chalisa by the light of their mobile phones. They wanted to finish the book, pray at the statue of Hanuman and return to their homes in Basti district by morning. 'We are Hanuman-ji's biggest bhakts. He helps those who pray to him honestly and earnestly,' they said. Also present on the terrace away from the stampede-like situation below was Faizabad-based businessman Ramesh Chaurasia. As the clock struck twelve, cries of 'Jai Hanuman' and 'Jai Shri Ram' rend the night sky. Chaurasia was a 'pucca bhakt' of Hanuman-ji. 'Me and my Bajrang Bali and no one else,' he said with a smile. To him and many others it's a miracle that a stampede hadn't happened already. 'There is no arrangement here, nobody to take care of crowd management, anything can happen anytime,' Chaurasia pointed to the chaos below. At midnight, the gold-plated doors were opened and Hanuman is born. This was a display of Saguna worship based on symbolism in its most powerful and real form. Devotees slowly pushed each other through the viewing gallery; the saints, Gyan Das included, left from the VIP door which was situated at the back of the temple fort. 'The one thousand people who came here are, you can say, the true bhakts of Hanuman-ji, they can do anything for him,' Chaurasia added on our way to get darshan. He certainly seemed to be one of them.

The exact moment of birth was marked by a huge display of fireworks, which continued for half an hour. The burning of crackers was not wasteful according to Sanjay Das, Gyan Das's disciple and his designated heir, 'There are so many villages around Ayodhya where people cannot afford expensive firecrackers. They also feel good when they see Ayodhya's sky lit up by the sparkling and dazzling lights.' Earlier in the day Sanjay Das, who is a trained wrestler, had explained that it is only in Ayodhya and a few other places that Hanuman Jayanti is celebrated a day before Diwali, as opposed to the rest of the country where it falls during the summer months. The next day, Ayodhya celebrated Hanuman Jayanti with gusto and devotion in temples across the town. Besides Hanumangarhi there are several temples dedicated to Hanuman. Prominent among these are Hanumat Niwas, Hanumat Sadan, Hanumat Vijay Kunj, Hanumat Kripa Kunj, Panchmukhi Hanuman Mandir Vasudev Ghat, Gujarati Panchmukhi Hanuman Mandir Ramghat, Anjani Gufa Mandir and Hanuman Gufa Mandir.

AYODHYA'S SIMPLE DIWALI
Ram's return from Lanka is a national holiday during which thousands of crores are spent by devout and non-devout Hindus on new clothes, cars, phones, homes, sweets and firecrackers. The grandeur of the festival

of lights is now regularly 'corroborated' by fake photographs of India, supposedly taken by the cameras of the International Space Station. All this notwithstanding, Ayodhya's Diwali celebrations remain simple and serene. Its temples are not packed with pilgrims, and its markets are not full of expensive lights and extravagantly priced firecrackers. This is not so much out of choice as out of compulsion. By the time of Diwali at the onset of winter, the earnings from the last fair, the Sawan Mela, are considerably depleted. The pilgrims from outside the state do turn up but in fewer numbers, and they are in any case not drawn to the smaller markets here. This time of the year, though, is well suited for a quiet appreciation of the town. The frantic hustle-bustle, the continuous honking on the streets and the perpetually crowded temples give way to an easy air. It's only the monkeys who become a little more alert to opportunities for snatching food.

On 30 October 2016, the day of Diwali, the banks of the Sarayu, Ayodhya's only constant through its history, are lit up by hundreds of mud lamps. A couple of hundred ascetics and pilgrims were praying. A family of four has travelled from Surat in Gujarat, to be here on Diwali. They were followers of the Swami Narayan sect which was founded by a Brahmin from Chappiya, a village near Ayodhya. Ramakrishna, the father of two young children, work as a labour contractor in a diamond factory. It was their second holiday as a family. Last Diwali, they wanted to go to Manali but were told it would be very cold. 'We can take a holiday only during Diwali, so I thought let's go and see Ayodhya,' he said.

In homes and shops, diyas were lit to attract Lakshmi, the goddess of wealth. The few LED lights that glowed garishly seemed out of place when compared to the low-key lighting of the diyas. Walking through its quiet lanes, Ayodhya bore scant resemblance to the bustling pilgrim centre that it is. 'These months are lean season for the town, melas are over and the next mela will be in April. So people here, who depend on pilgrims for a living, don't wish to blow money on firecrackers. As it is, we know that Ram-ji is here, we don't need to spend fortunes to celebrate his return,' said Pankaj Sahu, a jeweller.

Diwali is considered to be the onset of winter but the atmosphere in the twin towns of Faizabad–Ayodhya was slowly simmering with the upcoming assembly elections in Uttar Pradesh. And politics and the Ram Janmabhoomi–Babri Masjid dispute are two sides of the same coin in Uttar Pradesh. In the days leading up to Diwali, all parties had spoken of the Ram temple. The BJP government at the centre announced the setting up of a new Ramayana museum, and not to be left behind, the Samajwadi Party government quickly offered to allocate land for it. A few hundred metres from the Digambar Akhara—the birthplace of the Bajrang Dal, an RSS outfit launched in 1984—Mahant Satyendra Das was busy supervising the preparations for the evening puja on Diwali. Satyendra Das is an outspoken government servant—as the government-appointed head priest of the Ram Lalla temple, that is what he technically is. While playing with his grand-niece who kept pulling his flowing white beard, Satyendra Das weighed in on the announcement of the Ramayana museum and the renewed efforts for 'peaceful resolution' of the dispute. Cradling the child in his arms he said, 'It is nothing more than a lollipop ahead of the elections.' Linking the choice of his metaphor to the presence of the child, I asked him what he thought about the revival of media interest in Ayodhya's affairs. As the child toddled off, Das puts on a serious face and said, 'These things always happen, we are used to it; elections, calls for peaceful resolution, media stories, this goes on here. Those who are supporting these so-called mutual resolution schemes know that they will fail but they do it for the free publicity.'

The name of Satyendra Das's temple is Satyadham Mandir (temple of the abode of truth). During the course of several interviews my impression of him living up to the lofty meaning became stronger. Satyendra Das was not as antagonistic towards either the VHP or the BJP as his predecessor Mahant Lal Das, who, as we have seen earlier, was shot dead by unknown assailants in 1993. I asked Mahant Satyendra Das if he is afraid that being outspoken might cost him his job or even his life. Mahant Satyendra Das replied, 'Dharma protects those who protect Dharma. I have been told to get bodyguards and a government vehicle, but I have refused. Earlier I used to ride my own scooter [smiles]...now since some time I have been using a second-hand car. I am quite satisfied.' If Satyendra Das found the announcement of the museum the equivalent of a 'lollipop', Khaliq Khan in Faizabad irritatedly compared it with an accompaniment in Indian meals. 'You people [by which he either meant Hindus or journalists or both] are obsessing about the chutney instead of the main course. This is your problem!'

TULSI SMARAK BHAWAN: BATTLES OVER AYODHYA'S HISTORY

Ayodhya has three existing museums, the Kosala Museum in the Dr Ram Manohar Lohia University, the International Ram Katha Museum and the oldest of them—the craft museum in Tulsi Smarak Bhawan in Ayodhya's Shaheed Gali. Tulsi Smarak Bhawan is Ayodhya's premier cultural centre and houses the town's only functional public library. The office of the state-funded Ayodhya Research Institute also functions out of the same building. A daily staging of the Ram Leela used to happen here until it was stopped during the rule of the Samajwadi Party government in 2015, because of 'lack of funds'. This step immediately drew ire from the BJP, which said that, 'it is most unfortunate that while the government is making all efforts to appease minorities, it has overlooked the sentiments of Hindus'.[558]

The BJP conveniently forgot that it was the SP government that had started the Ram Leela in 2004. After Adityanath became the chief minister of UP, the Ram Leela was resumed in May 2017.

Like most buildings in Ayodhya, Tulsi Smarak Bhawan is also built like a temple. It was the setting of several meetings ('open' and 'closed') between 1990 and 1992 that were called by the VHP and affiliated organizations. The attempts at finding a mutually acceptable solution had never really taken off and negotiations between the Ram Janmabhoomi Trust and VHP saints on one side and the Babri Masjid Action Committee on the other had often descended into the sort of discussions that have come to characterize TV talk shows two decades later.

During the levelling and digging operations in July 1991, some artefacts such as the aamlak (a decorative piece) at the base of the shikar of a temple, other decorative pieces and stone objects like statues were found in one single pit. The Kalyan Singh government allowed VHP-allied experts like Professor B. R. Grover and Swaraj Prakash Gupta to make on-site inspections of this new evidence. The two experts set about making a new report based on this. Their argument was that these new discoveries were further proof that a temple had existed at the spot.

On the other hand non-VHP historians like Suraj Bhan and R. S. Sharma dismissed these findings as unscientific and unauthorized as they were conducted without the supervision of the Archaeological Survey of India. They also suspected that the VHP had planted the 'findings' to

---

[558]'Curtains down on longest-running Ramleela show in Ayodhya for first time in 9 years', *DNA*, 2 April 2013.

buttress its claims.[559] The scientific approach, or the lack of it, with which the 'karsevak excavation' was conducted mattered little to the VHP's plans to build public opinion for its case. This was sought to be achieved by increasing its budget for a mass campaign from Rs. 1.85 lakhs to Rs. 8.70 lakhs. Instead of having a sobering effect, the involvement of historians and archaeologists had only sharpened the divide. Labels such as 'Marxists', 'leftists', 'secular', 'communal', 'biased' and 'unprofessional' that were tossed around have remained part of academic and intellectual discourse in India, especially when it comes to Hindu–Muslim relations and their histories. It was against this tattered-to-pieces background of failed meetings that the dank conference room of Tulsi Smarak Bhawan was booked for a 'National Seminar cum Workshop on Ayodhya in History & Archaeology', to be held between 10 and 13 October 1992. The press release issued at the end of the seminar was typed on the letterhead of the Indian History and Culture Society whose president at that time was Swaraj Prakash Gupta. The statement emphasized the presence of nearly 'forty-five renowned historians and archaeologists' at the seminar. The statement also argued for a 'you do it or let us do it' approach to establish whether or not a temple existed beneath the mosque. It demanded an immediate excavation of the area under the mosque and challenged its non-VHP counterparts to accept the offer or conduct the excavations themselves.

It further stated that, 'now the time has come that instead of being defensive, we need to be aggressive. We ought to say that the existence of a temple is established by so many evidences. It is now their responsibility to prove that a temple did not exist.' In a way this was history making or remaking through numbers. The VHP historians were backed not just by a group of academics but by the millions of karsevaks who greeted each other with cries of 'Mandir wahin banayenge'. Their claim also found support in the sant community which had always backed the VHP. Less than two months later the Babri Masjid was demolished.

DEMONETIZATION IN AYODHYA

Shyam Das from the Maniram Das ki Chavni temple joined his friend Anand Gopal to take part in the 45-kilometre-long, 14 kosi (1 kos = 3.2 kilometres) circumambulation of the holy spots in and around Ayodhya. The

---

[559]'Historians challenge the VHP's "new evidence" People's Democracy', 25 October 1992, Noorani, ed, *The Babri Masjid Question, 1528-2003 Vol 1.* pp. 98–103.

auspicious time for the annual 'yatra' was at 7.32 a.m. and the two friends hurried to the banks of the Sarayu to make an early start. The start of the 14 kosi parikrama also marks the beginning of the Kartik Mela in Ayodhya. It is the last of the three annual fairs that attracts thousands of peasant families, mainly from neighbouring districts. Shyam Das and Anand Gopal joined thousands of other devotees taking their holy dip at the Sarayu, and made their way to Nageshwarnath, Hanumangarhi, Kanak Bhavan and Kale Ram temple (the temple houses idols made of black stone and is therefore called the Black Ram Temple).

This time of the year is very tense and hectic for the local administration. No accurate estimates are available but several thousand pilgrims come to Ayodhya to complete the 14-kosi yatra. They believe that besides earning them good karma, the circumambulation also increases their chances of attaining liberation from metempsychosis (the cycle of birth and rebirth, the transmigration of the soul from one body to another). It is boom time for Ayodhya's temples, temple-houses, shops, eateries and pandas.

The 45-kilometre journey is completed in two days. During this time pilgrims visit the many spots associated with the Ramayana like Bharat Kund, Nandigram, Janaura, Makhauda and other shrines located around Ayodhya.

On 8 November 2016, by the time the sun disappeared into the tall silver grass growing on the far bank of the Sarayu, thousands of people were well on their way around the holy cross-country mega-marathon. Thousands more had reached Ayodhya, even as busloads more were arriving. At 8 o'clock that night, Prime Minister Narendra Modi appeared live on Doordarshan, the State-run television channel, to make an important announcement. In the nearly half-hour-long speech the prime minister announced that Rs 500 and Rs 1,000 denomination notes would become invalid after midnight. The news was received with varying degrees of panic. For many of the pilgrims it was an unexpected bother, but since most of them were too poor to have bundles of currency stashed away, they took it in their stride. Unaware of its implications for them, many pilgrims celebrated that the prime minister had taken a step to end corruption. The next day onwards, demonetization's impact began to be felt on both pilgrims and shopkeepers of Ayodhya. Most shopkeepers had no choice but to refuse Rs 500 and Rs 1,000 notes and many pilgrims had to cut short their stay and return home before they ran out of their usable currency. In the immediate aftermath, temples too suffered as people held on to their money instead of putting it in donation boxes in the name of God.

Faizabad, the hub of economic activity in the region, was struck badly. ATMs remained shut in both towns till the beginning of December, and cash dependent businesses, which meant almost all businesses, were severely affected. Shyam Das and Anand Gopal had returned to Ayodhya the moment they heard of notebandi. 'We finished the parikrama, but we didn't stop at several places on the route.' Once back in Ayodhya, they got busy trying to deposit the little cash savings they had.

POST-DEMONETIZATION, DONATIONS POUR IN

The chowk is Faizabad's 'heart'. The chowk's heart is the Ghantaghar or the clock tower, which stands in the middle of a roundabout from where four roads lead out through arched gateways to Gulab Bari (the tomb of Asaf-ud-daulah), Bazaja, Ayodhya and towards Faizabad Collectorate. Like in many other Indian towns, the chowk in Faizabad has many reasons for people to throng there. Besides the markets that are stocked with all sorts of goods at 'wholesale' rates, there are confectionery stores, bookshops, street shops and paan shops. A paan shop of choice is a matter of serious concern for nearly every paan-lover. Comparisons could be drawn with bars or clubs but they don't really capture the culture of patronage of a paan shop that prevails in much of north India. Faizabad–Ayodhya and almost every town in Awadh is a paan-chewing town. The Bhanu Paan Shop at the Ghantaghar in Faizabad attracts patrons throughout the day, some in a hurry and others idling around. Evenings here are the time for the exchange of banter, information, and solicited and unsolicited views over the most pressing matters of the day. Though there is now very little space for motorists to halt for more than a few minutes, it doesn't stop them from halting by for a short catch-up with the proprietor of the paan shop and with other patrons. Being a small town, personal space has next to no meaning—everybody knows everybody.

On one such evening when the effect of demonetization was at its peak—around the time when the deaths of people standing in queues was animating discussions in Parliament—I found myself at Bhanu Paan Shop. Amid the honking which often starts and stops with the engines of vehicles, a man bristled away from the shop mouthing the choicest abuse at Prime Minister Modi's promise of 'achche din'. The sniggering of his friends and acquaintances provoked him even more. The man was extremely riled up about notebandi and had run into some notebandi-supporting friends. The discussion was taking on a paan-charged abusive tone. He now articulated his anger, 'If you deposit Rs 1 lakh in a bank you will earn interest on it. What will Modi give us, (expletive)!' This cracked up his friends, which only fuelled his tirade. 'They used saints and Janmabhoomi for twenty-five years, after that he used Gujaratis, and now he wants to feed on the poor, Modi (expletive), he is going to pay for this in 2019, you just see.' A cackle of laughter provoked by the choicest, most colourful and imaginative expletives followed, and the trader disappeared into the cacophony of honking, hawking and revving engines.

In Ayodhya, one of the people who felt the impact of demonetization most acutely was Kumri Devi. Her family of two married sons and their three children survived by selling milk, hawking newspapers and running a tea shack. 'People are still coming but instead of spending Rs 100 they are spending Rs 50 or even less. They are saving money and I understand that but we depend on this shop for a living, if they drink less tea we will have to eat less too,' she said while combing her granddaughter's hair and getting her ready for school. 'But if this is going to reduce corruption we will support,' Kumri Devi added.

The unofficial spokesperson in many public conversations in Ayodhya is either a white-clad Bairagi or a tilak-wearing man. Srilochan Das, a Bairagi, addressed a small gathering of four of us, 'Sacrifice is a prerequisite for nation-building.' Figures to measure the impact of demonetization were not shared by the managements of temples. In Ayodhya, discussing financial matters in an open and precise way is difficult at the best of times but became quite impossible after demonetization. 'We don't even count the money', 'Most of it is distributed back in society anyway' and the classic, 'We will have to go through the records, which will take time and we are always busy, but try next time!' were some of the reasons given by the mahants or their disciples.

The records of the Ram Janmabhoomi–Babri Masjid shrine were available. It received a major outpouring of donation in the days after demonetization was announced. Its 'earnings' in the first fifteen days of November 2016 (Rs 6.75 lakh) almost matched those through the whole of August (Rs 7.96 lakh). Mahant Satyendra Das, head of the government-run temple, arranged for this money to be deposited in the temple's bank account. Most of the money was deposited in Rs 500 and Rs 1,000 notes which were counted in the presence of a magistrate and the district treasury officer inside Manas Bhawan,[560] an adjacent building which was one of

---

[560] Arshad Afzal Khan, 'Post demonetisation, Ayodhya temple in "cash-22" situation', *Times*

the offices of the VHP till 6 December 1992. After the demolition it was acquired by the government and converted into a permanent office and a place to store antiquities and other items related to the Babri Masjid-Ram Janmabhoomi dispute.

Ramesh Chaurasia, the Faizabad-based businessman and Hanuman devotee, wasn't impressed by the collection figures. 'This is nothing. Other temples have received "gupt daan" [secret donation] worth crores but nobody will ever find out about them,' he said. Temples and religious trusts have been used for a long time as financial centres that lend, hoard and convert money from 'black' to 'white'. In February 2016, the Shankaracharya of Dwarka, Swami Swaroopanand Saraswati, alleged that the International Society for Krishna Consciousness (ISKCON) was a front for laundering black money.[561]

Interestingly, during demonetization, the temples and the money collected in the donation hundis (boxes) of temples remained exempt from any government scrutiny. In Mathura, believed to be the birthplace of Krishna, *India Today* reporters found the priests of a temple converting demonetized notes into white money by taking up to 35 per cent as commission.[562]

Ayodhya, though a smaller pilgrim centre, was under more heightened scrutiny than Mathura and did not report any such case of money laundering. A local reporter who covers the town for a Hindi daily sought to explain the absence of Mathura-like sting operations by saying that, 'Here people have become smarter. Everything is done in collusion with everybody important and powerful, so there are no leaks. Also Mathura is just two hours from Delhi, which has its own disadvantages.' He meant that the national media seldom ventures outside of a 200-kilometre radius of Delhi, therefore Mathura falls within their range of investigative stories. However, on its part, the local income tax office in Faizabad did its duty by issuing notices to local trusts and temples to maintain accounts for the money received post-demonetization. The hundis were exempt from this as per the guidelines of the central government. But not all temples laundered money or received stashes of demonetized notes.

Political parties were perhaps the only other 'public service organisations' who remained unaffected by demonitization. According to a report by

---

of India, 29 November 2016.

[561]Manmohan Rai, 'ISKCON front for money laundering: Swami Swaroopanand Saraswati', *Economic Times*, 9 February 2016.

[562]'Temple handi to NGOs: How launderers are still beating the govt on note ban', *Business Standard*, 3 January 2017.

the Association for Democratic Reforms, the BJP's earnings increased by 81.18 per cent (463.41 crore) between 2015–16 and 2016–17.[563] The same report showed that 'the total combined income of the seven national parties like the Congress, BSP, NCP, CPM, CPI and AITC increased by 51 per cent, from Rs 1,033.18 cr during FY–2015–16 to Rs 1,559.17 cr during FY–2016-17'. [564]

DIVINE MARRIAGE AND DEMONETIZATION

If poor families struggled to hold marriages across the country because of the sheer unavailability of cash, in Ayodhya, an extremely special marriage was almost jeopardized by demonetization. Just as the birth of Ram is celebrated as a festival in which the majority of Hindus participate in one form or another, the marriage of Ram and Sita too is one of the biggest annual festivals in Ayodhya. Temples belonging to the 'sweet devotion' or the Rasik tradition take the lead in the ceremonial re-enactment of the marriage of Ram, the solar clan's eldest prince, to Sita, daughter of Janak, the king of Mithila. The limits on cash withdrawal as well as on exchange of money created a major cash flow crunch. But it was somehow overcome through mutual trust and understanding between the temples and the vendors of various services necessary to conduct the festival, which is spread over five days.

In the Hanumanbagh temple known for its lavish and rich Sita-Ram wedding festival, every effort is made to re-enact the entire ceremony with the help of actors playing the roles of Ram, Sita and Vishwamitra, the family guru of Ram, and his brothers.

The Ram-Vivaah festival starts wth the ritual worship of Ram. On the second day the arrival of Vishwamitra for the wedding is staged. On the third day, Ram (enacted by a tinsel-clad young man wearing a crown and heavy make-up) strings the bow of Shiva, and on the fourth day, Ram's wedding procession, or baraat, is taken out after which the marriage between Ram and Sita (played by another male actor with more make-up) is consecrated with 'complete Vedic rituals'. Devotees too participate in this religious theatre by playing the roles of Ram and Sita's clansmen and clanswomen. VIP devotees, after giving large donations in cash or kind, get

---

[563]'What demonetisation? BJP revenue grew 81% to Rs 1034 crore in 2016-17; Congress, others earned this much', *Financial Express*, 11 April 2018.
[564]Ibid.

to play the role of the parents of the couple.

On the fifth day, a feast with fifty-six different varieties of dishes is organized for the two 'families', and a 'larger' reception is also held for whoever wants to partake in the celebration. Naturally, elaborate wedding festivals such as this require lakhs of rupees. The mahants of the temples of Hanumanbagh, Rang Mahal and Janki Mahal Trust along with other smaller Rasik temples were reported to have contemplated petitioning their local bank and the district magistrate to seek exemption from the Rs 24,000 per week withdrawal limit imposed by the government. Their logic, though rooted in religion, failed to impress the bank manager, O. P. Shukla, who cited the lack of Reserve Bank of India guidelines on divine marriage festivals.[565]

CITIZENS FOR PEACE

The impact of demonetization was both immediate and permanent on Chand Miyan, the owner of a one-room footwear factory in Faizabad. His 'factory', situated on the edge of Wazirganj, a working class neighbourhood, is one of several sandal-making units that supply to the small markets of Faizabad and neighbouring areas. After demonetization Chand Miyan's cash flow nearly dried up. 'For three months neither was I paid by the buyers nor did I pay my workers. We survived on what we had as savings, some of us borrowed money to run our household expenses,' Chand Miyan, a man with a toothy smile, recalled. As a member of the CPI(M-L), he is also active in the politics of his small neighbourhood and the day we met in his factory we came face-to-face with an unlikely phenomenon.

Inside the narrow lanes of Wazirganj, a group of young men, some barely of voting age, were animatedly discussing a 'peace move'. They were holding forms printed in Urdu and English and were being told by an elderly man to get as many signatures as possible on every form. Akram Chacha is a member of the Khaksar, a voluntary organization that boasts a proud history of participating in the freedom struggle. The now largely defunct Khaksar movement in India survives in some towns of UP. Akram is one such veteran of the movement. The forms that he was explaining to the youngsters were seeking to counter the moves to press for an amicable out-of-court settlement of the Ram Janmabhoomi dispute. 'We are not against peace and resolution through dialogue but we don't want

---

[565]'Demonitisation clouds over divine Sita-Ram marriage', *Jagran*, 21 November 2016.

our community to be fooled once again,' said Akram, as were being served tea in soft plastic cups from a nearby stall.

If conflict in Ayodhya was bolstered through the interventions of outside groups like the VHP, efforts to find a mutually acceptable solution are also the product of the efforts of 'outsiders', like retired Allahabad High Court Judge Palok Basu, who has been trying to organize 'peace dialogues' between the two communities. Under the latest 'peace formula', Muslims and Hindus are being asked to sign their consent to the Ram Temple being built at the spot where the makeshift tent-temple stands and the mosque being built at the edge of the acquired land. Akram, who calls himself a 'secular Indian', explains his opposition to this proposal. 'First, those behind this move are just publicity hungry people. They have only their own interest in mind. Secondly, we go by what more enlightened and knowledgeable community leaders tell us. We trust them more than these seasonal frogs,' Akram says.

Khaliq Khan, a nominee in the legal case and the convener of the local Hilal Committee, is one such community leader who is opposed to signature campaigns for the resolution of the dispute through dialogue. 'They do not know what they are talking about. Even if Muslims unite who should we talk to on the Hindu side? They are divided, and this signature campaign comprising 5,000 Hindus and 5,000 Muslims is not enough to resolve the dispute,' says Khan. In fact, the Nirmohi Akhara, the oldest litigant in the suit, is now seeing a public and ugly squabbling over who among its members should be the Akhara's legal representative. Besides, the Nirmohi Akhara maintains that the entire disputed site, including the deity Shri Ram Lalla Virajman, is their property.[566]

Fareed Salmani, a member of the Salmani community whose traditonal occupation has been that of a barber, is one of the local leaders backing the Justice Palok Basu-led Citizens Committee for mutual resolution. His inspiration in politics is Jawaharlal Nehru, India's first prime minister. 'My motivation is to get Hindus and Muslims to take the matter in their hands and find a solution. There is no doubt that ahead of the 2017 assembly elections the BJP will try to milk the issue of Ram temple but if we are successful we will be able to make this a non-political issue.' Salmani's words resemble the high moral speeches of his idol, Jawaharlal Nehru,

---

[566]'The disputed land in Ayodhya is not Ramji's, it's ours: Nirmohi Akhara', *Navbharat Times*, 17 April 2018.

when he says that it's his wish to see a politics without Ram and Rahim, mandir and masjid.

At the same time, he echoes the views of the VHP and the BJP when he says that 'Ram is worshipped by every Hindu but Babri Masjid is not, so Muslims should build their mosque somewhere else.'

In November 2016, the proposal, in the pipeline for nearly six years, was finally submitted to the commissioner of Faizabad who forwarded it to the Supreme Court.[567]

In all, three proposals, two for out-of-court settlements and one against out-of-court settlement, were floating in Faizabad–Ayodhya in the winter of 2016. The first one by Palok Basu, recommended that it should be left to the court to decide to allow or disallow whether or not the mosque should be rebuilt on the acquired land near Yusuf Ara Machine on the main road.

The Citizens Committee's proposal is that the Ram temple can be built at the disputed site, and that Muslims will not construct anything on one-third of 2.77 acres awarded to them by the Allahabad High Court in 2010. In return, the construction of both the Ram temple and the new mosque will start together. The mosque will be built near Yusuf Ara Machine in Ayodhya.

The third proposal is basically a counter to an out-of-court settlement. Khaliq Khan, who supports it, says, 'we want the court to decide whom the land belongs to'. The Sunni Central Waqf Board's title suit to the entire 2.77 acres of land was dismissed by the Allahabad High Court's 2010 verdict. As the nominee of Maulana Mahfoozur Rahman, a third-generation plaintiff in the dispute, Khaliq Khan says he speaks not just for Mahfoozur Rahman but the entire Muslim community. 'We have been betrayed again and again. First in 1949, then in 1986, then 1989, after that 1992, then the ASI excavations in 2003, and lastly by the Allahabad High Court's verdict in 2010 which summarily dismissed our suit. Through the years, the VHP scuttled all efforts to resolve the dispute through dialogue. Therefore, now only the Supreme Court can decide on this matter,' Khaliq Khan defends his stand.

Although an opponent, Mahant Nritya Gopal Das, president of the Ram Janmabhoomi Trust, agrees with Khaliq Khan on the 'peace moves', but adds an unwieldy twist. He reckons that people like Fareed Salmani and

---

[567]'Ayodhya dispute: petition filed to build new temple, mosque', *Indian Express*, 14 November 2016.

Palok Basu are 'interfering with the legal process pending in the Supreme Court'. The twist that he adds is that the new mosque will never be allowed to be built inside the 'cultural boundary' of Ayodhya. His view is shared by the VHP's local media incharge, Sharad Sharma, who adds that Muslims can build the mosque on the other side of the Sarayu River, but it cannot be called Babri Masjid. 'That can't be allowed anywhere in India,' he adds.

Given this position it is probably unthinkable that an out-of-court settlement can be worked out. The VHP's position, though, is quite consistent with its 1990's slogan of 'Babur ki santanon se badla le kar rahenge' (we will take revenge on Babur's children). Its movement was based on the belief that Babur was an 'invader who destroyed Hindus' places of worship' and that 'Babri mosque was a symbol of India's slavery'. Therefore, it is not surprising that it is opposed to any mosque in the name of Babur 'being built anywhere in India'. The VHP is perhaps unaware that several mosques built by Babur or during his time still exist in India. Just an hour's drive from the VHP headquarters in Delhi, there is a Babri masjid in Palam village. It was built in 1528 by Ghaznafar, a noble in Babur's service.[568]

VHP'S PLANS FOR THE 'REVIVAL OF AYODHYA'

Champat Rai Bansal, the VHP's general secretary, is a short man with a squeaky voice. His diminutive figure and somewhat mild bearing, however, is deceptive. After the death of Ashok Singhal in 2015, Rai has emerged as one of the faces of the VHP and the Ram Janmabhoomi movement. In November 2016, at a symposium titled 'Ram Mandir aur Bhartiya Asmita', in Delhi's Constitution Club, he addressed a crowd largely made up of the employees of the magazine that had organized it. His co-speakers were a couple of marginalized BJP leaders like Sanjay Joshi and Sanjay Pawar. Ram Bahadur Rai, a veteran Hindi journalist and the president of the Indira Gandhi National Centre for the Arts, was also present. Among those who skipped the symposium was Sudha Malaiya, member of the BJP's national executive. Champat Rai, Ram Bahadur Rai and Malaiya were deeply involved in the Ram temple movement. Champat Rai is a co-accused along with Advani and others in the Babri Masjid demolition case. Ram Bahadur Rai covered the movement and enjoyed unrestricted access to the BJP's top leadership of the time and was particulary close to former prime minister Atal Bihari Vajpayee.

---

[568]R. V. Smith, *Delhi: Unknown Tales of a City*, New Delhi: Roli Books, 2015.

Sudha Malaiya became famous among the pro-temple supporters as the 'budding art historian' who discovered the 'Vishnu-Hari inscription' from the debris of the Babri Masjid. This inscription, though not admissible as evidence because of the manner in which it was discovered, was used by the VHP to persuade the Allahabad High Court to order new excavations in Ayodhya in 2002–03. The poor turnout at the symposium, and the presence of only one television channel—TV18—did not deter Champat Rai from making more than an hour-long speech.

The theme of the symposium was 'Ram temple and Indian dignity'. Ram Bahadur Rai, as the chief guest, spoke last. He started by pointing out that the theme should have been 'Ram birthplace temple and Indian dignity'. He then dwelt at length on why the Ram Janmabhoomi movement could not sustain the momentum after the demolition. He shared the details of a meeting he had with Atal Bihari Vajpayee soon after the demolition: 'Vajpayee was sitting at the long table in his house. Phones were ringing continuously but he had asked not to be disturbed. We spoke for some time and I think he agreed with me when I said that...everybody present in Ayodhya on 6 December 1992—from Ashok Singhal to the common karsevak—should have given an affidavit to the Narasimha Rao government, saying that "Yes, we broke the Masjid, now punish us according to the law."'[569]

What had happened after the demolition was the complete opposite of an owning up of responsibility. The BJP's leadership, the VHP's office-bearers and its army of saints, had blamed the demolition on 'unruly karsevaks gone out of control'. Ram Bahadur Rai added with an air of self-righteous conviction, 'If those 2.5 lakh people had given these affidavits Ram Rajya would have been established. I don't want to go into why that did not happen.'

The meeting, which had started with few people in the audience, ended with even fewer who remained. But as the next few months showed, it would have been wrong to conclude that the Ram temple issue and Ayodhya were no longer relevant.

Champat Rai had himself said, 'There can never be a compromise on the temple', equating the construction of the temple at the disputed site with India's dignity.

Earlier during the Ujjain Mahakumbh in May 2016, the VHP had set 31 December as the deadline for temple construction in Ayodhya. On 5

---

[569]'VHP is trying to revive Ayodhya, but there is no momentum', *Rediff.com*, 26 September 2013.

October 2016, Prime Minister Modi attended the Dussehra celebration in Lucknow. He revived the Ram Mandir issue once again by leading the chanting of 'Jai Shri Ram!' by thousands of BJP supporters. 'Jai Shri Ram' is no longer an ordinary form of greeting like 'Jai Siyaram' or 'Jai Sitaram' (both of these acknowledge Sita) or the universal 'Ram-Ram'. Today, 'Jai Shri Ram' has become a call to arms for millions of supporters of the RSS and its various outfits. It is raised in the street, during rallies, as well as in the Parliament as a show of strength against their opponents.

STRUGGLING AGAINST AYODHYA'S ENTRENCHED PATRIARCHY

Saket Degree College is Ayodhya and Faizabad's most reputed institution of higher learning. Founded in 1951 by socialist leader Narendra Dev, his bitter rival Baba Raghav Das, barrister Parmeshwarnath Sapra and the former king of Ayodhya, Jagdambika Pratap Narain Singh, the college has an illustrious past. Its alumni are well placed in different government careers across academia, judiciary, police and civil administration.

Though Saket College remains a sought-after learning instituion, its glory days are long over. It continues to attract economically and academically better-off students. Outside the college, two south Indian dosaiwallahs do good business. Here locals and students can be seen relishing cheese dosais and other south Indian dishes cooked to cater to local palates. While a group of three second-year students were waiting for their dosas, I introduced myself and started a conversation. They were hesitant at first but started speaking freely and openly when the purpose of my questions became clear to them. 'Most of our parents would never let us live on our own, therefore we cannot go out to study like the boys,' was Asha's response, as to why she chose this college.

Like her, Asha's friends were doing a three-year graduation course in mathematics. Two of them lived in Faizabad, Asha is from Ayodhya. They came to college when 'necessary'. Today was one such day when they had to fill their forms for an upcoming examination. On most days classes are not held, and reading material or course books have been largely replaced with 'guides' and 'guess papers'. A few months later Asha agreed to meet my friend Prashansa and me at her home. During the course of several hours spent with Asha, what emerged was the similarity between her life and the lives of most Indian girls. She was usually cloistered inside the home, chaperoned when outside and made to adhere to a strictly enforced code of conduct. 'This is a religious place, Ram's own town, Buddha too lived here but do you think people here are holy and godly?' Asha asked. 'Nothing can stop a dog from barking, but at least men should not forget that they are in holy Ayodhya; Baba-Bairagi or householder, they stare at us up and down,' she said, disgusted.

The hollowness of a holy town is not easily seen through news reports or during visits, though sometimes certain sensational cases of excesses by Ayodhya's monks make it to local newspapers. One such incident of sexual crimes came to light in May 2017 when a middle-aged woman lodged a complaint of gang rape of her daughter and her by five sadhus of the Janki Niwas Mandir in Ayodhya.[570]

Asha's experience of oppressive patriarchy, though shared by most women, is complicated by the layer of religious sanctimony that covers all public and social aspects of life here. Asha knew that her parents, a middle-class business family, sent her to college because that's accepted social sanction in the town. Had she been a better student, they might even have considered sending her to study in Lucknow where her relatives live. But given her average academic performance, she was to stay with them till a suitable groom was found for her. 'When I was growing up my grandmother used to complain, grumble all the time about not having a grandson, "You are lucky the world has changed, in my time, girls used to be killed at birth itself,"' she recalled an early memory still fresh in her young mind. Her only solace in the town is the Sarayu. 'I like that the river is nearby. I like to go and sit there during the evening,' she said. The Sarayu is what redeems Ayodhya from its small-townness and the seasonal invasions by lakhs of pilgrims and tourists. Even during festivals and yatras it is possible to find a quiet space along the ghats and temporarily forget the din and crowds.

'Do you have a boyfriend?' Prashansa asked her. 'Yes I do, but if my family comes to know they will beat me and him both; he is from a different caste. I am a Brahmin, as you know,' she said. And a proud Brahmin at that. But her identity as a girl subsumes her caste identity. As our conversation drifted towards temples and mahants, Asha had snapped, 'Yes, there are many scholars of religion and scriptures here, but why are all of them men? The few women sadhus we see are old abandoned widows or those who come for special occasions.' It seemed she had given the subject serious thought. Having been brought up in a devout Hindu household, Asha savoured the

---

reverence for rituals and temple-worship. But what riled her up was the virtual absence of women in the religious life of Ayodhya. However, one of the leading kathavachaks (reciters/expounders of Tulsidas's Ramayana and the Bhagavad Gita) of Ayodhya is Mandakini Ram Kinkar, a disciple of Padma Bhushan recipient Ram Kinkar Upadhyay. Another upcoming woman kathavachak is Sunita Shastri, a disciple of Sitaram Sharma, who was the mahant of Laxman Qila. But these two seldom stay in Ayodhya, their proficiency with the Ramayana being much in demand throughout the Vaishnav Hindu diaspora spread across the world.

Mandakini Ram Kinkar had done very well as a preacher. Her guru, Ram Kinkar, appointed her the head of the three trusts that he ran. However, Asha's point still holds true. Being a city of renunciates, widows are abandoned here like in Banaras. However, now that there is increased social acceptance of widowhood in Hindu society, the number of widows living in Ayodhya has decreased. 'Maai vada' or the 'locality of mothers' is the only institution that has been taking care of widows for the last fifty years. And, reflecting the changing social norms, the number of widows living here has not increased. But for Asha and young women like her, women's roles are well defined as mothers, wives, sisters and widows, and she knows that nothing will change that. She said, 'I know my place, at least in this birth, I will have to swallow my dreams. If I am born a boy in my next life, I will also leave Ayodhya after school.'

AYODHYA'S PATRON AUNT: BADI BUA

A grove of neem, tamarind and banyan trees shrouds the tomb of Ayodhya's most revered aunt. Popularly known as Badi Bua (father's elder sister) or Badi Bibi, her tomb draws a continuous stream of committed and loving followers throughout the year. In the annual urs (death anniversary) held in her memory thousands of people gather to commemorate the piety and seek the blessings of Badi Bua, the older sister of the Sufi saint Nasir-ud-din 'Chiragh-e-Dehlavi'.

An interesting anecdote shared by her followers displays her singular dedication to God. Badi Bua was troubled by the mullahs for remaining unmarried. One day they confronted her and insisted that she must follow the customs of Islam and marry. The story goes that she agreed to marry but only to 'a truly pious man'.[571] The kotwal (chief police officer) of

---

[571]Yoginder Sikand, 'Ayodhya's forgotten Muslim past', *Countercurrents.org*, 5 August 2006

Ayodhya sent a messenger to Badi Bua expressing his wish to marry her. But she insisted that the kotwal present himself in person if he wished to marry her. According to legend, Badi Bua asked the kotwal why he wished to marry her and when he said that 'he was in love with her eyes',[572] she took out her eyes and gave them to him. The kotwal was so shaken by what he had witnessed, he fell at her feet and begged for forgiveness.

Ramdulare, a rickshaw-puller, has been praying at Badi Bua's mausoleum every week for the last forty years. To him Badi Bua is a personal saint, a benefactor and a powerful entity with whom he shares his problems. 'Last time my wife fell seriously ill, it was malaria and she would have certainly died if not for the blessing of Badi Bua,' he said. 'And did you not pray at Hanumangarhi?' I asked. 'Of course I did, for us, the actual residents of Ayodhya, there are three main goddesses, the Choti Dev Kali in Ayodhya, Badi Dev Kali in Faizabad and this dargah of Badi Bua. We worship here because they protect Ayodhya and its people.' Ramdulare didn't know how old his family's association with Ayodhya was but he insisted that they had been there for 'hundreds of years'. His faith in Badi Bua was unaffected by his being a Hindu. 'Badi Bua never tells me to stop praying at my Hindu temples neither does the caretaker of her shrine. My forefathers have prayed here. My father and mother used to bring us here. She is everybody's Bua,' he corrected himself, 'not just Bua, Badi Bua, if she was my father's Badi Bua and his father's and like that for generations before them, how can anybody have a problem. I am praying to my Badi Bua.'

Then I asked him a question often asked by Hindus, 'Have you seen Muslims praying at Hindu temples?' Ramdulare replied, 'Do you know Muslim women go and pray at Kanak Bhavan, they also go to Choti Dev Kali; they may not go inside the temple, but they stop outside and pray. Whenever my wife goes to Nageshwarnath, they tell her to pray for them too. In their religion idol-worship is not allowed so they can't pray openly, but I know they also believe in Hindu gods just as we Hindus believe in Badi Bua.' Ramdulare is part of the silent, invisible, poor section of Ayodhya. He had to leave for his forty-minute ride back home, but before starting off he shared another local belief, which according to him explained the lack of development, the absence of peace and the presence of strife in Ayodhya. 'Remember, Ayodhya lives under the curse of its two

<https://www.countercurrents.org/comm-sikand050806.htm>.
[572]Ibid.

great women, Sita Maiyya (Mother Sita) and Badi Bua. They were wronged
by Ayodhya's evil people. Till this curse lives, Ayodhya will also remain in
this state,' he said. He offered to drop me at the Ayodhya railway crossing
as it was on his route back home. On the way we crossed Mani Parbat,
another popular religious site. 'Now see this, here Ram and Sita used to
come in the months of Sawan. They used to put big jhoolas [swings] on
those trees and enjoy themselves.' Mani Parbat remains a place where the
idols of the gods from Ayodhya's temples come to 'enjoy', carried by their
devotees. The nearly fortnight-long Sawan Mela in Ayodhya commences
from the grounds of Mani Parbat. Deities of different temples are brought
here, sometimes in palanquins and sometimes in cycle rickshaws. Ramdulare
dropped me at Mani Parbat and pedalled on to his village. In 1871, in the
first-ever survey of Ayodhya, ASI's founder Alexander Cunningham had
concluded that the Mani Parbat was a Buddhist stupa which was built
during the reign of emperor Ashok.[573] Right behind Mani Parbat are the
graves of Hazrat Shish Alaih Salam and his family. Besides this dargah, there
are at least eighteen other important dargahs in Ayodhya. Some of them
bear names indicative of their origin, such as Hazrat Chup Shah (Vow of
Silence) and the two near the railway station that are called Hazrat Bijli
Shaheed Baba and Hazrat Line Shaheed.

AYODHYA'S RAMANANDI–RAMANUJI–MUSLIM FAULT LINE

In the month leading up to the Uttar Pradesh Assembly Elections that were
held in February–March 2017, Acharya Dharmendra Upadhyaya had been
very busy. As the candidate for the Ayodhya assembly seat from the Rashtriya
Lok Dal (RLD), he was constantly on the move campaigning with a
close circle of supporters and friends. The RLD has never been a serious
contender for this seat although in its previous avatar as the Bharatiya Kranti
Dal, it had stood second once, way back in 1967.

Acharya Dharmendra Upadhyaya, who is in his early forties, is a third
generation owner of a Ramanuji temple in Ayodhya's Vibhisha Kund locality.
His great-grandfather was the namesake of Swami Dharindharacharya, who
had traced the genealogies of the Kurmis and helped them campaign for
Kshatriya status in the 1920s. When I first met him, Upadhyaya was engrossed
in a heated discussion with a local journalist about the need for a 'youthful
and fresh face' to be elected as MLA from Ayodhya. He was arguing his

---

[573]Carnegy, *Historical Sketch of Tahsil Fyzabad, Zillah Fyzabad.*

own case, of course. As it turned out, Dharmendra Upadhyaya could not garner more than a few thousand votes. The BJP's Ved Prakash Gupta, a Faizabad-based businessman and a seasoned politician, won the election displacing the Samajwadi Party's MLA, Pawan Kumar Pandey.

But Upadhyaya's life does not centre around politics alone. As the head of Srinivas Kot Ramanuji temple, he commands the following of a number of disciples. Opposite his temple-house where he lives with his wife and children, stands another imposing building which also houses a Ramanuji temple. Its owner, Bhagvandas, is Upadhyaya's childhood friend.

Dharmendra moved to Ayodhya from Bihar when he was six years old. Bhagvandas was born in Ayodhya. Both studied in the Maharaja Inter College behind Upadhyaya's house. What was Ayodhya like when they were young, I ask them. Upadhyaya responds first, 'When I first came to Ayodhya, it was a quiet and peaceful place. The silence was so serene that it seemed Ram would have certainly lived here. You could only see monks and ascetics here, besides a lot of monkeys, of course. Around 3 p.m. every day, sadhus would be seen shopping at the vegetable market. Today nothing of that sort remains. A lot of householders have settled here.' He is himself one. 'Many householders have moved here since the first incident in Mulayam's tenure,' Bhagvandas adds. However, the actual population figures, not counting the considerably large floating population, for Ayodhya don't fully support their perception. From approximately 41,000 in 1991, Ayodhya's present population is nearly 56,000 according to the last census held in 2011.[574]

Bhagvandas is a boisterous and jolly character who sports a hairdo like the eponymous hero of the famous TV series, *Chanakya*. He narrates the story of his own temple. 'My name is Shri Bhagvandas Acharyaji, this temple [pointing across the road to his temple, a two-storey structure with its own well and a 10-feet-high gate] was founded by my father's elder brother Kaushalendra Prapannacharyaji. It is nearly 150 years old.' Both friends are steeped in the Ramanuji tradition and are proud of it. They also realize that they are part of a sect that lost its supremacy to Ramanandis long before they were born. According to them, the Ramanandis have grown because of their 'better marketing'. Both claim that since the 1990s Muslims have also grown in numbers. 'Earlier, at dawn you could only hear, "Sitaram, Sitaram", today all you hear is "Allah o Akbar", not "Sitaram",' Dharmendra

---

[574]'Ayodhya population census 2011' *Census 2011*.

asserts. 'Since the last ten years or so, even those mosques which were lying abandoned have been revived. Although no new mosques have been built, Muslims have put up loudspeakers on the old ones and are doing their namaaz there. All this is because they have been given patronage by the government,' Bhagvandas supplements his friend's point.

Before Adityanath became chief minister in 2017, the last time the BJP ruled Uttar Pradesh was in 2003. It was also the last time excavations had been carried out in Ayodhya. From 2003 to 2017, it was either the Dalit-backed Bahujan Samaj Party or the Muslim–Yadav combination centric Samajwadi Party that led the government in Lucknow. Naturally, they sought to allay the impression of being biased towards Hindus, and patronage of Muslims, who form 10 per cent of the state's electorate, was common to both parties. Ayodhya's Shias are even fewer in number and have come to align themselves with whichever party is in power. 'As we are less in number, we try to make up for it by focusing on educating our children so they can be in the mainstream,' says Sufi, a small-time businessman, who supplies cardboard boxes to the sweet and laddoo shops around Hanumangarhi.

But Ayodhya's Muslims are very few in number. There are almost 3,000 Muslim voters and their total population hovers around 6,000. Although there is no official data to support this, it could be said that there are more Muslims buried in Ayodhya's graveyards than living in its streets, homes or mosques. Hindus constitute nearly 94 per cent of the town's population of nearly 56,000 people, and Muslims have virtually disappeared from Ayodhya over the last 150 years. In fact, according to locals, most of Ayodhya's temple-houses have been built over and around land belonging to graveyards. Most pilgrims who line up outside the Ram Janmabhoomi temple are unaware that there are at least forty-five mosques in Ayodhya.[575] At least two of these are replicas of the Babri Masjid. The mosque known as Begum Barlas lies behind the Maharaja Inter College, Ayodhya's oldest higher secondary school. While the other one, much smaller in scale but similar to the Babri Masjid lies in the Moghulpura locality near the Ram Janmabhoomi–Babri Masjid. It's a neat structure with three domes and a water tank in front for ritual ablutions. Earlier known as the Shah Madar Mosque, it has been renamed Masjid Jalil Khali. On a visit there I met a young imam who had recently started living in a newly constructed room abutting the mosque. Behind the mosque lies the tomb of a now

---

[575]RTI reply from Office of the Municipal Corporation of Ayodhya, 9 August 2017.

forgotten personality; one of the graves around it is being used by a bunch of youngsters and their adult 'leaders' as a tabletop to play cards. The imam, emboldened by our presence, shouts at them, 'You will die for desecrating a holy grave, you fools.'

Coming back to Bhagvandas, he related a story about the three 'powerful and miraculous' graves next to his mosque. The story had emerged as an offshoot of a discussion about the intrinsic holiness of Ayodhya, which is why, according to Bhagvandas, Muslims had been burying their dead here. 'They wanted to make this their Mecca so that they can do Haj here itself,' he had argued. As Muslims left the city Hindus occupied their lands and graveyards. Bhagvandas's Shri Vedantacharya Ashram was surrounded by graves on three sides. Now, only the three graves on one side of the building remain as buildings have come up on other sides. He uses the empty space to dump cow dung and other trash.

'Why didn't you level these two graves?' I asked him.

'You cannot dig them up, you will go mad.' He then relates the story of a pot-smoking sadhu who used to live where the graves are. The sadhu, who belonged to the Tyagi tradition of Ramanandis, was lured by another more 'powerful and greedy mahant of neighbouring Ram Khilauna Mandir' into signing away the small piece of land, including the three graves. But soon after that, the proxy through whom the powerful mahant sought to take over the land went mad and ran away to Vrindavan. Bhagvandas appears visibly scared when relating the story. He was a young boy then but he believes that he too will go mad if he tries to encroach on the graves. This fear also helps him ward off any attempts at encroachment by anybody else.

Yugal Kishore Shastri, the 'secular mahant' and a well-known detractor of Ayodhya's godmen and their activities, says, 'Land grabbing, forcefully occupying ashrams and temples is the main business of the mahants of Ayodhya. Not a year passes without new criminal cases being lodged over properties. It's not just the Ram Janmabhoomi temple which is disputed here. Every second temple is under some sort of litigation.'

One of the ways that the land mafia 'grabs' strategically located spots is by changing their names, thus converting ancient public spaces into private properties. For instance, Ayodhya's ghats have undergone name changes, giving rise to objections from some locals. Mahant Pawan Das of Shatrughan Niwas temple has taken the matter to court. Pawan Das's Public Interest Litigation in the Lucknow bench of the Allahabad High Court alleges that out of the seven most significant banks by the river Sarayu, the local administration has permitted changes in the names of four. Rinmochan Ghat has been changed to Jhunki or Jhun Jhuniya Ghat, Paapmochan Ghat to Gola Ghat, Swargdwar Ghat to Naya Ghat and Shri Janki Ghat has become Chaudhary Charan Singh Ghat. The Lucknow bench had demanded answers from the UP government.[576]

Another Ramanuji grudge against Ramanandis relates to the fundamental difference between the two sects. They blame the lax rules of admission of the Ramanandi Sampraday for their own marginalization in the religious bazaar of Ayodhya. But they console themselves with chauvinist pride in their exclusivist Brahmin focus. 'Only Brahmins can become priests and gurus in the Ramanuji sect. Low-borns can become devotees but can never achieve the status of guru no matter how deep their devotion or knowledge of the scriptures,' says Bhagvandas with an undisguised sense of superiority.

Dwelling on the reasons for his sect's seeming failure at attracting devotees, Upadhyaya adds, 'We have certain customs that did attract the rich, upper-caste people. We have the "Panch Raagam" ritual, [wherein] only men are allowed to worship the idol of the deity, cook food for offering to devotees as well as serving it to the deity. Naturally, ordinary people found these customs difficult to follow.'

The Panch Raagam ritual involves branding oneself with a red-hot conch shell and a disc, both objects representing the God Vishnu, who manifests as Krishna, Ram and Parshuram, etc. Certainly, the process of becoming a disciple is simpler and quicker in the Ramanandi Sampraday: a guru whispers the guru mantra or the sacred words in the disciple's ear and that completes the process. The disciple could be from any caste. Once in the sect, the Ramanandis don't discriminate between high and low caste ascetics. Both Bhagvandas and Upadhyaya ruefully blame the pompous pageantry of Ramanandi temples for drawing in hordes of pilgrims like cattle. 'We don't know how to dress up our God in frippery clothes, how to decorate our temples and package them like the Ramanandis. They allow all castes to worship and pray and they "market" their temples better, so even if the majority of their devotees are poor, their number is so large that even if they donate ten rupees each, Ramanandi temples make a lot of money. If ten lakh people give ten rupees how much will it be?' Acharya Dharmendra Upadhyaya asks rhetorically.

Notwithstanding their inherent differences the Ramanujis and

---

[576]'PIL against changing names of Ayodhya ghats', *Hindustan Times*, 19 March 2017.

Ramanandis of Ayodhya today share much in common. They are part of the same Vaishnava culture, speak the same Awadhi dialect and cater to the same pilgrim market of Ayodhya. The Ramanujis may secretly despise the lack of differentiation of castes among Ramanandis, but they also submit to their guiding text: the sixteenth-century *Ramcharitmanas* by Tulsidas. Upadhyaya readily accepts that Tulsidas's Ramayana is also their supreme scripture. 'Be it any sect among Hindus, everybody wants to emulate the *Ramacharitmanas* in their lives,' he says. Even so, the latent feeling of being marginalized comes out through another grouse: 'a hardline Ramanandi will never say "Lakshmi Narayan Bhagwan ki Jai" [Lakshmi and Narayan being the names for their patron deities] even though I have no problem in saying "Siyavar Ramchandra ki Jai",' he says.

RELIGION: AYODHYA'S ONLY BUSINESS

Religion is the main source of income in Ayodhya. Until the 1960s, timber from the neighbouring Gonda district was sold from Ayodhya; but even that trade was limited to adjacent districts. Today, timber merchants have long disappeared and the town relies solely on pilgrims for their income. Most of the residents describe their profession as 'aakash vritti', which literally means 'what falls from the sky'. People depend on the gods for sustenance. Sufi, the businessman mentioned earlier who sells cardboard boxes to sweet shops near Hanumangarhi, swears by the local harmony that exists between Hindus and Muslims. What he worries about is the lack of jobs and livelihoods in Ayodhya. Sufi says, 'If the temples are shut for even one month for whatever reason, half of Ayodhya's population will face starvation. It's purely a pilgrim-based economy.'

The revenue model of Ayodhya's temples is fairly simple—donations from devotees and rent from properties. Donations are made by the poor and the rich in cash and kind. For instance, a poor peasant family from Bahraich district comes to the seasonal melas every year and they stay in a designated temple. At the end of their stay they leave behind the rations they carried with them along with a small amount of money. It is understood by both pilgrims and pujaris that this is a donation. The pujari has given the family shelter and a place to set up their temporary brick stoves. Richer pilgrims also come laden with sweets and make offerings of money, mobile phones, air conditioners, bed linen, etc., and some take care of various repairs or construction work that might be required in their guru's respective ashrams. This is in addition to the daily offerings of money that are made in the big, medium-sized and small donation boxes usually placed in front of the idols of deities. 'Pray and pay' is an unwritten code followed by the devotees here. Ascetics, priests and mahants are seldom engaged in any kind of profession and the devout pilgrims are only too happy to make contributions towards the sustenance of the religious gurus. Bigger temples run their own charities. Donations to religious trusts and charities is also a way of claiming tax deductions. By donating large amounts of money rich merchants are able to save income tax while earning 'good karma'. The melas attract mainly peasants and other rural folk from near and far. Busloads of pilgrims, on package tours, descend on Ayodhya, from as far as Andhra Pradesh, Madhya Pradesh, Rajasthan and Gujarat, and even as far as Nepal and Bengal during the mela months. The offerings of these pilgrims, and the money they spend on food and buying sweets and other knick-knacks is the real source of livelihood for thousands of people in Ayodhya. For richer temples like the Naka Hanumangarhi run by the Nirmohi Akhara in Faizabad, money is also earned by renting out their spacious buildings and grounds as venues for birthday parties, dinners and weddings.[577]

The Ramayanic tradition of primogeniture had been broken in the Ayodhya royal family with Man Singh's ascension in the late nineteenth century. The present heir to the throne of Ayodhya is a descendant from his grandmother's side, and therefore locals don't consider him as the true heir. Prince Yatindra Mohan Mishra, an acclaimed poet and author, met me at Delhi's Nehru Memorial Library & Museum where he was working on 'some research on his next project'. Mishra, who runs the Maharaja Public School in Ayodhya, illustrated the importance of the melas to Ayodhya's fragile, pilgrim-dependent economy. 'It is an ecosystem that really depends on the common farmer and farm labourer from neighbouring districts. When they have a good crop, they are able to spend more money in Ayodhya. If the harvest has been bad the income of Ayodhya's shopkeepers and businessmen also goes down. In the school that we run parents are usually able to admit their wards in August or later, because that's when they would have made some money during the Sawan Mela. I feel the economy of my town cannot be dependent only on the mela. We need industries and factories too,' he explained. Notwithstanding the negative views of the locals, the Mishra family continues to represent Ayodhya in India and abroad,

---

[577]Interview with Mahant Ram Das, Nirmohi Akhara.

particulary in Oyoto, a sister-city of Ayodhya in South Korea. Mishra is a writer and poet who recently authored a book on India's most celebrated singer, Lata Mangeshkar. Though the 'days of royalty' are long past, Mishra is aware of the weight and impact of his words, and chose to refrain from commenting on the Ram Janmabhoomi–Babri Masjid dispute. But he didn't hold back from saying, 'I am a proud Hindu and a proud democrat who believes in progressive values.' Like many locals who believe that writers and journalists highlight only the negative aspects of Ayodhya, Mishra too said, 'So far whatever has been written about Ayodhya, it has been negative.' Mishra seemed to hesitate while sharing his view about the VHP claims of Rama's historicity or the development of Ayodhya as an organized centre of Ram worship. But he talked openly about himself, 'I am a descendant of a royal family that patronized the legendary singer Begum Akhtar and artists like Pagal Dasji. More than anything else in my life, I want to preserve and enhance this intellectual, literary and artistic legacy of my family,' he said.

Ayodhya's royal family is one of the few Brahmin royal houses surviving in India. They have their own avenues of income, including a large amount of real estate and educational institutions, and are not directly affected by the ups and downs of the pilgrim bazaar of the town. Some of the biggest temples are also the biggest landlords and their landholdings are scattered in various states like Bihar, Uttar Pradesh, Chhattisgarh and Madhya Pradesh. Ramanujis once held control over the biggest land banks in Ayodhya. But with time the land holdings have shrunk as lands have been sold to sustain their temples and ashrams. 'The offerings from pilgrims are not enough and the richer devotees are too few in number,' said Dharmendra Upadhyaya.

Land may not be a source of income any more for Upadhyaya and Bhagvandas, but there are other ways to generate money for well-established families like theirs. Bhagvandas rents a portion of his ashram to an astrology firm. He offers religious counselling by way of providing guidance for rituals and even sending digital versions of religious mantras and texts. 'Just the other day, a lady devotee called me from Italy asking for a copy of the Hanuman Chalisa so I sent it to her on WhatsApp.' Did you charge her for that? I asked. 'No, but it's her wish if she wants to donate some money, she's from Chandigarh, we have an ashram there also.'

The astrology firm in his building operates like any other business process outsourcing or customer care centre. Horoscopes are made and shared over email and WhatsApp in return for payments via e-banking.

Besides, both Upadhyaya and Bhagvandas and other mahants travel across the country and stay at various temples and homes of devotees. At the end of each such stay they are showered with gifts of money, food and other items. Most of the devotees they have today have been associated with their respective temples over generations. A devotee's son becomes the disciple of the son of his father's guru. In this sense, unless the guru or the devotee break ties, inherited discipleship remains fixed. It is up to the ingenuity of the guru to attract more disciples.

The big Ramanuji centres like Asharfi Bhavan attract devotees throughout the year but even the combined footfall in all the Ramanuji temples is a fraction of those who visit Ramanandi centres like Kanak Bhavan and Hanumangarhi.

MOHAMMAD ANIS: A BELIEVER IN THE ONENESS OF GOD

Far from these sectarian concerns of the Hindus, Mohammad Anis, or Anis Bhai as he was addressed by all who knew him, lived on Faizabad's College Road. When I first met him, Anis Bhai was well into his seventies, living in a slightly different world. (He passed away on 18 December 2017 as the book was being written). His was a world where Nehru, Gandhi, the BJP and VHP were part of a larger Judeo-Christian attack on Islam and Muslims. Short and fair complexioned, he sported a well-groomed white beard and often wore the Afghani cap made famous by the legendary Afghan politician and military leader Ahmed Shah Masood. Despite having a heart problem Anis Bhai remained active before age caught up with him. His family has lived in Faizabad for the last 150 years. Giving a brief family history, he said, 'We are actually Khuranas from Multan, but about five hundred years ago our ancestor embraced Islam. In Faizabad, we were the first to open an optician's store.'

On a late morning in the winter of 2016, Anis Bhai took me on a conducted tour of mosques in Ayodhya. He was neither a trained historian nor an archaeologist but with years of involvement in the Ram Janmabhoomi–Babri Masjid issue, and through his own efforts, he had educated himself in the different histories of Ayodhya. His take on the entire issue revolved on the idea of the oneness of God and that 'the needless politicization of the dispute by the Sangh Parivar is to blame for all ills that plague Ayodhya and Faizabad'.[578]

---

[578]Interview with Mohammad Anis.

On two bikes, our party of four first headed to the Swargdwar area of Ayodhya. It is situated overlooking the Sarayu River and is the oldest locality in the town. Nawal Ray, the diwan of Safdarjung, the second nawab of Awadh, built a house here and the area came to be known as Nawal Ray ka Chatta. In the epic Ramayana, it is from Swargdwar that Ram ascends to heaven along with the residents of Ayodhya. Anis Bhai slowly climbed the steps from the banks and led us to a crumbling structure, which must have been a mosque, one of its minarets still standing atop the ruins. When viewed from the Sarayu Bridge, it is this minaret and the tall shikhara of the temple built by the chief of the principality of Kamiar in Gonda district that presents one of the more spectacular views of Ayodhya.

Swargdwar and its numerous big and small temples have either fallen into disuse or are now used as living quarters. Anis Bhai walked around the ruined mosque and bent down to examine the surviving wall. His theory is that when Aurangzeb's general built this mosque, he built it atop an existing mosque. 'You can see the bricks near the ground are larger, made of bajri [dried rubble] while the ones on top are of the Lakhauri type which are commonly found all over Awadh,' Anis Bhai pointed out. The other narrative is that Fedai Khan destroyed the Swargdwar temple and built this mosque on it. The minaret is badly damaged, and unless preserved, will sooner or later fall. Swargdwar is a warren of closely located buildings, the walls of the houses stand hardly a few feet from each other and it can only be entered by foot or on a two-wheeler. This is also the only part of Ayodhya that resembles other ancient Indian cities such as Banaras.

On an earlier visit to Swargdwar, a guide had shared a local myth about the old neighbourhood—it is believed that if a mentally disturbed person can reach Swargdwar on his own, he will be cured.

A short distance from Swargdwar lies the neighbourhood of Begumpura. Here, Anis Bhai led us to another ruined mosque; only its foundation was still visible. The small Eidgah next to the mosque was covered with Hindu symbols and the ubiquitous 'Sitaram'. The mosque was on a knoll, on a further slope, small one-room brick and mud houses have come up. Anis Bhai's demeanour was such that it evokes respect from most people. A small crowd of young boys gathered around us. Anis Bhai cut through the crowd as if they were not present and reached a cluster of houses on the slope. A few men and women were sitting outside their houses. He addressed an old woman and told Ashish, our companion, to ask her where her maika (mother's house) was and if she knew anything about the mosque.

Ashish: What is your name?

Woman: Sundari.

Ashish: Where is your mother's house?

Sundari: It was there, you know Janmabhoomi, over there.

Ashish: Do you know anything about the mosque?

Sundari: Yes, it is the mazaar of Kale Pahalwan Baba. His power is
          very strong.

The crowd had by now reassembled at Sundari's house. An old man dressed like a devout Muslim visiting a ruined mosque with young men with cameras had raised the locals' curiosity. Anis Bhai bade Sundari goodbye and started walking towards the parked bikes. As we were walking out, Afaq, another companion of ours, chipped in, 'Anis Bhai, while you were talking to the woman I was making small talk with some men. They were saying, if there was a mosque here then only a mosque ought to be rebuilt.'

None of us had even alluded to rebuilding anything let alone a mosque. But the abundance of mosques in Ayodhya (as has been noted, forty-five according to government records), and the ever-present issue of the Ram Janmabhoomi–Babri Masjid dispute, invariably leads public conversations back to the demolition in 1992. In Ayodhya, truth is seldom found on the surface, people here have learnt the art of saying what you want to hear over the last two decades. Opinions are custom-made, 'truth' is reinterpreted, history refashioned so many times, that it seems nobody believes in what they are saying themselves.

A large number of upper-caste Hindus, though, state only one truth: 'It is Ram's birthplace, Babur destroyed it, karsevaks from outside destroyed that mosque. But, what's done is done, now only a Ram temple will be built there.' And what about the crime of destroying the court's orders in the process and rioters killing Muslims?

Back in his house, Anis Bhai dwelled on the long history of the dispute. 'You must understand, it's an eternal struggle between shaitani (evil) and rehmani (good) forces. When our Constitution was being written, when India was about to become independent, evil forces were trying to sabotage us. Gandhi was murdered at that time, soon after that, idols were forcibly placed in the Babri Masjid, communal forces have been working since the very beginning. Nehru had wanted the structure to be sealed under high walls on all sides, that wasn't done. Things started to change after Indira Gandhi's visit in 1967.' Anis Bhai cannot be faulted for reading so much meaning into the late Indira Gandhi's visit to Ayodhya. The 1967 general election was held along with assembly elections in Ayodhya. After Nehru's death in 1964, the Congress had split into factions made up of Nehru's peers, called the Syndicate, and those who rallied around Indira Gandhi. It was also her first Lok Sabha election and she had chosen to contest from neighbouring Raebareli, her late husband Feroze Gandhi's constituency. Her visit to Faizabad seems to have been an unplanned one as not much information is available about it. The 1967 Ayodhya assembly elections, though, were a crucial threshold for the temple-town's later history. The Bharatiya Jana Sangh fought and won the election on the plank of 'reopening of the Babri Masjid and the eventual restoration of the Ram Janmabhoomi to Hindu sovereignty'.[579] The Congress, riven with factionalism lost the seat but, in the next elections held two years later in 1969, its candidate Vishwanath Kapoor wrested the seat back from the Jan Sangh's Brij Kishore Agarwal.[580]

Nearly fifty years later, Anis Bhai's attempt to read meaning into that short visit can only be explained by the tendency in people to create narratives retrospectively, to re-interpret the past in order to explain the present. But Anis Bhai is not alone in retrospectively amplifying the importance of minor events in history such as Indira Gandhi's visit.

Anis Bhai's involvement in Ayodhya's affairs was peripheral, his role limited to that of an influential adviser at best. But he hadn't given up and remained engaged with progressive groups in Ayodhya and outside. This was so because he was still hopeful that the vast majority of Hindus would one day see through the 'cynical religio-politics of the BJP'. He called himself a nationalist Muslim and lamented the present conditions of his co-religionists. Old age had made him cynical and also more religious, but he still related with joy and pride the little glimpses from his long life. 'On his visit to Ayodhya, Gandhiji had cradled my wife when she was a child... The first film I watched was *Dharam Putra* in 1963, it was about young Hindu and Muslim boys separated during Partition. The Hindu boy grew up as a Muslim in Pakistan and the Muslim as a Hindu,' his voice trailed off.

[579]Harold Gould, *Grassroots Politics in India: A Century of Political Evolution In Faizabad District*, New Delhi: Oxford and IBH Publishing Company, 1994, p. 417.
[580]Ibid., p. 464.

RAM NAVAMI IN 1902

In 1902, when the Babri Masjid was still being used as a mosque, Hindu pilgrims faced no problems in worshipping there. At the time it was the Janamsthan Chabutra that drew the most number of pilgrims, after Hanumangarhi of course. An account of the Ram Navami fair published in 1902 describes in vivid detail the popularity of Ram's birthplace. 'This spot has been the scene of fierce religious strife... In the present peaceful times the spot is sacred to both religions and the interesting and unusual site of a Hindu shrine within the enclosure of a Muhammadan mosque can here be seen.'[581] Bairagis belonging to the Nirmohi Akhara were in control of this shrine which was known as the Ram Chabutra till 6 December 1992, when it was destroyed by karsevaks. The account describes it as consisting 'of a platform about three feet high and ten feet square, built over the birthplace, and on top of this a little chamber, where an image of Ram, gorgeously robed, sits serene. On the left hand corner of this platform, near the ground is a small trap door, through which a peep into the heart of the original birthplace can be got.'[582]

The report then goes on to describe another spot (chauti) close to the Chabutra which was revered as the spot where Dasharatha and Kaushalya offered thankful prayers on the sixth day after Ram's birth. In 1902, both the Chabutra and chauti drew hordes of devotees. The chauti was much sought after by pregnant women who paid the pujaris for a little chuna (lime powder) to apply on their foreheads. In Awadh every mother wants to give birth to Ram, the ideal son, brother, ruler and husband.

RAM NAVAMI IN THE RAMANUJI QUARTERS

Ramanuji families living in Ayodhya also celebrate Ram Navami in their own way. Rangolis adorned the entrance of each house. The wide road, perhaps the widest in Ayodhya, that runs through the locality of Vibhishan Kund, was full of pilgrims returning from the Sarayu or going to the ashrams and temples where they were staying. Unexpectedly, a hand-drawn chariot appeared, accompanied by the sound of Carnatic music. Three men were playing mridangams (long South Indian drums) while two others blew hard on the nadaswarams (double reed wind instrument). Every Ram Navami, they come here from different Ramanuji centres in the South to

---

[581]'The Ram Naumi fair at Ajudhia, *Pioneer*, 19 May 1902, p. 3.
[582]Ibid.

perform during the Rath Yatra of the idols of Lord Vishnu and his consort Lakshmi. As the chariot stopped in front of a house people jostled with each other to receive the charanamrit, or holy water. The chariot pulled by devotees didn't stay for more than a few minutes and moved on to the next house.

Pradeep Dubey, a young law student who belonged to the Ramanuji sect, said that both the number of pilgrims and the duration of their stay has gone down. 'Earlier, Ram Navami was different, now the disciples don't spend more than a couple of days in Ayodhya.'

BIRTH ANNIVERSARIES OF RISHABHDEV, EMPEROR ASHOKA AND NISHADRAJ GUHA

It isn't just Ram's birthday that is celebrated during the months of March and April. Besides Ram, the Digambar sect of Jains celebrates the birthday of Rishabhdev, who is also known as Adinath. Rishabhdev is believed to be the first Tirthankar by Jains, and also considered to be an ancestor of Ram by some Hindus.

The Digambar Jain Mandir is one of the largest in Ayodhya. Situated inside a massive walled compound in the Raiganj neighbourhood, the temple houses a 31-feet-tall statue of Rishabhdev. The Jains, though few in number in Ayodhya, uphold their well-established reputation of being wealthy merchants and generous patrons of religion. One of India's richest Jain families has a strong connection with Faizabad–Ayodhya. Indu Jain, the matriarch of the Sahu–Jain family that runs the *Times of India* newspaper and other companies, comes from a family that was once based in Faizabad. Indu Jain herself was born in Faizabad in 1936.

Besides Ram and Rishabhdev's birth anniversaries, the birth of ancient India's most famous king, Emperor Ashoka, was also being celebrated in Ayodhya on the eve of Ram Navami. Ashoka's story of disillusionment after the gory war of Kalinga is taught to children in India's schools. A grandson of Chandragupta Maurya, Ashoka converted to Buddhism. Chandragupta had embraced Jainism towards the end of his reign. One of the main organizers of Samrat Ashoka's birthday celebrations was Vineet Maurya, an activist working towards establishing the Buddhist roots of Ayodhya. Vineet embraced Buddhism when he was in college. Even though many Indians take much pride in Ashoka's achievements, his birth anniversary is neither well known nor celebrated nationally. Vineet explained the reason behind celebrating an ancient emperor's birth anniversary. 'Dr B. R. Ambedkar, a convert to Buddhism, used Ashoka's teachings while drafting the Indian Constitution. I too converted to Buddhism after getting disillusioned with the casteist Ram Janmabhoomi Movement. As a Buddhist, I feel we should teach our children about Ashoka's greatness. There was no other king like him,' Vineet emphasized. The birth anniversary function was being held in a half-built building in a small compound covered with overgrown wild grass. The neighbourhood in which it was located was celebrating Ram Navami with songs being played on loudspeakers, giving a somewhat surreal touch to the dinner hosted in honour of Ashoka.

At a distance of a few hundred metres from where Vineet was busy with his celebrations, lies the temple-cum-dharamshala of the Nishad community. The legendary Nishad King Guha is remembered for the help he provided to Ram, Sita and Lakshman in crossing the river Ganga in the early days of their exile. His birth anniversary was also being celebrated on the same day as Ram and Ashoka's. Nishads are an important vote bank for political parties. In fact, the BJP's unprecedented landslide in the 2017 assembly elections in Uttar Pradesh is widely credited to its success in bringing Nishad, Rajbhar and OBCs communities into its fold. However, a few days after the local BJP MP Lallu Singh participated in the anniversary celebrations on 5 April 2017, the Uttar Pradesh government removed King Guha's birth anniversary from the list of official holidays.

Among the non-Hindu birth anniversaries that are celebrated in Faizabad–Ayodhya are those of dead saints like Shah Ibrahim, whose mazaar is thronged by an equal number of Hindus and Muslims; and Hazrat Ali, Prophet Muhammad's nephew and son-in-law, one of the first to embrace Islam. Revered more by the Shias, Hazrat Ali's birthday is celebrated on 11 April each year. The main chowk of Faizabad is decorated with lights on the occasion.

Despite it being mela time, Muslim neighbourhoods of Ayodhya remain undisturbed by the thousands of pilgrims milling around them. And locals see nothing remarkable about this. During the tumultuous years of the Ram Janmabhoomi Andolan, the presence of karsevaks was like a sword hanging over their heads. 'We had lived together before 1992 and we live together now. Hindus do their worship and we do ours,' says Hashim, who was thirteen years old when the Babri Masjid fell.

Hindus and Muslims are indeed still living together now in many of the older neighbourhoods like Gola Ghat. The dream of some VHP saints like Acharya Dharmendra to drive away Ayodhya's Muslims and turn the place into a Hindu Vatican lies in tatters now. Muslims (though few in number) and Hindus continue living together, though perhaps not as closely as before.

Outside Kanak Bhavan, the streets and bylanes of Ayodhya are bustling with pilgrims. Most of them are from the rural areas of Uttar Pradesh, Madhya Pradesh, Rajasthan and Bihar. The majority of them have come from the neighbouring districts. Every shop is open and every open space is turned into a temporary shop selling religious accoutrements, snacks, ice creams and the mela speciality—grains of rice with one's choice of words written on it.

Kuldeep Pandey from Sitapur has come with his five cousins in the hope of doing good business during the mela. He has laid out his wares on a concrete platform outside a shop that has 'disputed property' pasted on it. In all, he is selling twenty-seven different items. These include malas or garlands made by stringing together small pieces of the wood of the tulsi plant, revered by all Vaishnavas and believed to be the king of all plants for its medicinal properties, as well as framed pictures of gods and goddesses like Lakshmi, Ganesh, Shiva and family and Ram and his family. Framed photos of the two actors who played Ram and Sita in the 1987 television series *Ramayan* are still being sold thirty years later.

It is the women who are doing the shopping, asking Pandey the prices of different rings, earrings and small cases for keeping sindoor (vermilion). No shop displays the price of the items on sale and Pandey too charges his customers based on a quick assessment of their purchasing power.

The permanent shops of the town are overflowing with items meant for religious use as well as for the needs of rural people. It's their time to relax and forget about the worries of daily life. And the little money that they have brought with them is carefully spent on small indulgences. All the shops store the same wide range of products: thread for tying on the wrist (kaleva), red loincloth, bundles of yagyapavit (the white-thread worn by upper-caste men around the torso), sandalwood paste, vermilion powder, incense sticks, toys made in China, miniature millstones and rolling pins (to make sandalwood paste), garlands made of plastic flowers, incense-stick holders, small polished shiny stones (to be worshipped as different gods), photos of Hanuman holding his fleshy chest open (inside his chest can be seen the smaller images of Ram and Sita), stoles with Jai Shri Ram printed on them, and small brass idols of Ram, Sita and Hanuman.

Ladies carefully untie the knots at the end of their saris where they keep their money while haggling until the very moment of handing over the cash. Pandey finds the business below his expectations and fears that he won't be able to recover his costs. Old sadhus covered in dust and matted hair seem to have come out from hibernation to make an appearance at the fair to mark Ram's birthday. A crippled sadhu lies on the road in an ochre-coloured loincloth, the drain flowing inches away from his matted hair. Except for his missing left leg, the rest of his body is covered with tattoos of the trishul, Ram and the shivling. As he is lying virtually in the middle of a narrow road, pilgrims cannot avoid him. He plays his small kettledrum and lets out a loud 'Jai Shri Ram' every now and again.

At the Sugriv Qila hilltop, a free kitchen is being run by a wealthy family. Its well-dressed and perfumed members are earning 'good karma' by feeding the poor pilgrims; a few SUVs are parked outside. Food is at the risk of rotting in the 42° C heat, so they are frantically ladling oversized servings onto small styrofoam plates. 'We want to feed as many different people as we can,' says Manoj, one of the organizers who has flown in from Mumbai just for this 'social and religious service'.

Kanak Bhavan is one of the several big and small temples built by royal families in the first quarter of the twentieth century. Others include the Raj Dwar and Darsheneshwar temples built by the royal family of Ayodhya; Kanchan Bhawan, built in the 1930s by the Bijawar royal family (related to the Orchha and Tikamgarh royal house); Balrampur temple; and the several small temples built by principalities like Kamiar.

At Hanumangarhi, the rush of pilgrims is most ferocious. Its stone steps are covered by a heaving, sweating, energetic and breathless mass of humanity. It might be his master's birthday but Hanuman's pre-eminence remains undiminished.

The Ram Navami festival in 2017 was special also because the newly elected chief minister, Adityanath, himself a monk of a Shaivite sect from nearby Gorakhpur, was expected to visit Ayodhya during the Ram Navami fair. To render the place 'visit worthy' for the chief minister-cum-mahant, nearly 1,000 'cleaning workers' were to be deployed by the nervous district administration. But the chief minister's trip was cancelled at the last minute. A relieved officer who didn't wish to be named remarked later, 'Thankfully he will now visit during the birthday celebrations of Mahant Nritya Gopal Das.' It was prudent of the chief minister to cancel his trip because melas often turn into deadly overcrowded places prone to stampedes. In the Ram Navami mela of 2017, a sixty-five-year-old woman died after she fell down and was trampled upon by more able-bodied survivors of the mini stampede. The police recorded it as a 'death caused by heart attack' and ordered a probe. One of the worst stampedes to occur in Ayodhya was in 1986, the year when the locks of the Babri Masjid were opened. That year, during the Kartik Mela held in November, thirty-two people were killed in an early morning stampede. The dead included twenty-three women, eight men and an eighteen-month-old baby.

Eyewitnesses in both incidents had apportioned the blame for the deaths to fate. Hanuman Prasad Gupta was recorded as saying in 1986, 'These things happen. Those who died came here to die.'[583]

Most people though come to Ayodhya to live. For the farmers, the Ram Navami mela coincides with the harvesting of the rabi crop, sown in winter and harvested in spring. In a lucky year of a good harvest, an average family is able to afford the trip to Ayodhya. The trip is one of the few times that poor families and especially women get a break from the back-breaking drudgery of working in fields and at home. But it's not like they are on a vacation. Most of them camp in private and public open spaces where the women are in charge of setting up a makeshift stove and preparing the meals. Pilgrims from the same village stick together. 'Last time I had come with other people from my village. This year I have got my parents and my own children with me,' Parshuram, from Raibareili district, told me. His wife was cooking khichri, which would be eaten with some pickle.

RAJ DUTT PANDEY, TANTRIC 'DOCTOR'

During every fair, 'Dr' Raj Dutt Pandey sets up his table and a few chairs outside the one room clinic that he runs on the premises of the ashram of the late saint 'Paltu Das'. The ashram is located down the road from Ayodhya's only post office. On his rickety plastic table stand an assortment of bottles and medicine boxes. Pandey is usually found sitting with a few policemen who avail of the chairs lying around and do their duty from there. Finding him alone, and drawn by the word 'tantric' on the doctor's board that hangs behind him, I asked him about the Ram Navami Mela, and the kind of ailments that he has to deal with as a doctor. Just then a pilgrim arrived asking for a painkiller for his injured foot. 'Rs 10 for two tablets,' Pandey told him. Some prosaic chatter about Prime Minister Narendra

---

[583]Dilip Awasthi, 'Ayodhya Kartik Mela tragedy: crucial lapses on part of district administration main cause', *India Today*, 30 November 1986.

Modi not visiting Ayodhya followed. Two heavyset women climbed up the steps to the clinic. They appeared to be in pain and even before they reached his desk, one of them requested, 'Doctor Sahib, please give me medicine, my stomach hurts as though on fire.' Without enquiring about the patient's medical history or asking if she had eaten stale food, the tantric doctor simply said, 'Give me ten rupees. Here is the medicine, take one now and one in the night and don't eat oily food.'

Another group of men approached him for pills for 'gas problems'. Pandey offered them two tablets for Rs 12. 'Is it Aciloc? Give me Aciloc,' one of them said. The doctor told the group of men, 'This is a clinic not a medical store where you demand medicines. Here treatment is given not just tablet.' The men reluctantly agreed to buy his 'treatment' after haggling successfully and bringing down the price from Rs 12 to Rs 10. The 'doctor' now started talking about his hernia problem and brought up the subject of tantra, an occult science quite popular among Indians. 'I am a tantric too and I have some special powers but there are side-effects,' he said, adding that he could have been a great man, but his stars did not favour him. It had been close to an hour at Dr Pandey's makeshift clinic, during which time most of the patients complained of stomach-related ailments that cannot have been attributed to the rigours of travelling alone. Ayodhya, without proper sanitation and drinking water, turns into a breeding ground of illnesses like diarrhoea, bloating and other stomach problems during melas. Clearly, not much has changed since the Pilgrim Committee's Report of 1913 was submitted.

The other danger pilgrims have to contend with is from monkeys. Accompanied by a male relative, two young girls come up to the clinic. A monkey has bitten one of the girls and she needs treatment. On hearing about the monkey bite, the policemen who had been ignoring Pandey and his patients, now sat up and asked the girl to show them where she had been bitten. The girl, hesitant at first, rolled up her salwar when both Dr Pandey and her male relative told her, 'Show it child, it's all right, it's police uncle.' The girl had been bitten on her left thigh when she and her sister had gone to defecate. The wound was serious and Dr Pandey readily admitted that it was beyond the scope of his clinic. The policemen and the doctor now shouted at the male relative for not taking her to Shri Ram Hospital straight away. They turned to the girls and said, 'Go, hurry now, don't keep standing here.'

◆

Meanwhile, the queue outside the entrance to the Ram Janmabhoomi–Babri Masjid was hopelessly long. The shrine is open to darshan from 7 a.m. to 11 a.m. and from 1 p.m. to 5 p.m. during the summer months. In winter, the shrine opens at the same time but shuts down earlier. Thus, during the designated hour of Ram's birth the shrine remained closed, leaving many pilgrims disappointed.

Mahant Satyendra Das does not endorse the disappointment voiced by some pilgrims because of the disputed Ramjanmabhoomi complex being closed for darshan during the hour of birth. 'In any case we keep the curtain drawn during that time (hour of birth) and by the time we open it darshan is resumed. People always look for a reason to complain,' he says.

BANKING ON RAM'S NAME

The late spring sun was setting fast behind the establishments owned by the Maniram Das ki Chavni Trust. The trust runs an eye hospital and a free kitchen where anybody can walk in. In terms of Ayodhya's sacred topography as well as Ramanandi traditions, Maniram Das ki Chavni is not as favourably located as the Nirvani Akhara at Hanumagarhi or the Rasik temples of Kanak Bhavan, Laxman Qila and Bada Sthan (Dashrath Mahal). But the alliance with the VHP and association with the Ram temple movement has brought much material property and influence to the trust. A recent example of this appeared in the Sawan mela of 2017. Uttar Pradesh, being the home of the rivers Ganga and Yamuna, Shiva devotees pass through the state to pray at various holy places like Haridwar, Rishikesh and Ayodhya. These devotees are called kanwariyas and some of them are known to be a nuisance to public peace and order. From playing loud music on massive loudspeakers mounted on trucks to blocking roads and indulging in random hooliganism, they rule the routes that ply on towards their journey to fetch the waters of sacred rivers like the Ganga, Yamuna and Sarayu. To regulate kanwariyas, the UP government declared a ban on the use of DJs by kanwariyas. One of the first and most prominent sants to speak against this ban was Mahant Nritya Gopal Das, who asked the government to reconsider its decision.

In Ayodhya, his words had immediate effect. The kanwariyas not only continued to blast eardrum-destroying music, they challenged the police and dared the locals to have a 'DJ war' with them. A truck mounted with forty speakers, some of them arranged in the shape of a heart, stopped for a few minutes in front of the Ayodhya police station and the DJ shouted,

'We will give Rs 11,000 if there's any other DJ who can play louder than us.' The police escorting the young and energetic crowd of trident-wielding kanwariyas, meekly ignored them. A bystander plugged his ears with his fingers, and once the procession moved on he said, 'There is a ban, but in Ayodhya, there is no ban. You can do anything in the name of religion.'

Mahant Nritya Gopal Das's influence is not only political; under his leadership the Maniram Das ki Chavni Trust has successfully marketed its innovative ideas like the Ram Naam Bank (Name of Ram Bank) which has created a name for itself in the pilgrim bazaar of Ayodhya. The Ram Naam Bank runs on a simple yet effective principle. Ram devotees are encouraged to write the word 'Ram' as many times as they can. They can also write 'Sita Ram' or 'Siya Ram' or any other name of Ram. An account holder in the Ram Naam Bank is assured full return of his or her labour on Judgement Day. Ram Naam Bank occupies the top floor of the Valmiki Ramayana Bhavan, which is situated right opposite the Maniram Das temple on the first floor of which Nritya Gopal Das lives in a small room. The manager of this 'bank' is Mahant Punit Ram Das, a short, elderly man who likes to wear fashionable spectacles. He lives in a two-room house just behind the bank and was kind enough to delay his lunch so he could answer some questions.

Q: What is the purpose of this bank?
A: The only purpose is to promote Lord Shri Ram's name.
Q: How does the bank encourage that?
A: When a person comes to open an account here, we give them free stationery, so that even poor people who often can't afford to buy a pen and a notebook are not deterred from writing the Lord's name.

His disciple, who refused to reveal his name, was in a hurry and probably hungry too. But Mahant Punit Ram Das patiently continued, 'The bank has branches in USA, Canada, Poland, Nepal and India.' Filling notebooks with Shri Ram or Shri Sita Ram in 'red ink only' might seem like an odd way to spend time but for the devout Ram bhakt nothing is as redeeming as remembering Ram and his name. Simple and often uneducated Bairagis and other sadhus sometimes only know how to write 'Sita Ram', being unlettered otherwise. The bank came up in the post-demolition years nearly twenty years ago. One can't help but think of it as an innovative way to keep the millions of Hindus that the VHP had mobilized engaged in Ram bhakti.

Today, there are online versions and also an Android app of a Shri Ram Naam Bank that allows users to fulfil their devotion by tapping their favourite God's name on the screen of a smartphone. Printouts of these entries are then taken to Ayodhya and 'shown' to an idol of Hanuman before being deposited in the Ram Naam Bank, which acts as the central bank of Ram Naam, to which smaller branches send in their deposits. The treasury of this bank is a neatly arranged set of bundles of notebooks. The Ram-Naam notebooks have also been filed in Arabic, Urdu, English, Marathi, Gujarati and Hindi. This is the most innovative idea being executed under the guidance of Mahant Nritya Gopal Das, whose name has been implicated in cases of land grabbing. The 2001 bomb attack on him was the result of one such attempt—the forcible eviction of Mahant Devram Das of Radha Ballabh Kunj Temple.[584]

Devram Das was himself a notorious criminal who had been caught with a minor girl in a Bhagalpur hotel enjoying pleasures forbidden to Ramanandi Bairagis. Later, he had been charged with rape.[585] Once 'Das' is affixed to a name it means the person has taken a vow of celibacy.

Chandra Bhushan Upadhyay, who is in his sixties, is well built and fit. He left the army in 1990 and settled in Ayodhya where his father had come to acquire considerable property. After coming to Ayodhya in 1990, Upadhyay was 'blown away' by Mahant Nritya Gopal Das. His father, Pandit Devdutt Sharma, was also close to him, a 'simple' saint from Vrindavan who had made Ayodhya his spiritual home.

Upadhyay is one of the many disciples of Mahant Nritya Gopal who blames the 'crab' mentality of Ayodhya's people for degrading his guru's name and reputation. To him, and many others, Nritya Gopal is the 'only real saint in Ayodhya'. And Upadhyay realized this quite early on as within a year of moving to Ayodhya, he took diksha, or was initiated as a disciple, of Nritya Gopal. Among the reasons why he chose him to be his guru, he cites the selfless charity of Maniram Das ki Chavni Trust which runs several Sanskrit schools, an eye hospital and free kitchens for sadhus and laity both. 'I have seen with my own eyes how more than one lakh people used to be fed there in the 1990s,' he asserts.[586]

The various accusations of land grabbing and other cases registered

---

[584]Brijesh Singh, 'The guns and godmen of Ayodhya', *Tehelka*, 29 November 2013.
[585]Ibid.
[586]In an interview to the author, 27 February 2017.

against his guru are dismissed by him as motivated and baseless. According to ancient Indian wisdom, truth is many sided. In Ayodhya's case, its history—like all history—is many-sided and multilayered. And so too are the histories of the mahants and monasteries and temples in Ayodhya. According to Upadhyay, the land grabbing that was widely reported to have triggered the bomb attack on Nritya Gopal Das in 2001 (which Nritya Gopal Das claimed was a ploy by Pakistan's Inter-Services Intelligence) is a baseless charge against his guru. Upadhyay says, 'There can be any number of reasons for which an existing owner or mahant of a temple cannot run it anymore. In such cases, many of them willingly hand over their temples to Maharaj-ji because they know that he has the ability to run them well.'

According to Upadhyay's version, the bomb attack was planned by Devram Das 'who had put a blot on his guru's name and that of the sant community'. His guru, Gopal Das, the mahant of Radha Ballabh Kunj, had approached Maharaj-ji to accept control of the temple, as he did not want it to fall into the hands of a criminal like Devram Das. Therefore, Maharaj-ji was attacked to prevent him from taking over.

Now, Upadhyay seeks to buttress his guru's reputation as a humble and simple sant, devoid of any material greed. 'More than twenty years ago, when I used to visit Maharaj-ji more often, a gentleman from Calcutta pleaded with Maharaj-ji to accept the "donation" of a vehicle. Till then there was not a single vehicle in the temple. Maharaj-ji refused his offer and told him that in Ayodhya he uses cycle rickshaws and when he travels outside, devotees like the Calcutta gentleman (we call men like him "dhanpashu", or a very wealthy man), send their cars for his convenience. It was after the bomb attack that a vehicle was purchased for Maharaj-ji, because the police wanted him to have it for his own security.' The narrative provided by Upadhyay weaves in explanations for both the 'land grabber' reputation and also enhances Nritya Gopal Das's image of a selfless sant with few needs.

However, despite all the assertions of transparency made by various members of the trust, they could not provide a concrete number of the establishments owned and managed by the trust. 'Indifference' towards matters of money was reiterated as the reason for the inability to provide clear details.

On Nritya Gopal Das's seventy-eighth birthday celebrations on 10 January 2017, the list of VIPs reflected the importance the BJP and VHP still attach to Ayodhya. His well-wishers included, among others, Kalyan Singh, and Ram Naik and K. N. Tripathi, the governors of Uttar Pradesh and West Bengal respectively. Both have been senior leaders of the BJP and

RSS. From the central government, Prime Minister Narendra Modi made up for his absence by sending eight senior ministers, including another former chief minister of UP, Rajnath Singh, currently the home minister. Also in attendance were Uma Bharti, the young, firebrand sadhvi best remembered for her ecstatic photograph taken against the backdrop of the smoke rising out of the rubble of the Babri Masjid, and for urging karsevaks by saying, 'Ek dhakka aur do, Babri Masjid tod do (give one more push, destroy the Babri mosque)'. She was then the minister for water resources and was leading India's Clean Ganga Mission. The chief minister of BJP-ruled Madhya Pradesh, Shivraj Singh Chauhan, was accompanied by his minister, Jai Bhan Singh Paneriya, a Bajrang Dal star in the 1990s.

Curiously absent were A-listers and the co-accused with Nritya Gopal Das, like L. K. Advani and Murli Manohar Joshi. The VIP guest list was topped by Amit Shah, president of the BJP, widely held to be the most powerful man in India after Prime Minister Modi. Modi and Shah have been inseparable since Modi became chief minister of Gujarat in 2002.

The stage made for the eight-day-long celebrations brought back for many golden memories of the 1990s. Besides the bevy of politicians, also on the stage was an impressive horde of VHP-allied holy men, each one known and addressed by his multi-hyphenate title, including Jagatguru Shankaracharya Swami Vasudevanandji, Maharaj Jyotishpeeth Jagathguru Ramamanandacharya Rambhadracharyaji, Chitrakoot Jagatguru Ramanandacharya Swami, Hans Devacharyaji Maharaj Jagannath Dham, and a dozen other VIP 'saints' from north India.

The VHP was represented by its working president, Pravin Bhai Togadia, and general secretary, Champat Rai. Dozens of other office bearers of the RSS, VHP, BJP and other Sangh Parivar outfits occupied the front rows.

Contrary to expectations, Chief Minister Adityanath Yogi, who had just completed his first hundred days in office, would only talk about the resolution of the dispute through mutual consensus and dialogue. His visit to Hanumangarhi and Ram Janmabhoomi took place amid much chanting of the VHP's war cry, 'Mandir wahin banayenge', 'wahin' being the disputed site of the Babri Masjid, where the tent-temple now stands. Ayodhya's locals though were far from united in insisting on 'temple first'. Vikas, a local shopkeeper, asserted, 'We want our town to be developed first. We want industry, drains, electricity, roads and jobs. That's what we want from respected Yogiji.' And you don't want the temple? He paused for a second, and said, 'Who would say no to the Ram temple in Ayodhya, but first we want to see our town developed.'

Mahant Nritya Gopal Das was given Y-category security by the BJP government in 2015. This was a massive upgrade from the lone police gunner that was assigned to him by the Government of UP following the bomb attack in 2001. At that time, Chief Minister Rajnath Singh had flown to Faizabad the same day in a government chopper to ensure that Nritya Gopal was well cared for in the district hospital. After 2002, the BJP went out of power in both UP and at the centre and Nritya Gopal Das's stock too went down with it.

Despite the security and the high profile that he enjoys, Mahant Nritya Gopal Das is easily accessible to those who seek an audience with him. After a body search (bags have to be left outside) by friendly CRPF guards, a short flight of stairs leads to the small rectangular room where Ayodhya's richest mahant is seated amidst an assortment of unopened gifts, bags of wheat brought as prasad and boxes of sweets. At one end of the room is the bathroom while the other end functions as a kitchenette. The lack of frills suits the man himself who has the reputation of being a 'simple sadhu', and who, unlike many other sadhus and mahants, is not given to launching into lengthy monologues.

During an interview that took place less than a week after the end of the birthday celebrations, I asked Mahant Nritya Gopal Das about his relationship with BJP politicians.

Q: You are a monk, a mahant, why do so many chief ministers, central ministers, governors and politicians want to be present at your birthday? What is your relationship with them?

A: (nodding his head and rocking back and forth) First, many of them have known me for decades. Secondly, they come to me out of their reverence, love and trust.

Q: People say that you help politicians electorally as you have lakhs of devotees, and that's why they remain so close to you.

A: That is a different aspect. But they come here out of reverence, love and trust.

Q: As the head of the Ram Janmabhoomi Trust, how hopeful are you of the construction of the temple?

A: Modiji at the Centre, Yogi in the state. Waah! Waah! Now the work of the construction of the Ram temple will start as soon as possible. If not, now, then when?

Q: The Chief Justice of India, Justice J. S. Khehar, had said that parties
    should resolve the matter through dialogue. You have welcomed
    that. What do you think of certain out-of-court settlement efforts
    that were being made last year?

A: Our stand is clear. Muslims should give up their claims and allow
    the construction of a grand Ram temple. They can build their
    mosque anywhere on the other side of the Sarayu River, not in
    Ayodhya.

Q: But Mahant-ji you are not even a party to that case...

Mahant Nritya Gopal Das grinned and vigorously nodded his head. I
took that as a gesture of 'no comment' and of his acceptance that neither
he nor the Ram Janmabhoomi Trust is a litigant in the legal dispute. He
was one of the twelve accused in one of the two cases pertaining to the
demolition of the Babri Masjid. Taking my question to be about that case,
he started talking about it, but I clarified that I meant the title suit, in
response to which he fell silent again; he was a bit hard of hearing, but I
think that also allowed him to evade questions he didn't want to answer.

A couple entered the room, sensing that my 'darshan' time was about
to end soon, I threw him one last question.

Q: Mahant-ji, after the Supreme Court revived the conspiracy charge
    against L. K. Advani, M. M. Joshi and Uma Bharti, another accused
    in the case, Ram Vilas Vedanti, told the media that it was he who
    led the demolition of the mosque. What do you think of this
    sudden zeal to take credit for a crime?

A: Look here, it is not one person who was responsible. Therefore,
    nobody can say that he led the demolition. The karsevaks had
    been told to bring a fistful of sand and put it on the designated
    spot outside the disputed area. But karsevaks who had come from
    outside Ayodhya wanted to demolish the mosque. Advani, Joshi and
    others who are named in the conspiracy case tried to stop them
    by making announcements from the stage but the karsevaks did
    not listen to anybody and did what they had to do. We all are
    being wrongly charged with conspiracy to demolish the mosque.
    Those who did it are nowhere to be seen. Vedanti making such
    statements is an attempt to get some publicity. It is rubbish.

The interview was over. As the fidgeting by his designated-heir, Kamal

Nayan Das, increased, Nritya Gopal Das gave me some sweets and said goodbye with a big smile.

TWENTY-FIVE YEARS LATER

In some cases, the perpetrators and victims of the riots of 6 December 1992 continue to live in their old homes. One of the survivors of the violence, which began with the burning of Muslim homes and shops, is Mohammad Shahid. Shahid was barely out of his teens in 1992. The last imam of the Babri Masjid, Haji Abdul Ghaffar, was his grandfather. 'My grandfather had a very good standing in Ayodhya and neighbouring regions. We had a profitable timber business. It was named after my father, Mohammad Sabir.' Timber stores are locally known as 'Aara Machines', aara being the local word for the saw used to chop the wood.

Sitting outside a mosque on the main road to Naya Ghat, the sound of passing trains momentarily drowns out the constant whirring of the saws from a nearby metal workshop. With his eyes red and puffy as if he had been crying the entire night, Shahid recounts the day he lost his father, Mohammad Sabir, and his uncle, Mohammad Nazir. 'The previous day karsevaks had damaged some mazaars and graves. On 6 December, they entered this mosque—it didn't have a gate then—and ransacked it. The Quran was torn and thrown on the road. They were in thousands.' Shahid pauses and looks up towards the other side of the road. 'Then they started setting shops, including our shop, on fire. My father was with other older men, they ran towards our house. We were just boys.' That was the last he saw of his father.

He and other boys ran across the road to the house of Haji Mehboob, a local landlord. Many Muslims were already there. His father and uncle were lured out of their Muslim neighbour's house and killed. 'My uncle had a gun, they snatched it and killed them. On their faces especially they poured kerosene and burned them. All the dead bodies were found burnt,' he says.

Fayaz, an elderly rickshaw puller and recent Mecca-returned Haji, joins us. 'I knew his grandfather very well, I used to take him to Faizabad, the court there, Civil Lines...' Shahid sends him off to bring his pocket clock and rosary that most Hajis carry with them as souvenirs from Mecca. Shahid resumes talking, 'If I had gone with my father he would have been alive today,' he says, as though annoyed both with himself and his father. That day changed his life forever.

The night of 6 December was spent in the police station where he and others had escaped as mobs of karsevaks set Haji Mehboob's house on fire. On the evening of 7 December, the dead bodies of Muslims were collected under police protection and taken for burial in a graveyard in Raunahee, a Muslim-majority village on the Lucknow road. Earlier that morning, Shahid had set out hoping to find his father and uncle, 'I was calling out, "Abbu!" "Chachajaan!" Our house was still on fire, all the timber had been set on fire, it was still smouldering. Then a Hindu neighbour told me where the bodies of my father and uncle were lying. They were charred black,' says Shahid.

How did they know which houses belonged to Muslims and that your father and uncle were Muslims? I ask Shahid. 'They kept beards and my father was known as the son of the last imam of Babri Masjid. Locals, mainly Khatiks, were acting as guides for karsevaks and after the killings, a Khatik neighbour looted our house; he still lives there,' Shahid answers, the pain rising in his voice.

Old and toothless Fayaz, who has been patiently waiting to join the conversation, now speaks, 'The crowds that I have seen at Medina are bigger than the number of pilgrims who come here for Ram Navami.' Fayaz wasn't present in Ayodhya on 6 December 1992. He lived in a village nearby but now lives in the mosque as a caretaker. He has his own 'feel-good' version of the events of 6 December 1992. 'I was present in our village. CRPF came soon after the rioting and told the karsevaks that they should leave as soon as possible because Muslims are coming from all around Awadh. By 9 p.m., only dogs, burning shops and trees lying on the roads remained in Ayodhya. They escaped in buses,' he says.

Shahid received the nearly two-lakh rupees compensation for his father's death. He dropped out of college after the riots and despite his wish to leave Ayodhya, stayed back at his mother's insistence. As we are about to leave, the conversation turns to the renewed buzz around the dispute. Settling back in our chairs, Shahid weighs in on the fallout of Yogi Adityanath as Uttar Pradesh's new chief minister. 'They don't want to resolve it,' Shahid says. How do you want it to be resolved? I ask. 'As a Muslim, I will never say you can build your temple there. A mosque was demolished and another mosque should be rebuilt. The temple can be built where the Ram Chabutra was,' he replies.

The official VHP position is that the mosque can be rebuilt anywhere outside the 'cultural boundary of Ayodhya', and it cannot be named after Babur.

MUSLIMS FOR RAM TEMPLE

In a significant change of strategy the RSS is projecting that it has the support of Muslims for the construction of the Ram temple. It is doing this through the Rashtriya Muslim Manch or National Muslim Forum, an organization the RSS founded in December 2002. In the wake of the BJP coming to power in Uttar Pradesh, the manch has increased its activities in Ayodhya. On 14 June 2017, its patron Indresh Kumar flew in from Delhi and attended an iftar with Muslims. The programme was organized by Babloo Khan, a local Muslim leader who has emerged as an outspoken supporter of the Ram temple. At the event, Indresh Kumar told the attendees, 'India is the country of Khuda and honesty is the only means to reach heaven according to Islam.' Indresh Kumar's history—he was one of the accused in the 2007 Ajmer blast case (he was let off in 2017 while three other co-accused were found guilty)—was not brought up either at the meeting or its coverage in local newspapers. A day later, Kumar took the customary dip in the Sarayu along with some Muslim boys. There he appealed to Muslim youth 'to leave the path of violence, of hatred and come forward for the construction of Ram temple'. In the characteristic RSS fashion of teaching Muslims about their religion, he said that 'to advocate for Babri Masjid is an insult to Islam'. Emulating the RSS-backed Muslim Manch's pro-temple advocacy, Azam Khan, a little-known builder in Lucknow, has also founded his own organization called the All India Muslim Karsevak Forum. The VHP denies any association with this outfit. That, however, doesn't deter Azam Khan from descending on Ayodhya from time to time. In April 2017, Azam Khan made news for trying to enter the Ram Janmabhoomi–Babri Masjid complex after the gates had been shut. The dejected group of Muslims raised slogans of 'Ram Lalla hum aaye hain, Mandir wahin banayenge' and 'Jai Shri Ram' outside the barricade near Hanumangarhi. An amused shopkeeper commented, 'It's a Hindu government so they are compelled to do this drama.' A few days before RSS's Indresh Kumar's visit, the Muslim Karsevak Manch's activists participated in an elaborate yagna to pay tribute to those karsevaks who died in 1990 and 1992. They also prayed for the speedy construction of the Ram temple.[587]

---

[587]Sachchidanand Shukla, 'Muslim kar sevaks take oath to construct Ram Temple in Ayodhya', *Hindutsan Times*, 21 April 2017.

PSUEDO-JOURNALISM: AYODHYA'S BANE

The glossing over of Indresh Kumar's past as a terror suspect by many local newspapers in Faizabad and Ayodhya underlines the biased role that most Hindi media outlets have played in widening the gap between facts and fiction and in misinforming the public about the motives and ideologies of players like the RSS and the VHP. Throughout the Ram Janmabhoomi movement in the 1980s and 1990s, Hindi media houses remained willing accomplices in the perversion of history and facts. Ayodhya and Faizabad have a rich publishing history as centres of Urdu and Hindi literature. However, the only local daily that has survived the onslaught of capitalism and communalism on public interest journalism in the twin towns is *Jan Morcha*.

Jan Morcha was launched in 1956 by Mahatma Hargovind, a close associate of Mahatma Gandhi. For a newspaper that was started with a seed fund of Rs 75 collected through personal donations, *Jan Morcha*'s continuing survival in the twenty-first century is nothing short of a miracle in Indian journalism. Its office in the Bazaja area of Faizabad occupied by severely underpaid journalists is a picture of slow decay—a stinking staircase, creaky doors, exposed electrical wiring and old furniture. Beneath this depressing veneer lies the untold story of the struggle of a cooperative-run Hindi newspaper in the ocean of family-owned newspapers and media corporations. Sheetla Singh has been the captain of this ship through the last five decades. It is a testament to its high ideals and rich world view that the yellowed and dust-soaked archives of *Jan Morcha* provide as much of a glimpse of the region of Awadh as of the country and the world.

During the course of the Ram Janmabhoomi movement, *Jan Morcha*'s strident commitment to journalistic and democratic ethics turned it into an 'enemy mouthpiece' for the RSS and the karsevaks. What had riled the Sangh Parivar and its local representatives was *Jan Morcha*'s adherence to 'non-communal' and factual reporting. Its resident editor, Krishna Pratap Singh, gives the example of the firing-related deaths on 2 November 1990 when Mulayam Singh was the chief minister. 'The day most other newspapers and certainly all the local ones published head;ines of "Ayodhya Bathed in Blood", *Jan Morcha* carried the report about twelve people who died in police firing. That number still stands,' he says.

This intransigence to align with the press notes of the VHP angered the karsevaks and their leaders, prominent among them, Vinay Katiyar, the president of the Bajrang Dal and now a Member of Parliament. 'After the

1990 firing incident the Sangh Parivar ran a house-to-house campaign to stop people from reading *Jan Morcha*,' says K. P. Singh.

Jan Morcha's 'golden age'—or at least when it was the newspaper with the highest circulation figures in many districts of Awadh—is long over. Since the late 1980s most national dailies have opened offices in Faizabad. Today, Ayodhya, and because of it, Faizabad, are permanently sensitive spots on India's media map. A new generation of journalists has come up since the demolition of the Babri Masjid in 1992. After an interim lull, Ayodhya is once again in the spotlight. BJP-majority governments both in the state and at the centre have the construction of the Ram temple in their manifestos, although unlike in the 1990s, they have refrained from setting a deadline for it.

Jan Morcha still remains in circulation but its readership has fallen as steadily as the stagnant salary increments its team have received. Its existence itself though is a form of resistance, a cocking a snook of the journalistic kind. Reporters from other local dailies, weeklies and bi-weeklies envy its editorial quality but are happier writing reports based to a large extent on the overflowing calendar of religion-based stories and VIP visits. Birthdays, the waning and waxing moons, religious festivals, yatras, deaths of saints, urs of Muslim fakirs and visits by publicity-hungry godmen are the staple stories in the newspapers of Faizabad and Ayodhya. Amidst this, *Jan Morcha* still enjoys respect and credibility. 'This newspaper has not been rejected by the readers. People still turn to *Jan Morcha* to verify important news,' K. P. Singh says. In the times of WhatsApp and a plethora of dubiously funded media outlets, the paper's continuing survival sends a ray of hope to democratic forces in the region.

CELEBRATING THE BIRTH OF RAM

In Ayodhya, no other day is celebrated with as much fervour as the birthday of its favourite God, Ram. According to the Ramayana, Ram Navami marks the end of the nine-day-long ritual that was conducted by the childless King Dasharatha. It usually falls in the months of March and April and is celebrated like the birth of an actual baby. In the epic, Ram and his three brothers, Lakshman, Shatrughan and Bharat, were born together to a childless Dasharatha, Ayodhya's lord, after a long struggle and tapasya.

In 2017, Ram Navami fell on 5 April. During the Ram Navami fair in Ayodhya, the deep devotion to Ram manifests itself in the form of carnival. Every temple and household marks it by preparing special sweets, performing pujas, setting up community kitchens, buying new clothes for the idols, and organizing music and dance performances. The fair starts nine days prior to Ram Navami and climaxes at the moment when Lord Ram is born. The district administration begins preparations for the fair—in which lakhs of people participate (no precise government data on number of attendees is available)—weeks in advance. In Kanak Bhavan, the large mansion built in 1891 by the royal family of Orchha and Tikamgarh, the number of pilgrims steadily increases as the time of Lord Ram's birth draws closer. When the gates are opened at the 'actual moment of birth' a torrent of pilgrims begins flowing up the steps of the temple, passing through the area in front of the sanctum sanctorum and finally exiting on the side that overlooks the Ram Janmabhoomi–Babri Masjid complex. The 'climax' of the birth is artfully crafted at Kanak Bhavan. Velvet curtains are kept drawn since the previous day. As the clock approaches 12 noon, the large iron gates at the main entrance of the Kanak Bhavan are shut by the police, who are deployed in large numbers and are heavily armed. Meanwhile, a large screen starts projecting a static shot of the velvet curtains. Live commentary by a local expert in the Ramayana works the throng of devotees. Ten minutes before noon, the main gates of the building are shut. Now the crowd, comprising men, women, children and toddlers on the shoulders of their parents and grandparents, eagerly awaits the opening of the curtain so they can witness the birth of Dasharatha and Kaushalya's son. The eyes of the devout are transfixed to the screen (the ceremony is also broadcast live on Doordarshan and All India Radio) and so are those of the policemen and media persons.

The curtains are drawn to wild cheering as people break into joyous dancing and singing. The crowd outside is now getting restive to enter the temple. When the gates are finally opened after another ten minutes, Kanak Bhavan turns into a massive birthday festival.

Inside the black-and-white checkered quadrangle, men, women and sakhis (women dressed as men) are singing and dancing in three different groups. As the summer sun beats down on devotees, three pairs of dholaks, harmoniums and cymbals are played in different corners of the large open-air courtyard and the tempo is kept up by singing songs using the different names for Ram like Raghuraiyya, Dasharatha-putr and Siyavar (Sita's husband). Thankfully, there is no DJ at work here. Some people are immersed in reading their Ramayanas. A few women, mostly middle-aged or older, are so moved that they burst into tears. For most Hindu mothers, son-worship comes embedded and internalized in the epic's narration of Ram's birth.

The songs sung during Ram's birth are called sohars. The sixth day (Chauti) and the twelfth day are celebrated with special fervour.

One of the many songs still sung at Hindu homes relates the story of a female deer and Kaushalya, who is blinded by her love for the newborn Ram. It poignantly describes the pain of a doe when Kaushalya refuses to let her take the skin of her partner who was sacrificed for Ram's Chauti celebrations. While some see in the folk song the pathos between the ruler and the ruled, the dominant species and the inferior species, others find in it the inherent nature of folk songs, which always question the establishment and try to represent the voiceless.

Be that as it may, the song is most powerful in its original dialect. In Awadhi, it moves many white-haired men and women to tears. Kaushalya, immersed in her happiness of motherhood achieved after a special yagna, refuses to let the doe take the skin of the deer, her partner. She tells the doe that the skin will be used to make a small hand-drum for her son Ram to play with. The song ends with the doe crying with the pain of separation each time she hears the sound of the hand-drum being played. The song is fast fading away from popular culture, though it survives in Awadhi folk literature.[588]

6 DECEMBER 2017

Three days before the twenty-fifth anniversary of the destruction of Babri Masjid, Faizabad's Ghosiana became tense along communal lines over an incident of road rage. A Muslim couple's car had grazed past a couple of Hindu baraatis, who then dragged the man out and beat him up. It so happened that the baraat's route passed through the neighbourhood in which the couple lived. The Muslim man extracted quick revenge with the help of his cousins and friends and in the ensuing melee, a leg was broken on the Hindu side. Violence related to road rage is common in north India, and every year dozens of people are injured or killed because of it. The incident in Faizabad instantly took a communal turn. Ghosiana has traditionally been home to a large number of Ghosi Muslims, who have been cattle-and milk-farmers. It is also the village in which the muezzin of Babri Masjid took refuge in the intervening night of 22–23 December 1949, when the idol of Ram Lalla had been forcibly implanted inside the Babri Masjid.

---

[588]For a description of the poem, see 'Tehin tashe tashi hariyan', *Ramyantar.com*, 15 December 2009 <http://blog.ramyantar.com/2009/12/blog-post_14.html>.

With 6 December 2017 approaching, the Faizabad police and administration took no chances, and swooped down to arrest the young Muslim men who had assaulted the Hindu baraatis. The police also stationed anti-riot vehicles and scores of armed personnel in Ghosiana to prevent any Hindu attack on the locality. The accused Muslim boys were on the run. Until they were arrested, tension was likely to prevail.

Though by no means a serious communal incident, its shadow, along with the renewed assertion in the form of the ban on buffalo meat and slaughterhouses by RSS-affiliated Hindu outfits like Bajrang Dal, formed the backdrop of 6 December 2017. Locals know that most tourists come to Ayodhya out of curiosity about the demolition of Babri Masjid. Raju, a young, well-dressed, e-rickshaw driver says, 'If it was not for the Janmabhoomi issue, I don't think people would come here from Haryana, Himachal Pradesh and even Sikkim. The first place they ask us to take them to is Babri Masjid-Ram Janmabhoomi. We tell such tourists to see other temples too but they are not very interested. All they want to hear about is the 1990 firing, the Shaheed Gali, the demolition and how it all happened. I was a little kid in 1992 but I tell them whatever I have heard from elders.' As an e-rickshaw driver-cum-guide Raju relies on such tourists for livelihood. However, both devotees and tourists (there is a thin line dividing them) stay away from Ayodhya in December. On the eve of the twenty-fifth anniversary of the demolition, there was a palpable excitement among cadres of RSS outfits like VHP, Bajrang Dal and the BJP. The small town's abiding relevance to Indian politics also loomed its shadow a day before 6 December.

During the first hearing on the Ayodhya title suit on 5 December 2017, senior advocate and Congress leader Kapil Sibal, who was representing the Sunni Central Waqf Board, told a three-judge special bench headed by the Chief Justice of India that the title dispute should not be decided until the 2019 general elections are over. He also pleaded that the case be heard by a Constitution bench of the Supreme Court. Later that day, the Sunni Central Waqf Board would distance itself from Sibal's remarks in the Court. However, BJP leaders instantly picked on Sibal's remarks in the Court. On the campaign trail in the soon to be held assembly elections in Gujarat, BJP President Amit Shah targeted his Congress counterpart Rahul Gandhi and dared him to make his party's stand clear on the construction of a Ram temple in Ayodhya. Shah also used the opportunity afforded by Sibal's comments to dismiss Rahul Gandhi's much-publicized visits to Gujarat's temples. He said the statement by Sibal showed the 'double standards' of the Congress whose president on one hand is on an 'election tours of temples' while it opposes a Ram temple in Ayodhya. The Supreme Court special bench headed by Chief Justice Dipak Misra rejected both demands made by Sibal.

While Ayodhya was once again back as an election trope in true earnest, in Faizabad a function to mark the sixtieth anniversary of *Jan Morcha* became a platform for veteran journalists and academics to reflect on the role of the media during the Ram Janmabhoomi movement and its continuing fallouts. Anand Pradhan, an associate professor in Delhi's Indian Institute of Mass Communication weighed in on the post-truth world we live in, saying, 'Instead of fact-based opinions and beliefs, today we have belief-based facts and opinions. New media like WhatsApp and social media have belied the expectation that they will empower the young and the weak'. Listening to him, one couldn't help but think about how from the very beginning alternative facts had been the backbone of the VHP's campaign to 'free' Ram's birthplace. On the stage, unaccompanied by any senior politician or even journalist, sat *Jan Morcha's* founder-editor Sheetla Singh, a known opponent of RSS's ideology and the temple movement. The absence of national-level prominent personalities underscored the near-complete isolation of independent and secular newspapers like the *Jan Morcha*.

Among the audience sat local politicians of all hues, and also those like Khaliq Khan and Vineet Maurya, who consider *Jan Morcha* an ally in their respective struggles. Uniting them both is the unending and seemingly irresolvable dispute over Babri Masjid's destruction and the construction of a Ram temple.

Vineet Maurya converted to Buddhism after having flirted with the temple movement in the late eighties and early nineties. Today, Vineet is an active Dalit activist in Ayodhya and against all odds on 23 July 2018, his writ petition demanding that the disputed site be declared a Buddhist site was accepted by the Supreme Court; his contention being that since it is a Buddhist site it should be declared a Buddhist Vihar like Shravasti, Kapilvastu, Kushinagar and Sarnath.[589]

On 6 December 2017, I set out early to visit the disputed complex along with a friend. The day had begun like any cold December day, much

---

[589]Arshad Afzal Khan, 'Now, plea in SC claims disputed Ayodhya site is Buddhist land', *Times of India*, 14 March 2018.

like how it must have been twenty-five years ago. A thin fog hung in the town's lanes, the streets were empty as they had been on several preceding anniversaries of the Babri Masjid demolition. The small groups huddling around tea shops had other matters on their mind; the Babri Masjid's demolition was just one of them. The previous evening, the police had taken out their own yatra through the town. This was done to reassure the town's people as well as the media that the police were ready to ensure nothing would disturb peace and law and order in Ayodhya. Dharamshalas and hotels were checked and the details of guests verified. Local officers of the police led the march through the city dressed in their leather jackets and tan leather shoes while the troopers followed in riot protection gear.

On our way we passed sadhus returning from their bath at the Sarayu River, rickshaw pullers pedalling into town from neighbouring villages, and the unceasing chanting of Sitaram Sitaram from the loudspeakers atop Hanumangarhi temple. It was a cold morning like any December morning in Ayodhya. However, the VHP's call for 'grand celebrations' on 6 December had made us anxious enough about being in the magma chamber of right-wing Hindu communalism, and that too, on the twenty-fifth anniversary of its eruption. My friend, unaccustomed to wearing a bindi, had carried a pack of bindis in her bag. The Babri Masjid-Ram Janmabhoomi complex was largely empty apart from stray visitors like us. After some routine questions we were allowed to go through the iron cage and after viewing the idols of Ram Lalla and his brothers, came out without any incident. While the devotee might feel a religious connection with the place, for many others it is like witnessing the theatre of the absurd. My friend's initial reaction was that she couldn't help but feel a great injustice had been done. A medieval-era mosque, which was more a derelict monument, had been razed to the ground and replaced with a place of worship for another community. 'Where was—no, where *is* the rule of law?' she wondered aloud. The streets lined with shops were not buzzing as they used to during other times of the year and there was hardly any rush at the Hanumangarhi temple, the totem-pole of the pilgrim town of Ayodhya.

A kilometre away, outside Hashim Ansari's house (who passed away during the writing of this book), members of the Babri Masjid Action Committee and other Muslim groups besides other local Muslims had gathered to observe the day of the demolition as 'Yaum-e-Gham', or day of mourning. Every year they congregate here and interact with local and national media to decry the demolition, call for the reconstruction of the mosque and demand the resolution of the dispute in court. It's a ritual that they have been conducting for the last twenty-four years. The few functional mosques in Ayodhya display banners painted with words of mourning, calling 6 December a 'Black Day'.

On the twenty-fifth anniversary of the demolition, there were no special programmes nor a significant crowd of Muslims. In fact, compared to last year, which was the first 6 December without the toothy-grinned Hashim, there were only a handful of Muslim men seated on a few plastic chairs. Afaq Ahmad Khan, the chairman of the Babri Masjid Action Committee was among them.

A well-known face, seventy-eight-year-old Afaq Khan was happy to meet us—journalists from Delhi. Soon, he was joined by Khaliq Khan. In 2016, Khaliq Khan and other prominent Muslims of Faizabad and Ayodhya were part of emotional scenes that unfolded at the same place. For the first time since 1992, the Black Day was observed without Hashim Ansari, who is still remembered with fondness, even by his legal adversaries like Mahant Ramdas of Nirmohi Akhara.

Soon after Khaliq Khan joined our conversation, we were surrounded by a group of onlookers and a few policemen in uniform and some in civilian clothes.

Me: After Kapil Sibal's demand to defer the case till 2019, the BJP and others are claiming that your case is not strong enough and therefore you want to stall the case. Has it not backfired from your perspective?

Afaq Khan: Whatever be the judgement, whether it is in favour of Hindus or Muslims, there will be a sharp reaction across the country. Moreover, the benefit will go to the ruling party, the BJP. Their policy is like the British, they want to divide Hindus and Muslims and continue to rule.

Me: We have just visited the disputed site. Why don't you ask the Court to let Muslims worship there like the Hindus do?

Afaq Khan: Yes but that has been the status quo since 1986, rather, since 1949. But it's not as though we haven't tried to win our legitimate right to pray there. In 1986, when the locks to the mosque were opened, I had appealed to my seniors in the community to issue a call to all Muslims across India to come and pray there, but in their wisdom, they refused to issue such a call. Now we can't even enter there.

Khaliq Khan: Muslims can enter if they don't think you are a Muslim.

Khaliq's sharp interjection made us all laugh. He was stating a fact, which they have learnt to live with, and humour makes it easy to accept it.

Twenty-five years after the destruction of the mosque and the riots that followed, there is not a single government sign that reflects the disputed nature of the site. From being the name of a Police Station (Thana Ram Janmabhoomi), to large boards showing us the way, it is only Ram Janmabhoomi that survives. The government signboards bore directions only to Ram Janambhoomi, and not Ram Janambhoomi–Babri Masjid. As if with the demolition, the more than five hundred years of history was also erased.

◆

Getting hold of Vineet Maurya is not easy. A tireless community mobilizer he is always on the move on his bicycle. Today, he is at home, which stands at the edge of the acquired area—about 500 metres as the crow flies—from the Muslim gathering at Iqbal Ansari's (Hashim Ansari's son's) house.

From the terrace of Vineet's house one has a clear view over the fenced-off buffer land acquired under the Acquisition of Certain Area at Ayodhya Act, 1993. Vineet wouldn't let us go to the terrace for fear of harassment by the police. 'If somebody sees there are outsiders on the terrace, the police will be informed and it will just lead to a lot of problems for me.' So we sat in the alley outside his house and chatted. He had not yet filed his petition claiming Ayodhya as a Buddhist site in the Supreme Court, but was excited to talk about it. He said, 'We have four ASI reports that say that the artefacts and remnants found in the excavation at and around the disputed site are similar to those found at sites like Sarnath. Therefore, I want the government to declare this site as Buddhist and provide the protection allowed under the Ancient Monument and Archaeological Sites and Remains Act, 1958.' But, aren't you a little too late? I ask him. 'Yes I might be, but other Buddhist groups have tried to enjoin the matter before as well. The Allahabad High Court did not let them become a party, for example.'

A post-graduate degree holder in Ancient Indian History, Vineet insisted that if a thorough and fair excavation was conducted, it would be proven that all of Ayodhya was a Buddhist Vihar.

The sun had risen but its rays eluded us in the alley, so we decided to venture into an open space near the fenced-off area. One of us started taking photos of the general area where all one could see were large mango trees and a couple of armed guards sitting in the sun by their watch tower. Upon seeing us the guards became agitated and asked us to stop clicking photos and go away from the fence. As if on cue, the crackle of their wireless radio became louder. One of them had started walking towards us. 'There is Section 144 in place throughout the year. Whoever you are, wherever you are from, we don't care. Don't you know where you are?' he yelled. I do know I said, and walked away along with Vineet, who had all through this exchange maintained a 'safe distance' from me.

'They don't let anybody stand near the fence, not even us who have lived here for centuries,' said Vineet.

'So, this is extra-alertness is not because of it being 6 December?' I ask him.

'You can come tomorrow and see if they let you stand there. This is normal,' he said wryly.

Back on the main Ayodhya–Faizabad road, life seemed to go on like any other day. Schools and colleges were open and so were most shops and other commercial establishments. The VHP's workshop where the building blocks of their proposed model of a future Ram temple are stored and carved was devoid of tourists as was the rest of the town. Other than a reporter memorizing his walkthrough piece to the camera, a stonecarver who was gently chiselling leaves on stone and a group of gawking monkeys, there was only a saffron clad man who doubled up as a guide in return for a voluntary donation.

Not too far from the workshop lies the VHP's sprawling campus called the Karsevakpuram, from where a large number of cars and motorcycle-borne Bajrang Dal and BJP members had left sometime back for their 'victory march' through Ayodhya and Faizabad. The VHP's media incharge in Ayodhya is forty-four-year-old Sharad Sharma. He had been busy since early morning, organizing a public meeting to be held later in the day. Unlike in 2016, when both VHP and Muslim groups marked the day of demolition of the Babri Masjid with token pledges and resolutions, this year it was to be celebrated by local units of the VHP and Bajrang Dal with unrestrained fervour.

Sometime later, driving past them, we heard their supporters shout slogans that were offensive and threatening towards Muslims. Later, after prominent Muslims from the town protested to the police, a case for breaking prohibitory orders (Section 144) and disturbing 'peace and communal harmony' was registered against fifty unknown persons.[590] In characteristic

---

[590]Arshad Afzaal Khan, 'In Ayodhya 25 years after Babri Masjid demolition, VHP organises

style, police had acted with deliberate delay, but because a case was registered, they could not be accused of being partisan towards Bajrang Dal, an RSS outfit that was formed in Ayodhya at the peak of the temple movement.

Almost every bike bore a saffron flag, many foreheads were streaked yellow with sandalwood paste, and all chanted 'Mandir wahin banayenge', and more incendiary slogans as they had passed through Ayodhya and Faizabad. Some of these men also passed through Ghosiana, which was still tense in the wake of the road rage violence involving Muslims and Hindus. In Faizabad, the men were not stopped but moved about with a police vehicle in tow.

Compared to previous years, 6 December 2017 had been very eventful. The Shia Waqf Board's plea to be made a party in the case had been admitted by the Supreme Court a day earlier, and things seemed to be moving at a pace faster than ever before.

The same day, Prime Minister Modi addressed four election rallies in Gujarat. One of them was at Dahod, the twin city of Godhra where more than fifty karsevaks were killed in a fire that engulfed their coach of the Sabarmati Express train in 2002. Hindu groups alleged that the coach had been set on fire by Muslims from a locality near Godhra station. What followed for the next several weeks was an anti-Muslim carnage that hadn't been witnessed in independent India. Dozens of Hindus also died in pitched battles but Muslims bore the brunt of violence both in terms of lives and livelihoods. The riots were followed by state elections in which the BJP rode to power with a clear majority.

Fifteen years later, on the campaign trail for his party as the prime minister and its strongest leader, Narendra Modi made it a point to 'thank' the Sunni Central Waqf Board for distancing itself from Sibal's appeal pertaining to deferment of the case till the 2019 general elections. He said, 'I give compliments and express my thankfulness to the Sunni Waqf Board for the solidarity they showed on the Ram Mandir issue. They released a statement and said that they were not happy with the stand of Congress leader and lawyer Kapil Sibal, which he presented before the Supreme Court. When the Sunni Waqf Board and the entire nation wish an amicable solution of the Ram Mandir issue, the Congress is trying to create impediments against the construction of Ram Mandir.'[591]

"Day of Bravery" while Muslims observe "Black Day"', *The Wire*, 6 December 2017.
[591]'PM Modi thanks Waqf Board for solidarity on Ayodhya', *DNA*, 7 December 2017.

Ayodhya's place in Indian politics remains largely unchanged. So far the RSS and BJP have carefully managed the rhetoric around temple construction. They have sidelined vehemently pro-temple VHP leaders like Pravin Togadia, and made others fall in line. The symbolism of a Ram temple at the place where Hindus believe he was born remains an important and unifying force. Within Ayodhya, people's cynicism towards politicians is undiminished. They have been here many times before. But have they?

The BJP is in power at all the three tiers of government: the municipal corporation of Ayodhya, the state government, and in New Delhi. And yet, the party under Narendra Modi and Amit Shah, and RSS supremo Mohan Bhagwat, has not taken any overt steps to indicate that the government is partisan in the matter. An Act of Parliament, with judicial approval, could be one way to clear the way for building a Ram temple—as promised by the RSS and the BJP. However, that can only happen once the case is heard and decided by the Supreme Court of India.

At present, political calculations for the BJP do not clearly indicate that the cost of bulldozing their way, either through legislation or through popular mobilization, will be redeemed by the electoral benefit that would accrue from such a step.

Therefore, for now, the town's people, and observers in the rest of India, are playing the wait and watch game.

◆

The people of Ayodhya now have a standard set of replies to inquisitive outsiders depending on their perception of what the outsider wants to hear. When asked if they took part in the karseva on 6 December 1992, most of them, from shopkeepers to the omnipresent and omniscient bystanders, will say, 'Hum dekhe sab kuch, lekin kare kuch nahin' (I saw everything but I didn't do anything). If they perceive you as being 'mandirvadi', or pro-temple, you'll be told, 'Hum kiye karseva sab ke saath' (I did karseva along with everybody else). Some will even tell you that they carried back with them bricks and other masonry from the debris. But very few will be able to produce those souvenirs. One obvious reason for the reluctance to share any physical evidence of their actions on 6 December 1992 is the far-fetched but real fear of being implicated in the demolition. It is perhaps this fear that also makes most of them call the demolition 'a miracle' or 'an act of God'.

The one person whose life changed just as much as the idol Ram Lalla's did on 6 December is Satyendra Das, the government-appointed head priest of the Ram Janmabhoomi–Babri Masjid shrine. 'From a huge, well-made building where Ram Lalla was protected from rain, water, heat and cold, now he is in a tent, and I am fortunate that I still serve Him. For me, 6 December is a day to be reminded of Ram Lalla's suffering,' he says. 'Is there going to be a special puja?' I ask him. 'There is no effect of 6 December either on Ram Lalla or on his pujari. I will follow my usual routine,' Das replies.

Yet another 6 December passed peacefully, the twenty-fifth since the Babri Masjid was razed to the ground and its rubble thrown away, some of it taken home by karsevaks. The emotional pull of the Ram Janmabhoomi movement rested on the belief of millions of Hindus in saguna (idol) worship. That is why idols and deities are treated like actual beings who feel the vagaries of weather just as humans do. Which is why the RSS–VHP's campaign to 'free Ram Lalla' from a Mulism invader's mosque had appealed to the sensibilities of millions in the 1980s and 1990s. After winning the UP elections, the VHP revived this tactic to win certain comforts at the disputed shrine. On 23 December 2017, a hot-air blower was installed inside the tent that houses the deities of Ram Lalla and his three brothers on the appeal of the VHP.

AYODHYA, 1992

O Rama
Life is a bitter fact
and you are an epic.

> You cannot win over
> the unthinking
> that now has not ten or twenty
> but a million heads and hands;
> and who knows with whom your ally
> Vibhishana too now stands.

What more can our misfortune be
that your kingdom lies shrunk
to a stage of dispute so petty.

Ayodhya is not your war-free realm now
but a warrior's Lanka of old,
and 'Manas' not your virtues
but slogans that elections hold.

O Rama, where are these times
and where your golden days:
where your noble glory
and where these wily ways!

We humbly pray, O Lord, that you return
securely, with wife and home,
to some scroll – some sacred tome;
these jungles are not the jungles of yore
that Valmiki used to roam.

—Kunwar Narain (1927–2017)
Translated from the Hindi by Apurva Narain

EPILOGUE

Ayodhya remains a pilgrim centre that draws the renunciates, seekers, escapists, destitute runaways, criminals as well as sinners trying to start anew. Runaway children still end up in Ayodhya and like soldiers of fortune, wage their struggles for survival and supremacy in the ashrams and temples of Ram's city.

In 2008, Arun Das was nine years old when he ran away from his home near Gonda and came to Ayodhya. A kind woman took him to work in her small shop that sold religious items and fruit juice. One day, he met Mahant Bajrang Das, an ageing Ramanandi ascetic, who offered to take him on as a disciple. Arun agreed and started living in his ashram in Laxman Ghat. Over the years, Arun Das learnt the scriptures and practised rituals for conducting religious ceremonies. Bajrang Das was pleased with him and declared Arun Das his heir in 2013. But before the ashram's property could be transferred in Arun's name, Bajrang Das died at the age of ninety-five.

Like so many others, this ashram and its lodging house too remain stuck in a legal dispute between Arun Das and an older tenant. Mukedmebaazi, or litigation, is a fact of life in Ayodhya, and it doesn't deter Arun Das from dreaming about a better future for himself. 'I would like to go to a big city like Mumbai or Delhi and serve the religious needs of the people,' he says while fiddling with his rip-off Apple earphones. Like many locals he believes that Ayodhya will be developed only when the Ram temple is built. 'Because, the world over, Hindus know about the issue, they are waiting for the temple to be built. Once it is built then they will visit Ayodhya and everybody will benefit from that,' he says.

I proffer the counter-theory that floats under the surface in Ayodhya: what about those who believe otherwise, who say that once the temple is built, pilgrims will come but won't visit other temples; some even hold the opinion that if the temple is built Hindus will visit for a couple of years but will forget about it once the euphoria fades away? 'I don't believe that. These are the views of selfish and petty-minded people. When Hindus will come from the US, Canada, UK, they will see not just the Ram temple, they will go to other temples too, they will buy from the shopkeepers here, they will stay here, so there is everything to gain,' he reasons. His argument though compelling, is contestable. Most pilgrims from abroad or even the well-heeled ones from other states in India, don't spend more than a day here. They come in taxis from Lucknow or Banaras, where there are good airports, and return the same day. Hardly any foreign tourists ever come here besides the annual government delegation from South Korea.

As the 2019 national elections draw near, the RSS supremo Mohan Bhagwat has repeatedly made statements claiming that only a Ram temple will be built in Ayodhya, and that even opposition parties cannot openly oppose its construction.[592] Indifference to the ongoing judicial process in the case is nothing new for the RSS as it knows well that the issue's sentimental appeal needs to be kept alive among devout Hindus. The Congress called the RSS chief's statement a 'frog's cry during rains' and accused the RSS-BJP of sending Lord Ram to '"exile" after every election'.[593]

The VHP too has revived its community of sants. On 5 October 2018, it held a meeting of fifty sadhus at its headquarters in Delhi, where the seers and sadhus passed a resolution detailing a month-wise plan to create favourable public opinion for the construction of the Ram temple before 2019. Mahant Nritya Gopal Das later led the panel of seers to present their demands to the President of India. Characteristic of the VHP's diminished ability to unite Ayodhya's sadhus behind it, only five of the fifty seers who attended the meeting were from Ayodhya. These seers castigated the BJP for not fullfilling its promise to build a Ram temple in Ayodhya and demanded that the government bring in a special legislation that would allow the construction of the temple.[594]

In Ayodhya, a VHP-supporting mahant started his fast unto death. He demanded that Prime Minister Modi announce the construction of a Ram temple by bringing in a special Act of Parliament.[595]

---

[592]'Opposition can't oppose Ram temple: Mohan Bhagwat', *Times of India*, 2 October 2018.

[593]'"Frog's cry": Congress on RSS chief's remark on Ram temple', *Hindustan Times*, 5 October 2018.

[594]'Ram Mandir push:VHP passes resolution on Ram temple, to submit memorandum to President', *Times Now*, 5 October 2018.

[595]'"Modi can give assurance, then end hunger strike": Mahant Patamahansa Das', *Punjab Kersari*, 7 Ocotber 2018.

While too much cannot be read into the VHP's periodic moves ahead of elections, their threat of a nationwide agitation cannot be ignored either. It is not inconceivable that the hordes of young men who are often seen gyrating to the beats of techno-bhajans cannot be diverted to Ayodhya, to finish the task that began on 6 December 1992—construction of a temple at Ram's Janmabhoomi.

Hindus in Ayodhya–Faizabad definitely want a Ram temple and have been waiting for the last four years to see some tangible movement towards its construction. As Ramesh Chaurasia, a Hanuman devotee said, 'If Hindu governments at the centre and the state cannot build it, then who will?' The government is also active and its intelligence department is busy conducting 'feasibility studies' and 'impact assessment surveys' to ascertain the reaction of people if the temple were to be built through an Act of Parliament. Now that the VHP-backed sants have once again given a call for karseva to build a temple, it remains to be seen if the mobilization of Hindus will be easier than before. BJP governments or BJP-supported governments are in power in nineteen states in India, including in all but one neighbouring state of UP (Delhi has an Aam Aadmi Party government). Mahant Satyendra Das, though, believes otherwise. He believes that 'neither the BJP government at the centre nor in the state have the "icchashakti" or will to build the temple. We have been waiting for Modiji to at least visit Ayodhya to see how Ram Lalla lives in a tent, but he hasn't. We have given the BJP everything, they have a full majority now, power in 19 states, and still they don't keep their promise of a Ram temple. It is Ram Lalla who gave them everything, and it is He who will teach them a lesson,' an agitated Das, told me over the phone. Muslims are used to the headlines and the VHP's posturing before every election and are keeping a cautious watch on these developments.

However, the only democratic and constitutional possibility to clear the way for the temple is if the Supreme Court upholds the Allahabad High Court verdict of 2010 or decides the title suit in favour of Hindu parties. In that case the temple will have to be built and the Muslims will comply, as the Sunni Central Waqf Board has stated many times. But if the Supreme Court decides that the land where the Babri Masjid stood belongs to Muslims, will the VHP and the Sangh Parivar comply?

They have maintained since the beginning that the courts cannot decide this matter; what's the guarantee that they won't mobilize Hindus against the Supreme Court verdict?

In July 2017, the Uttar Pradesh Shia Central Waqf Board revived their claim on the Babri Masjid. As mentioned earlier, the Shia claim over the mosque had been dismissed by the Faizabad Civil Court in 1946. If the Shia Waqf Board's appeal to join the case is admitted by the court, it will add a new dimension and additional delay to the nearly sixty-year-old legal dispute. It is not yet clear what motive lies behind the move to become a party after more than seventy years. The desire of the board members to ingratiate themselves to the Yogi and Modi governments cannot be ruled out. The chairman of the board, Wasim Rizvi, denied that this is the case.

MUTUAL SETTLEMENTS THROUGH TALKS

This suggestion is premised on the assumption that everything can be solved through dialogue and 'give and take'. But when neither the VHP nor the Nirmohi Akhara nor other Hindu parties (eight in all who appealed against the 2010 verdict of the Allahabad High Court) nor the Muslim parties led by the Sunni Central Waqf Board are ready to 'give' or give up, dialogues of mutual settlement are meaningless.

'It is an ego clash, a conflict between Hindus' inferiority complex and Muslims' superiority complex,' a seasoned observer (who wishes to remain anonymous) of Ayodhya had commented. Where ego rules and rationality has failed it is naïve to expect that talks will solve the problem. If the Hindu parties agree to vacate the land presently occupied by the makeshift shrine of Ram Lalla, the Sunni Central Waqf Board may agree to have the temple constructed at the spot where the Ram Chabutra stood inside the outer courtyard of the mosque. Another way to solve the dispute would be for the Muslim parties to give up their claim and agree to build the mosque outside Ayodhya. 'But how can we let that happen; it means tomorrow a mob can destroy another mosque or any other Waqf land. It would legitimize the forcible occupation in 1949 and the demolition in 1992,' is the response of Zafaryab Gilani, the Sunni Waqf Board's lawyer. In any case, he says, Waqf land is a grant made in perpetuity and its nature cannot be changed. The disputed land cannot be cordoned off nor can a public amenity be built on it. This 'compromise' solution of building a hospital or a museum has been floating about since the dispute's early days in the 1990s. But it is not acceptable to the VHP or to the Sunni Central Waqf Board.

Will the courts decide one way or another by 2019? Will the temple be built by 2019? From RSS functionaries to BJP ministers to the common Hindu on Ayodhya's streets, the answer is a resounding 'yes'. The BJP proved that it didn't need the support of Muslims by winning a landslide majority without fielding a single Muslim candidate in the 2017 assembly elections in UP. The political emasculation of Muslims as a 'vote bank' is also all but complete at the national level. However, on the shifting sands of Indian politics, itself shaped both by economic issues like inflation and unemployment, and religion, the BJP of winter 2018 doesn't appear as strong as it did when it took power four years ago in May 2014. The legislative route itself of enacting an Act to allow the construction of a temple is fraught with both political and constitutional risks. As has been pointed out earlier, even Parliament cannot pass a law while the dispute is pending in the Supreme Court. Therefore, until the Supreme Court of India passes a verdict, it will be unconstitutional to pass such a law. The BJP has officially and repeatedly emphasized that the temple will be built through the court's verdict and constitutional processes. Certain experts also hold the view that the BJP can change the Constitution. Until a solution is found or forced, the Ram Janmabhoomi–Babri Masjid dispute will remain unresolved. Perhaps, the resolution of this bloody dispute lies not in the hands of our present generation of leaders, seers and people, but in the hands of future generations who would think of it differently and not as a Hindu versus Muslim issue.

Ayodhya has come a long way in its journey over millennia, and while today it is called the graveyard of India's composite culture and rule of law, I am hopeful that this label, too, will not stick forever. Ayodhya will keep changing its course with the river Sarayu as its eternal witness.

ACKNOWLEDGEMENTS

A book is never written only by its author. A book such as this one is often a collective effort with contributions from a vast range of people. I am thankful to numerous people in Ayodhya, Faizabad, Delhi and Lucknow for sharing their stories and perspectives. I am also grateful to many people whose courage, hospitality, and knowledge helped me sail through the twists, blind spots, and whirlpools that mark the process of writing such a book.

I'd like to start by thanking Simar, my friend of many years, for her faith in me, without whom this book wouldn't have been possible.

Arjun and Indranil, with whom I shared the first draft of the first chapter, and whose encouraging words helped me in the early stages of writing this book. Shireen, for her counsel and support whenever I needed it. Lucie, for being the first one to read the draft manuscript, her comments proved critical in improving the text. Pallavi, for her support while transcribing and typing out the manuscript, and for being a rock of a friend. Panini, for his friendship and for being an excellent source of ideas over the years. Qubool, for his selfless friendship and support. Revati for her morale-boosting conversations. Sam Miller, for his wise and pointed suggestions on how to approach a subject like Ayodhya.

Shabnam for keeping me well-fed and keeping the house together. Raamprasad, for giving me company every evening, and letting me recite the Ramcharitmanas to him! Isabelle and Jasmine, for their optimism and friendship. Seetharaman for keeping things grounded.

Professor William Pinch for his generous suggestions on background research on Shaiva-Vaishnava relations.

Professor B. B. Lal for reliving his time in Ayodhya for my sake during the course of a late afternoon. Certain archaeologists and retired government officers who cannot be named but who have my gratitude for putting their trust in me and sharing their stories.

The good folks at Nehru Memorial Library who help many like me in their quest for books, films, and other archival material.

Mr Chandrashekhar Gaur for guiding me to people who were key to the legal development of the Ayodhya case. Tarunnuum Cheema for her cheerful resourcefulness and legal aid. Prashant Gaur for his help in navigating the corridors of the Supreme Court.

In Faizabad and Ayodhya, Mahant Satyendra Das, Mahant Gyan Das, Yugal Kishore Shastri, the late Mohammad Anis, Vineet Maurya, V. N. Das, Mahant Nritya Gopal Das, Khaliq Ahmad Khan and Mahant Ram Das and Sharad Sharma.

Afaqullah Lashkari for his joie de vivre and reliability. Dinesh Singh for his counsel and support. Anil Singh (Sir) for his insights on Faizabad–Ayodhya and Hindi literature. From *Jan Morcha*, founding editor Shitla Singh, for his help each time I asked for it; K. P. Singh, for his toothy grin and spirited journalism; and Shivnath Sharma, for making sense of the archives.

Ashish and his friends, for their company and for sharing their stories of growing up through the 1990s' Ayodhya–Faizabad.

At Aleph, my brilliant editors, Aienla Ozukum and Rosemary Sebastian Tharakan, have my eternal gratitude. Any errors and omissions that remain in the book are mine.

Finally, I owe it to Aban for being a co-traveller in this fascinating journey.

BIBLIOGRAPHY

Advani, L. K., *My Country My Life*, New Delhi: Rupa Publications, 2008.

Ali, Darogah Haji Abbas, *An Illustrated Historical Album of the Rajas and Taluqdars of Oudh*, Allahabad: North-western Provinces and Oudh Government Press, 1880.

Ansari, Zoe, ed., *Firaqnaama: Commemoration Vol.*, National Amir Khusrau Society, 1999.

Bakkar, Hans, *Ayodhyā: Part I*, Groningen: Institute of Indian Studies, University of Groningen, 1984.

Bakhsh, Muhammad Faiz, *Tarikh Farah Bakhsh*, Hoey, William, trans., Lucknow: New Royal Book Co., 2005.

Basu, Amrita, *Violent Conjunctures in Democratic India* (Cambridge Studies in Contentious Politics), Cambridge: Cambridge University Press, 2015.

Bhatnagar, Pushkar, *Dating the Era of Lord Ram*, New Delhi: Rupa Publications, 2004.

Bossy, John, *Christianity in the West, 1400–1700*, New York: Oxford University Press, 1987.

Bulcke, Camille, *Ramkatha: Utpatti aur Vikas*, Prayag: Hindi Parishad Prakashan, 1950.

Dani, A. H. and Masson, V. M., eds., *History of Civilizations of Central Asia*, Vol. 1, Paris: UNESCO Publishing, 1992.

Das, Sisir Kumar, *A History of Indian Literature, 500–1399: From Courtly to the Popular*, New Delhi: Sahitya Akademi, 2005.

Dasgupta, Sanjukta and Basu, Raj Shekhar, eds., *Narratives from the Margins: Aspects of Adivasi History in India*, New Delhi: Primus Books, 2012.

Dasji, Pandit Ramtahal, *Shri DevMurariji ki Jeevani Tatha Shri Guru Parampara Prakash*, 1938, p. 74.

Digby, William, *'Prosperous' British India: A Revelarion from Official Records*, London: T. Fisher Unwin, 1901.

Dimmitt, Cornelia and Buitenen, J. A. B., *Classical Hindu Mythology: A Reader in the Sanskrit Puranas*, New Delhi: Sri Satguru Publications, 1998.

Dubey, Scharada, *Portraits from Ayodhya: Living India's Contradictions*, New Delhi: Tranquebar Press, 2012.

Elst, Koenraad, *Ayodhya: The Case Against the Temple*, New Delhi: Voice of India, 2002.

Foster, William, ed., *Early Travels in India*, London: Oxford University Press, 1921.

Gopal, Sarvepalli, ed., *Anatomy of a Confrontation: Ayodhya and the Rise of Communal Politics in India*, New Delhi: Penguin Books India, 1991.

Gould, Harold A., *Grass Roots Politics in India: Century of Political Evolution in Faizabad District*, London: Oxford & IBH Publishing Co. Pvt. Ltd., 1995.

Griffith, Ralph T. H., trans., *The Rámáyan of Válmíki*, London: Trübner & Co., 1870–74.

Guha Ranajit, ed., *Subaltern Studies I: Writings on South Asian History and Society*, Delhi: Oxford University Press, 1982, pp. 143–197.

Hamilton, Walter, *The East India Gazetteer*, Vol. II, London: Parbury, Allen and Co., 1828.

Hasan, Zoya, *Congress after Indira: Policy, Power, Political Change (1984-2009)*, New Delhi: Oxford University Press, 2014.

Hawley, John Stratton and Narayanan, Vasudha, *The Life of Hinduism*, New Delhi: Aleph Book Company, 2018.

Iness, McLeod, *Lucknow and Oude in the Mutiny: A Narrative and a Study*, London: A. D. Innes and Co., 1895.

Jadunath Sarkar, *History of Dasnami Sampraday*, Daraganj: Sri Panchayati Akhara Mahanirvani.

Jaffrelot, Christophe, *The Hindu Nationalist Movement and Indian Politics: 1925 to the 1990s: Strategies of Identity-building, Implantation and Mobilisation*, London: C. Hurst & Co, 1996.

————, *The Hindu Nationalist Movement in India*, New York: Columbia University Press, 1993.

Jain, Meenakshi, *Rama and Ayodhya*, New Delhi: Aryan Books International, 2013.

Jha, Krishna and Jha, Dhirendra, *Ayodhya: The Dark Night: The Secret History of Rama's Appearance in Babri Masjid*, New Delhi: HarperCollins India, 2012.

Kaur, Surinder and Singh, Sher, *Hanuman Gurhie Ayodhya: Incident, 28th July, 1855 (Root Cause of Babari Masjid Dispute)*, New Delhi: Institute of Objective Studies, 2011.

Kishore, Kunal, *Ayodhya Revisited*, New Delhi: Ocean Books, 2016.

Malla, Kalyan, *Suleiman Charitra*, Haksar, A. N. D., trans., New Delhi: Penguin Books, 2015.

Mishra, Ranjana Sarvesh, *Shri Ram Janmabhoomi ka Raktranjit Itihas*, Ayodhya: Ram Milan Tiwari, p. 6.

Mishra, Yatindra, ed., *Shehernama Faizabad*, New Delhi: Vani Prakashan, 2016.

Montogomery, Bernard Law, *The Concise History of Warfare*, New York: William Morrow & Co, 1983.

Muhammad, Malik, ed., *Amir Khusrau Bhavamatmak Ekta Ke Agradoot*, 1975.

Nagar, Amritlal, *Gadar ke Phool*, New Delhi: Rajpal & Sons, 2012.

Nandy, Ashis, et al., *Creating a Nationality: The Ramjanmabhumi Movement and Fear of the Self*, New Delhi: Oxford University Press, 1998.

Nath, Rai Bahadur Lala Baij, trans., *The Adhyatma Ramayana*, Allahabad: Oriental Books Reprint Corporation, 1913.

Newboult, A. W., ed., *Padri Elliott of Faizabad: A Memorial*, London: Charles H. Kelly, 1906.

Noorani, A. G., *The Babri Masjid Question, 1523–2003: A Matter of National Honour*, New Delhi: Tulika Books, 2004.

Oldenberg, Veena Talwar, *The Making of Colonial Lucknow—1856–77*, Princeton: Princeton University Press, 1984.

Oude: Papers Relating to Oude, London: Harrison and Sons, 1856.

Pandey, Gyan, *The Construction of Communalism in North India*, New Delhi: Oxford University Press, 1990.

Pandey, K. M., *Voice of Conscience*, Lucknow: Deen Dayal Upadhyay Prakashan, 1996.

Panikkar, Raimundo, *The Vedic Experience: Mantramanjari: An Anthology of the Vedas for Modern Man and Contemporary Celebration*, New Delhi: Motilal Banarsidass, 2016.

Pattanaik, Devdutt, *My Hanuman Chalisa*, New Delhi: Rupa Publications, 2018.

Pauwels, Heidi, ed., *Patronage and Popularisation, Pilgrimage and Procession: Channels of Transcultural Translation and Transmission in Early Modern South Asia; Papers in Honour of Monika Hortsmann*, Wiesbaden: Harrassowitz Verlag, 2009.

Pemble, John, *The Raj and the Indian Mutiny and the Kingdom of Oude—1801–1859*, New Delhi: Oxford University Press, 1960.

Pinch, William R., *Peasants and Monks in British India*, Berkeley: University of California Press, 1996.

———, *Warrior Ascetics and Indian Empires*, Cambridge: Cambridge University Press, 2006.

Qanungo, Kalika-Ranjan, *History of the Jats: Contribution to the History of Northern India, to the Death of Mirza Najaf Khan, 1782*, New Delhi: Low Price Publications, 2003.

Rajagopalachari, C., *Bharat Milap: From the Tamil Ramayana of Kamban*, New Delhi: Publications Division, Ministry of Information and Broadcasting, Government of India, 1967.

Richman, Paula, ed., *Many Ramayanas: The Diversity of a Narrative Tradition in South Asia*, New Delhi: Oxford University Press, 1994.

Sankalia, H. D., *The Ramayana in Historical Perspective*, New Delhi: Macmillan India, 1982.

Sharma, Gopal, *Karseva se Karseva Tak*, Jaipur: Rajasthan Patrika Limited, 1993.

Singh, Arvind Kumar, *Ayodhya Vivaad: Ek Patrakar Ki Diary*, New Delhi: Shilpayan, 2010.

Singh, K. S. and Datta, Birendranath, eds., *Rama-katha in Tribal and Folk Traditions of India, Proceedings of a Seminar*, Kolkata: Anthropological Society of India and Seagull Books, 1993.

Singh, Kaur, *Hanuman Gurhie Ayodhya Incident, 28th July, 1855: Root Cause of Babari Masjid Dispute*, New Delhi: Qazi Publishers & Distributers, 2012.

Sitapati, Vinay, *Half-Lion: How P. V. Narasimha Rao Transformed India*, New Delhi: Penguin Books, 2016.

Sitaram, Lala, *Ayodhya ka Itihas*, New Delhi: Arya Book Depot, 1932.

Sleeman, William Henry, *A Journey through the Kingdom of Oude in 1849-1850*,

London: R. Bentley, 1838.

Smith, R.V., *Delhi: Unknown Tales of a City*, New Delhi: Roli Books, 2015.

Srivastava, A. L., *The First Two Nawabs of Awadh*, Agra: Shiva Lal Agarwala and Co. Ltd., 1954.

Srivastava, Sushil, *The Disputed Mosque: A Historical Inquiry*, New Delhi: Vistaar Publications, 1991.

Taqui, Roshan, *Lucknow 1857: The Two Wars of Lucknow, Dusk of an Era*, Lucknow: New Royal Book Company, 2001.

Thapar, B. K., ed., *Indian Archaeology 1976–77: A Review*, New Delhi: Archaeological Survey of India, 1980.

Thapar, Romila, *The Past as Present: Forging Contemporary Identities through History*, New Delhi: Aleph Book Company, 2014.

———, *The Past Before Us*, New Delhi: OrientBlackswan, 2013.

———, *The Penguin History of Early India: From the Origins to AD 1300*, Vol. 1, London: Penguin Books, 2002.

Tiefenthaler, Joseph, *Description Historique et Géographique de l'Inde*, Berlin: Spener, 1786.

Trivedi, Shikha, *Ayodhya: A Place Without War (More News is Good News)*, New Delhi: HarperCollins India, 2016.

Twining, Thomas, *Travels in India a Hundred Years Ago, With a Visit to the United States*, London: J. R. Osgood, McIlvaine & Co., 1893.

Valmiki, The Ramayana, Arshia Sattar, trans., New Delhi: Penguin Books India, 2000.

Veer, Peter Van Der, *Gods on Earth: The Management of Religious Experience and Identity in a North Indian Pilgrimage Centre*, New York: Bloomsbury Academic, 1988.

Yule, Henry and Burnell, A. C., *Hobson-Jobson: The Definitive Glossary of British India*, Clarendon: Oxford University Press, 2013.

REPORTS, ARTICLES

Bakker, Hans, 'The rise of Ayodhy as a place of pilgrimage', *Indo-Iranian Journal*, Vol. 24, No. 2, 1982.

Bennett, Leanne, *The Origins of the Peasant Agitation in Oudh: The Awakening of the Peasants*, Montreal: Concordia University, 1997.

Burghart, Richard, 'The founding of the Ramanandi sect', *Ethnohistory*, Vol. 25, No. 2, 1978, pp. 121–39. JSTOR <www.jstor.org/stable/481036>.

Diskul, Subhadradis, 'The difference between Valmiki Ramayana and the Thai version of Ramayana (Ramakirti) of King Rama I of Thailand (1782–1809)'.

Horstmann, Monika, 'Visions of kingship in the twilight of Mughal rule', *2005 Gonda Lecture*, Amsterdam: Royal Netherlands Academy of Arts and Sciences, 2006.

Prior, Katherine, 'The British administration of Hinduism in North India, 1780–1900', Ph.D. diss., Cambridge: St Catherine's College, Cambridge University, 1990.

Sarkar, Tanika, 'Who rules India? A few notes on the Hindu right', *Revista Canaria de*

Estudios Ingleses, 76; April 2018, pp. 223–39.

Saxena, A., et al., 'Holocene vegetation and climate change in Central Ganga Plain: A study based on multiproxy records from Chaudhary-Ka-Tal, Raebareli District, Uttar Pradesh, India', *Quaternary International*, Vol. 371, February 2015.

Tripathi, R. P., 'Bhitari pillar inscription of Skandagupta—a note on Ganga-Dhvanih', *Proceedings of the Indian History Congress*, Vol. 39, 1978, pp. 1010–14.

Vajpeyi, Raghavendra, 'A critique of the Huna invasion theory', *Proceedings of the Indian History Congress*, Vol. 39, 1978, pp. 62–66.

FURTHER READING

Alam, Muzzafar, *The Crisis of Empire in Mughal North-India: Awadh and the Punjab, 1707-48*, Oxford India Perennials, New Delhi: Oxofrd University Press, 1986.

Anderson, Benedict, *Imagined Communities: Reflections on the Origin and Spread of Nationalism*, London: Verso Publications, 1983.

Asher, Catherine B., *The New Cambridge History of India: Architecture of Mughal India*, Cambridge: Cambridge University Press, 2008.

Bakshi, Fasihuddun, *Wahabi Movement*, New Delhi: Classical Publishing Company,.

Bates, Crispin, *Subalterns and Raj: South Asia since 1600*, Abingdon: Routledge, 2007.

Brockington, J. L., *Righteous Rama*, New Delhi: Oxford University Press, 1984.

Desai, Santosh N., *Hinduism in Thai Life*, Bombay: Popular Prakashan, 1980.

Dhar, Maloy Krishna, *Open Secrets: India's Intelligence Unveiled*, New Delhi: Manas Publications, 2005.

Dodson, Michael S., ed., *Banaras: Urban Forms and Cultural Histories*, New Delhi: Routledge India, 2012.

Fisher, Michael H., *A Clash of Cultures: Awadh, The British and the Mughals*, New Delhi: Manohar Publications 1987.

Geiger, Wilhelm, *Culture of Ceylon in Medieval Times*, Stuttgart: Franz Steiner Verlag Wiesbaden GMBH, 1986.

Ghurye, G. S., *Indian Sadhus*, Bombay: Popular Prakashan, 1953.

Godbole, Madhav, *Secularism: India at a Crossroads*, New Delhi: Rupa Publications, 2016.

Godbole, Madhav, *Unfinished Innings: Recollections and Reflections of a Civil Servant*, Hyderabad: Orient Longman, 1996.

Habibullah, A. B. M., ed., *Nalini Kanta Bhattasali Commemoration: Essays on Archaeology, Art, History, Literature and Philosophy of the Orient*, Dacca: Dacca Museum, 1966.

Karlekar, Hiranmay, *Independent India: The First Fifty Years*, New Delhi: Oxford University Press, 1998.

Krishnamoorthy, K., ed., *A Critical Inventory of Ramayana Studies in the World*, New Delhi: Sahitya Akademi, 1993.

Lal, Vinay, 'The discourse of history and the crisis at Ayodhya: reflections on the production of knowledge, freedom and the future of India', *Emergences*, Vol. 5, No. 6, 1993–94.

Legge, James, *A Record of Buddhistic Kingdoms*, New Delhi: Oriental Publishers, 1971.

Nizami, Khaliq Ahmad, *State and Cultural in Medieval India*, New Delhi: Adam Publishers & Distributors, 1985.

Padgaonkar, Dileep, ed., *When Bombay Burned*, New Delhi: UBS Publishers and Distributors Ltd., 1993.

Pandey, Gyanendra, *The Ascendancy of the Congress in Uttar Pradesh: Class, Community and Nation in Northern India, 1920-1940*, London: Anthem Press, 2002.

Pathak, Vishuddhanand, *History of Kosala upto the Rise of the Mauryas*, New Delhi: Motilal Banarsidass, 1963.

Pollock, Sheldon, 'The divine king in the Indian epic', *Journal of the American Oriental Society*, Vol. 104, No. 3, July–September 1984, pp. 505–28, 1984.

Pollock, Sheldon, *Ramayana and Political Imagination in India,* Chicago: The Committee on Southern Asian Studies at the University of Chicago, 1995.

Powell, Avril A., *Scottish Orientalists and India: The Muir Brothers, Religion, Education and Empire*, Woodbridge: Boydell Press, 2010.

Prajapati, R. S., *Ramanand Sampradaya aur Sahitya*, Agra: Pragati Prakashan, 1984.

Qanungo, Kalikaranjan, *Sher Shah and His Times*, Calcutta: Orient Longmans Limited, 1965.

Seervai, H. M., *Partition of India: Legend and Reality*, Bombay: N. M. Tripathi Private Ltd., 1994.

Seshadri, H.V., ed., *R.S.S. A Vision in Action*, Bangalore: Sahitya Sindhu Prakashana, 1998.

Singh, Arjun, *A Grain of Sand in the Hourglass of Time: An Autobiography*, New Delhi: Hay House Publications, 2012.

Singh, S. N., *The Kingdom of Awadh*, New Delhi: Mittal Publications, 2003.

Swaroop, Devendra, *Ayodhya ka Sach*, Granth Akademi, 2007.

Vasudha, Dalmia and Stietencron, Heinrich von, *The Oxford India Hinduism Reader*, New Delhi: Oxford University Press, 2007.

INDEX

Adityanath, Yogi, 266, 280, 283, 287, 306, 324, 338, 345, 349

Advani, L. K., 213, 218–220, 240, 242, 251, 270, 273–74, 316, 345, 347

Akbar, 28–29, 42, 59–60, 70

Al Hassani, Syed Nasiruddin Mahmud or Chirag–e–Dehlavi, 66, 75, 320

Ansari, Hashim, 205–06, 277, 357–59

Archaeological Survey of India (ASI), 5–6, 267–73, 315, 322, 359

Asaf–ud–daulah, 84–90, 94, 99, 112, 123, 279, 309

Ashoka, 55, 335–36

Aurangzeb, 58, 70–71, 75, 78–79, 83–84, 145, 231, 331

Aurobindo, 300

Awadh Kisan Sabha, 169–71

Babri Masjid, 75, 90, 101–02, 110, 145, 204–07, 227, 287, 296–97, 300, 324, 332–34, 336, 339, 350, 352, 354–57, 363
   ASI excavations 5–7, 268–69, 271
   Conflict over ownership, 97–98, 143, 148–50, 180, 185–86, 188, 190–95, 197–202, 207, 215, 217, 219–21, 229–32, 239, 253, 255–56, 272, 275–76, 306, 315–17, 367–68
   Controversy regarding construction, 19, 29, 67–71
   Demolition, 54–55, 63, 222–25, 233–34, 236, 238, 240–41, 243–52, 260, 274, 278–79, 283, 293, 307, 345, 347–49
   Hanumangarhi dispute (see Hanumangarhi: Ram birthplace dispute)
   Ram Chabutra 148, 149, 182, 188
   Ram Lalla, 7, 188, 193–94, 198, 201, 204–05, 207–10, 213, 216–17, 223, 228–30, 232, 238, 241, 245–46, 252, 255–56, 258–59, 262–63, 267, 269–70, 273, 275–78, 281, 283, 286–89, 298, 300–02, 305, 314, 350, 354, 357, 363, 366–67
   Sita Rasoi, 7, 53, 145, 243, 276–77, 298–99

Babur, xiii, 28, 54, 68–70, 76, 97, 149, 180, 196, 235, 240, 250, 267, 316, 332, 349

Badi Bua, 75, 284, 320–22

Bahujan Samaj Party (BSP), 214, 258, 266–67, 324

Bairagis, 72–73, 78, 83–84, 87, 90, 97–99, 101, 106–07, 110, 115, 117–18, 129, 141, 43–144, 148, 154, 80–181, 185–89, 193–94, 196, 197, 199, 201, 264, 291–93, 334, 342–43

Bajrang Dal, 202, 211, 229, 232, 247–48, 253, 259, 261, 305, 345, 351, 355, 360–61

Bakker, Hans, 14, 17–19, 56, 63

Balanand, Swami, 71, 84, 292

Banaras, 15, 23, 28, 35, 53–54, 56, 71, 75, 79, 82, 89, 97, 151, 153, 164, 168, 180, 207, 217, 259, 296, 320, 331, 366

Bano, Shah, 203, 208–09

Bansal, Champat Rai, 316–17, 345

Baqi, Mir, 28, 69–70, 180, 221, 227, 251, 276

Bharatiya Janata Party (BJP), xiv, 57, 189, 195, 210, 213–15, 217–22, 227–28, 230–232, 234–236, 239, 241, 247, 249, 251, 253, 257–67, 270–74, 277, 279–283, 287, 293, 299, 301, 305–06, 312, 314–18, 323–24, 330, 333, 336, 344–46, 350, 352, 355, 358, 360–62, 366–69

Bharti, Uma, 231, 237, 258, 345, 347

Buchanan, Francis, 94–95, 173

Burghart, Richard, 74

Carnegy, Patrick, 130, 134, 145

Chitrakoot, 25, 31, 33, 259, 288, 345

Cunningham, Alexander, 5, 16, 322

Dalhousie, Governor General, 104–05, 112, 114–15, 118–19, 124–26
Dalit, 73, 212–14, 265, 296, 324, 356
Dalmia, V. H. , 231, 240, 258
Dalrymple, William, 48
Das, Abhiram, 188–89, 194, 197–98, 287
Das, Baba Raghav, 185–88, 199, 318
Das, Mahant Devram, 343–44
Das, Mahant Gyan, 252, 265, 289–94, 302–03
Das, Mahant Lal, 233, 258, 305
Das, Mahant Nritya Gopal, 225, 231, 246, 265, 277, 287, 289, 315, 338, 341–48, 365
Das, Mahant Raghubar, 148–50
Das, Mahant Satyendra, 53, 210, 246, 283, 286–87, 305, 310, 341, 363, 366
Das, Pandit Ramtahal, 59–61
Das, Sudarshan, 189
Dashrath Mahal, 53, 182, 265, 285, 341
Dev, Narendra, 185–86, 318
Devmurari, 59–61
Digambar Akhara, 188, 197–98, 202, 220, 224, 264, 285, 288–90, 305
Digby, William, 160
Diskul, Subhadradis, 44
Dixit, S. C., 202, 222

Elliott, Padre John Alexander, 151–59
Elst, Koenraad, 29

Faizabad, 3, 43, 55, 67, 78, 81, 84–87, 89, 99–101, 104, 106, 108, 111, 117–18, 122, 128–131, 133–34, 143, 148–57, 162–64, 167, 169–71, 181, 185–86, 189–90, 192–93, 195, 198–99, 201, 204–07, 211, 213–14, 220, 224–27, 232, 237, 241, 263, 265–66, 275, 279–84, 294, 297, 303–05, 309, 311, 313, 315, 318, 321, 323, 328, 330, 333, 335–36, 346, 348, 351–52, 354–56, 358, 360–61, 366–67

Gahadvala, 19, 56–57, 61–62, 64
Galta conference, 73, 99, 174, 285
Gandhi, Indira, 200–03, 240, 332–33
Gandhi, Mohandas Karamchand, 52, 170–72, 180, 186, 212, 253, 330, 332–33, 351
Gandhi, Rahul, 259, 282, 355
Gandhi, Rajiv, 203–05, 208–11, 213, 230, 232–33, 240–41, 272, 298

Godhra, 262–63, 266, 361
Golwalkar, M. S., 71, 189
Gosain, Anupgiri, 80–81, 83–84, 89
Gupta, Shekhar, 250
Gupta, Swaraj Prakash, 15, 306–07

Hamilton, Walter, 96–97, 147
Hanuman, 40, 54, 73, 83, 98–99, 121, 154–55, 201, 223, 264, 274, 288, 294–95, 300, 302–03, 311, 337–38, 343, 366
Hanuman Chalisa, 302–03, 329
Hanumangarhi, 53, 89–90, 97–99, 101, 124, 126, 128–31, 133, 138, 143, 146, 154, 170, 174–75, 178, 180–81, 185, 197, 201, 287, 324, 327–28, 345, 350
    Ram birthplace dispute, 105–09, 111–19, 121–22, 188, 195–96, 223, 225–26, 265, 357
    as a pilgrim centre, 182, 285, 288–91, 294–96, 302–03, 308, 321, 330, 334, 338
    commissions of enquiry, 104–06, 107, 109, 117
Haridwar, 71, 74, 97, 163–64, 203, 215–16, 266, 288, 341
Harishchandra, Bharatendu, 146–47, 195
Hastings, Warren, 88, 95
Hussein, Shah Ghulam, 100–03, 107, 114, 119, 128, 143

Indian National Congress (INC), 168, 170, 172, 181, 185, 187, 193, 199–201, 204, 208–09, 211–14, 227, 230, 232–33, 239–41, 249, 257–60, 266, 272, 280, 282, 290, 298, 312, 333, 355–56, 361, 365
Iness, Lieutenant General McLeod, 129–31

Jahangir, 42, 48, 70
Jan Morcha, 224, 226, 247, 249, 351–52, 356
Jan Sangh, 195, 199, 214, 333
Janata Dal, 214–15, 220–21, 224, 227, 258
Joshi, Murli Manohar, 232, 239, 251, 345, 347

Kanak Bhavan, 53, 142, 172, 174–75, 182, 285, 308, 321, 330, 337–38, 341, 353
karseva, 216, 219–21, 227, 237–38, 240–43, 362, 366
karsevaks, 19, 216–17, 220–23. 225–29, 233–34, 236–39, 242–52, 258, 261–62,

264, 270, 274, 285, 295, 300–01, 307, 317, 332, 334, 336, 345, 347–51, 361, 363

Kartik mela, 164, 308, 339

Kashi, 15, 77, 79, 187, 200–01

Katiyar, Vinay, 202, 232, 234, 236, 238, 241–42, 258, 263, 266, 351

Kaushalya, 13, 43, 334, 353–54

Khan, Aghai Ally, 103–05, 107–08, 112

Khan, Khaliq, 207, 224–25, 257, 268, 270, 278, 305, 314–15, 356, 358–59

Khusrau, Amir, 65–66

Kishan, Pandit Hari, 148–50

Kishore, Kunal, 63, 67, 69–71

Kumbhakarna, 50–51

Kurmis, 87, 173, 179, 293, 322

Lakshman, 9, 24–25, 27–28, 30–31, 37–41, 45, 50–51, 97, 121, 196, 300, 336, 352

Lakshman Qila, 78

Lal, B. B., 5–6, 8, 18, 268–69, 271

Lawrence, Henry, 134, 138–39

Lodi dynasty, 35, 68

Macdonnell, Sir Antony, 160–61, 163

Mahabharata, 5–6, 58, 289

Mahatmyas, 62–63

Mahavira, 9, 15–16

Mandal Commission, 215, 217, 227–28, 260

Mani Parbat, 54–55, 322

Maniram Das ki Chavni, 220, 224, 285, 287–90, 307, 341–43

Manthara, 30

Mantle, Rev. Gregory, 155–57

Mathura, 54, 84, 163, 187, 200–01, 217–18, 224, 232, 239, 311

Mayawati, 258–59, 266, 272, 275, 279, 282

Mehboob, Haji, 180, 244–45, 251–52, 283, 348–49

Mishra, Sir Kunwar Pratap Narayan Singh, 130, 142, 163

Modi, Narendra, 219, 251, 266, 279, 282–83, 308, 310, 317, 339, 345–46, 361–62, 365–67

Nageshwarnath, 55, 58, 61, 78, 97–98, 294–95, 308, 321

Nair, Shakuntala, 190, 192, 194, 227

Nath, Mahant Digvijay, 187–88, 191, 193

National Democratic Alliance (NDA), 261–62, 264, 272–73

Nehru, Arun, 203–04, 208, 211

Nehru, Jawaharlal, 34, 181, 185, 190–91, 240, 259, 314, 330, 332–33

Newstrack, 247–49

Nirmohi Akhara, 188, 198, 224, 276–77, 288–89, 314, 328, 334, 358, 367

Nirvani Akhara, 188, 197, 288–89, 291, 302, 341

Nishad, 9, 24, 31, 281, 335–36

Orr, Captain A. P., 101–06, 107–15, 119, 128

Outram, Major General G. B., 100, 104–10, 112, 114–20, 122, 124–26, 138

Paramhans, Ramchandra, 188, 193, 197–98, 200, 225, 262–65, 268, 277, 288

Penberthy, Jeff, 247–48

Pinch, William R., 72, 88, 92, 173, 179

Prayag, 60, 71–72, 74, 77, 79, 89, 288

Puranas, 11, 13, 62–63

Rai, Ram Bahadur, 163, 316–17

Ram bhakts, 56, 215, 219, 224, 228, 231, 239, 244–45, 249, 259, 264, 342

Ram Janmabhoomi, 53, 71, 75–76, 111, 189, 193, 196–200, 209–10, 214, 221, 228, 233, 236, 239–40, 249, 265, 268, 274, 286–87, 295–97, 301, 313, 316–17, 324, 325, 333, 336, 351, 356, 359, 363

Ram Janmabhoomi–Babri Masjid, 71, 97, 196, 200, 215, 220, 222–25, 232, 234–36, 241, 253, 256, 265, 272–73, 275, 283, 285, 287, 289, 295–96, 298–99, 302, 310–11, 324, 329–30, 332, 341, 345, 350, 353, 355, 357, 368

Ram Janmabhoomi Mukti Yagna Samiti, 200, 207

Ram Janmabhoomi Trust, 235–36, 265, 277, 287–88, 306, 315, 346–47

Ram Naam Bank, 342–43

Ram Navami, 146–47, 164, 296, 334–36, 338–39, 349, 352–53

Ram Rajya, 52–53, 212–13, 228, 230–32, 272, 282, 317

Ram Shila, 210–12

Ram, Babu Priya Dutt, 192, 195, 198

Ramayana

    Adhyatma Ramayana, 22, 25–26, 28

    Bengali Ramayanas, 21, 27

Buddhist Ramayana, 23, 49
Jain Ramayanas, 21, 23, 26–27, 29, 51
Kamban's *Ramavataram*, 22, 25
Nalayira Divya Prabandham 23
Pauma Cariya by Vimalasuri, 21, 26–27
Rama Retold, 34
Ramakien, 29, 44–45, 47, 49–50
Ramayanas in folk literature, 40–42
Shilappadikaram 23
Suleiman Charitra, 35
Tribal Ramayanas, 36–40
Tulsidas's *Ramcharitmanas*, xi, 22, 25, 28–29, 50, 73, 75–76, 169, 188, 282, 296, 327, 369
Urdu and Persian Ramayanas, 42–43
Valmiki's Ramayana, 3, 9, 11–14, 20–33, 39, 41–42, 44, 50–51, 58, 220, 230
Ramanandis, 63, 72–75, 77–78, 87, 89, 91, 94–95, 99, 107, 150, 168, 172, 174–79, 182, 188, 199, 280, 289, 291–92, 323, 325–27
Ramanujis, 72–73, 77, 168, 172, 175–79, 182, 193, 199, 291, 326–27, 329
Ramchandra, Baba, 126, 168–70, 172–74, 196, 300
Ramkot, 18, 244, 285, 287–88, 299
Rao, P.V. Narasimha, 233–34, 239–42, 253–55, 257–58, 260–61, 317
Rashtriya Swayamsevak Sangh (RSS), xii, 52, 71, 75, 188–89, 202–03, 208, 215, 217–20, 224, 227–31, 235–36, 239, 241, 243, 247, 251, 253, 257–61, 266, 278–79, 281, 285, 290, 305, 318, 344–45, 350–51, 355–56, 361–63, 365, 367
Rath Yatra, 207, 218–20, 228, 335
Rithambara, Sadhvi, 231, 241

Safdarjung, 78–81, 85, 99, 124
Sahay, Subodh Kant, 236
Saheb, Nana, 127–28, 133, 140
Saket, 14–18, 55, 57
Samajwadi Party, 258, 266, 279–80, 290, 305–06, 323–24
Sangh Parivar, 202, 220, 230, 330, 345, 351–52, 366
Sankalia, H. D., 12–14
Sarayu, 3, 9, 18, 20, 40, 52, 55–56, 61, 66–67, 70, 75, 78, 98, 100, 146–48, 150, 162, 203, 220, 222–23, 225, 241–42, 252, 272, 288, 291–94, 304, 308, 316, 319,

325, 331, 334, 341, 347, 350, 357, 368
Scindia, Vijayraje, 231
Shah, Amit, 189, 345, 355, 362
Shah, Maulvi Ahmad Ulla, 128–29, 135, 140
Shah, Wajid Ali, 90–91, 100, 104–08, 113–18, 124–28, 138, 140
Shahabuddin, Syed, 207, 224
Shaiva Gosains, 80–81, 92
Shaiva Sanyasis, 73, 87, 99, 292
Shaivas, 30, 58, 60, 73–75, 78, 98, 182
Sharad, Ram Gopal Pandey, 196–97, 300
Sharqi dynasty, 68–70
Shastri, Yugal Kishore, 290, 325, 370
Shekhar, Chandra, 227, 229–30, 232
Shilanyas, 210–13, 215, 265
Shiva, 17, 19, 25, 30, 37, 45, 49, 55, 58, 61–62, 73, 98–99, 150, 187, 197, 312, 337
Shri Ramanandi Vaishnava Mahamandal, 175–76
Shuja-ud-daulah, 80–82, 85, 89, 99, 111
Singh, Kalyan, 232, 234, 236–37, 239, 241, 254, 258–59, 274, 297, 299, 306, 344
Singh, Raja Man, 70, 103–05, 111–13, 117, 127–28, 130–43, 162, 328
Singh, Rajnath, 262, 345–46
Singh, Shatrughan, 264–65
Singh, Sheetla, 351, 356
Singh, Vir Bahadur, 204, 206, 208
Singh, Vishwanath Pratap, 203, 208
Singhal, Ashok, 71, 201, 220–21, 223, 225, 235, 237, 258, 264, 316–17
Sitaram, Lala, 46, 81–82, 89, 146
Skanda Purana, 62–63
Somnatha, 187, 213, 218–19
Sorabjee, Soli, 256–57
Srivastava, Sushil, 16, 18, 20, 69
Sumantra, 24, 31
Sunni Waqf Board, 181, 198, 205, 254, 276–76, 289, 315, 355, 361, 366–67
Swargdwar, 56, 61, 67, 326, 330–31

Telingas, 135–36
Telugu Desam Party, 263
Theravada Buddhism, 23, 47, 49–50
Thongduang, 46, 48
Tiefenthaler, Joseph, 82–83, 145, 148, 244
Tirthankars, 26, 56, 335
Treta Yug, 14, 91, 142
Tughlaq, Firoz Shah, 66–68
Tughlaq, Muhammad bin, 67–68

Umat-uz-Zohra or Bahu Begum, 84–86, 88, 130
United Progressive Alliance (UPA), 272–73, 282
Urmila, 40–41

Vaishnavas, 25, 30, 58, 60, 63, 71–74, 78, 91–92, 98, 101, 176, 337
Vaishnavism, xiii, 57, 59, 63, 72, 92, 172, 174, 182
Vajpayee, Atal Bihari, 57, 242, 261–62, 264, 268, 272, 316–17
Vamdev, Swami, 225, 227
Vedanti, Ram Vilas, 287, 347
Vibhishan, 24, 50
Vikramaditya, 17, 53, 57, 142

Visharad, Gopal Singh, 188, 191, 193, 197–98
Vishva Hindu Parishad (VHP), 7, 53–55, 71, 75–76, 145, 180, 200–02, 204–08, 210–13, 215–23, 226–31, 233–43, 247, 249, 252–53, 257–59, 261–66, 268, 270–74, 279, 281–83, 287–88, 290, 293, 296, 301, 305–07, 311, 314–17, 329–30, 336, 341–42, 344–45, 349–51, 355–57, 360, 362–63, 365–67
Vishwamitra, 24, 312

Weston, G. K., 102, 108, 111–13

Yadav, Mulayam Singh, 214, 220, 222–23, 226–27, 231–32, 234, 258, 266, 272, 279–82, 323, 351

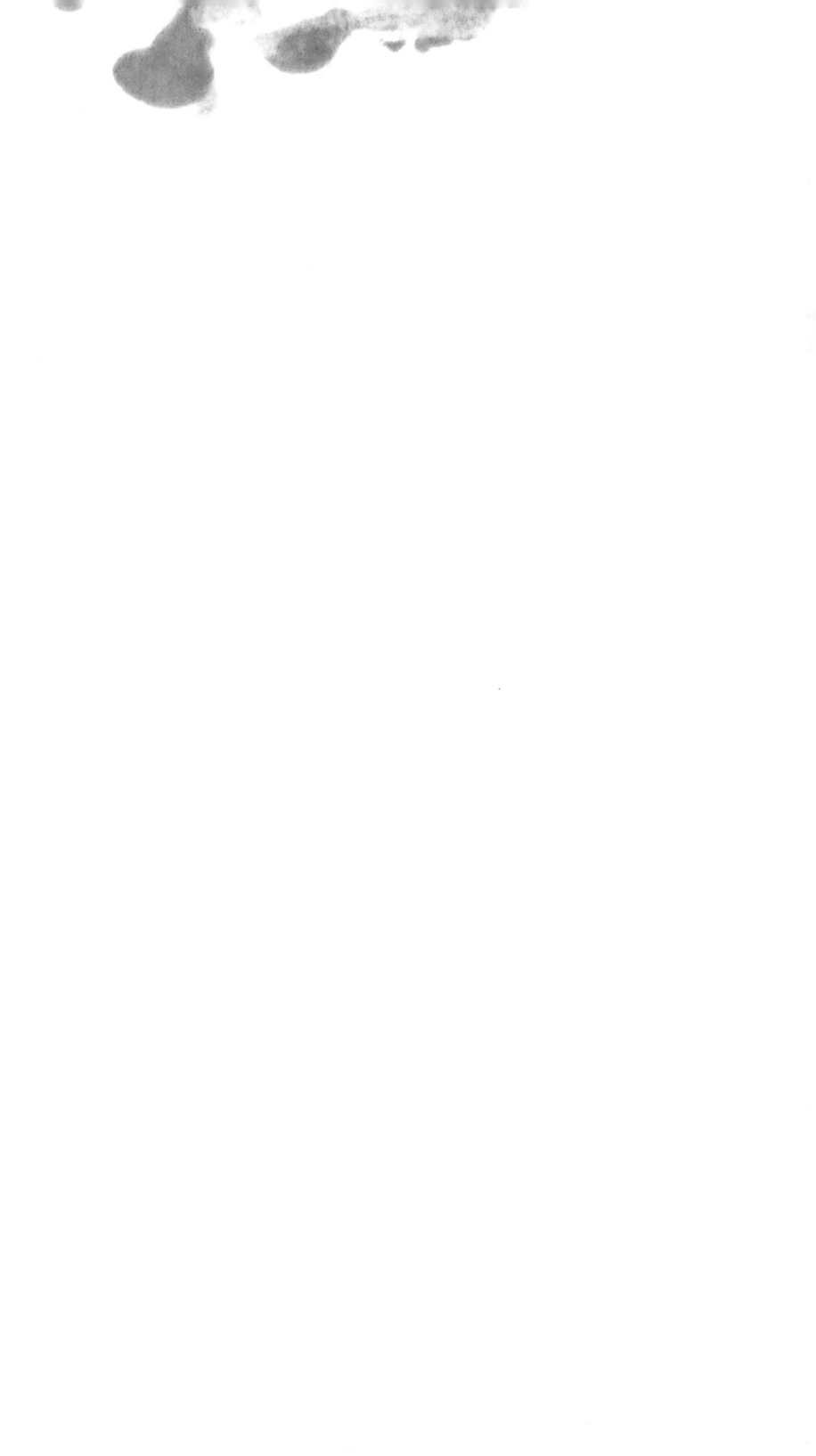